Primary Documents

Primary Documents

A Sourcebook for Eastern and Central European Art since the 1950s

edited by Laura Hoptman
and Tomáš Pospiszyl

with the assistance of
Majlena Braun and Clay Tarica

Foreword by Ilya Kabakov

The Museum of Modern Art, New York

Distributed by The MIT Press, Cambridge, Massachusetts, and London, England

Contents

Foreword

The publication of this anthology is very important for understanding the process of art-making in Eastern Europe over the past forty years, and particularly of the place occupied by texts, discussions, commentaries, etc., in that process. The abundance of such verbal material and of what might be called its emotional saturation is so great that it can be discussed as a unique, but highly specific segment of the overall artistic production of that region.

In many respects, the texts included in this collection could turn out to be strange, confusing, and difficult to understand for the outside observer. As a rule, it is not clear who the writers of these texts are: art historians, critics, cultural scholars, psychoanalysts, essayists, artists? On the one hand, there is an intentional, estranged, descriptive "outside" perspective present in them; on the other hand, there is some sort of nervousness, a desire to "break free," to utter some long-known truth that seems to be brewing in them. These are texts in which the author wishes to express "everything," his entire lifelong conception, a truthful description of himself and of those surrounding him.

A knowledge of the context is not just desirable for reading this collection of texts, it is essential. Unfortunately, that context is not familiar to many, and as a result of certain circumstances, it still does not provoke special interest. What is recounted in these texts happened in distant, closed countries, that—at least in the case of the former Soviet Union—virtually did not exist on the artistic map of the world from the 1930s until the 1980s. Nevertheless, certain painful circumstances and reasons for the emergence of these texts should be elucidated. I shall attempt to say a few words about the nature of such texts using the artistic life of Moscow at that time as an example, since it is this city and this milieu that I know from personal experience. Although generalizations are difficult to make, it is hoped that such a specific example can give at least a hint of the circumstances under which much of the work in this volume was generated.

Most of the authors of the Russian texts included in this anthology come from the "unofficial world," an extraordinarily strange and paradoxical phenomenon that existed in the "former" Soviet Union in the 1960s and 1970s. On the one hand, this world experienced pressure and the constant threat of extinction by the surrounding monolithic Soviet world, and on the other hand, its emergence was imperative given the conditions whereby artists were in total internal isolation and deprived of opportunities to publish, exhibit, and exchange works and texts with the outside world. There was a need to elaborate one's own means for intellectual "survival."

This was not a genre of "manifestos" by which the artists of the beginning of the century in Russia wanted to destroy and silence the "decaying world of the bourgeois environment." The completeness and finality of the "Soviet environment" in the 1960s and 1970s were many times more severe than in the previous "bourgeois" environment. Under these conditions, a unique genre of "self-description" emerged, whereby the author would imitate, re-create that very same "outside" perspective of which he was deprived in actual reality. He became simultaneously an author and an observer. Deprived of a genuine viewer, critic, or historian, the author unwittingly became them himself, trying to guess what his works meant "objectively." He attempted to "imagine" that very "History" in which he was functioning and which was "looking" at him. Obviously, this "History" existed only in his imagination and had its own image for each artist. One artist might imagine a "world of contemporary Western art," for others it was the "Pantheon of great masters of the Renaissance," and still others imagined this to be the "Russian avant-garde of the 1920s." This is to say nothing of the fact that reproductions served as the material for these fantasies, and in the case of "Contemporary Western Art" or the "Russian Avant-garde" these were extremely rare in those years. But this was no misfortune at all! What was important was that these images which had nothing to do with reality burned rather brightly and constantly.

A multitude of texts of a cultural nature emerged through this kind of fantasizing about the outside, "beyond-the-Soviet" world. The original impetus came from an understanding that the Soviet world, no matter how complete and finished it might appear to be to its inhabitants, was still not the entire world, but rather only a part of the surrounding human universe. In the same way, Soviet art appeared not as a river, but as a swamp drying up and located far away from contemporaneous artistic life elsewhere.

Therefore, many texts written at that time were attempts to see how "our place," "our situation," looked from the perspective of that outside world, that external culture. The artist had already become not only the author of his own works, but also the "cultural observer" standing beyond the walls of the Soviet home and peering in through the window. Naturally, any story about what this observer saw here was also attributed to some other outside observers and interested parties. Such was the nature of Moscow Conceptualism, the basis of which is precisely a collection of observations of a cultural nature of various aspects of Soviet life, Soviet consciousness, and so-called art, including that unofficial art produced in this very community.

But in contrast to a normal medical situation based on the opposition of "doctor-patient," our situation was different in that any artist was simultaneously both the observer and the object of observation. This is where the fluctuating point of view—"first here, then there" (the Russian poet and artist Dmitri Prigov's definition)—comes from. This is also what leads to the mixture of various styles in texts and works, reflecting attempts at creating what is ostensibly a combination of objective description and passionate personal utterances. The result is that strange combination of sounds and noises described at the beginning of this essay. Hence, the texts in this collection represent simultaneously criticisms and memoirs, theoretical notions and analyses of each other's works, descriptions of artistic events and utopian desires.

—*Ilya Kabakov*

Introduction

While "Western Europe" has been a recognized designation for that part of the world for a long time, there is no such comparable designation for Eastern Europe, at least not in that region itself. Interviewing passersby in the streets of Ljubljana, Sofia, or Riga reveals that most people identify with their city or nation, but the concept of "Eastern Europe" sounds like a foreign and antiquated term. This relatively undefined region east of Germany and south of Scandinavia comprises many different traditions and languages, and furthermore it is liberally subdivided into inner borders that shift hither and thither as nowhere else. The various countries and nations of this broadly defined Eastern Europe do not relate to one another; instead, they tend to relate to other cultures and regions: parts of former Yugoslavia to Mediterranean culture; the Czech Republic, Slovakia, and Hungary to the history of the Austrian Empire; the Baltic countries to Scandinavia; and the southern Balkans to the Near East.

The concept of "Eastern Europe," as it has been understood in the past several decades, then, is neither geographic nor social; it is economic and political. A product of the Yalta Conference of 1945, it was created with the intention of outlining zones of influence in Europe. Subsequently, the territory between Germany and Russia fell under the influence of the Soviet Union and soon became isolated from the rest of the world, and, in the eyes of the world, politically homogenized. Imported Stalinism or homegrown socialist experiments of one kind or another—together with the various attempts at shaking them off—could be found in every nation. But the former socialist facade is not the most important bond uniting Eastern Europe.

Eastern Europe is a place of great intellectual capacity, where men and women of letters speak any number of languages while sharing a related sense of humor and skepticism — among the few tools available to help them survive the cruel and often bizarre political escapades in their countries. For several decades, artistic freedom in Eastern Europe was singularly suppressed, creating conditions for the development of artistic expression markedly different from those of the West. First, censorship made the publication of every independent thought, no matter how politically remote, extremely difficult. Many writers had to censor themselves in order to be officially published. Some decided to put out a samizdat, or self-publication, but this strategy radically limited their audience. Criticism in the Western sense of the word existed only in a limited number of countries and only for a limited number of years. It should come as no surprise, then, to note that much of the most interesting art writing comes not from art historians or critics but from the artists themselves. Nevertheless, many writers and artists continued to write about art and to create artworks that were relevant to the international cultural discourse. Many of them were truly dual citizens: they were both from the country where they resided and part of an international community of modern art.

A large percentage of the most important Eastern European art forms remains virtually unknown outside of their own milieu—never translated, never staged abroad, rarely exhibited. Internationally, visual art is the least-known element of Eastern European culture, which does not diminish its significance; however, access to it has proved to be the most difficult obstacle.

The overriding reason for publishing these essays and texts on Eastern European visual art forms from the past four decades is to provide English-speaking readers with original historical documentation, primary source materials for serious academic research on the subject of Eastern European visual culture. Many of these texts have heretofore been available only in their original languages. These English translations thus fill a gap. Creating the parameters of such a task was a challenge in itself. In order to give the publication the widest possible scope, we decided to take into consideration not only the countries of East and East Central Europe, but also all post-Communist European countries, including the former Yugoslavia. Russia is an independent superpower with its own strong culture and traditions, but because the conditions under which Russian artists struggled for free expression were comparable to those in the rest of Eastern Europe, we decided to include this large area as well. We opted to arrange the anthology according to thematic chapters organized in roughly chronological order rather than deal with each region separately. This allows us to present information about visual art from the many diverse countries, with an eye to both comparison and contrast. Each chapter concludes with a case study that focuses on either a selected important exhibition, or a significant controversy or polemic.

We hope that this book will serve as a general introduction for American and other English-speaking readers to major figures in the artistic and the critical realm. However, this is not a collection of monographs identifying the most major of Eastern European artists over the past thirty years. Although these texts concentrate on both art and theory, the emphasis in this volume is on the latter. Our criteria for inclusion were straightforward: we chose landmark texts that labeled movements, challenged received ideas, and changed the way art was made and thought about by influential writers respected in their communities and nationally. With our focus on primary source material, we have, for the most part, avoided retrospective regional assessments, monographs, and art-historical chronologies.

Our decision to focus on primary source material rather than on retrospective situational analyses written over the past decade is a conscious one, made with the knowledge that contemporary critical discourse is dominated by work that deals with the intellectual reacquaintance of West and East. There have been many essays, several of them important, written by scholars from the region over the past decade that deal specifically with the problem of the reception of East Central European cultural production by Western European and American intellectual consumers. Inspired by the groundbreaking analysis of the Oriental Other in nineteenth-century Europe published by Edward Said, scholars like Igor Zabel from Slovenia, Nada Beroš from Croatia, and Piotr Piotrowski from Poland have lucidly examined and dissected the motivations behind Western interest in Eastern European culture. This discussion of postcolonialism has been necessary during the past decade of identity-building in the East and discovery in the West. It is the position of the editors of this anthology, however, that understanding is the foundation of critical analysis, and that critical theory is shaky indeed without it.

After more than thirteen years since the end of Soviet domination of this region, it is time to add to this rich discourse of self-examination a helping of historical information in the belief that the understanding of cultural production begins with the revelation of its sources. It is with this that a history—or many histories—can be built.

As more and more contemporary art from Eastern Europe becomes accessible to the West through the proliferation of information systems like international exhibitions, print publications, and the Internet, it becomes increasingly necessary to provide a context for what we can see for the first time. It is hoped that with access to these texts, English-speaking readers can begin to have a more complex understanding of the very different issues that surround contemporary art in this region, and the circumstances that contributed to its making.

—Laura Hoptman and Tomáš Pospiszyl

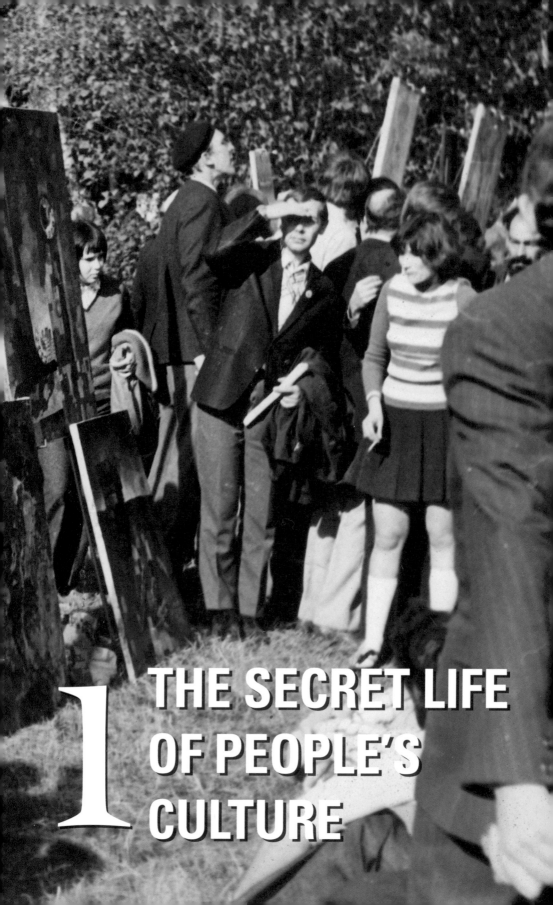

1 THE SECRET LIFE OF PEOPLE'S CULTURE

Before the fall of the Iron Curtain, art in many countries of Central and Eastern Europe existed under the more-or-less repressive conditions of the totalitarian State, with the level of oppression varying in intensity and from place to place. The rigid rules of Socialist Realism, the only official art doctrine, were quietly loosened in most countries in the late 1950s, aided by the Twentieth Congress of the Soviet Communist Party, where Stalin's dictatorship was criticized. However, it took several years before more liberal policies reached all aspects of society, including the arts. In some countries, limited independent cultural activities were tolerated, in others not. In general, culture remained under the control of the State, and, when needed, ideologically defined Socialist Realism was used to discredit artists or prevent them from freely publishing or exhibiting their work.

Contact with Western art was suppressed, and efforts to organize progressive exhibitions were rejected if not criminalized. Young people were denied access to art schools, not on the basis of their talent but according to their political profile; art magazines were under constant censorship; and museums and galleries showed only those artists whose work was sympathetic to the official politics of the time. It was possible to control and regulate access to State galleries and museums and to influence and "guide" many artists, but it proved impossible to stop some artists from making the kind of art they wanted to make. A complex network of alternative avenues of distribution and operation, which included self-published books and private exhibitions and concerts, was established, built directly on a tradition developed during World War II and earlier in reaction to a history of repressive regimes in the region that had existed for decades in various forms. Between the two oppositions—official and unofficial culture—there existed a so-called gray area in which these two extremes overlapped and sometimes even collaborated.

Autonomous artistic expression, therefore, came to be understood both by the authorities and the artists themselves not as something belonging solely to the sphere of aesthetics, but more as an act with political consequences. If Western postwar modernism up to the 1960s displayed an inordinate concern for artistic form over content, a large part of artistic expression in Eastern Europe inevitably had political motives, beside which formal experiments paled. This led to difficulties in creating criteria by which to judge such art, because it tended to play an important role in the larger struggle for political freedom.

This chapter begins in the 1960s, when the most difficult period of Stalinism was over. However, in most cases it was still impossible for artists and critics to express themselves freely in the public arena. Contact with Western art was obstructed or strictly forbidden, and in some regions it was even difficult for artists and theoreticians to communicate with one another, as official platforms for such interactions had not been established or were completely controlled by the State. Nevertheless, under the seemingly homogenous surface of official art, there persisted many lively attempts to create an autonomous visual culture.

It is important to understand that many Eastern European intellectuals were politically oriented to the Left, and some of them, even at this time, believed that their political system could be reformed. But history brought one disillusionment after another, and, as the essay "The Intellectual under Socialism" by the Czech critic Jindřich Chalupecký demonstrates, in time left-wing political beliefs were disassociated from Soviet power. The recollections of Russian artist Yuri Sobolev illustrate not only the uneasy struggle for free expression of his artist friends—the Estonian Ülo Sooster and the Russian Ilya Kabakov—but detail the everyday problems that artists living under socialism had to face. Ivan M. Jirous, a Czech critic and activist, writes mostly on rock music, but his essay "A Report on the Third Czech Musical Revival" served as a manifesto and theoretical base for creation of a parallel culture in many different mediums. Coriolan Babeti's essay on the Romanian artist Stefan Bertalan conjures the isolated atmosphere in which independent-minded artists had to work in that country.

A case study, which supplements the chapter, consists of a description, timeline, and selection of articles and comments about the so-called Bulldozer show, an independent, open-air art exhibition in Moscow in 1974 that was violently terminated by Soviet State authorities. The show became a symbol for the state of contemporary art in Eastern Europe, and although widely reported by Western media at the time, it remains relatively undocumented.

—*Tomáš Pospiszyl*

YURI SOBOLEV

Born in 1928 in Moscow, the artist and writer Yuri Sobolev has played an essential role in the development of Russian art for many decades. In the 1960s and 1970s he was a prominent member of Conceptual art circles, and it was against this backdrop that he wrote the following essay on the occasion of an exhibition about the Moscow-Tallinn art axis. Written as a lyrical memoir of Sobolev's friendship with Ülo Sooster (1924–1970), an Estonian modernist artist living in Moscow, the text describes the romanticized notions that artists living in Moscow harbored about Tallinn, Estonia, which to them retained some semblance of openness in contrast to Moscow. Sobolev captures the mythological and often surreal dichotomies between home and isolation, nostalgia and reality.

Virtual Estonia and No Less Virtual Moscow: An Essay on Island Mythology

Strictly speaking, I cannot claim to have any sort of objective knowledge of Estonian mentality, of the artistic environment of Tallinn, or the problems of interrelations on the Tallinn-Moscow axis.

These notes do not strive to be either scientific or documentary, or even less — documentary research. I am merely trying to figure out how this cluster of concepts, feelings, and notions gradually established itself in my mind, born as it was from misunderstandings, conjectures, projections, and metaphors, all disguised as logical deductions.

It seems to me that fundamental and scientific treatments of many topics often lack this kind of intimate approach. Far from being objective or exact, this is a result of a free play of archetypes, which are intertwined to form a mythologeme entitled ESTONIA.

Where did we get to?

My penetration beyond the unknown boundary dividing the "line of alienation" of the Leningrad October railway station from Estonia proper was accomplished as on a computer: I needed a password which would open up the access to a certain sphere inaccessible to the uninitiated, an incantation.

For me, as for a great number of Moscow artists and critics, there was a definite password, which made the protected area accessible, the password was: **sooster.**

The place where we then found ourselves was not, in fact, the real, authentic Estonia; it was a *virtual* Estonia, which each of us perceived as his or her own personal version of the country. I know only mine, and this is what I am trying to describe.

Virtual Estonia . . .

But first of all, [Ülo] Sooster himself had to make his appearance on the Moscow scene. His story was the following: In 1956 Sooster was released from the camp in Karaganda.[1] Lida had joined him in the zone — being released earlier; so there, in the zone, the romantic prison love came to its happy ending. The newlyweds traveled to Tallinn. But the official Estonia received them coldly, showing no sign of being pleased. For the Union of Artists Ülo Sooster was a *persona non grata.*

Sooster took offence and went back to Moscow, to Lida's home place. In October 1956, the young couple came to my flat on Kazak Lane.

This was when we became friends.

In fact, Ülo was the first person from abroad I had ever met. His foreign origin did not manifest itself through unusual manners or the strange Georgian-Baltic accent (he had learned Russian from Georgians in the prison camp). He confirmed the existence of a space called **abroad** by his entirely unusual approach to the problems and occurrences of my reality and his foreign rituals of everyday life in which I imagined to hear the echoes of an exotic magic. It all reminded me of the ancient travelers' treatises about countries whose inhabitants had dogs' heads, or only one foot, or snakelike arms, about islands beyond the boundaries of reality. And beyond those boundaries I, too, felt at home . . .

One sunny day, Sooster and I were lazily strolling along Tver Boulevard sipping Bulgarian wine from a wicker bottle and benevolently observing very young girls in their early spring bloom — a blissful state for a seaman on leave. Suddenly I noted how Sooster's gaze became tense, his face changed, he looked around anxiously and asked with genuine amazement: "Yuri, where are we? What sort of a town is it? Where have we got to?" This was a breakthrough to the reality with which we refused to identify.

Virtual time

We had problems with time and space. We were both looking for a lost time. Sooster's time continuum had a gap of about thirty years. And it was not only the time in the camp and at war. He had experienced this asynchronous state already in bourgeois Estonia. The more so was the case with me!

Now, in order to "mend" the gaps in his time, Sooster invented a somewhat naive ontogenic literal method. He suggested (or, to be more correct, demanded) that we should restore, in a compressed way, the whole chain of development of art of the last thirty years: the principles of deformation of Cubism and Expressionism, the spatial inventions of Picasso, Braque, de Chirico and Morandi, the abstractions of Mondrian and Pollock, the Surrealism of Max Ernst and René Magritte, the poetics of Klee and Miró . . . It was a kind of sophisticated theater performance. We wore holes in our trousers sitting in libraries, studying monographs and journals about the drama of art and the great masters of the twentieth century. And later, standing in front of our easels in the studio, we kept trying on their costumes and masks and assuming their roles. We sought to experience the births, deaths and transformations of these artistic strategies. Above all it was an alchemical idea of being a disciple of a wizard. To carry out all the reactions described in the books, to perform all magic rituals, restore the lost sequence of transformations and purification in the hope of summoning a potent spirit of time and space and obtaining from it the recipe of the philosophers' stone. This was the essence of the Estonian "island" strategy.

"Jeder ist ein Ausländer . . ."

The discontinuity or discreet nature of time was also a source of one of our spatial problems: We were living in an isolated, curiously indeterminate space. Like the irresolvable contradiction of Zenon where the arrow can neither be found where it is nor where it is not.

Normally we were in a third place: on a fictitious island in a virtual space in another country. We were yearning to find our organic place in time, removing ourselves from the one that was occurring around us. We wanted to live in a way we thought we should live. We were not transferring situations from abroad; we were the carriers of foreigners' sincere viewpoints. These were not the points of a crew of dissidents, but rather of escapists — very frank and natural.[2]

For me and Ülo Sooster, the principal spatial problem was determined by a search for our own virtual island where we could hoist our flag and which we could reach easily any time. In reality, Ülo had discovered a multitude of such islands: Wednesdays or Fridays on Krasin Street, then the Nolev's Ark[3] on Kirov Street, the Artistic Café, the studios in Southwest Moscow and on Leningrad Road. And Sooster's last island in his Sretenie Boulevard studio which he left twice a week to visit the reality of his home, family, and Moscow, and whence one day he disappeared for ever . . .

Beyond this dry patch of land surrounded by oceanic waters existed another reality — abroad. And according to our theory of relativity it was the place where foreigners lived . . . or perhaps we ourselves as foreigners. This was a feeling I first experienced in Tallinn among a throng of people speaking a foreign language. "Foreigners!" I thought and corrected myself at once: "Oh no, they are at home here, I am a foreigner."

"Jeder ist ein Ausländer. Fast überall"

Three decades later I read this noble slogan on a street in Cologne: "Everyone is a foreigner. Almost everywhere." An island is not only a blissful refuge in the ocean of an alien reality; it is also a place of solitude and seclusion. This is why the inhabitants of virtual islands long to populate them. The aborigines were happy to receive any visitor. That was how groups were formed. It meant a large number of steady visitors at cafés; those who were closer gathered regularly at each others' homes; and those closer still were artists, scientists, and musicians who shared each other's views. In 1958, I first met [the Russian sculptor] Ernst Neizvestny on a plane. We kept talking all through the flight and on our way from the airport I took him to the Artistic Café. There, at his usual table near the window, with countless coffee cups and a plate of peculiar sculptural biscuits called Brushwood, Ülo Sooster was sitting and drawing something on pieces of paper. I introduced them. The first visitor had landed on the island. In 1960 came more visitors: young graduates from the Moscow Printing Institute, Vladimir Yankilevsky and Viktor Pivovarov. Temporary refuge was given to a Harkov artist Brussilovsky and in 1960 Ilya Kabakov joined the islanders. Some other names could be mentioned but the native islanders remained the same: Ülo and Yuri.

Bottom Ice. Mythologeme No. 1

We both came from islands. This is why we immediately understood each other and appreciated the fact that many things never needed long explanations.

But in order to better understand the mentality of virtual islands, it is necessary to introduce a mythologeme which is fairly essential for the understanding of virtual Estonia. It is directly linked to the cordiality and openness but at the same time with the protected nature of its inhabitants. This also determines many stylistic peculiarities of its art.

This is the mythologeme of underwater ice. These island people possess something that I could never manage to develop — a special strategy of communication.

You submerge yourself in water and it seems warm, then it begins to get colder and colder and then, all of a sudden, you touch something chilly and impenetrable: the crust of bottom ice. This is what a Russian usually keeps hitting his nose against in contacts with foreigners. It is discouraging. But there is also a constructive side: it creates a very comfortable, I would even say, productive framework for communication. Because within the space between the surface of water and the bottom ice you can feel totally secure. You will be warned in due time when you cannot go any further. This is a part of the Estonian mentality and I think one of its noble qualities. This reservation protects not only your partner's inner world but your own as well. It does not let you overflow in the wrong direction or by mistake. It also creates the impression of a magic secrecy, inexpressible in words. Through the ice you seem to discern the outlines of the most important, the eternal . . . The ultimate truth!

Ülo and Ülo. A Secret Brotherhood: Mythologeme No. 2

Sooster had a global project for overcoming the island desertedness and isolation: the concept of brotherhood.

It was based on a fact of purely accidental similarity. At the first sight Ülo and I were very much alike which sometimes led to comical mistakes. On the island we were brothers. I think I have never felt a deeper affinity with any other male being in my life. It was more than friendship and something different from a relationship of a teacher and a disciple because we kept exchanging our roles. It could be better described as a blood relation. And that is how Sooster's rela-

Ülo Sooster. Untitled. 1963. Oil on illustration board, 13¹³⁄₁₆ × 19¹¹⁄₁₆" (35 x 50.1 cm). Jane Voorhees Zimmerli Art Museum, Rutgers, The State University of New Jersey, The Norton and Nancy Dodge Collection of Nonconformist Art from the Soviet Union

tives treated me and how my elderly parents treated him. And Sooster's island mentality—the curious mixture of sober determinism, cool and eccentric nihilism, and mighty emotions of a mannerist type—turned the accidental into the magical. The island myths were supplemented with the myth of twins. Twin brothers, coupled according to the principle of difference and complementation, the harmonious binary of black and white, affirmation and negation, praise and depreciation, birth and death, permanent variability and variable permanence. With deadly seriousness and fits of earnest mirth, Castor and Pollux from a Moscow basement studio literally collected people with identical appearance: snapshots from magazines, reproductions of paintings, or just information of someone having amazing similarity with the exemplary pair—either living or dead, old or young, of whatever field of activity or place of birth. They were incredibly numerous. From the Polish film star Zbigniew Cybulski to an anonymous Buddhist monk from a snapshot in the magazine *Ogoniok.* All of them, without knowing it, were part of a universal brotherhood of islanders, something like a secret affiliation, a worldwide conspiracy of noble allies, a dream of Teilhard de Chardin. I refuse to judge what was prevailing in the concept—the absurd fun-making or the nostalgia of a forsaken island.

Bardo

Ülo died unexpectedly, enigmatically, and in solitude on his island on Sretenie Boulevard in October 1970.

His remains were displayed in the hall of the animated cartoon film studio Multifilm. His soul was going through the ordeal of descending into the Ugric Chonyid Bardo[4]—a landscape scarcely illuminated by the North Star. Swift transformations were soundlessly quaking that world. The skeleton of a juniper was being covered with ornamental flesh of a fish, the inner framework of which was restructuring itself into an egg already pregnant with a bird growing fins, submerging into water and bursting forth again with the needles of a bush— the endless Sansara of Sooster's lifelong dreams.

But already the lights of Paris streets were extinguished by the Superbird Hornebom who dashed away like a swallow, the "thousand-faced woman" dissolved in the darkness of the lifelong dreams of an island artist. The outlines of a virtual world were melting away. And the frosty reality was coming into view: boulders where Kalevipoeg had left the runic marks of his hands and feet, the thistles which had grown of the drops of his sweat, the perfect hemispheres of ice-age hills, the traces of a giant's fertile plough or the feeding breasts of Earth Mother Maaema.

Through the crust of bottom ice faces of thunder gods and demiurges, the gods of the heavens and their heavenly wives were making their appearance— the simple gods and spirits, rulers of nature and the elemental powers, guardian spirits of crafts . . .

And the publican remembers them, the long-forgotten ancient names. They sound patriarchal and familiar: Vanaisa—Grandfather, Taevataat—Heavenly Father . . . The ice was completely melted. Sooster had returned to his homeland. Alone.

"Poor Ülo!" cried Moscow sculptor Ernest Neizvestny bitterly, standing by his coffin.

The Abroad is Tallinn: A Virtual Flight to Paris via China

In 1957 Sooster and I went together to Estonia for the first time.

Understandably, I arrived in Estonia with a pronounced sense of guilt. I came from the invader's country, from among the occupants who had destroyed the peaceful and comfortable life of a lovely little state. I could not help feeling ashamed and sharing the responsibility for the deportations, arrests, and persecutions that my empire had brought onto the Estonians. (I had a similar gruesome feeling of guilt with respect to Czechs. In spite of having many opportunities I never went to Prague after 1968, although I had close friends among the artists in Prague.) So when I was kindly received in Estonia — it happened very quickly — I experienced the joy of being forgiven, a great influx of gratitude, which may have begun to operate as a feedback. I was able to enter very cordial relationships with many people, which led to close, almost blood-related ties. These people belonged to the hapless generation of Sooster and also younger artists, the circle of [the Estonian printmaker] Tõnis Vint. I think that our relationships were being formed at the greatest possible distance from the surface of water, and sometimes even deeper.

My personal attitude toward Estonia was, of course, brotherly. I was perhaps one of the few Russians accepted into the Estonian artistic community. And I would never have entered it if it were not through the back door, as a friend of Sooster . . . It seemed to me that I was really trusted. I could easily dive right to the crust of the underwater ice. And I found myself in the virtual space. It seemed that Estonians, too, had their spatial and temporal problems.

In Tallinn the atmosphere was very peculiar: Life had stopped in 1940 — people were wearing clothes and hats dating from the beginning of the 40s. They sat on the first floor of the old-fashioned, time-worn café called Tallinn, in the daytime drinking weak coffee and listening to the quiet murmur of chamber music on stringed instruments and, as it seemed, were holding the same leisurely conversations of the dreamlike mythical time of 1938, or 1939, or 1940. But the ground floor of the café Tallinn was the meeting place of the bohemian subculture of the town. Here, not only weak coffee but also beer and smuggled-in vodka were drunk by the picturesquely ragged, marginal characters, students wearing their corporation caps called tekkel, and artists. It was the simulated prewar Paris with its Montmartre and Montparnasse. The bourgeois Estonia was virtually present along with the space of a typical Soviet town with the republican subordination. This second (or first) reality was testified not only by groups of shamelessly noisy drunken Russian aliens on the streets but also the painfully familiar signs of typically Soviet desolate and dangerous tedium. The amazing beauty of a medieval seaside town was also an existing reality — the sign of a romantic foreign land of Zurbagan, a harbor for sailing ships ready to receive the star stowaways of Vasili Aksionov. Very near the café Tallinn, Sooster used to have his studio on the top floor of a gothic tower. Once on a spring night in 1949 he arrived there, happy after a first date, exhilarated by the spring and wine. Within two hours he was forced to come down the same steep staircase, arrested by the KGB for an attempt to escape abroad: "to Paris via China," as was written on the papers of accusation.

"Poor Ülo!"

A Virtual Flight: To New York via Helsinki

And still real life was showing through the nostalgic virtual reality. Tallinn kept in step with the times. And in the most advanced way at that. Estonia was the first, and perhaps the only one of the Union's republics that was blessed with access to electronic information. Transmissions of Finnish television could be received in every Estonian house adorned with a T-shaped aerial cross. This kind of cross represents the balance of opposing forces. Balanced and free of contradictions, the remembrances and expectations converged at one point: here and now, which conquered space and time. Because the "here" did not mean the streets of Tallinn, and the "now" was taking place in virtual time. Traveling through the dusky Bardo of Soviet actuality, it was becoming possible to encounter the reality where "pure light and achievement of freedom" are experienced.

[Jean] Baudrillard's "phobia of reality" was being overcome. The somatic aspect was dying and being transformed into the psychic one, and so the television viewer, dying in this sense, acquired Maya-Rupa — the "Luminous illusory body." True, just as in Bardo, the psychosomatic *simulacrum* of a person asks himself: "Am I dead or alive?" — and is not able to give an answer. He sees his relatives and friends as he saw them before, and hears them weep . . . But it is all vague and indistinct. The important thing was that the virtual reality replaced the actuality and was itself transformed into actuality. In nonvirtual queues Estonians discussed the prices of virtual goods and bought stale Soviet margarine: Finnish TV was transmitting the margarine advertising campaign.

I think this unique invasion of reality into the virtual world, the earliest in the history of civilization (thirty years before Baudrillard's *The Gulf Wars Did Not Take Place*), embraced practically the whole population of Kalevipoeg's land from the ministers to the eccentric marginal characters. The unique fact was that they all lived in two virtual countries at the same time. I visited one of them on my first trip to Tallinn: it was the canned life with a prewar passport. The other was the space of the *simulacrum* — the electronic actuality full of archetypes, ideas, protagonists, fashions, and news of the television world. "This beer is far from being beer but it is balanced by the fact that this cigar is no longer a cigar. If the beer was not beer but the cigar was still a cigar — then it would be a problem." (I am citing Brecht cited by Baudrillard.)

This paradigm naturally also included the young artists from Tönis Vint's circle whom I actually visited during all my subsequent trips "abroad." They certainly saw and criticized the hopeless idiocy of the electronic messages but within the confines of this same virtual reality. They set themselves and their way of life against the pettiness of Finnish bourgeois society but not against their own Tallinn one. They were ironical toward the Philistine prewar cultural canons and silently ignored the Soviet provincial reality. It was the reverse, negative version of the Finnish petty-bourgeois society, the nostalgic *simulacrum* of the Tallinn of 1939 and the everyday life in the capital of Soviet Estonia.

Yet the electronic media also included messages of a different kind. In homeopathic doses the foreigners in Tallinn managed to extract from it particles of alternative information much the same way as we did in Moscow when reading between the lines in publications like the "criticism of bourgeois philosophy" or the "crisis of the deformity" of modernist art. In this way our thirst for a different kind of information and a different life was quenched and, limping, we kept in step with the times. Virtual Finland, though, lived synchronously with the events taking place in the galleries of New York and Berlin, transmitting in real time the newest artistic texts to the studios of Mustamäe. For us, foreigners from the capital, where all the artistic trends and ideas from the end of the last century to the middle of this one existed simultaneously, Tallinn was perhaps, up to the middle of the 70s, our principal guide to the context of real culture and art.

My Tallinn friends, though, had one more strong antidote for the Finnish Maya-Rupa. It was the healthy immunity of the people who were firmly tied to their land.

Soil. Mythologeme No. 3: Family and Roots

Ülo Sooster was brought up on an island farm. He ate fish right after it was taken from the fishing net, and eggs which were freshly laid, and he drank, according to his own words, the warm milk brought to the table right from the cow's udder. After graduating, Tönis Vint dealt with designs for advertising milk products. He and other members of the Vint clan were already a bit further removed, by a generation of intellectuals, from the natural Estonian farm life. And their art as well seemed to lie in the further sphere of the international avant-garde. Yet these nonconformists clearly continued to identify with their family and roots.

The Christian culture had ousted the archetypes of Estonian ancient myths into the national unconsciousness. This is why there is no ground for serious hypotheses, and only irresponsible and very tempting speculations are possible. Let us agree that they are related to the virtual and not to the objective Estonia.

The Estonian mentality does not seem to have a clearly noticeable Oedipus complex.[5] The son of Kalev was not an adversary to his father and did not try to kill his mother.

All my Estonian friends had strong family support, which is not character-istic of us Russians and of many other nations in the world where there is always a barrier, a confrontation of generations. I did not notice this in the inhabitants of Tallinn, who showed traditionally supportive feelings toward their children who in turn had normal relationships with the older generation. On the street or on a bus you may note how respectfully an elderly Estonian addresses an unfamiliar child. During my first visit to Estonia I was amazed by the close con-tact that existed between the prominent artists and the "young." In the café, where artists gathered, I demonstrated to my friends some blurred photographs of my not very outstanding works. All of a sudden, someone asked from behind my back: "May I have a look?" I gave my permission, he looked, made some re-marks and left. I asked who he was? And I was told that it was [Evald] Okas, the member of the Academy of Fine Arts of the USSR. By the way, his son Jüri Okas, one of the extreme radicals of the 70s and 80s, was not only recognized by his father as an artist, but he also influenced his father, who started painting things unacceptable by Soviet academic standards. The young generation did not re-ject the life style of their parents altogether. Neither did the parents reject the way of life of their sons and daughters who were seeking alternative techniques.

Family and roots—the primary mythologemes of Estonia—escape the ficti-tious games of the virtual world. This is the sphere of authentic reality. These texts do not lend themselves to simulation, just as it is impossible to falsify the shaman's drum or runic signs on a stone: they simply will not work and will lose their magic.

Identity[6]

With pride, softened by his usual ironic reflection, Sooster once cited to me an excerpt from Hemingway's *To Have and Have Not:* "And in every harbor you will find two Estonians with their sailing boat preparing for a trip around the world." "Two Estonians in a harbor" at once became an important idiom in Ülo's and my language of the birds. "Floating islands" — the islands drifting around the ocean of the world, always retaining their island sovereignty and the flag of their registration port.

The Estonian classic artist Eduard Viiralt belonged to the École de Paris and spent half of his life in the Rotonde café and still remained a national Estonian artist. The young Estonian artists of the 70s were sitting at home. Besides the short visits to Moscow, they never traveled in the usual sense of the word. But, staying at home, they constantly traveled in time, from the real Estonian time to the virtual time of the "abroad." A large number of international exhibitions and awards confirm the success of those voyages, the synchrony of their work with the trends on the international art scene, the actuality of their strategies, and also their relative independence and originality.

On my walls I have some graphic works of the Estonians of the 70s. The conceptual silk-screens of Raul Meel, which against the dark blue background the incisively white system of lines predetermines the curvatures which describe with precision and clarity the progress of unknown events. They can equally be changes in the level of hemoglobin in the blood of a rocker escaping from the police in New York, fluctuations of currency rates in the Tokyo stock exchange, or the distribution of root words in the Uganda language in relation to explanatory words or thousands of other processes — for such is the international universality of informatics. There is no trace of real Estonia besides the title of the series "Under the Estonian Sky." And besides the visual presence of this sky. The mandala of Tõnis Vint: in a black, void, circular sphere, delicate white and red shapes are formed which then dissolve into darkness — a continuous text of a "calm mind," a record of lyrical meditation. It does not have a nationality or a postal code. And still these sheets are infallibly Estonian. This kind of metaphysical decorativeness, fictitious objectivity, and poise of lyrical minimalism is unique.

When I think of dozens of other works by the artists in Tallinn twenty years ago, the meaningless concern about the establishment of the "boundaries of the individual national ego" comes to my mind. For [Leonhard] Lapin, [Jüri] Arrak, [Andres] Tolts, and Jüri Okas this concern about national "identity" was superfluous. The organic connection these artists had with their native land automatically guaranteed the "national sovereignty" and its localization in visual arts.

The Experimental: Transplantation of an Estonian into an Unfamiliar Ground

In Moscow, Sooster found himself in an environment, which, although surrounded by the Iron Curtain, was intensely non-Estonian; it was a cosmopolitan mentality, traditionally typical for Russian intellectuals, which easily acquired forms of whatever it communicated with in the process of the exchange of ideas, without any risk to national identity which in Russian history traditionally characterizes only the retrograde nationalists and reactionary officials.

Our circle—the Moscow Russians, Ukrainians, Jews, Armenians, Abhasians, Tartars, Georgians—organically identified with the Russian culture. You may have been deeply immersed in Buddhist, Tantric, or cabalistic discourse, be a skeptic or an atheist or a mystic, and still remain in the all-pervading vigorous context of the Russian Orthodox continuum. Suffice it to mention such different personalities of the Moscow artistic scene as [Ilya] Kabakov and [Eric] Bulatov, [Eduard] Shteinberg and [Vladimir] Yankilevsky, [Mikhail] Shvartsman and [Andrei] Monastyrski, [Ernst] Neizvestny and [Viktor] Pivovarov, [Dmitri] Plavinsky and [Vagrich] Bakhchanyan. Sooster had mastered the full course of prison-camp internationality and felt at ease among the cosmopolitans of Moscow. It was easy for him to remain Estonian in Moscow because the Moscow scene never made an attempt to Russify him. For the Muscovites he was valuable and interesting as one more salient form of mentality—the foreigner's. But first and foremost as a dissimilar and strange personality—another being.

It seemed to me that Sooster never felt a need of elaborating, a specific Estonian discourse within the polylingual Moscow environment. One is, of course, free to project the junipers of his pictures to the landscape of Western Estonia, the fish to his childhood dreams of fishing on the island, and to correlate the egg with the mythical primordial egg, which, having dropped from Ilmatar's (Väinämöinen's mother) knee, fell into pieces and formed Water, Earth, and Sky. For Sooster all these archetypes were the crystallization of metaphors in the flux of the metalanguage of virtual Moscow which ignored frontiers and nationalities. This was one of the interesting lessons that the Estonian apprentices traveling to Moscow were experiencing at the beginning of the 60s.

Trips of Estonian Masters and Apprentices: Moscow Abroad

The artists of Sooster's generation, who had studied with him either in Tallinn or in Tartu (all of them had also been to prison camps), started visiting him in Moscow to seek information and an alternative way of life. After exile they lacked the dynamism of life. The artistic climate in Tallinn was, at that time, rather stagnant and uninteresting. Exile had been a more vehement situation than the one that surrounded them now. And they felt the need to go abroad—to Moscow. They visited us periodically: Valdur Ohakas and Heldur Viires had shared Ülo's fate and were his classmates from Tartu. With the generation there was also change of apprentices: Jaan Klõsheiko, Malle Leis, who, even after acquiring the masters' skills, still continued their pilgrimages. Still later, a new "independent" generation joined them: Raul Meel and Leonhard Lapin. On every visit they discovered a new situation in the virtual reality of "unofficial art"—the Moscow scene was in the process of rapid, effervescent development. Every now and then new characters appeared, old residents matured, and newcomers joined them, groups and large groupings were formed like that of the "Liazonova Group" and the school of Beliutin.

First Sooster and I escorted the visitors to the artists' studios. Later they all came to know each other and the initial apprehension and uneasiness of the pilgrims disappeared. They started to visit the studios on their own. There was one compulsory route. It first remained within the limits of the island of Ülo and me. But it kept gradually expanding.

By the beginning of the 60s a topographic grouping had formed in the area of Sretenie Boulevard and Sretenka Street. My Novel's Ark was situated right by the Kirov Gates, and in the Russia House were the studios of Kabakov and Sooster. Neizvestny was initially sculpting on Sretenka Street until he, too, moved to a studio in Sretenie Boulevard. Brussilovsky — an immigrant from Harkov — lived on Stopani Street. And so it continued until the Manezh exhibition.[7] There we exhibited together as a compact group: Neizvestny, Yankilevsky, Sooster, and I, your humble servant.

In 1964 a typical "geographical adventure" took place: I moved to Bauman Street and a studio in Trubnaya and, deprived of telephones, found myself in topographical isolation. For Sooster and me, the occasions of landing on our island became rather rare. Yet on Sretensk Boulevard the forming and re-forming of groups went on as before. In the 70s, after Ülo's death, the historical grouping was formed which became the crest of the "Moscow wave" in 1988–89.

This digression into history was necessary to outline the Moscow routes of the Estonian visitors, which they followed with a critical interest. My works were found to be inadequately finished, the straightforward pathos of Neizvestny's symbols left them puzzled, Yankilevsky could not be completely trusted: the complicated refined form did not match the simplicity of his metaphors. Kabakov's lessons we poorly understood in the beginning. And this misunderstanding was natural. His language was radical from the very start and it differed from other texts of the Moscow school.[8]

Later the lessons he communicated were understood and absorbed.

Without doubt, the main guide and mediator was Sooster. Independent, equally different, and similarly authoritative for Moscow as well as for Tallinn, he stood in the middle of the bridge connecting the two cities. He was admirable in his profound simplicity and tolerance. The most important fact was that the lessons he taught concerned the content, not the form, and even if the form was involved, it was the thought forms, the strategy of conceptions, not solutions. Members of both groups learned from him. And quite a number of people managed to learn a lot.

I did not often discuss the results of the pilgrims' expeditions, especially during the period of their independent visits. That is why I can only presume, although it would be very interesting to know for sure, their reaction to the metaphysical [Dmitrii] Krasnopevtsev, Shvartsman, the mystical translator of supreme messages, the megacephalic [Oleg] Tselkov, the unruly [Anatolii] Zverev, the refined [Boris] Sveshnikov, and the majestic Bulatov. A reaction was certainly there, the dialogue was actively sustained, and the coexistence between the two areas was developing within the framework of the independence of each. Both consisted of self-reliant personalities. That is why it would not be right to talk of direct influences or imitations of one another. Everyone knew his worth and therefore deduced from the communication its meaningful part, not the outer form. This was evident already at our first joint exhibition in Tallinn, naively and spontaneously organized by me in 1967.

Design of a Trap to Capture the Emptiness

The process of understanding a text is in itself the text of paramount importance, a determinant of the meaning of a work of art. It was something that many of us Muscovites sensed by the middle of the 70s. It was becoming clear from this process of peeling off the layers of meaning that these layers do not conceal the ultimate truth but one aspect of absolute silence and emptiness which has the ability to generate a presentiment (pre-expectation) and expectation of the truth outside a work of art.[9] This state of mind is essentially introspective, it is turned inward into the consciousness of the spectator and excludes the material reality with its objects, and it includes an experience of the void. This is what we kept saying with the self-confidence of Eurasians who had briefly encountered the Buddhists' paradigms.

"Emptiness," "void" — these terms entered the slang of the Moscow artists. And everyone was seeking the methods that could supply his work with this quality. I happened to develop a method that could be called "it is not that." In short, it was an attempt to create a maximally many-layered structure consisting of fictitious meanings. Every layer was to induce the expectation of a "core meaning." Having entered it, the spectator would understand that "it is not that," the layer would be peeled off and the spectator would be led to the next one, etc. Until the fictitious nature of the whole structure was revealed and the spectator would be left with the expectation of an encounter with himself. This complicated structure was found to be a phantom, a disappearing mirage and the graphic work thus became a manifold imitation. Such a minimalist gesture, which did not mean anything beyond the gesture itself, seemed to bring my strategy nearer to the strategy of Vint. Vint and his school rejected the aggressive gesture in drawing and also the emotion in the organization of composition.

The space of minimal messages was designed according to the principles of European rational geometry, the module, which excludes even the least artistic willfulness. This space could nominally also possess the quality of the notorious emptiness. I would say that this void was created by the strictly reglementary actions of the artist, beginning with the format of the paper chosen by him. He had a permanent module, a window within which he placed his world, it was almost a square and yet not quite a square. I would say that this format of the module was rigorously followed by all Vint's disciples and the artists of his circle.

The ritual discipline of creating an object decided the size of the module and predetermined the arrangement of its parts. Tönis seemed to declare: I feel that I need to establish a module, in principle, it does not matter which. The fact that I feel the need for this module is my communication with something superior to you and me. And the nature of the module is my business.

"I decided the size of my module and restricted my artistic language so that I could operate with, say, only black and white, or, once in a while, to add a little red. I set myself limitations determining that the surface of the canvas or paper may be either black with white forms and red dots, or white with black lines. I set myself limitations in the sense that my gesture must not be emotional. If these limitations are set rigorously and if they are reproduced from one sheet to another with the steadfast tenacity of a ritual, a special meaning is found." You toil hard to forge your work, you never think of voluntarily violating the module, you fight the imperative of this module and thus a powerful aggregation of energy is achieved which has nothing to do with the things depicted. It has to do with overcoming the chasm between my own reality and the reality of the thing. As soon as this new reality is materialized — and for Tönis it meant to accomplish his task according to the precepts of the strict imperative of the module — the work became impersonal. The only personal quality of it is the evident fact that this is the work of Tönis Vint or someone of his school. After that this fact can be dismissed. The next thing to dismiss is the layer of iconography and subject. And we are left with the mirrorlike surface of underwater ice in which the spectator is faced with the risk of seeing his own reflection; we are left with the expectation of emptiness because nothing is left, yet the energy flow is there. While describing this process of "minus reality plus energy" it occurs to me that to a large extent I am projecting my own strategy on Tönis Vint's. This is understandable as we are both working within the limits of the modular system. And this system leads us, in spite of ourselves, from the realm of objects to the realm of objectivity. The European Tönis seems to be less radical and more decorative in the sense that he tried to transmit thought contents. He tried to actualize them through a form, instead of obliterating them. But for me it is now important to state with gratitude that the very significant idea of a strictly regimented magic ritual, the principle of a module, I received straight from Tallinn.

"Where is Maria Nikolayevna?"

As I begin this chapter I cannot but repeat to the reader my total inability to be objective. I cannot decide if it is at all possible. In my case I lack the distance, the "going over the borders" of the system of Godel.[10] And also the conviction of an objective existence of Moscow and Tallinn outside my personal experience. I prefer to remain in the safe virtual waters that wash the shores of two independent islands. We have repeatedly stated the sovereignty of these two artistic schools, those of Moscow and Tallinn. Each has its own space and destiny. Tallinners were by far the first to make a step from virtual to mundane reality. There are lots of reasons for that. Some are rather banal. For instance, despite all the hindrances the Estonian "avant-garde" started to exist in real time and space: they had exhibitions in their own country, a legally acknowledged journal, they could legally participate in exhibitions abroad, which all meant undeniable socialization. With us, the most desirable success at exhibitions still had a virtual quality. We talked about the reception of our works abroad as we would talk of the phenomena of "indifferent nature," as one would say at sunrise: "it's getting light," so we said "it's being exhibited." . . . Thus all the facts of an artist's biography slipped from the existential sphere to Heidegger's impersonal "Man" sphere. We did not use the active voice of the present or past tense "I exhibit my works" or "I exhibited my works," but a passive phrase "my works were exhibited." I regularly found invitations in my mail, delayed about 20 to 30 days, to the openings of exhibitions of artists unknown to me and sometimes even to exhibitions of my own works — these were passwords which would open an access to virtual reality. You had only to press ENTER to find yourself in a virtual street of a virtual city, to see the entrance to a virtual gallery with its halls and black-and-white reproduction of an exhibition: and you see your virtual self wearing a smock and feeling lonely in a corner of a hall, forgotten among the crowd at the opening of your virtual exhibition.[11]

In the summer of 1985 in a real glade by the motorcar route from Tallinn to Moscow I cut the ribbon tied to the branches of dusty bushes and opened, in real time but virtually, a personal exhibition of Ilya Kabakov in Bern. "No reality for exhibiting works exists," Ilya Kabakov noted in a conversation with Monastyrski, "things manifest themselves in their absolutely indeterminate indifference . . ." For the authorities who held us under lock and key, we, too, existed in a form of virtual abstraction, "in an absolutely indifferent state." The parental wrath of the authorities was aimed at the figure of a stylized "abstractionist" as a shooting target. The lordly rage was very rarely if ever able to discern a person of flesh and blood and almost never his particular works. I dare to state that after the Manezh exhibition nobody in power, except the specialists of the KGB, ever saw any works of unofficial artists.

The book designers Ilya Kabakov and Viktor Pivovarov were among the five best illustrators of the Soviet Union whose works were exhibited at pompous official exhibitions at home and abroad and shown to art history students as examples of Soviet graphic art. But the conceptualist artists Kabakov and Pivovarov did not exist in the reality of Soviet art of the 70s and 80s. "The Death of the Author" was implicitly inherent in the very system of this reality. "Where is Maria Nikolayevna? Where is Boris Ignatyevich?" — an impersonal voice asked from the void of a picture by Kabakov. And a similarly impersonal voice as the former answered with suppressed melancholy: "They are not . . ." This cosmic name-calling could last forever, including the names of the entire NOMA and no-NOMA . . .[12]

The names did not correspond to the information in the passports. The words and images did not belong to anyone: they were hanging in virtual emptiness, as trash tied to ribbons in one of Kabakov's installations entitled "A man who never threw anything away." The structuring of life into Conceptualist texts was conditioned by the context of life itself. This operation in Moscow was put in effect not only with respect to Conceptualist art but also with respect to all unofficial (and consequently virtual) art. In contrast, the Estonians started working with actual models of art and philosophy quite early. They reacted to the experiences of Moscow artists of the 60s and 70s and by the beginning of the 80s took over the strategies of contemporary art while confidently finding their own place or niche as this process was called there. I believe their originality was organically preserved during all this time. Not a single artist, a Sooster or Kabakov, was born in the Tallinn arena. The dialogue was proceeding on the level of exchanging texts, not formal languages, and information about strategies, not the strategies themselves. In my opinion it could not be otherwise. The specific characteristics of island mentality described above could not be applied or reproduced in another climate. The Tallinners and Muscovites placed the notions of structure, construction, and destruction, void and emptiness, mythological space, etc., into different contexts. The value of our communication is in the very act of relating itself, in the fact that its text is "forever written here and now."

Notes:
1. He had been arrested and falsely accused in 1950 and was sent to Kazakstan for six years.
2. By the way, such "foreigners" were quite numerous on the Moscow scene at the time. Let us remember one of Sooster's refrains expressing utter surprise: "What sort of a town is this? Where have we got to?"
3. Reference to Y. Sobolev's second family name Nolev.
4. Period of hallucination between death and rebirth, as described in the *Tibetan Book of the Dead*.

5. The three psychological levels of Berne seem to be more productive here than the purely psychoanalytic approach. According to Berne, the Parent level includes not only parents but also the country, the homeland. This is your heritage, that which as a Child you receive as a groundwork. The Adult level is the level of a person who has transcended its boundaries and achieved a healthy state in which he is able to integrate himself, find his center, his own self, to define himself as a personality responsible for his actions and able to take the responsibility off his parents and, to return to the psychoanalytic interpretation, shake them off his back. Therefore, if my guess about the son of Kalev being integrated to the level of an Adult through the characteristics of a Parent is right, the Oedipus rebellion is excluded, but at the same time it brings the Adult all the neuroses of a child living under the dominance of a Parent at the level of a Parent.

6. It is funny that there is no such word in Russian; one has to use a loan from English or a lengthy description.

7. The inclusion of abstract experimental paintings at the 1962 exhibition of the Moscow Artists Union at the Manezh exhibition hall angered Khruschev and caused a tightening of controls on culture in the Soviet Union.

8. It was not by chance that in the catalogue of our first great international exhibition *Alternativa Attuale II* in Aquila, Italy, in 1965 its curator, Chrispoldi, set Kabakov apart and grouped together Yankilevsky, Sooster, and myself.

9. "What was demonstrated to us was, in fact, the demonstration of our perception — and nothing more. This pure expectation was exactly what was going on, and it was an expectation that came true. The thing that came true, or happened, was not something that we were expecting, not a particular event that would be opposed to us; it was just the expectation that came to pass" (A. Monastyrski, "Trips to the Countryside," Moscow, 1980).

10. Kurt Godel's "undecidability theorem" states that in any logical mathematical system, there are problems that cannot be solved by any set of rules.

11. By the way, later, at the time of real exhibitions in real time and space, the poignant feeling of our marginality and virtuality did not disappear but became rather more obvious and vivid, perhaps because we never wore a smock.

12. The term "NOMA," originally proposed by the artist Pavel Peppershtein, is used to describe the circle of Moscow Conceptualist artists whose work deals with linguistics.

Written in 1996. Originally published in *Tallinn-Moskva (Moscow-Tallinn) 1956–1985* (Tallinn: Tallinn Art Hall, 1997). Reprinted here in abbreviated form. Translated by Inna Kustavus.

•●

JINDŘICH CHALUPECKÝ

Jindřich Chalupecký (1910–1990) was one of the formative Czech art historians and theoreticians of the second half of the twentieth century. He was a founding member of, and a major theoretical and organizational force behind, Group 42, an association of poets, painters, and photographers named for the year of its inception. Group 42 sought to link the self-referential avant-garde with the needs of the common people. Recognized as a leading critic of his time, Chalupecký later embraced Happenings and Conceptualism, which he was able to promote in his position as curator of the Gallery of Václav Špála in Prague in the late sixties. His last years were devoted to an expansive study of the work of Marcel Duchamp, which remained unfinished at the time of his death.

The following essay depicts the disillusionment of a Leftist intellectual just months after the Communists took power in Czechoslovakia in 1948. Formerly sympathetic to Communism and the Soviet Union, Chalupecký discovered that the current regime offered only two possibilities for leading an independent cultural life: emigrate or work outside official circles.

The Intellectual under Socialism

I think it is difficult for Western scholars to imagine the position of an intellectual in a country that has fallen under Soviet domination. Take, for example, an intellectual of the political Left. Just as in other countries, intellectuals in our country [Czechoslovakia] did not only sympathize with the Left, but also attempted to a greater or lesser degree to participate actively in its success. The majority tended to identify with the most radical faction, represented by Communism, or at the least respected its position. This does not mean that these intellectuals did not harbor certain reservations or misgivings, for even at that time there was sufficiently clear evidence of pressure exerted by the party on the arts and sciences in the USSR. Moreover, the arrival of Soviet troops [in Czechoslovakia in 1945] provided further evidence that the propaganda heralding the high cultural development of the broad Soviet masses had been greatly exaggerated. Despite this, we created our own explanations and found excuses for these unpleasant facts, as we tried to convince ourselves that we needed to consider the particular conditions of a backward country, the greater part of whose territory lay in Asia and is, moreover, endowed with a different cultural tradition from that of our own country.

It appeared self-evident to us that Communism would take on a different form in our country, especially as far as its cultural aspects were concerned. After all, would we not have a say in this decision? Assuming that the majority of us would decide to work in the Communist party or at least cooperate with the Communists, should that not be the best guarantee that things would develop differently from in the USSR? Add to this the fact that the most influential functionaries of the Communist party kept telling us how they respected our needs and intended to protect and support our work. And, indeed, did they not promise to give top priority to cultural questions in their program, and to nominate a number of distinguished cultural personalities as candidates for parliament, apart from looking after our material needs and asking for our support in elections? Did not all this show how much they valued both the arts and the sciences?

We knew that a Communist regime did not mean paradise on earth, and we realized that conditions in the USSR were far from perfect. Still, it seemed clear that if we had to choose between life in the bourgeois order with its cultural indifference, its social injustices, economic inequalities, and life under socialism — culturally engaged, socially just, and economically steered by a firm hand — there could be no doubt as to what choice we should make.

No matter whether we chose to collaborate actively, or merely engaged in wishful thinking, or just tacitly tagged along, the Communists persevered in their quest for power and eventually captured it unconditionally and absolutely. And so we woke up in a world that had never been anticipated and that was, perhaps, really not possible to anticipate.

Before we realized what was happening, the world around us changed not only in all its material aspects, but also in its intellectual complexion. People who previously had not been taken seriously by anyone — all sorts of mountebanks who abound in the cultural world — suddenly gained key positions in various official functions and public positions. People with integrity became speechless. Almost overnight, it was possible to utter the most outrageous nonsense and spread lies without anyone raising his or her voice in opposition. Any distinction between truth and falsehood, genuine values and counterfeit ones, seemed suddenly to have vanished. In place of a diverse and sophisticated culture we were presented with something so incredibly barren, monotonous, and base as to defy reason. How was this possible? How could this have happened? Here we were, ready at all times, and now, instead of socialism they had foisted upon us *this*. What made this possible? In order to find an explanation, we must first put on record two specific subjects and correct a few misunderstandings.

The first serious mistake is to assume that the Communists came to power and maintained power solely by the use of force. Daily experience shows that even though the majority of the population does identify with socialism in principle and basically does not oppose even some of its more radical forms, the prevailing Communist version of socialism is able to rely only on a small and constantly shrinking minority of the population. Still, they cannot rule by police power alone, however pervasive. In fact, violence is just one of the instruments used to maintain Communist power, and then only as a last resort.

The primary means of gaining popular assent is, without doubt, the use of the power of persuasion. The party is continually training a great number of propagandists. Not very intelligent, uneducated, loud-mouthed, self-assured, and ignorant of anything except that which they had learned in the party institutes, they act as sort of traveling salesmen, peddling Communist ideology. And it has to be admitted that their syllogisms are rather skillfully designed to gain the confidence of the unprepared and uneducated—at least for a short while. Incidentally, this ever-growing horde of agitators is presently already becoming more and more unpopular. Short of any ideas of their own and lacking any sense of humor, they drone on endlessly, repeating constantly the very same phrases that have been printed and broadcast a thousand times somewhere else. Their only success—if one can call it that—is to bore everybody to death with their endless chattering. Even this tends to benefit the regime, for their smooth and ceaseless rhetoric permeates all aspects of life and renders futile any attempt by an ordinary citizen to formulate his or her own views.

However, if these attempts at persuasion fail—and that happens quite rapidly—a second strategy has to be applied, namely, intrigue and deception. Tenacious, determined, and firmly relying on each other, Communist functionaries are quite skilled in exploiting human weaknesses. Not only do they know how to exploit the ambition and greed of those whom they need to win over to their side, or how to trap others whom they want to get out of their way, but equally they do not shrink from exploiting their indifference, ineptness, ignorance, or carelessness and, above all, their lack of tactical experience. They know how to be patient and wait for the opportunity to act resolutely and quickly whenever and wherever an opportunity presents itself. Thus, the experience gained in capturing power on the national scale is applied at a smaller scale at each and every opportunity in order to enlarge and consolidate their power. To achieve success, they know no scruples, and any resistance that cannot be co-opted or corrupted one way or another is eliminated, preferably at the very moment the opposition appeals to their integrity, since its supporters cannot imagine that they will be eliminated by lies, fraud, and deceit. We shall examine this tactic in more detail later. In the meantime, it should be kept in mind that it is another mistake to accuse the Communists of moral turpitude, for their lack of moral rectitude in these matters rests on a different foundation.

The third and most powerful tool of Communist government is its organizational ability. No one is more skillful than they are in exploiting the potential of modern organizational techniques, which make it possible to control everybody expeditiously from a small and frail center. This system, labeled "democratic centralism" by the Communist party, is superbly contrived. It is used within the organization of the party itself, and is equally applied to the building up of so-called popular mass organizations, whose main mission is to control non-Communists (such as trade unions, youth and women's organizations, etc.), whose membership is dispersed throughout a number of small and insignificant local units.

These local organizations are the only place where an individual can voice an opinion. Those seeking a forum for expressing a critical opinion find it impossible to locate any other place to gather, and being thus dispersed, their opinions inevitably get lost. Not only have these dissidents no chance to come to know each other, but they are routinely denied the opportunity to learn other views. So it becomes impossible to create any kind of coherent or significant critical mass.

These local organizations are also the only place where delegates can be elected to the district centers and from these to the regional and national centers. This provides an additional guarantee that any kind of criticism that may have emerged in any one of the local units — even if it expresses generally positive or genuinely constructive views — will be silenced long before it reaches the national center, which remains the only place where actual decisions are made. And that is the reason why it becomes futile to advance any kind of divergent opinion, even if it is presented in the most positive manner or based on sound evidence. Everybody understands this, and so people just remain silent and listen with utter boredom and resentment to the interminable speeches of the agitators sent by the party to their meetings. Instead of considering these grass-roots organizations as the wellspring of the will of the people and a place for the party to build up its internal strength and evaluate daily experiences and their ideological significance, they are turned into a breeding ground for distasteful and base personal interest peddling, greed, and spite. Neighborly disputes, which in the past took place in the halls and stairways of private apartments, have now at long last gained the status of an officially sanctioned platform, where they are allowed to play themselves out in the guise of a distasteful but nevertheless dangerous political game.

Since attendance at these meetings is mandatory, they have become not only one of the most bizarre, but also one of the most aggravating burdens for the citizens of all Stalinized countries to bear. In spite of this, these meetings do fulfill a certain purpose, for above all they rob people of their time. Most people are compelled to attend at least two meetings a week, and those attending are often assigned small but demanding tasks. If one adds to this the mandatory participation in various celebrations, manifestations, parades (and there are many of these), and the so-called brigades [nominally "voluntary," unpaid work brigades], the result is that no time is left for anyone to stop and reflect on what is really happening to his or her life. And, let us not forget the diabolic invention of collective "organized leisure," which makes sure that people are unable to devote themselves to their own private concerns even during their vacations.

Moreover, these meetings do not only rob people of their time, but—and what is even worse—strip them of their integrity and their capacity to contemplate any kind of principled resistance. Recognizing not only the danger, but also the utter futility of any criticism, just about everybody pretends to agree to anything they are told and vote for or sign anything. If compelled to speak up, such as during mandatory debates or political screening proceedings, the affected party will automatically repeat memorized rote sentences, even though nobody believes a word of what they are parroting. And so people are taught to become mean-spirited and devious. It is very difficult to describe the suffering thus inflicted on the great majority of the population and the evil and hopeless loathing evoked by this strategy.

Only after all the preceding machinations have failed, direct terror is called into action. This ranges from so-called soft terror—as, for instance, the forced attendance at the above-mentioned hated meetings and manifestations, or the mandatory purchase of books and newspapers (here the governing motive of the party is more often than not financial gain)—to more menacing types of terror, such as potential loss of employment and, ultimately, brute police force.

Thus, only after the more moderate expedients begin to fail will the leadership of the party feel compelled to rely on the use of its ultimate instrument of power: unadulterated terror. Nor is there any attempt made to hide its presence, since it is clear to anybody that the number of police both in and out of uniform is rapidly increasing, while popular hearsay spreads the news of ever-increasing cases of sadistic torturing of prisoners, people sentenced without trial, sentences being delivered by the central committee of the party to the courts before the actual trial date, and people being beaten to death in police stations or while in court custody.

If the Communist press likes to tell its readers that capitalism is creating its own gravediggers, then their system is surely preparing for its own funeral as well. The truth is that any kind of organized opposition is impossible and that any dissenting voice is unremittingly silenced, no matter whether it is sounded by ordinary folk or articulated by intellectuals. Eventually, another class of enemies begins to emerge that is much more dangerous and difficult to identify because of its cunning ability to dissimulate. The deadly, stupid, and interminable propaganda eventually renders people indifferent toward any action or initiative proposed by the Communist party in its efforts to gain the support of the population. Its devious tactics create an overwhelming sense of mistrust among the broadest segments of the population toward anything proposed by the party, even if it is positive. Its inhuman organizational mania, suffocating all sense of what is right and wrong, ends up fomenting an atmosphere of petty and servile spite. But, while terror may well break the spirit of many, it can also produce individuals with great courage. In the end, there will always be people who arrive at a point where they no longer care what happens. Having said all this, it may sound strange if I add to the above another warning, namely, that it is a mistake to assume that all the Communists ruling the countries under Soviet control, their party leaders, and the sizable number of their functionaries—from top to bottom—are made up entirely of dishonest, corrupt, and unscrupulous individuals. Like everywhere else, here too we can find examples of all manner of human wickedness and vice. But one can also find high-minded individuals—especially among the prewar generation—who cannot be suspected of base mercenary motives. They make an honest effort to be of service to the people, and even though they may not shrink from sacrificing somebody else's life to achieve their political goals, they do this with the deep conviction that their actions are not a matter of personal whim, but necessary for creating a better and more beautiful future world for everybody than any that may have existed in the past. In the deepest recesses of their heart they still harbor the chiliastic belief that humanity is capable of realizing paradise in this world with peace, prosperity, happiness, freedom, and good fellowship for all, provided, of course, that everybody accepts their teachings and submits to their leadership.

How is it possible, then, that by seeking to do only good they have brought about so much evil? It seems to me that the cause of this is not to be found in their individual personas, but in the ideal they have sworn to follow. A bit of Hegel still permeates their inner self, best exemplified by the story that when confronted by the accusation that the facts did not conform to his theories, he reportedly answered: So much the worse for the facts. The only difference between Hegel and Marx is that the former was content to merely interpret the ways of the world, while the latter believed that the task of philosophy was to change it. And so it happened that Marx's disciples have decided to do away with any fact that does not conform to their philosophy. They refuse to see reality. They are not interested in what is, but only in what ought to be, and have declared their theory to be the only valid version of a truly "scientific world view." In practice this so-called science has become transformed into a system of unadulterated ideology in the worst sense of its meaning. Even their officials admit that it is not cognition and experience, but the proper acquisition of ideology that must be assigned first place in their order. The notion of a future ideal condition for humanity takes precedence over anything else. In effect, such a notion clearly violates the fundamental requirement of science, namely, careful observation of reality. To the extent that we regard reality as something observable, and thus something concrete, particular, and extant, their view essentially maintains that reality is essentially worthless and uninspiring.

Communist ideologues prefer to teach and think primarily in universal and futuristically colored categories. Anything concrete or real represents for them a kind of lower level of hypostasized reality, something to be used only as a means to an end and only if it has value in terms of their general future goals or as an idea to be made real. Moreover, theory thus interpreted carries with it the danger that its supporters have become incapable of correcting their own mistakes and controlling the actual, concrete, and living consequences of their actions. Hence, nothing can stop them. Obsessed with their ideal of a future good, they have become impervious to any evil they may have perpetrated, however monstrous. If any facts surface that are at odds with their theory, they are either summarily dismissed as being without significance or declared as irrelevant. To legitimize this approach, they have invented the term "party-line science." In practice this means that for any interpretation of facts, truthful content or empirical inclusiveness become irrelevant. Instead, the more important point is which interpretation can be brought better in line with their ideological position. For example, even the latest theories in psychology and anthropology are labeled bourgeois pseudo-sciences and are summarily dismissed without further study. And so they cling to their own conception of man, which recognizes as human only those individuals who are willing to live in the realization of an idea whose future is yet to be implemented.

The question to be asked is this: What if there are people who will not find happiness in such a world, or others who are not at all attracted by its vision, and who therefore have no desire to live and work for its realization? Well, so much worse for the truth and so much worse for the dissenting individual. Moreover, even if the world contrived by the Communist party, in which everybody is expected to prepare for his or her own future, and even if this world reveals itself as a wretched and hopeless desert devoid of anything that would make life desirable, the blame is invariably placed on the backwardness and lack of awareness of these people, their prejudices and anachronistic beliefs, thus making it necessary to make them over, whether they like it or not. In this context it should be remembered that even Marx and Engels believed that it would be possible to transform bourgeois pseudo-democracy into a genuine democracy, where all matters concerning human well-being would be truly decided by the people themselves. In contrast, the Communists never ask the people for their opinion for they consider them not only unenlightened, but, moreover, inherently incapable of creating their own happiness. Thus, it becomes their duty to think for them and act for them.

Their mission is to redeem them, whether they like it or not. No longer do people have to worry about creating their own happiness. Instead, the party takes care of it for them and its ideologues make sure that everything is implemented correctly. There are no more laws created by the will of the people; instead, laws are decreed by ideologues. This exceeds by far any reasonable conception of the dictatorship of the proletariat, but resembles instead a distorted vision of Plato's rule of philosophers. And, since the people are considered to be deficient in philosophical thinking or, as the ideologues like to say, are ideologically ignorant, the end result comes to resemble more and more the utopia of Plato's *Republic,* where the "caretakers will have to use much deception and many lies for the benefit of their wards . . . in order to assure everybody's well-being."

Inexorably, such rationalistic utopias, whether Plato's or Marx's, end up corrupting any sense of integrity that may still survive. If even Plato did not hesitate to consciously make use of untruth and deception in his ideal commonwealth and accept it as efficacious, then the Communists certainly have arrived at the same conclusion. Lies, deception, and ruthlessness are thus presumed to lead to truth, honesty, fraternity, and peace. With their vision of a noble goal somewhere far away in the clouds and in the future, they fail to see that as they keep on deceiving, defiling, cheating, and teaching hate, they sink into evil ever more deeply themselves. It is in this way that the inhuman abstractions of the ideologues fall on their own heads with a vengeance, for in spite of their pursuit of what are supposed to be pure and sensible ideas, they prefer to ignore the obscure and fathomless presence of lived reality, and dismiss it as nonexistent or existing only in a "state of imperfection."

They spout lies as a matter of course and pretend that these lies can be separated from the person uttering them. They forget that lies make for liars, who fail to see that even when telling a "white lie" with the best of intentions, lying eventually becomes habitual and, either from laziness or custom, establishes lying as a common practice, while those uttering them become incapable of distinguishing between truth and falsehood. Conversely, those who are fed these "white lies" as a cure for their ignorance and stubbornness become inured to their effects, and gradually turned into individuals who are taught to accept the constant barrage of lies as something normal and habitual, until they abandon any effort to seek truth both in life and in spirit. All this is perpetrated in the name of some abstract general ideal and some promised future benefits, eventually leaving everybody with a feeling of indifference toward truth and lies. In the end, these liars, deceivers, and bullies lead the confused and indifferent, the deluded and the slavish, the brutalized and the spiteful to — what? Socialism?

What then is the situation of the intellectual in this monstrous world? Shouldn't he or she be the first to rouse the conscience of both the government and those governed by making his or her voice heard and by sounding an alarm? After all, this is not a question of some abstract idea of the future, but a question of what is happening to people now and what they are becoming. In contemplating this Tower of Babel, constructed of blunders and stupidity and patched together by the cement of good intentions, the intellectual, along with everybody else, is obliged to inhabit it. And so one may well ask what he or she is able to accomplish in such a situation. The answer is: nothing.

First of all, there is no opportunity to say anything anywhere to anybody. Neither is this a question of risking persecution. Not at all. The reason for this is much simpler and essentially banal, for no newspaper or journal will print a single statement that does not conform to the official party line. Furthermore, no forum is allowed to exist that would provide an opportunity to be heard. Even assuming that the intellectual may find some kind of opportunity to voice an opinion, he or she will immediately be accused of being an enemy of the state, a traitor, an *agent provocateur,* a paid agent of a foreign power, or a spy. Soon the most ridiculous, loathsome, and slanderous reports will appear in the press, along with distorted and entirely false reports of what he or she had said. Moreover, there is not the slightest chance of defending oneself. The result? The propaganda machine cleverly uses any material of dissent put forward by anybody for its own purposes as a means of furthering the very cause that has been attacked.

The intellectual is well aware of this trick and therefore remains silent. In the end, he or she can confide in only a few close friends and that is all. The writer ceases to write because his or her work will not be published, nor will the vital stimulus of collegial support continue. But there is more. Cut off from receiving books and journals from abroad and denied permission for study trips and attendance at conferences, the intellectual will find private life untenable. Even if conformity is outwardly feigned, he or she will eventually fall prey to the dreadful convoluted logic of the system, which transforms anyone who lives a lie and tries to hide behind a façade of deception into a liar and a cheat. A single act of obeisance will not suffice either. Soon more and more will be asked of them. Alternatively, one may decide to keep silent, but this too will provoke suspicion. Why is he or she keeping silent, and why have writing and publishing ceased? Charges are bandied about: What is the use of a scientist or an artist who keeps sitting on the sidelines? He or she must be either an enemy or simply incompetent. In either case and under no circumstances should one expect to be supported in keeping a job and maintaining a lifestyle, however modest.

The result is despair. Perhaps, the intellectual will contemplate the dangerous and illegal act of getting out of the country. But failure in doing this can mean imprisonment and penury. Or, if he is no longer young and has a family with children, he may lose courage and decide to stay put. Perhaps he will take the path of lies, deception, and turpitude; perhaps he will succeed in finding refuge in some innocuous job where he will eke out a meager living in passive anticipation, where both hope and despair define an existence that has become meaningless. How many of such intellectuals languish in the Soviet Union, and how many have been added to their number in its satellites?

Written in 1949. Originally published in *Tíha doby (The Burden of Our Times)* (Olomouc [Czech Republic]: Votobia, 1997). Translated by Eric Dluhosch.

•●

ANDREI EROFEEV

Born in Paris in 1956 into a family of Russian diplomats, the curator and art historian Andrei Erofeev received conservative art-historical training at Moscow University, while privately acquainting himself with the nonofficial art scene of his time. In 1989, as curator at the Tsaritsyno Museum, he was assigned the task of building a collection for a planned museum of contemporary art. Following protracted bureaucratic and political wrangling, the works were eventually integrated into the permanent collection of the State Tretyakov gallery in Moscow, and Erofeev became head of its Contemporary Art Department.

This essay presents a general overview of Soviet artists working underground in the 1960s. Erofeev describes the evolution of Russian art during this time as evidence of the mercurial status of artists under Nikita Khrushchev, since they were awarded some freedom after the "thaw," albeit inconsistently. In response to these freedoms, unofficial artists took distinct paths. Some employed geometric abstraction, ironically reminiscent of the first Russian avant-garde of the 1910s and 1920s. Others tended toward a unique brand of Pop art and Conceptualism forged by artists Ilya Kabakov and Vitaly Komar and Alexander Melamid.

Nonofficial Art: Soviet Artists of the 1960s

"We are the children of Socialist Realism and the grandchildren of the avantgarde." This manifesto-style phrase of Vitaly Komar and Alexander Melamid, leaders of the Moscow underground of the 1970s, was meant to emphasize the idea of succession in the Russian-Soviet artistic conscience. However, at the very least it is inexact. Moreover, it is a fine example of an inattentive, and perhaps even contemptible, attitude to their own past, of a self-interested manipulation of this past, a feature which, not without reason, is considered to be typical of the Russian mentality.

It reiterates the fact that the Russian conscience is unfavorably disposed to the cause and ideology of its immediate predecessors, the "forefathers." This, in fact, defines the specific rhythm of respiration that is typical of Russian history: it comes in spasmodic gasps, like the breathing of a tuberculosis patient. Each of its phases equates to twenty or thirty years, that is, the active life cycle of a generation; it is regularly followed by an attack of convulsions, a paroxysm of the entire social organism, a crisis which opens up a new epoch in politics, public consciousness, and art.

It is precisely a twenty-year period of Soviet culture (from Khrushchev's thaw to Brezhnev's "détente") that Komar and Melamid have ignored, a period that made it possible for them not only to adapt themselves relatively painlessly to the demands of the artistic scene of New York, but also to survive in the USSR in the first place. Having somehow escaped imprisonment or a term in the mental hospital, they were able to engage in their mocking art, parodying sacred writings and state symbols and emblems. The start of that twenty-year period was marked by the epoch-making Twentieth Congress of the CPSU [Communist party of the Soviet Union] (1956). The totalitarian regime, which had not long before buried Stalin, disowned the cult of that leader of the people, but left intact the mighty machine of police surveillance and ideological pressure, the principle of institutionalizing any sort of personality-based initiatives and of uprooting all criticism. It left intact the meek society, too—society that placed all its hopes on the renewal of socialism. Culture was dominated by clichéd images, which had long lost their pathos and aggressiveness, having been polished to absolute anonymity.

Toward the end of this historical period, in the mid-1970s, quite a different picture can be seen: Society, contaminated by nihilism and criticism, viewed the values on which it was built and according to which it existed with sarcasm (a turn which left the Leftist intellectuals in the West flabbergasted). Everything proclaimed by the authorities was rejected out-of-hand, while whatever they renounced was passionately endorsed, as if in a childish spirit of contradiction. The ever-growing worship of the fairyland of the West resulted in the rejection of everything Soviet—be it ideas, objects, or behavioral patterns. It took a further twenty years for this type of mentality to burst out of the boundaries of the intellectual and capital-city circles and permeate all walks of life in the empire, finally depriving the regime of any serious support and chance of survival. New values crystallized, being acknowledged and finding their expression in the texts and images of a new cultural phenomenon that appeared at the turn of the 1960s and became known as nonofficial art.

Ilya Kabakov, an outstanding Russian Conceptual artist, briefly characterized this period in art as follows: "In their spontaneity and suddenness of explosion, in the multiplicity of causes and twists, which all came together at one and the same time and locked around the phenomenon subsequently called nonofficial art, the 1960s will be, possibly, comparable to the 1920s."[1] That is, to the peak period of the Russian radical avant-garde. Kabakov is perhaps a little extreme here, and underlying this statement is his filial commitment and gratitude to the time

Ilya Kabakov. *The Queen Fly*. 1965. Enamel on plywood, 22¹/₁₆ × 27⁹/₁₆" (56 × 70 cm). Collection Erna and Paul Jolles, Switzerland

when he himself emerged as an artist. However, there are some grounds for drawing comparisons between these two periods, which are so much opposite in spirit.

Both in the 1920s and in the 1960s, it was not people of letters or philosophers, not architects but artists who became the epicenter of a live, developing culture; it was artists who were the first to grasp the spirit of the times. They were the first to reorient creative activities in the 1920s from purely aesthetic goals to political pragmatism. And, to a certain degree, the time of the thaw was justifiably considered to be the spiritual successor of the utopian life-building of the artists of the 1920s. Social programs were generated in the bowels of art. Even poetry was carried into the sphere of political pamphlets. Passionate people of action, oracles who were imbued with global ideas, moralists and teachers of humanity came in the stead of the overfed past masters of Socialist Realism. They appealed to the masses and, moved by compassion for them, tried to lecture the authorities on their behalf. And it was artists, again, who readily perceived the thrust of a new culture, one which was personality-based and alien to social adventurism. They left the squares and stadiums and came back to the enclosed space of private life.

The home—for the most part, a flat or even a single room in a communal flat, in which the whole family, and, in that period of communal life, sometimes several families lived—this peripheral zone, exposed least of all to ideological X-raying and the stringent control of authorities, became the springboard for the development and manifestation of new cultural values. Something akin to live, individualized speech was resurrected in this domestic environment. Here it was appropriate to concentrate on the inner world, imagination, ideals, and subconscious inclinations of an individual and to make the private individual the main hero of creative art, immersed in the context of everyday life, so that the world was presented through their eyes.

Painters were the first to confine themselves to the limited space of a living room. They based their communication with one another and the public on the model of a communal flat, a kind of family hostel. Cultural life was presented as a series of everyday domestic acts and rituals, while the community of single-minded creators was itself shaped like that of a family clan, where blood ties and friendly relations were held in higher esteem than professional roles and links.

From a political point of view, this domestic intercourse, with its underlying free thinking and debates on certain works of art, was seen as the classical strategy used to conspire toward dissidence, a strategy which was well recognized from the descriptions of the heroic past of the Communist party that abounded in all textbooks on Soviet history. For this reason, the powers-that-be were well versed in this kind of camouflage, the more so because these meetings of artists and their fans were not kept secret. This is how Oscar Rabin, an outstanding figure in nonofficial art, described his domestic jours-fixé in Lianozovo, a Moscow suburb: "Our receptions were a great success. Guests walked, sometimes in whole groups, along the narrow road leading to our barrack from the railway station. Foreigners came, too. It was a fine sight to see their splendid limousines, reminding one of 'blue cigars' . . . parked beside our dark, squat barrack. Our neighbors, no doubt, have long ago reported us to 'where they should know it.' So we have been expecting a visit from militiamen any day now."[2]

The spy mania had not yet disappeared from the mind of the authorities. It was still only possible to communicate with foreigners on an official footing. As many artists were not employed at any Soviet institutions, and on this ground fell under the civil code article relating to parasitism,[3] from the point of view of the authorities there was no question about the criminal nature of these new cultural communities; nonetheless, they abstained from physical reprisals. The history of nonofficial art, though, is full of administrative reprisals, such as the closing of semilegal art exhibitions, the expulsion from the Union of Artists of those who presented their work there, their detainment for short terms by the militia on some false pretext, and their being summoned to the KGB for interrogations. The artists were constantly under threat of having extreme measures taken against them, an impression which was thoroughly cultivated, but, with a few exceptions (Viacheslav Sysoev's arrest and the suspicion that Evgenii Rukhin fell victim to a trumped-up murder), never materialized.

It would be a mistake to think that nonofficial art was a by-product and unforeseen result of the totalitarian state's pressure on the creative intelligentsia. While the Stalinist regime was in complete control of all spheres and forms of a person's self-expression, including children's creativity and amateur folk art, and nipped in the bud any sprouting of the cultural frond, the situation changed in the late 1950s, when Khrushchev's thaw set in. Freedom, which up to then was interpreted as the penetration of political cults into the emotional sphere, as the transformation of ideology into love, was now viewed from a position approximating liberalism. Within the framework of one's domestic private existence, an individual was freed from playing the hierarchical and ideological role assigned to him or her in the public "performance" staged by the authorities.

Naturally, the luxury of independence was first of all granted to the elite, who enjoyed the right of access to broader information (Western periodicals and books supplied through specialized book-distributing agencies), to an expanded range of entertainment and to individual whims, queer fancies, and caprices. Thus Vladimir Kemenov, vice-president of the USSR Academy of Fine Arts, used to demonstrate his love of Impressionism and Symbolism before his friends at home, and even hung the works of Pierre-Albert Marquet and Alexandre Benois in his study, while in public he never tired of deriding them, often making short shrift of their young fans in his department.

This kind of behavior was not only a matter of special privileges enjoyed by the "bosses," the 1960s were noted for "double-thinking," which spread in waves from the top echelons of society down, so that it became a generally recognized cultural norm, the model of a developed, unfettered conscience. Students were at that time suppressed only on account of the fact that they demonstrated the "free" substance of personality in public, for their attempts to transfer private values, behavioral norms, ideas and intimate emotions into the social sphere, which was an area for devotion and servility to the authorities. It should be stressed that both forms of conscience were considered equal, and therefore relative, being adapted to suit a certain cultural situation; the social conscience is finely illustrated by the famous "carnival" concept developed by Mikhail Bakhtin, a concept that was acclaimed far and wide at the turn of the 1970s. Bakhtin held that during a carnival, people are not just indifferent spectators of a performance; they take part in this performance, where life is turned inside out. "The laws, bans, and restrictions, which defined the structure and order of ordinary — that is, noncarnival life — are lifted for the term of the carnival; eliminated to begin with are the hierarchical system and all forms of fear, awe, piety, etiquette, and the like, which are connected with it."[4]

In ordinary everyday life, in the rooms of communal flats, the "world turned inside out," the carnival principle of life turned the wrong side out was acknowledged, and looked like blasphemous, paranoid behavior. Any kind of monistic conscience, whether true to orthodox Communist or, vice versa, to religious dogmas in any area of existence, seems to be infantile and uncultured. The figure of a fanatic turns into a glaring anachronism, while the concept itself assumes a clearly disdainful implication during the thaw. Therefore it would be hardly justifiable to identify opposition between official and "underground" art with an ideologically determined and free personality of the 1960s.

"People were not divided into black and white," wrote Gennady Aigi, one of the first Leftist poets of the thaw, "They belonged to both underground and official varieties of culture."[5] At the peak of liberalization (1956–61), when it seemed that the authoritarian regime was about to be replaced with a civil society, with "socialism with a human face," sometimes the same artists and even the same works of art were representative of both new official art and the new cultural opposition, the only difference being one of interpretation. "Remove Lenin from banknotes!" exclaimed Andrei Voznesenski, a famous Soviet poet, and the crowd burst into applause, drunk with the seditious meaning of the first two words of this sentence; representatives of the authorities nodded with understanding also, thinking the sentiment was pronounced in defense of the leader's sacred profile, which in their opinion was somehow profaned by being printed on paper money. And even after the authorities once again resumed the stand for a stringent and meticulous regulation of culture, after artistic life split into two parallel but opposed lines, double-thinking and the position of creative servitude, as well as that of individual freedom and the manifestation of a personalized vision, characterized the dual mentality of both those who were driven "underground" and those who succumbed to the shackles of officialdom.

December 1, 1962, was a critical, fatal moment for fine arts: on this day, Nikita Khrushchev paid a visit to a large retrospective exhibition dedicated to the thirtieth anniversary of the Moscow Union of Artists, where "Leftist art" was presented as a natural outcome of the processes of liberalization. Naive avant-gardists met him at the entrance with stormy applause. But the "Father of the Thaw," suddenly faced with the prospect of pronouncing a political verdict on the works of new culture — either by renouncing or supporting them — resorted to a diplomatic ploy, to a compromise: he simply declared them to be private psycho-pathological distortions of the public conscience. This event marked the beginning of the ever-increasing domestic isolation of independent artists; they were consistently denied the right to show their works to the public in any place and form. For this reason, this date can justifiably be seen as the birth date of nonofficial art. Over the entire period of its existence, clinical metaphors were key terms in describing its unregulated, nonformalized relations with the authorities. Even though the latter had already discarded cardinal surgical methods with respect to the "disease" at hand, they could not reconcile themselves with the irreversible impact the disease had on the self-conscience of the "patient" — society.

The end of this phenomenon, or, rather, its transformation into a generally recognized cultural trend, an alternative to official art, even though severely censured and criticized, came during the mid-1970s — the period when the first legalized exhibitions took place and a kind of shadow union of nonofficial artists, the so-called Graphics Moscow City Committee, was formed. "No matter how strange it may sound," as twenty high-placed KGB officers declared in the period of glasnost, "it was our stand which in the final account played a noticeable role in the formation of the Section of Painting at the United Committee of Graphic Artists."[6] This refers to the fact that after a large and highly symbolic error that met with a worldwide negative resonance — the bulldozer attack on a nonofficial art exhibition and the burning of what was left of it in September 1974 — the authorities at last decided to regulate and legalize their relationships with "underground" art; this was entrusted to the most flexible and pragmatic of Soviet structures — that is to the State Committee for Security, or the KGB.

No matter what the forms and situations in which nonofficial art made its appearance in artistic life, a room in the communal flat remained, as of old, its habitual abode. The limited space and everyday environment accounted for the actual artistic context and meaning of individual creativity: here it came into interaction with both partners and opponents, and turned into a fact of culture. It was in a single room in the communal flat that Russian nonofficial art was mentally measured against the world avant-garde, as well as that of art in other epochs. It was here that information flowed, as if to a library, where it was doomed to a clandestine existence, as were the artistic creations which testified to the artists' awareness of its existence. Yet the most important function performed by the artist's single room was perhaps the creation — in terms of space, color, and material — of an ideal aesthetic reality about which he or she dreamed and which was rendered on their canvases. The artist created his or her works in the same quarters where the family eked out its meager existence, which differed only slightly from the poverty of the war years. There was no distance, not even a symbolic one — no partition or screen to set the sacral tools of creativity and the cult apart from domestic utensils, like, for instance, in a communal kitchen, when man eats his meals at the same table at which he writes the manuscripts of his future book; from time to time he has to cry out: "For God's sake, move away a little! Don't you see I'm working? Why must you put the soup right here, Mom?"[7]

The utopian idea of art merging with life, taken so closely to heart by Russian avant-gardism of the 1920s, fully materialized under these conditions in a chain of episodes which were sometimes funny, but for the most part ugly, humiliating, and dramatic, and which presented the modernistic interpretation of creativity as an immersion into the world of pure forms and ideal entities in a laughable and even indecent light. The gloomy background of everyday life, typical of the creative activity of a nonofficial artist, and their constant forced return to the plane of a routine perception of life put into question and discredited the generally recognized conventionalities of the artistic world and primarily the specific, symbolic status of artistic creations. Products of nonofficial art remind one of a huge family archive, where you might come across genuine masterpieces among heaps of all kinds of rubbish: useless papers, "trifles," rough sketches, "trinkets," and random unfinished drawings. It would be a mistake to ascribe this to provincialism or a lack of artistic will, generally inherent in Russians. In all evidence, we should rather emphasize the fundamentally different nature of this creativity as compared with the West. Confined within a narrow circle — family environment — it bears little resemblance to any form of well-adjusted commodity production, a manufacture whereby the market is regularly supplied with standard-quality goods. This creativity was rather like playing music at home: it may be very skillful, and the musician may be talented, but it still does not go beyond being a mixture of a divertissement and an emotional confession; it is always improvisation, a hint at the possibility of a high-standard performance, which is out of place in the privacy of the home.

Within this kind of creativity, the greatest value was placed on sincerity, lyricism, and the author's original style, on the harmony between the artist's inner disposition and his or her emotional state. Hence the vagueness of style and the violations of the canons of genre, the absence of any clear-cut professional method when approaching formal tasks, the polyphony of languages and the host of coded hints at some profound relationships, to which only members of a given community have access. This state of affairs is not to be reduced to the absence of the means or opportunities alone; the intentionally pitiful form, typical of artistic work belonging to nonofficial art, is to a large degree explained by the fact that it would be absurd to hold forth in high style at home, in one's family. So if some artist all of a sudden began to create large-scale "real" pictures or sculptures, he or she immediately found themselves in the role of a doctrinaire, delivering a high-flown sermon to a circle of astounded friends.

The material product born of such domestic creativity was not taken seriously either. There was no market for works of art in the country, and practically no collectors of artistic works, so pictures, piled up in overcrowded rooms, were sold for a song or given as a gift to friends. The process of creativity and meditations and moments of bliss connected with it were considered more valuable than their result—a self-valued aesthetic object; the former were artificially prolonged and relished. And the plastic form was perceived in the first place as a means of rendering all sorts of observations, anecdotes, and ideas, as an intonation of speech, inviting the spectator to discussion and comment. No wonder that the whole of nonofficial art, including its abstract trend, is generally highly narrative. It tried to call forth words, remarks, and statements, and the lengthy explanations that were provided at the exhibitions passed in time to the surface of the canvases themselves, and in certain extreme avant-gardist trends, even ousted all other components of an artistic image.

Nonofficial art tried unequivocally to avoid serious statements and pompous postures: it cultivated self-irony. This was attributable to the ambiguous status of the artist, which was in many ways dangerously similar to that of a dilettante, since more often than not the artist lacked a regular education, was alienated from the local institutions of artistic life, and was cut off from the world process of creative art which was so manifest abroad. The generation of spiritually crushed avant-gardists of the Stalinist era and of cultured artists in general, who were in contact with the historical movement of Modernism, had long since dispersed all around the world, and there were no longer any links with them. The artists succumbed to the sensation of a complete and hopeless loneliness, which still reigned in their souls even when they became free, first in the West and, later, here in Russia as well. When they were at last free to communicate with the world at large, they could not overcome the psychological complex which made them feel like bastards deprived of any support from the fundamental traditions of twentieth-century art.

Typical of the avant-gardists' mentality and behavior were opposition to official art, dissociation from aesthetic clichés imposed by the authorities, provocation and rebelliousness, as well as Bohemianism. The same features were inherent in the Russian artists who belonged to the 1960s underground. This is why their fans and critics, and not infrequently the artists themselves, began to present nonofficial art as a variety of avant-gardism, as a hard, torturous activity aimed at resurrecting the Modernist artistic school that had been devastated during the Stalinist era. But if you leave aside this trend's pathos and have a look at the artistic results of underground creativity, the shallowness of such an interpretation comes into bold relief. Some works of nonofficial art are outwardly very close to those of contemporary trends in Western modernism. But as a rule, these appeared at the earliest stage of its inception, at the stage when neither the creative work of a concrete underground artist nor the movement as a whole were independent; in the subsequent evolution, this similarity was eradicated.

It seemed that everything moved backwards—from modern and radical forms of expression of visual experience toward compromise, stylized pictures, and, later, even toward bizarre, pseudo-museum artifacts. Pseudo-avant-gardism proved to be a convinced, programmed conservatism—an apology for a perception of reality in aesthetic terms, as a consolidation of traditional imitative techniques, and classical, even academic genres and methods of work. This strange, illogical metamorphosis finds its explanation in the cultural mission voluntarily undertaken by underground artists, a form of unofficial program that they presented to society.

A shift to the position of underground creativity actually spelled the rejection of long-tested and canonized cultural norms in favor of a new, nontrivial interpretation of art. It was accompanied by the formulation of a highly original project of artistic creativity. Yet, as distinct from Western or classical Russian avant-gardism, this action was not focused on a search for an unprecedented image of art. In the proposed innovations, emphasis was put on its personalized, individual nature. Any work that had an unquestionably individualized form was counterpoised to the collective, anonymous principle in art; it could even be a traditional one, as long as it epitomized personal freedom and a departure from submission and obedience. As for the traditional ethical or aesthetic cults, which had struck firm root in the public consciousness and were invariably a target for criticism by any form of avant-gardism, these frequently provided a fine object for the work of nonofficial artists.

It was not conservatism but conformance to which society sacrificed many traditional cultural values, which they tried to overcome. These downtrodden values were resurrected through the acts of individual artistic insight. They were ascribed the features characteristic of an artist's individual vision. They served as an object of zealous service and worship. In other words, nonofficial art was in many respects characterized by a restorative nature. Religion, mysticism, philosophy, cultural pursuit, sociology, branches of knowledge which were all under a ban during the reign of despotism were now being resurrected in the context of individual creative concepts of the artists working within this trend. However, to impart these to the viewer, it was necessary to reveal and master new forms of speech and substitute them for the commonly practiced realistic ways of describing reality learned at artistic schools and academies.

Poet Joseph Brodsky recollected: "As I look back, I can see that we started from scratch — to be more precise, we began from a place which was startlingly devastated, and we tried, intuitively rather than consciously, to resurrect the effect of the continuity of culture, to restore its forms and tropes, and to fill in the few forms which survived but were mostly compromised, with our own, novel or seemingly novel, modern content."[8]

Artists were faced with a difficult dilemma. They could either recognize the existence of this devastated space, their own loneliness and lack of continuity, and start from scratch, relying on an active world outlook, their own intuition and subtle emanations of the times; or they could seek support in abstract thinking, in a certain public project of art. The former option opened the road toward a creativity that would be truly modern and adequate both for the creator's personality and for the situation at hand. In the latter option, a variety of utopian art would again come in the footsteps of the avant-gardism of the 1920s and of Socialist Realism. The vast majority of artists chose the latter option — a result of professional inferiority complexes, provincialism, and a wish to join the artistic environment of international art by seeking similarity with their idols in creativity. Before nonofficial art could formulate its specific approaches and take the path that uncovered the nature and goals of the creative process, it had to undergo a long period during which the underground trend in official creativity was first carefully fostered and then outlived. This was not, by any means, a servicing of the authorities' interests, but the formulation and objectifying of the cults, myths, and manias that spread in Soviet society in the 1960s.

Everyone began to study. All of a sudden Moscow was covered with a thick network of underground academies, each of them boasting up to several dozen students. A cohort of astounding-looking mentors gave lectures; despite the fact that they may have seemed like imbeciles and charlatans, they possessed "genuine" knowledge about what should be done, and how to partake of the life-giving sources of real art, to overcome one's own ignorance, and assimilate culture. The only way was to copy certain models: these differed according to the personal tastes and stock of information possessed by each particular lecturer. Thus Eli Beliutin, the leader of the largest school of the underground, saw genuine art in exalted figurativeness as in the work of Jean Dubuffet; Boris Birger saw it in the brown paintings of Rembrandt's imitators; Vasilii Sitnikov in pointillism, as in the work of Giovanni Segantini . . . and the list goes on. Most of these irreproachable oracles, and their pupils and disciplines, have produced virtually no fruit; they have made no tangible contribution of creative work to the treasury of nonofficial art, but their method of gaining access to culture through stylization has, however, been in general use since. The worship of an artistic model assumed the scale of a pagan cult. A model was seen as the embodiment of universal artistic values, its regional or historically specific characteristics being totally ignored. Approaches of a secondary nature were greeted warmly. A borrowed manner was viewed as an opportunity to learn a free and nonideologized language. Different kinds of stylization, accompanied by changes in behavior, forms of activity, style of dress, and even the entire image, did not, as a rule, reflect self-importance; they were simply an attempt to describe contemporary life in a language that was different from the official one.

After a long period marked by single-mindedness, Soviet society, which had at last won freedom, split into a multitude of home-based groups with diametrically opposed political and cultural orientations. Under these conditions, no general utopia of art was possible. At one and the same time, several incompatible professional clan projects appeared, but none of them was recognized by the public. Still, if we try to identify similar moments in their evolution, we can trace a common descent from utopian dreams about the future to the grass roots, to sources, and lost traditions.

The late 1950s works of Vladimir Slepian, Boris Turetsky, and Yuri Zlotnikov are motivated by the wish to break radically not only with an individual manner in painting, but also with easel painting as such. Their creations are in fact a type of color-and-rhythm composition, which act as signals upon the human organism centers, though they could equally come from any other means, technical ones included. They are not pictures, nor are they lists of drawings; rather, they are plans of some possible plastic performances. They can perhaps be seen as an extreme point of radicalism in nonofficial art, which was just emerging. At the same time, they were the first attempts at resurrecting abstract art, which was long banned in the USSR and which all young artists of the period of the thaw identified with the style of supermodern civilization.

Other neophytes of nonfigurative creativity were already confined purely to the boundaries of easel painting and subjectivist aesthetic searches. Each of them presented, as if in a competition, his own project of modern art, modeled after a particular variety of Western abstract art. Lev Kropivnitsky and Nikolai Vechtomov, for example, gave preference to Jean Arp's biomorphism and Abstract Expressionism, while Vladimir Yankilevsky preferred the graffiti of the CoBrA group. They felt themselves to be catapulted into the world's avant-garde through this single act of sharing alien traditions.

The creativity of the group known under the name of Dvizenije was the most international in spirit. This community of artists, which emerged in 1962, was led by Lev Nusberg and had close ties to Kinetic art. Its creations were in fact an alloy of light and color, motif and musical effects with the cinematographs and theatrical performances, a mixture made up of contemporary Western design and the spatial structures of Russian Constructivism; it gave birth to the last utopian project of mass public modern art in the USSR. The trend focused its attention on the contemplation of perfect technical engineering forms, devoid of any initial functions, which dominated the urban environment, nature, and the globe as a whole. In his early works Francisco Infante presented the globe as encircled in fiery spirals and surrounded by stars that he arranged in the simplest geometrical figures. The Dvizenije group directed its projects into a nonartistic environment, into the space inhabited by life, which it wished to permeate with aesthetic values, an ideal geometrical plasticity, light, and electronic music.

Regrettably, Soviet society was reluctant to recognize not only Kinetic art, but Constructivism itself, the nostalgic echoes of which gave the Dvizenije group's projects a somewhat outmoded, museum hue. To induce the state to recognize the opuses of his group as a new public style, Nusberg tried to put these projects to the service of political propaganda and agitation. The "movement's" utopia relied on the erroneous assumption that the public conscience had already undergone radical changes and that following Yuri Gagarin's feat, the entire Soviet system had soared high into outer space and from those heights was taking a universal look at the world, one which the young avant-gardists claimed to express.

After the failure of their Kinetic projects, which were not put to any use, all other attempts to resurrect on the territory of the Soviet Union a positive, aesthetic creativity of form, based on the actual stylistics of world avant-gardism, failed also. Isolated desperate attempts to make the Russian underground look like Modernism and in this way to confirm the cultural similarity of new Russia to the West were, as a rule, of no consequence either. Up until the early 1980s Soviet "Westerners," who were at a huge distance from the centers of world art, had to eke out a miserable existence as provincials, doomed to peep with envy now and then over many barriers to obtain a glimpse of the West in order to find food for their own creativity.

Another remarkable trend of the 1960s, which accounted for the choice of image and styles, was born of the pathetic desire to resurrect culture. The semantic borders of this word, deemed to be a magic one in those years, were eroded as a result of overuse. It was widely applied to denote the aggregate heritage of all civilizations, all museum art, and old things in general. In fact, there was only one taboo: no one among those who saw culture as a tool for the renewal of artistic creativity ever used the word to indicate the spiritual experience and material reality of either Stalinist or contemporary Russia. They were convinced there was no culture there. Hence, to pass from the profane environment to the spiritual sphere, to rise above everyday life, one had to make an imaginative trip in time and space and enter into a dialogue with one's own alter ego.

Beginning with the 1960s, Boris Sveshnikov and Dmitrii Krasnopevtsev ennobled their genre scenes taken from Soviet prison or army life by using the stylistic means of the Dutch school of painting, old German xylography, and classical French drawings. This method was later taken on by Dmitri Plavinsky and Viacheslav Kalinin, whose genre scenes and landscapes portraying Moscow gateways and suburbs were executed in the stylistic manner of old masters. Sometimes different styles were piled one on top of the other, resulting in an eclectic, complicated mixture of styles; this mode is exemplified perfectly in the works of Oleg Tselkov (early twentieth century), who combined Fauvist experiments with color and light searches typical of Fernand Léger and Kazimir Malevich, and with attempts to make the form dynamic, first launched by Italian Futurists. However, as soon as the artists ceased to comment on the surrounding reality and tried to express their own existential and social experience, it became clear that the delicate conventionalities of "museum" art did not help at all, and were, in fact, obviously harmful. Oscar Rabin, Vladimir Yakovlev, and Anatolii Zverev only used stylization as a short-term transitional stage from immature naturalism to confessional expressive painting, which violated and distorted the canons of cultural rhetoric. A sad paradox arose from the fact that, by this time, world art had already discarded this self-dominant artistry as a trite drawing-room cliché; this exalted and rough manner of painting, which produced such a great impression on Soviet viewers sick and tired of the glossed-over paintings executed in the style of Socialist Realism, was already outmoded.

However, the vast majority of nonofficial artists firmly renounced the attempted murder of the clarity and beauty of form, even if it was made in the name of confessional and didactic goals. It was no accident that their interest in "museum" art coincided with the emergence of American Pop art and its European counterparts onto the world scene. The Moscow underground interpreted this as a betrayal of culture for the sake of playing up to the vulgar vernacular of everyday life, as bowing to the worst traditions of commonplace conservatism typical of Central Europe. The rift between the human stand and the artistic principles of the "nonconformists" became ever wider. As soon as these sworn rebels and daredevils stood at the easel, they began to see as their goal the defense of a reverential attitude toward culture and traditions, and to hold forth enthusiastically about spirit, truth, and beauty.

For this reason, it was not the outcry of half-blind Vladimir Yakovlev but the dry and stiff aestheticism of Eduard Shteinberg that best reflected the main line of development — and degeneration — of nonofficial art. Shteinberg can be regarded as the most consistent stylist. At first he, like all the rest, tried to divorce his painting from the prison of nature; he borrowed geometric aestheticism from Constructivism, and it served him perfectly as a tool to schematize landscapes. However, it subsequently prevailed over everything else in his creative manner and even usurped the central place of the hero in the picture. From

Oscar Rabin. *Still Life with Fish and Pravda*. 1968. Acrylic and oil on canvas, 35 7/16 × 43 1/2" (90 x 110.5 cm).
Jane Voorhees Zimmerli Art Museum, Rutgers, The State University of New Jersey, The Norton and
Nancy Dodge Collection of Nonconformist Art from the Soviet Union

that moment on, the artist began to create ever more stylized and scholastic pictures, in which the aestheticism of Russian avant-gardism is crossed with its antithesis — "bourgeois" *valeur* painting. Vadim Zakharov, an artist who belonged to the next generation of the underground, called him "a powdered Malevich." For Shteinberg, the visible engendering of Suprematism with museum values was a symbolical reflection of the sacral code of the national spirit.

Plavinsky interpreted culture as synonymous with objects that bear an imprint of historical times. He scrupulously restores the ruins of ancient civilizations, destroyed and almost assimilated by nature: the time-eroded surfaces of buildings, all kinds of things in everyday use, and manuscripts describing the life of people long gone and long forgotten. The metaphor of immortality is embodied in the very structure of his works, in which the sight of fine, multilayer painting is shut off from the viewer by a rough crust and wax.

"I often instinctively paint over an almost finished picture," he confessed, "with a new composition: it may be a variant of the first one, or an entirely new composition. Thus it may be repeated again and again — several times on one and the same canvas. For instance, my large picture, *The Wall of the Novgorod Church in Autumn* is painted over an almost finished work, *Remnants of Noah's Ark*. At first I was confused and bewildered by this method of doing an artistic work. And only as several years passed by, did I realize the inexorable logic of art, according to which the 'cultural layer' is created gradually, by applying temporal layers of independently organized compositions."[9]

Thus both Shteinberg and Plavinsky did not in fact reflect culture, but actually resurrected it in direct, material terms, the former by imitating the patina of a museum piece, and the latter by copying archaeological layers. In both cases, the result of these efforts is that their creations were consistently and purposefully deprived of characteristics that are intrinsic to a newly created work of art.

In addition to sacramentality and immortality, there was a third key epithet for culture that was widely applied by representatives of nonofficial art — spirituality. Vladimir Veisberg and Dmitrii Krasnopevtsev were dedicated seekers of its visual equivalents. First of all they forcibly pumped an atmosphere of spirituality into the space of life itself, into rooms that were thoroughly shut off from the outside environment and cleaned of the elements of everyday Soviet life — into rooms, in fact, that were turned into a kind of holy chamber or sanctuary, where time came to a standstill and where the individual, having abstracted himself or herself from the hustle and bustle of everyday life, could plunge into meditation over a set of simple objects, not weighed down by any ethnographic semantics. The main topic of their pictures is unsophisticated still lifes. As they are immersed into a specific spatial environment — achromatic and as though filled with vapor in Veisberg, and sterile and airless in Krasnopevtsev — inanimate objects lose their bodily substance and turn into ghosts, into some metaphysical prototypes of themselves. More than anything else, this variety of creativity brought to mind some form of ritual, some cult act, in which the artist played the role of a hermit monk and, at the same time, of a preacher: the work itself was a substitute for an altar before which the viewer lapsed into a specific mystical state and acquired a fundamental knowledge about the nature of being.

In no way was nonofficial art preoccupied with formal problems and pure plastics, although always striving to impose upon the latter a profound philosophical meaning. This comes into bold relief in the work of so-called Surrealists — Vladimir Yankilevsky and Ülo Sooster. Each object in their creations portrays some metaphysical notion, the meaning of which the artist tries to explain in a simple language; for example: "Woman Is an Erogenic Bosom," "Man is an Aggression Machine," "The City is a Labyrinth of Geometrical Figures," "Horizon Is a Chink in Space," "The Socium is a Crowd of Monsters and Mutantsk," and so on. A concrete motif was turned into a sign or notion by schematizing it using the creative method promulgated and applied by Pablo Picasso, Paul Klee, and René Magritte. In this way, the frame of mind of artists in the underground was realized in a search for a genuine, free, and philosophical interpretation of life in the "genuine" pictures of other artists.

Quite suddenly the cult of museum art became a source of subject matter for the creative work of Ilya Kabakov, a younger member of the group of "Surrealists." His work *Ruysdael's Hand and Reproduction* (1956) meticulously presents a true-to-life situation in which the nonofficial artist (his role is offered to any viewer) closely scrutinizes a poster which is made from the Dutchman's picture and is glued to the bottom of a large white box. The reproduction can also be seen as a view opening out from a window; in this case the white box turns into a windowpane. The author provides yet another interpretation as well: the picture, like a curtain, shuts off an endless Suprematist space. Or it prevents one from plunging into the metaphysical reality of this other world, which is indicated by a shining enamel coloring. And, finally, there is a third and rather sad version: there is a paper picture and a box, and all the rest is just a product of one's inflamed imagination, caused by sitting for too long in the underground. This first attempt at realizing the collective syndrome of nonofficial art within a cultural framework and describing it ironically testified at the same time to the fact that an extremely profane, philistine approach to the products of artistic creativity attached to the idea underlying a work of underground art. These artistic products were dealt with as if objects placed on the ordinary plane of life, like those of a cook or plumber, on a par with other functional objects in everyday use.

The works by Mikhail Roginsky also demonstrate the likeness of art to things in everyday use, a concept so graphically presented in Kabakov's "boxes" and later in his "stands." Roginsky rapidly advanced from ornate "museum" fantasies to still lifes and genre scenes from the life of communal kitchens, and to the imitation of all kinds of visual aids—that is, to an anonymous rendering in paint of fire-prevention rules or railway-station announcements. Roginsky's *Red Door* is undoubtedly his most radical creation (1965). This was the first readymade of Russian art and the only one of the 1960s. The meaning of this work, in which depletion is replaced with a real, appropriated object, and painting is reduced to a crude and monotonous coloring, is revealed exclusively through a variety of visual and mental correlations: that of a certain artistic tradition (in this case, of a monochrome abstraction) with the commonplace environment of underground creativity: that of the title with the object's initial semantics, and so on.

Both Kabakov and Roginsky took to the line in nonofficial art that ran counter to a thrust into the other world and into eternity: they were more aligned to the circle of artists belonging to the so-called Lianozovo group, who preferred unsophisticated, laconic, and ironic comments on Soviet reality to a breakthrough to avant-gardism or an immersion into meditations. They depicted life in a barrack, of which they possessed firsthand knowledge, since they lived there themselves; they also portrayed undernourished prostitutes from the nearby neighborhood, drunkards, and all other human "refuse," a category in which—to a certain extent and with certain artistic stylization—they placed themselves. Of course, a particular program can be detected here—to provide a nonofficial image of reality, to cast a glance at it through the eyes of ordinary people; but we also see that the artists, like foreigners, kept a safe distance from this by means of delicate stylistics, and shut themselves off from the miasma of everyday life by painting, using it as a form of protective mask. Over time their painted anecdotes became loaded with slang, and their stylistic means were also influenced by the nature of the things they depicted. Thus Oscar Rabin created a painted version of a "picturesque" double banknote, and, somewhat later, of two inner pages of the newspaper *Pravda*.

The notorious Pop art, as the trend was now commonly known, stuck to purely topical references, which did not involve the work's initial parameters. As in the past, it remained an authorized imitation. And it was anything but simple to overcome its hermetic, self-centered nature. The convincing proof of this can be found in the desperate attempts initiated by Aleksandr Kosolapov, a young sculptor who subsequently evolved into a famous Conceptualist. At the turn of the 1970s, he wished to identify life with art, proclaiming everyday things to be sculptures and producing monumental, stylized replicas of a meat chopper, a window latch, and a door handle. He made the space of a painting open for the viewer to enter by creating picturesque replicas of the furnishings and inhabitants of a whole room — a husband and wife, and a shameless mistress; this is the first installation in Soviet art made up of flat contours of the human figure and of things executed in cardboard and painted.

Painting and sculpture grew ever closer to everyday life and were its continuation in thematic terms. They were nonetheless severed from it by the barrier created by the conventionalities of artistic language. The aesthetic reduction of the meanings of any of the objects, even the most repulsive, within a given space of an artistic work was clearly demonstrated by Boris Turetsky. Following in the footsteps of Arman, he demonstrated the relevant mechanism by using an extreme example — the contents of a slop pail. Immediately calling to mind the objectified abstraction of Vasily Kandinsky, the *Rubbish Heap* did not, however, call into question the inexorable transforming power of the picture's plane; on the contrary, it confirmed it.

Roginsky in his *Red Door* had made a radical step, which in many respects was definitive for the nature of mature nonofficial art: an artistic creation was deprived of its specific ontology. Although initially being simply an ordinary object, it was turned into an artistic phenomenon as a result of the mental act involved in changing the angle of visual perception. The unique nature of the *Red Door* consists in that its contemplative artistic status is not strengthened by anything at all in the plastic terms — it has no frame and is not placed in a gallery; it is just the limit, or, if you like, the ideal of art undistinguishable from life.

The concept of an ambivalent and obscure artifact was mainly developed by the second generation of the Russian underground, which gave birth to local varieties of Conceptualism and Pop art. However, it was already popular enough in the 1960s, being exemplified in Mikhail Chernyshov's abstract-geometrical series made of wallpaper. The creative activity of this "naughty boy" of nonofficial art is a graphic illustration of an ever-mounting irritation with, and repulsion for, the metaphysical sermons typical of the leading figures in the underground. "It just came to my mind," said this young man, who since his early days had imbibed the cultural charge of 1960s Western youth, "and what if illiteracy is just a new value? What if the works, which are hopelessly below standard, are perfect precisely for this reason?"[10] This is pronounced by a normal, perhaps somewhat over-Americanized student, who has not gone through the tortures of provincialism, hunger, or timidity inherent in a neophyte. Nevertheless, these artistic values, reminiscent of a child's scribbling, and a kind of a challenge to artistic pursuit, which is completely out of place in the underground, did not result in a break away from nonofficial art, but on the contrary, crystallized it, giving it the clarity of a formula. In these values, as in the work by Ilya Kabakov called *Death of Ali, a Little Dog,* dilettante, homemade renderings of all kinds of joyful or sad family events, so characteristic of the Lianozovo group (Evgenii, Lev and Valentina Kropivnitsky, Oscar Rabin, Vladimir Nemukhin, Nikolai Vechtomov, and Lydia Masterkova) and their friendly meetings in the presence of their wives, parents, and children, who were also all given to fine arts, were elevated to the status of encompassing the specific quality and generic property of new Russian art.

It was only after the oppressive impact of a beggarly existence and hopeless dilettantism, flaws that were so painful for the underground, were removed by means of satirical reflection and proclaimed to be cultural values that the basis appeared for the inception of genuine avant-gardism, adequate both to the artist's personality and the epoch of modern creativity in the Soviet Union. The nonofficial art of the 1960s became a launching pad, a point of reference, and a phenomenon to be overcome.

Notes:

1. I. Kabakov, "The Seventies," manuscript, p. 2.
2. O. Rabin, "Other Art: Moscow, 1956–76" in *Chronicle of Artistic Life* (Moscow, 1991), p. 48.
3. Artists who were not members of an official artists union and did not have other employment could be arrested for "parasitism."
4. M. Bakhtin, *Problems of Dostoyevsky's Poetics* (Moscow, 1972), p. 207.
5. G. Aigi, cited in "Other Art: Moscow, 1956–76" in *Chronicle of Artistic Life,* p. 122.
6. V. Vlasov, A. Mikhailov, N. Kovalyov, et al., "Are You Ashamed Now, Colonel Karpovich?" *Ogonyok,* no. 34 (August 1989), p. 25.
7. I. Kabakov, Rooms, MANI addition, manuscript, Moscow, 1987, p. 75.
8. J. Brodsky, *Poems* (Tallinn, 1991), p. 15.
9. D. Plavinsky, Diary for 1979–80, manuscript, p. 84.
10. M. Chernyshev, *Moscow 1961–67* (New York, 1988), p. 53.

Written in 1995. Originally published in *Non-Official Art: Soviet Artists of the 1960s* (East Roseville, Australia: Craftsman House and G + B Arts International, 1995).

•●

CORIOLAN BABETI

The Romanian art historian and curator Coriolan Babeti (born 1944) was appointed Deputy Minister of Culture after the fall of the Communist regime in Romania, and served as Commissioner for the Romanian pavilion at the Venice Biennale from 1990 to 1995 before becoming Director of the Romanian Cultural Center in New York. In this essay, he writes about his encounters with the Romanian artist Stefan Bertalan, who was a founding member of the Sigma Group, based in Timisoara. Beginning in the 1960s, young Romanian artists began to contest state-sponsored Socialist Realism by abandoning any representation of the figure. The artists of the Sigma Group investigated Western art and developed a Romanian formalism that was quickly adapted into a highly spiritual approach to abstraction. Bertalan's work is a testimonial of his own personal tragedy, readily understood by other artistic voices suppressed at the time. Babeti describes the psychological and spiritual repercussions of existence in the marginalized, yet parallel universe of dissidents. By treating Bertalan as a case study of sorts, Babeti evaluates what, in his opinion, were the two primary reactions to Communism: to accuse history or to evade it.

The Bertalan Case: The Artistic Experiment as an Exercise and Neurotic Sublimation

The old house in Fabric [Romania], inhabited by Bertalan, his wife, Karin, and their two children, Bastel and Buber, was a picturesque living space-studio.

Little by little the studio intruded into the living space, displacing it, and when Bertalan was left alone here at 1 Chopin Street, everything around, including the kitchen, became a bric-a-brac laboratory-warehouse where your first temptation was to clean it up, your second to treat it as an archaeological site, your third to give up, silently contemplating this decay of creation in the weft of quotidian existence.

We walked out into the courtyard and Bertalan said: "Let's salute the sun." I did so, moved by his request. He seemed so convincing in the execution of his Mithraic ritual that I surprised myself expecting the day's heavenly body to reply. He took a sheet of white paper, placing it behind the vine leaves that clambered over the trellis in front of the door that faced the courtyard. "Look, Babeti, how colorful the shadows of this drawing are!" Like the lover's silhouette on the wall in the Greek legend of the origin of drawing, Bertalan showed me the shadow of his lover—a plant. "Look over there at those holes," he shared with me another time, pointing to the vacant knotholes brought on by age in the boards of the fence that separated his courtyard from that of his neighbors, nameless and hostile. "I am being watched at every step," he added, "watched through those holes," which I began to picture as photographic viewfinders or as an Argus-like secret-police spy whose one wakeful eye was vigilant, even when the remaining ninety-nine were slumbering. With Bertalan beside me, it was difficult not to believe as he did! "Disguised as tractor operators and lumberjacks, they prevented me from drawing, even up in the mountains at Rasinari," he told me, pointing to a stunning suite of sanguine drawings. "While I was working in the Apuseni Mountains an airplane followed my every move during the whole time I was there."

Finally, one night, during a period when he visited me nightly, he struck me in the dark, in front of the gate where I had just dropped him, adding to the violence of his act a reproach, that he couldn't leave the country because of me. It

Stefan Bertalan. *Padurea Verde, Timisoara* (detail). August 6–10, 1976. Floral-shaped textile membranes suspended by strained strings. Courtesy the artist

was my turn to be blamed; he had already suspected everyone else who was close to him. Just like the neophyte initiated into Zen, the moment Bertalan's request was forcefully rejected in front of the monastery gates that were slammed tight on his foot, I had a revelation about the solitude that he wove around himself. A Robinson Crusoe inhabiting tragically an island populated by the inextricable mix of fiction and reality; the social environment was the last great arena for his experiments. Harassed by humans and phantasms, he nourished himself on the tragedy of his seclusion and alienation. He eventually managed to get to Germany, and we saw each other again in Venice, where I invited him to exhibit his 1985 work *13 + 1* at the Biennale Centennial of 1995. "They follow my every step," he told me, describing the 'electronic assault' to which his house in Öringen was subjected, and the insomnia forced upon him by the insidious clamor. Undesired, frightened on his floating island, Bertalan persists in the drama of his neurosis, which belongs not so much to the place he left behind as to the time that he traverses, disbelieving that "we are all aboard." Tethered to these times, one artist will continually attempt new solutions, another will be a witness. Bertalan is a witness whose experiments are sublimations and islands of neurosis.

Setting aside subtle distinctions for the moment, Bertalan appears like a paroxystic case in point of the creative neurosis that pervaded the arts in Romania during the years 1960 to 1980. At Gataia, protected by his psychiatrist friends, he recorded daily, in abstract drawings — he told me so upon his return — the paths the patients of the wards followed along the hospital grounds. Bertalan's panels showing extended wires or reticular structures drawn with colored pencil dissimulate, in their ludic exercise, these observations about the mechanics of alienation.

His stylistic leaps, disconcerting for those around him, went from Sigma's structural rationalism to drawings from nature and from activities on the shores of the Timis River. The protean nature of his studio has the trans-stylistic coherence of wounds and traumatic episodes, which he records as if they were oppressively re-experienced reality. As a kind of ritual, he assists the fate of a plant — be it a beanstalk, a cauliflower, or a sunflower — from its creation to its dying. Nothing of the didactic ecologism of Joseph Beuys, within the European sphere, could the artist from Timisoara claim kinship with; only on the surface of their performances were they allied. Almost none of the pedagogy of the public shaman gathering devotees in his native country, or his adopted one — Italy — could be found in this practitioner of intercontinental peripatetics with his "Eurasian walking stick." Little of the thaumaturgy of his social agenda is set forth for his Düsseldorf disciples. Bertalan's work is a record of his inability to adapt and his sense of being perplexed by history. He is, purely and simply, the sensor for his fellow creatures, history experienced dramatically in the first person. His "progress," experimental and yet open to scholarly suggestions, surfaces in these drawings that are like a seismograph, recording his encounters, his fundamental contacts with the Bauhaus, with nature, with the drama of history. No attempt at synthesis follows this uninterrupted succession of observations, registered by his very existence. In a sense, Bertalan obstinately refuses his own "museumification." It is difficult to find an object that he would propose to a museum. He is tempted neither by the aesthetic finish of an object nor by its imperishability, and certainly not by its "eternity." Here and there are a painting —

an *Homage to Brancusi* from 1976 — studies for drawings, diagrams tracing the growth of the dicotyledon, photographs and film, slides of performances or the memorable architectonic structures constructed of willow twigs, a form of sacred space which renders the magnified veins of a leaf (present in *13 + 1*). I barely make out this "ignited bonfire" from which they emerged.

Posterity means nothing to an artist so intensely attuned to the present. In his fervent experimentation, Bertalan has not explored the limits of his art, its forms, and he seems to have no desire to pay any attention to the novelty he has introduced. This novelty simply matches the drama he wishes to communicate. The modern sacrifice of stylistic constancy is in itself the natural result of this exhalation. The formal eclecticism of his readymade installation of the *Ping-Pong Table* is just as expressive as it is confusing. Bertalan does not investigate the limits of artistic language, but the limits of existential endurance. And, unarguably, the unifying fiber of all his experiments is Expressionism. For this reason I ventured to regard this trajectory of his life not as an exercise in its transfiguration but as a metaphor of its disfiguration, scars of his wounds, incurred in the rush of reality and fiction — the two never entirely detached from one another.

Bertalan, the "Beuys" of Eastern Europe and the exemplar of his fellow beings' neurosis, intruded into a conference held by Andrei Plesu at the Gallery Pro Arte in Lugos, scattering grains of golden corn over the assembled crowd like a sower, a hierophant. He marvels over a biblical text, reciting to us the passage about Jacob's dream at the altar of Bethel. During the years, he had discovered this biblical text with an amazement that made me feel this book had been written only for him, and that its events had occurred only of late. He had discovered it with the same amazement that in the 1960s he had studied Kandinsky, Klee, or Gropius, or that in the 1970s he had discovered Leonardo. Experimentation carries an expressive force and the authenticity of this amazement before the common locus, be it a landscape, a flower, or human destiny. Its freshness is the experiment's most natural and direct form, its capacity to redeem from banality even the dogma and dramaturgy of alienation.

Written between 1990 and 1995. Originally published in *Experiment in Romanian Art since 1960* (Bucharest: Soros Center for Contemporary Art, 1997). Translated by Julian Semilian.

•●

IVAN MARTIN JIROUS

Ivan Martin Jirous (born 1944) is a poet, critic, and publicist, known by his pen name Magor. In the late 1960s he was instrumental in promoting Czech underground and independent culture, and in 1969 he became the artistic leader and manager of the rock group The Plastic People of the Universe. Under his influence, the group combined psychedelic rock and avant-garde music, and their stage performances resembled playful rituals or Happenings. He was also a charismatic leader of youth, organizing numerous unofficial concerts, exhibitions, performances, and festivals of underground culture. Jirous, along with other band members, was repeatedly imprisoned in the 1970s and 1980s, due to his association with the Plastic People and his involvement with the underground press.

"A Report on the Third Czech Musical Revival," first distributed in 1975 in samizdat form, was widely read by young people in Czechoslovakia, and during the 1970s and 1980s

it became a kind of manifesto, or credo, for independent Czech culture. Although the text focuses on rock music, it describes the general cultural situation in a totalitarian state and demonstrates the impossibility of destroying independent thinking and artistic expression.

A Report on the Third Czech Musical Revival

In great cultural revolutions, the only correct way for the people to liberate themselves is never to use any method that attempts to accomplish things on their behalf. Trust the people, have confidence in them, and respect their initiative. Banish fear! Do not be afraid of confusion. Let people be their own teachers in this great revolutionary movement. — Mao Tse-tung

I

Late in 1974, just one day before New Year's Eve, we traveled by train to attend a concert in Lišnice, a small village west of Prague. We disembarked at the nearest train station and walked the remaining four kilometers [about three miles]. It was shortly before dusk, and we chose the shortest route across a stretch of half-frozen marshland to the village. There were forty-five of us. We knew that some of our other friends were arriving in Lišnice from another direction by bus, and many more were expected to come in their own cars. We were all in a joyfully expectant mood. The year was at a close, and there was a palpable prospect of celebrating its end with music. We were going to hear the first concert performance of the groups Umělá hmota [Synthetic Matter], DG307, and others. As we trudged through the desolate countryside, many of us experienced a feeling of profound anticipation, difficult to put into words. Our walk reminded us of the trek of the first Hussites up into the mountains. We picked up this theme, made some jokes on the subject, and speculated on its portent in our situation. Was it conceivable that upon arriving in Lišnice, the minions of the village overlord—now the hirelings of today's establishment— would be waiting to disperse us?

That was indeed what happened. Never mind that this was planned as a New Year's party of friends—in this case some musicians and members of the village fire-brigade band—who had been playing soccer together and who were to meet in the hall of a public restaurant. Never mind the fact that the local council had given its tentative approval for such a meeting. All of us who had assembled in the hall were asked to disperse immediately, or else force would be used to break up the gathering. We dispersed. Why? Because people who decide to go out of their way to hear music they like are similar to the people who in the past trekked up into the mountains to hear a good sermon, except that in our day we have no other choice but to give in to violence. Incidentally, when our crowd was being forced to clear the hall of the restaurant, another party was in progress in the bar of the same establishment, consisting of a group of hunters who were being entertained by a brass band whose decibel level was at least as powerful as that of a regular rock band. A candlelit Christmas tree completed the scene as a symbol of that gentle season. A member of that party had been instrumental in banning our kind of music, and he refused, in a rude manner, to discuss the matter with our representative. Instead, he called the police. He turned out to be the deputy to the secretary of the local Communist village council of Líšnice.

In the [Hussite] past, he would probably have been called a servant of the Anti-christ. Today he is called the deputy of our [Communist] establishment. Actually, he hardly deserves the attention given to him in this report, except that he is a typical example of the countless bureaucrats who, since the early 1970s, have either prohibited or called the police to disperse a number of similar musical events. It is symptomatic of our time to direct hate and suspicion against people who want nothing more than to create their own art, an art they feel compelled to express in an era that stubbornly refuses to concede that the first and foremost mission of art is to serve people who wish to live together in truth.

II

Be that as it may, this report is not meant to concern itself with what these musicians are doing—for, above all, it is the music that should be listened to—but rather the how and why of what they are doing. I will call this the third Czech musical revival, which started during the first half of the 1970s, in all probability around 1973. The exact time of the first Czech musical revival (if there was one) is not really important in this connection. The use of the term "third musical revival" can be traced back to a statement of Karel Voják, who was associated with The Primitives Group. He observed that the second Czech musical revival took place during the late 1960s, a time when rock music (which then went by the name Big Beat) took off with unexpected vigor all over Czechoslovakia, especially in Prague.

In Prague alone there were a few hundred bands, but most of them did not achieve popular recognition or become well known. However, this is not the point. What is important is that many different people had the opportunity to make music, people who had formerly been prevented from doing so either due to the restrictions imposed by class or origin, lack of formal education, or their unwillingness to submit to an educational process that was perceived as too difficult to fit into under the prevailing conditions of that period. The important

The Plastic People of the Universe in concert at Havlíčkův Brod. 1969. Courtesy Jan Ságl

fact is the number of active rock bands in existence during those years. Regardless of their quality, they created the seedbed for a natural weeding-out process. Many groups were formed, but quickly disbanded and re-formed into new ones. How else would people be able to come to know each other and share mutual interests and personal predispositions than by performing and showing their work before an interested public audience?

The information blockade [imposed during the late 1960s] that affected all young people between the ages of sixteen and nineteen must be considered one of the most serious crimes perpetrated by the ruling establishment, because it is during those formative years that essential character traits become established for the rest of one's adult life. It infuriates me when I hear that if somebody is predestined to a certain fate that somehow his destiny is bound to find him and help him reach his goal. How is it possible to achieve anything when we are surrounded by an impenetrable wall of stupidity and subterfuge?

Josef Janíček, the present leader of The Plastics, performed for three years in The Swimmers band before he became a member of The Primitives Group. Milan Hlavsa, who founded The Plastic People of the Universe at age nineteen, had gained his experience with the group The Undertakers and put together two short-lived bands of his own in-between. How can our young be expected to establish any new viable groups in the present situation when they are denied the opportunity to develop a solid and spontaneous musical base, where musicians, guided solely by their musical sense and their mutual affection, can compare, come together, and disband as they wish? At any rate, these days are gone forever.

This brief review of the history of Czech rock music has been presented here primarily in order to compare it with the current situation, to be discussed later. Other, formerly famous Czech rock groups have purposely not been mentioned, simply because the main intention of the above was to focus primarily on the incredible spread of rock music in the Czech lands during that time. However, there is one Prague band that cannot be ignored: The Primitives Group.

III

When the mode of music changes
When the mode of music is changed
When the mode of music changes
The walls of the city shake. — The Fugs

In retrospect it can now be stated, without exaggeration, that with the founding of The Primitives Group, the phenomenon of a real musical underground emerged in Prague, perhaps not consciously, but certainly on some level of awareness. This is also the main reason why we did not mention any other "famous" bands from the era of Czech beat music. Unfortunately, they wasted their potential, along with the trust imparted to them. It was amazing to watch how quickly the representatives of this new type of music managed to overtake well-established, older, but less up-to-date genres in the commercialization of their art, how the driving force of their effort became the desire to make a career by performing on the stages of so-called experimental theaters, how they craved academic recognition, and how they worried about the opinion of pious and impotent critics who tend to judge rock music on the basis of obsolete criteria, which have become useless even for judging those domains of the arts from which they had been borrowed in the first place.

Only The Primitives Group stood apart from the spiritual emptiness that had engulfed all the other officially recognized bands. It was a rough and savage group, far removed from any kind of nicety, and, in fact, it probably subconsciously was aiming at the very opposite. The group did not create its own repertoire, but instead demonstrated a perfect feeling for the works of Jimi Hendrix, Eric Burdon, The Grateful Dead, The Pretty Things, The Doors, The Mothers of Invention, and The Fugs. During the late 1960s the playing of Anglo-American rock music on the Czech scene was considered absolutely essential if the next generation of Czech rock was to achieve world-class standards. Incidentally, at that time the market had not yet been saturated with a flood of foreign records as it is today. For example, when The Primitives played Frank Zappa's music for the first time, only a small number of initiates had any knowledge of his existence.

But this alone would not have been enough to transform The Primitives into a group which was to emerge as a legitimate icon of the underground movement, a movement that succeeded in creating its own self-contained world with its own inner dynamic and aesthetics and thus also its own ethic, distinct and separate from established society. It was primarily their orientation toward a single facet of contemporary music, i.e., the so-called psychedelic sound that set them apart. In this respect, The Primitives succeeded in being quite creative, especially if one considers that when they adopted this genre, they did not really know the exact meaning of this term. Nevertheless, they interpreted it correctly, by using their music to induce in their audience a special mental state, which succeeded, at least for a moment, in producing a feeling of absolute release from everyday concerns and which laid bare the most elemental wellsprings of a person's inner being. Apart from music, a number of other means were used to achieve a direct impact on the senses: water (fish feast), air (bird feast), and, above all, fire. Optical effects were borrowed from the visual arts or from the related movement of so-called Happenings. This has been described elsewhere, but survives primarily in the form of legendary tales.

One more brief remark about The Primitives Group should be made. Once the official critics of Czech rock music started to take this *enfant terrible* seriously, the group decided on its own initiative to dissolve. This did not mean the end of the evolution of psychedelic music in Prague, however. The Primitives disbanded in May of 1969. At that time Plastic People of the Universe had already been performing for the last five months.

IV

The world is beautiful
But the Plastics don't see it
Flowers are beautiful
But the Plastics don't see it
Sunset is beautiful
But the Plastics don't see it
Their eyes behold only one thing
Only one thing they see as beautiful
Plastic People of the underground. — *"Cosmic Symphony"*

The allegiance of The Plastic People of the Universe to the underground was deliberate. Not unlike The Primitives Group, who had created their distinctive version of psychedelic music on the basis of a certain naiveté and paucity of information, the notion of underground was perceived by The Plastics entirely on an emotional level and according to the literal meaning of the word "under" or "below" ground. Another significant factor in the development of rock music in Prague was the fact that its founder, Milan Hlavsa, emerged as an outstanding composer. His original music was accompanied by equally original lyrics, which during the first phase of The Plastics' existence managed to achieve a kind of mythological synopsis of the cosmology of the underground.

The underground is perceived here as mythological, as a world of a distinct mentality, different from the mentality of people of the establishment. The lyrics of Michal Jernek and Věra Jirousová, resonating with the spirit of the cabala of Agrippa of Nettesheim (whose symbolism had been used by The Primitives Group for their Feasts of the Elements), presented the followers of the underground with a situation that fully deserves the designation "of the Universe" as part of the name of the group. A characteristic line in their "The Sun" phase goes like this: "All the stupid brains are on the sun, while our mighty tribe lives in a velvet underground." In the composition entitled "The Universe Symphony and Melody about a Plastic Doctor," all the planets circling the sun were celebrated, with one part dedicated to the planet earth with the title "Plastic People Underground." In a song about two extraterrestrial worlds and a mythical bird called Fafejta, there are allusions to mythological themes, especially Celtic mythology and the cabala of Agrippa, apart from allusions to the universe of rock music (John Lennon and Yoko Ono), which were also given a mythological interpretation.

To the extent that the Plastics turned their attention to concrete worldly matters, as in their composition "A Ball of Lightning," which celebrates a favorite character in the group's lyrics—the eccentric inventor Prokop Diviš (for example, Diviš sits in a shack in the Canadian bush with his friends, among whom are Roy Estrada, the bass guitarist of the group The Mothers of Invention), they made sure that this too was interpreted primarily as a mythological vision of reality.

The Plastic People continued consciously in the manner of The Primitives Group by enhancing their musical numbers with various visual effects. For example, a fire, tended by costumed pyromaniacs, was burning on the stage, with the members of the band playing the piece "A Ball of Lightning." The performers wore colored makeup on their faces, and a character spitting fire joined the tableau. During the opening performance of the "Cosmic Symphony" in the artists club Mánes [in Prague] the Plastics sacrificed a chicken to the god Mars. On the day of the manned moon landing, they hurled fiery disks across the stage, which later became a permanent feature of their performance.

Apart from their original creations, The Plastic People also forged links with The Primitives Group in their "educational" activities. For example, they introduced to the Prague scene the unforgettable compositions of Andy Warhol's group The Velvet Underground, and familiarized the public with most of the repertoire of Ed Sanders's and Tuli Kupfenberg's The Fugs. It goes without saying that they also played the more recent Frank Zappa compositions. This represents a fairly accurate snapshot of what was happening during the time when the designation "of the Universe" was truly a symbol of their commitment. Faithful to their past, they still use the name today.

But, in the meantime, the situation had changed, compelling them to plant their feet firmly on the ground. The underground of mythology became transformed into an underground responding to the cultural and sociological changes of the early 1960s, which became embodied in the works of Sanders, Ginsberg, Nutall, Leary, and other pioneers of this movement. I should add that it required the special conditions of our own political situation for our underground to eke out its existence in the literal sense of the word.

V

Again, the devil took him to a very high mountain,
And showed him all the kingdoms of the world and the glory of them;
And he said to him, "All these I will give you,
If you will fall down and worship me." — Matthew 4:8–9

During the early 1970s the Prague authorities took drastic measures to curtail the rock movement. It was forbidden to sing English-language lyrics, English-sounding band names had to be changed, etc. Regrettably, a number of rock musicians decided to quit and chose to act as pitiful accompanists for commercial pop stars. Only The Plastic People of the Universe refused to make any changes, either in their name or in their repertoire or appearance. On the contrary, they resisted any interference from the outside that would compromise the character and basic convictions of the band members. As a result, the group lost its professional status; some of its less-committed members left, with the core of the next incarnation of the Plastics gathered around Hlavsa and Janíček. This group had to start again practically from the beginning, without equipment, instruments, or a definite home base. Nonetheless they had a clear idea of what they were all about: to play only music that the conscience of its members compelled them to play and to create joy. Only thus can the joy of a musician's calling be passed on to the listening public.

After a prolonged period of silence, during which The Plastic People regrouped into a new ensemble and was enhanced by the presence of the virtuoso violinist Jiří Kabeš (and, for a time by the vocalist Paul Wilson), they staged a performance during a dance festival in Ledeč nad Sázavou in 1971. It became clear that this was the only significant rock group that managed to prove it was possible to play rock without lowering its musical standards or compromising its artistic qualities. Dozens of rock fans from Prague, Carlsbad, and other cities came to listen. This brought about the atmosphere of what we earlier referred to as "trekking up into the mountains." When Milan Hlavsa in Ledeč nad Sázavou saw this cross-country crowd, who had traveled by train or bus, and others who had hitchhiked to hear his concert, he made his now-famous remark: "We can't give up now, even if we wanted to. What else will people want to do for fun?"

The Plastic People band thus occupied the exceptional position of being the only real underground rock group in the Czech lands. It demonstrated by its very existence that the term "underground" was not just a superficial label to be attached to a new musical trend, but above all a way of life with its own special attitude. I must confess that I always held a grudge against other fairly decent Prague rock groups that decided to compromise their positions during the early 1970s by giving in to certain conditions imposed by the establishment in return for permission to perform their music in public, even if that music precluded the creation of a genuinely new art form.

Why did they do it? I think they lacked and still lack a legitimate feeling for their art, its function in society, and the duty of those who are privileged to create it. Those who fail to understand this will easily go astray. The Plastics stuck to their convictions not only because they were good musicians—even though at that time there may have been better musicians in other rock groups in the technical sense—but also because even during the worst times, when they had no equipment, no audience, and nobody to help them, they knew one thing and one thing only: it is better not to play music at all than play music that fails to spring from the performer's deepest musical convictions. Above all, it is better not to play than play according to the wishes of the establishment. Even that is putting it too mildly. It is not only better but essential. To give up everything is one of the fundamental requirements for anybody who wishes to be called an artist in today's society. Integrity must always take precedence over any other consideration in the realm of the spirit. Moreover, It is usually too late to opt out when things have already become too obvious. Once the first concession has been made, whether under the guise of some phony excuse or the honest belief that it does not really matter, all is lost.

As soon as the devil (speaking today as the spokesperson for the establishment) proffers his first concession, and asks you to trim your hair back just a little in order to obtain permission to play, it is time to say no. And, just as soon as the devil (speaking as the spokesperson for the establishment) asks you to change your name and promises in turn that you will be allowed to play again as you played before, it is time to say no again—no, we will not play.

Be that as it may, in the end this is not the real issue. The real question to be asked is: Why should the establishment have the power to prevent those from performing who have renounced all privileges usually afforded to a professional musician? The establishment is surely capable of putting pressure on those who want to be better off than their peers. But for those who pursue a better life not in the sense of material security, but solely in the pursuit of seeking and following the truth, the establishment inspires little fear. Only those deserve to be called true artists who come to understand that the gift of art has been bestowed upon them not in order to live better than their neighbors, but to use their talent to celebrate their fellow human beings. Marcel Duchamp said it best shortly before the end of his life: "The great artist of tomorrow will go underground." Here, I am not using the term "underground" as some kind of label designating a new style, but as standing for a new spiritual attitude of an honest artist, who has decided to react to the dehumanization and perversion of all values in today's global consumer society.

(**VI–XII** not included)

XIII

We have to act reasonably in this world of evil, in a situation into which God has irrevocably placed us. —John Milton

The word "underground" has been mentioned frequently in this essay, and we would like to clarify what we mean by this term. The word is not to be interpreted as being tied to a specific artistic movement or style, in spite of the fact that in music it manifests itself primarily in the form of rock. Instead, it represents the spiritual position of intellectuals and artists who consciously and critically confront the world in which they live. It is a declaration of war against the establishment, against things as they are. It is a movement that operates primarily with artistic means, even though its representatives are conscious of the fact that art is not and should not be the end-all of an artist's effort. The underground produces people who understand that by relying on so-called legal means, nothing can be changed and so they do not even try to become part of the "legal" establishment. Ed Sanders of the New York Fugs expressed this attitude most succinctly when he announced his "total assault on culture." Only people who are not part of "official" culture can launch such an assault.

In a nutshell, the term underground stands for the activities of artists and intellectuals whose works are deemed unacceptable by the establishment, and who refuse to become martyrs or remain passive in the face of their difficulties, but instead try to bring about the demise of the establishment by their works and actions. Anger and humility are indispensable qualities for those who have chosen the underground as their spiritual home. Anyone lacking these qualities will not be able to survive inside the underground for long.

The idea of the underground had its origin during the early 1960s in the West, where it became established as a distinct movement. At the same time, one must note the sad and common practice of the Western establishment to co-opt and embrace enthusiastically any new musical fashion, just as it would embrace a new automobile design or any other fashionable innovation. And so, having once achieved recognition and fame, a number of rock musicians acceded to the lures of official mass culture (we shall call this the "first culture" for our purposes), and conjoined with its representatives.

Things are fundamentally different in our own situation, and in many ways much better than in the West simply because we live in an atmosphere of clear-cut alternatives: the first culture does not want us. In turn, we do not want anything to do with them either. Period. This eliminates the major source of temptation for anyone, including the most resolute soul: the longing for recognition, success, awards, and titles, and, last but not least, material prosperity gained by fame. In contrast to the West, where a number of people with a mind-set very close to ours live in a state of constant confusion and might conceivably be considered our potential friends, things are much more clear-cut here. Anything that we are doing goes against the grain of those who represent official culture. Why is this? Because anything we do is useless in creating the impression that things are as they ought to be. And indeed, things are not as they ought to be.

Of course, it is true that in the history of humanity there has never existed a time when things were perfect and everybody was happy. Nevertheless, it has always been the role of a true artist to take note of things that are not as they ought to be. It is for these reasons that one of the most important tasks of art is to stir up trouble. The goal of the underground in the West is the outright destruction of the establishment. In contrast, the goal of our underground is to create a second culture, a culture completely independent from all official communication media and the conventional hierarchy of value judgments put out by the establishment. It is to be a culture that does not have as its goal the destruction of the establishment, because by attempting this, it would—in effect—mean that we would fall into the trap of playing their game. The real aim is to overcome the hopeless feeling that it is of no use to try anything and show that it is possible to do a lot, but only for those who are willing to act and who ask little for themselves, but instead care a lot for others. Only by such means will it be possible to survive in dignity the rest of one's life according to the prophetic words of the chiliastic Táborite Martin Húska: "The faithful person is a thousand times more valuable than any kind of ritual sacrament."

Written and distributed in samizdat form in 1975. Selections from text, officially published in I. M. Jirous, *Magorùv Zápisník* (Prague [Czech Republic]: Torst, 1997). Translated by Eric Dluhosch.

A CASE STUDY: REPRESSION

Bulldozer Exhibition, Moscow, September 15, 1974
Izmailovsky Park Exhibition, Moscow, September 29, 1974

From the late 1920s on, in the Soviet Union, the Communist party used art as a propaganda tool to portray the positive aspects of life and work under the newly formed political system, an endeavor which called for tight control over the kinds of art produced and presented to the public. Socialist Realism became the standard mode of representation, while abstract art, art with religious or erotic themes, and art critical of the political system were decreed unacceptable. Restrictions were enforced through a network of artists' unions, the official Academy, and the ministries of culture. Artists had to be official union members to be allowed to exhibit, receive commissions and studio space, and membership was restricted to those artists whose work conformed to Party ideals.

Temporarily, under Khrushchev's reign in the late 1950s and early 1960s, the Party broadened its definition of acceptable art and literature. Works by Western artists were exhibited in 1956 and 1957 for the first time,[1] stores for the sale of art were established, and artists were generally given greater freedom, all of which contributed to the emergence of a small, unofficial art community. However, after abstract experimental paintings, included in the Manezh exhibition of 1962 drew the ire of Khrushchev, the Party again tightened its control on cultural production. Freedoms were curtailed but underground activities continued, with artists and writers presenting their works in samizdat publications and private apartment shows.

In 1969 the Neo-Expressionist painter Oscar Rabin proposed holding outdoor exhibitions, exploiting a loophole in government regulations. But the idea failed to find supporters, and it was not until a few years later, when a new generation of younger artists had emerged in Moscow and Leningrad, that the idea took hold. A recent wave of police intimidation, which included interrogations, arrests, property damage, and interruptions of private exhibitions by police, left many underground artists feeling as if they had nothing to lose and needed to mount a counteroffensive.

Under the direction of Rabin and Aleksandr Glezer, a poet and collector of unofficial art, a small group of artists, which included Nadezhda Elskaia, Vitaly Komar, Lydia Masterkova, Alexander Melamid, Vladimir Nemukhin, Aleksandr Rabin, Evgenii Rukhin, Viktor Tupitsyn, and Yuri Zharkikh, decided to hold an open-air exhibition on an empty field in the Cheryomushki district on the outskirts of Moscow. The site was chosen for its remoteness so as to avoid possible claims of "public disturbance."

—*Majlena Braun*

Chronology of Events[2]

Sept. 2, 1974	Artists send letter to Moscow City Council announcing their intention of putting their paintings on view on Sunday, Sept. 15.
Week of Sept. 9	Mikhail Shkodin, deputy head of the Department of Culture at the Moscow City Council, suggests during a meeting that the artists mount the exhibition at the local artists' union, and arranges for a meeting with union officials.
	The artists present their paintings for review to the union officials but receive no definite answer on an exhibition. At a

Invitation to the Bulldozer Show. Text: You are invited to the first autumn Open-Air Art Exhibition. The following artists will participate: O. Rabin, E. Rukhin, V. Nemukhin, L. Masterkova, N. Elskaia, Y. Zharkikh, A. Rabin, B. Shteinberg, A. Melamid, V. Komar, A. Brussilovsky, V. Sitnikov, V. Vorobiev, I. Kholin. The exhibition will be held on September 15, 1974, from 12 to 2 P.M. at the end of Profsouzmaya and Ostrovitianov streets. Courtesy Komar & Melamid

	subsequent meeting with Shkodin, they make clear their intention to proceed with the proposed outdoor show. Shkodin informs Rabin that he cannot forbid the exhibition but would not recommend that it take place either.
Sept. 14	Glezer and Rabin meet with *New York Times* correspondent Christopher Wren to describe the general situation and negotiations with authorities.
	The artists meet to plan for the following day. The main objective is for the artists not to be detained before the exhibition.

The New York

"All the News That's Fit to Print"

VOL.CXXIII..No. 42,604   © 1974 The New York Times Company   NEW YORK, MONDAY, SEPTEMBER 16, 1

A water truck pursues crowd from the scene of an outdoor art show in Moscow after authorities halted exhibition

United Press International

RUSSIANS DISRUPT MODERN ART SHOW WITH BULLDOZERS

Unofficial Outside Exhibition Dispersed—Bystanders Hit and Paintings Confiscated

By CHRISTOPHER S. WREN
Special to The New York Times

MOSCOW, Sept. 15—In a dramatic confrontation over nonconformist art, Soviet authorities used bulldozers, dump trucks and water-spraying trucks today to break up an outdoor exhibition of unofficial art as it was being set up in a vacant lot.

A crowd of several hundred people, among them artists, Western diplomats, correspondents and curious neighborhood residents, scattered when dump trucks and a pair of bulldozers overran what the artists had billed as the first autumn outdoor art show in the Soviet Union.

Two water trucks, normally used for street-cleaning, pursued the fleeing crowds across the street. A handful of people pelted the trucks with clods of dirt.

Three Americans Struck

Three American correspondents—two men and a woman—were beaten by young vigilantes who roamed the scene intimidating people to move on. Several uniformed police looked on impassively and made no effort to stop the violence.

The young men who appeared to be organized into teams, ripped up, trampled and threw more than a dozen paintings into a dump truck to be covered with mud and driven away. Artists who protested were roughed up and at least five were arrested. An unknown number of angry spectators were taken to a nearby police station.

Later, one spectator who was released, Aleksei Tyapushkin, reportedly a member of the official Union of Artists and a decorated World War II veteran, said the police had told him that all the confiscated paintings had been burned.

Thirteen organizers of the exhibition sent a written protest to the Communist party Politburo protesting lawlessness, arbitrary misuse of force and violation of constitutional rights. They demanded an investigation, the return of their works

Continued on Page 10, Column 1

Terrorists Free 2, Hold 9 At Embassy in The Hague

By TERRY ROBARDS
Special to The New York Times

THE HAGUE, Monday, Sept. 16 — Two women hostages were released early today by the Japanese terrorists who have been in control of the French Embassy since Friday afternoon.

70 on Saigon Plane Die as It Explodes During Hijacking

By JAMES M. MARKHAM
Special to The New York Times

SAIGON, South Vietnam, Sept. 15—Sixty-two passengers and eight crew members were killed today when an Air Vietnam Boeing 727, apparently hijacked by a man demanding to go to Hanoi, exploded near a provincial airfield on the coast of South Vietnam.

According to several accounts, the plane exploded about 1,000 feet above the airfield at Phan Rang, 175 miles northeast of here, after the hijacker detonated two powerful M-26 hand grenades.

But a telephone operator at Phan Rang, who said he had witnessed the crash, reported the plane had gone down at a steep angle and exploded on impact at the edge of the run-

A Dutch police official said the release showed that significant progress had been made in the negotiations with the terrorists to turn over the remaining nine hostages seized in the raid on the embassy.

The two women, each 22 years old, were allowed to walk from the door of the French Embassy to Dutch police officers who were waiting by the wall of the American Embassy about 50 yards away. The women then were assisted into the American Embassy, where they were examined by a doctor and a psychiatrist.

One was identified as a telephone operator and the other was identified as a secretary. Both women appeared to be weak.

The terrorists were still holding Ambassador Jacques Senard and eight other hostages. The invasion of the embassy by three armed men who said they were members of the Japanese Red Army, a terrorist group, captured national attention.

Among earlier signs that offi-

LEBANON REPORTS 2 ISRAELI ATTACKS

Says Planes Strike in South, Killing a Village Leader and Causing Damage

Special to The New York Times

BEIRUT, Sept. 15 — Israeli fighter bombers struck today at targets in southeast Lebanon, killing one civilian and wounding two others, the Ministry of Defense said in a communiqué.

The dead man was identified as Fuad Abou Saleh, the mukhtar, or local leader, of Hasbaya, which is the largest township of the region, known as the Arkub, on the slopes of Mount Hermon.

The communiqué said a military jeep had overturned during the raid, which lasted 10 minutes. It mentioned no Lebanese military casualties but reported damage to houses and farms.

The targets attacked were listed as the outskirts of Choya, Zaglah and the Morani Bridge, all in the Hasbaya area.

The attack was carried out by eight Israeli Phantoms flying at a high altitude, the communiqué added.

The Ministry of Defense in a

Grenade Explosion Kills 2 and Hurts 26 In Paris Drugstore

Special to The New York Times

PARIS, Sept. 15 — A hand grenade exploded in a crowd on the lower sales floor of the Saint-Germain-des-Prés drugstore late this afternoon, killing two persons and wounding 26.

Some of the injured were reported in grave condition.

The prefect of police said that according to witnesses a young man had tossed the grenade from a balcony onto the crowded main floor of the sub-basement. The man—described as 25 to 30 years old, dressed in a gray suit—escaped down a staircase in the panic caused by the explosion, the prefect, Jean Paolini, said.

A Popular Store

The "Drugstore Saint-Germain," as it is known, is one of the most popular attractions of the Left Bank and includes a cafe and shops. It is on a main thoroughfare from the government and embassy district to the university section and Latin Quarter. The store is owned by Marcel Bleustein-Blanchet, a successful advertising man who is a well-known supporter of Israel.

Two of the 26 injured were children

It is therefore decided that the participants will split into two groups: one will stay overnight at Rabin's and take the subway to the site; the other will stay at an apartment within walking distance of the site.

Sept. 15 Police arrest Rabin and Glezer at the subway stop, accusing them of robbery but let them go twenty minutes later.

The "First Fall Outdoor Exhibition" lasts thirty minutes, in light drizzle. When the artists arrive with their paintings, they are met by militia, several dump trucks, bulldozers, and a group of "volunteer workers," who announce that a park is being built. The roughly four hundred spectators—mostly artists, local residents, including journalists and diplomats—are asked to leave immediately. When several of the artists attempt to hold up their paintings for view, the workers charge at them, knocking them and their paintings to the ground. American embassy official intervenes and demands that worker in charge identify himself. The man replies, "We are the working class, the international proletariat." Several paintings are burned on a bonfire. Fights break out and three bulldozers move across the field, rolling over paintings and toward artists. Rabin is thrust into the air by the blades of one bulldozer. Several foreign journalists are beaten, their cameras broken; Christopher Wren has a tooth knocked out. Police arrest Oscar and Aleksandr Rabin, Rukhin, Elskaia, and Tupitsyn, and twelve spectators are taken for interrogation.

The remaining participants are forced to leave the site. They regroup at Glezer's in the evening to write a letter of protest to the Politbureau (see p. 72).

The arrested artists, whom police threaten with one-year prison sentences, go on a hunger strike.

US embassy in Moscow sends three-page telegram with account of events to US Secretary of State, noting that American correspondents had been "roughed up."

Sept. 16 American and European radio stations and newspapers make the event the main news story of the day.

The official Soviet news agency TASS issues a statement denouncing the exhibition as "cheap provocation with the sole intent of creating anti-Soviet sentiment."

American embassy official files oral complaint about treatment of American journalists with Mikhaylov, Acting Chief of Soviet Ministry of Foreign Affairs, USA division. Mikhaylov denies knowledge of events but agrees to investigate.

US embassy sends telegram with report of complaint to US Secretary of State and several other US embassies.

Authorities inform foreign correspondents that Jagodkin, vice director of culture at the city council, has been found solely responsible for the decisions leading to the scuffle.

Rabin and Ruhkin are tried in court and fined. They are released although they refuse to pay the fine. Elskaia and Tupitsyn are let go later that day.

About thirty foreign journalists attend a press conference at Glezer's apartment, which is surrounded by KGB agents who photograph everybody leaving the building. Glezer announces that a letter has been sent to the government, detailing the artists' intention of holding another exhibition in two weeks.

Sept. 17   Mikhaylov arranges a meeting at Rabin's. He assures Glezer and Rabin that his agency was not involved in the events, and says that the responsible police chief has been reprimanded and the party functionary who gave orders has been assigned to Vietnam.

Invitation to Izmailovsky Park Exhibition, 1974. Courtesy Komar & Melamid

Unofficial art on display at the Izmailovsky Park Exhibition, 1974. Courtesy Aleksandr Glezer

He asks what the artists hope to achieve. When told that they merely want permission to show their paintings and the release of Aleksandr Rabin, he promises to arrange this.

Sept. 18   Aleksandr Rabin is released from prison.

Sovetskaia kul'tura publishes a letter to the editor written by the "workers" from the Bulldozer event (see pp. 72–73).

Week of Sept. 23 Shkodin, representing the Moscow City Council, enters into negotiations with artists, offering them permission for an exhibition if only Moscow artists take part. Artists insist on including painters from Leningrad.

Artists and their parents are threatened with loss of employment if the artists take part in what is labeled a "Jewish" exhibition. Glezer is attacked near his apartment by undercover agents, tied to a tree, and beaten. He phones Mikhaylov and threatens to call a press conference. The KGB agent promises to ask for police protection for Glezer.

Sept. 25   After artists promise not to display anti-Soviet, religious, or pornographic paintings, Shkodin signs a permit for a four-hour official exhibition in Izmailovsky Park but refuses to give artists a copy of the statement. Eventually he agrees to let foreign journalists photograph the permit.

Groups of young artists call the city council asking to be included in the exhibition. A committee is set up to review the work; Rabin and Glezer approve the inclusion of all applicants.

Sept. 28   The deputy chairman of the Moscow City Soviet organizes a press conference for foreign correspondents and reproaches them for exaggerating the Bulldozer battle. He then informs them that the Izmailovsky exhibition will only be open to friends of the artists and those with invitations.

Artists learn that the site of the exhibition is surrounded by barriers and that bulldozers and street-cleaning machines are waiting in woods nearby. Rabin reads a declaration to foreign correspondents over the phone, warning that should admission to the exhibition be limited and there be provocation, the artists will exhibit their paintings for ten minutes but return ten days later. The KGB overhears this declaration and subsequently gives instructions to allow the event to take place without disturbance.

Sept. 29   The "Second Fall Outdoor Exhibition" at Izmailovsky Park lasts four hours, in sunny weather, without any interruption by authorities. More than seventy artists set up paintings of diverse styles in a long line across the field with some ten thousand spectators crowding around them. Lively discussions ensue. It is the first uninterrupted public display of unofficial art in the Soviet Union.

Week of Oct. 6	Artists submit a request for premises for an exhibition in December and file charges against those who destroyed their pictures during the Bulldozer event.
	Two participants of the Izmailovsky exhibition are drafted into the army and sent to the Altai, near western Mongolia. Three artists are put in insane asylums, and countless others are threatened with commitment to an asylum if they continue exhibiting their art. The police threaten others with arrest unless they take full-time employment.
Oct./Nov.	The Russian press publishes articles against the nonconformist artists.
Dec. 12	KGB agents break into Glezer's apartment and confiscate material regarding the two exhibitions as well as recorded interviews with artists. Glezer is taken to the Lubyanka headquarters and told he will be tried for anti-Soviet activities unless he agrees to emigrate.

International reaction concerning the Bulldozer events forced Soviet authorities to change their treatment of unofficial artists. Following the Izmailovsky Park show, further exhibitions were mounted with state approval, and selected artists were allowed to travel and exhibit abroad, but state aggression toward unofficial artists persisted in less-overt ways and did not end until Gorbachev's *glasnost* reform period in the late 1980s.

The fate of some of the artists who participated in these exhibitions is worth noting. Nadezhda Elskaia: died under mysterious circumstances in 1978, just before emigration; Aleksandr Glezer: exiled in Feb. 1975, moved to Paris; Vitaly Komar: emigrated in 1977 and settled in New York; Lydia Masterkova: emigrated to Paris in late 1970s; Alexander Melamid: emigrated in 1977 and settled in New York; Vladimir Nemukhin: exiled, moved to Berlin; Aleksandr Rabin: exiled with his father in 1978; Oscar Rabin: exiled in 1978, moved to Paris; Evgenii Rukhin: died under mysterious circumstances during a fire at his Leningrad studio in 1976; and Yurii Zharkikh: exiled.

Notes:

1. In 1956 there was a Moscow exhibition of Picasso's works from Soviet museum collections; the 1957 Sixth World Festival of Youth and Students in Moscow included works by artists from fifty-two countries.

2.. This chronology is based in part on information and documentation provided by Aleksandr Glezer, coorganizer of the Bulldozer and Izmailovsky Park exhibitions; his assistant, Yuri Volkogonov; Vitaly Komar and Alexander Melamid, who were artists and participants in the exhibitions; Alfred Friendly, Jr., *Newsweek* magazine's Moscow Bureau Chief from 1974 to 1976; and David Nalle, Counselor for Public Affairs at the US embassy in Moscow from 1973 to 1975. International newspaper reports as well as the following publications were consulted: Alexander Gleser, *Kunst gegen Bulldozer: Memoiren eines russischen Sammlers* (Frankfurt: Ullstein Verlag, 1982); Alexander Glezer, *Contemporary Russian Art* (Paris: Third Wave Publishers, 1993); and Oscar Rabin, *L'Artiste et les Bulldozers: Etre peinture en URSS* (Paris: R. Laffont, 1981).

Letter sent to the Politburo by the Bulldozer exhibition artists, September 16, 1974

Twenty-four artists from Moscow, Leningrad, Pskov, and Vladimir planned to hold their autumn exhibition in the open air on September 15. They gave the Moscow City Council advance notice of their intention in a letter dispatched on September 2. Moscow Council officials, headed by K. A. Sukhinich, failed to give the artists any indication that the spot they had chosen for the showing of their pictures, on wasteland far from any city streets, was unsuitable or forbidden. Yet at twelve noon on September 15 the artists and numerous spectators were met at the exhibition site by police in civilian clothes with dump trucks and bulldozers. The artists' pictures were taken away and their arms twisted and dislocated. The bulldozer drivers literally chased artists and spectators. One bulldozer driver, after running over pictures by Oscar Rabin, knocked the painter off his feet, and another plowed into a confused crowd of people. Water cannons scattered artists and spectators with powerful jets of water. Eighteen pictures were mutilated and burned by uncontrolled young thugs. Five artists were detained by the police, who to our surprise took a most active part in the assaults on artists and the destruction of their works.

We demand an investigation of these events, which are a disgrace to our country, the punishment of those responsible, and the return of the surviving pictures. We also inform you that in two weeks' time, on Sunday, September 29, in the same place, we shall re-erect the open-air exhibition of our pictures which was sabotaged by mischief makers.

We ask you to remind the police and other guardians of public order that they are there not to encourage barbarism and hooliganism, but to defend others from it—in this case spectators, artists, and works of art.

Originally published in *Museum of Soviet Unofficial Art* (Jersey City, NJ: C. A. S. E., 1980). Translated by Michael Scammell.

Letter to the editor published in *Sovetskaia kul'tura,* Moscow, September 18, 1974

Are you aware of what happened on September 15 in our borough of Cheryomushki? On the morning of that day, we, residents and workers of local companies, gathered together for a mass meeting of volunteers—a *voskresnik*—and dedicated ourselves to turning a park into a greener and better-equipped place for our neighborhood. We were perplexed and indignant when cars, one after another, began to stop at the lot across from the park at the intersection of Profsouzmaya and Ostrovitianov streets at about twelve o'clock. A handful of disheveled, brazen people began to drag from their cars very strange and colorful framed and unframed canvases with the intention of exhibiting their artworks right there in the open air, despite the fact that we and the other volunteers were still working. When they descended on the scene, our work schedule was disturbed. Crowds and commotion started at the quiet crossroads. These uninvited guests behaved provocatively. They wrenched shovels and rakes from the workers, pushed them off the lawn, and tore posters that appealed for participation in the *voskresnik*. They disturbed the traffic and cursed obscenities. It is interesting, however, that some foreigners came also, before the "artists," and then with them. They arrived in cars clearly marked with license plates from embassies of capitalist countries. Shockingly, some of the paintings arrived in those very cars. Among the foreigners, we discovered later, were many journalists who came, not to merely report on "the artistic event," but to aggressively take pictures of the chaos and to actively interfere. A correspondent from the Norwegian newspaper *Aftenposten*, Udgord Nils Morten, punched a volunteer police officer in the face, while the officer castigated him for his offensive act. There were many other similar incidents. The indecent behavior by the group of artists-formalists turned out to be a planned political provocation.

Upon the request of the participants of the *voskresnik*, the volunteer police intervened in the situation and asked for help from the militia. Some organizers of the "exhibition" were delivered to the militia with the purpose of identifying them. They turned out to be "liberal artists," "nonconformists" like Rabin, Kropivnitsky, Sychev, Elskaia, Tal, Slavutskaja, Tupitsyn, and others—about fifteen in number. The paintings that they brought were, in our opinion, contrary to artistic intentions and elicited nothing but disgust and disdainful laughter. Since all these people called themselves artists, we contacted the Artists Union to ask for clarification and were told that none of them were members of the Artists Union of the USSR. And so the artists clearly acted on their own accord without permission from the union. One week ago, they apparently contacted the Moscow City Council, which explained to them all of the procedures required for mounting and organizing an art exhibition in Moscow, but they did not pay attention to any of the instructions. The Moscow City Council requested that the artists contact the Moscow Artists Union. The union explained all of the necessary requirements, but the artists never followed them.

It became clear that some of these "artists" who conspired to arrange an exhibition in such a strange way managed to have had exhibitions abroad and to sell their paintings there. They did not do it for the money, but rather for the prestige of being known as unrecognized artists in their own country.

As everyone knows, the manipulation of their reputation here as "unrecognized artists" has not yet awarded any of them a laurel wreath. Even worse, they violated public order, committed acts of unbridled hooliganism—things not to be tolerated from anybody. We residents of Cheryomushki who witnessed this mayhem protest categorically against similar "artistic" actions and require that the law of our country and public order in the capital be respected by so-called liberal artists who seemingly know nothing about real art, and by their foreign friends and patrons.

Participants of *voskresnik*:
V. Federov, metal turner, winner of an exemplary worker competition
E. Swistunov, radio technician, winner of an exemplary worker competition
V. Polovinka, Director of the Department of Road Management and Equipment of the Borough Cheryomushki, Deputy of the Borough Union of Worker Deputies
B. Timashev, electrician

Translated by Tetyana Kasyanenko.

E1

Date Printed:
18 Jan 2002   DOC_NBR: 1975MOSCOW12385

CHANNEL: n/a
HANDLING: n/a

RELEASED IN FULL

1

<<<<.>>>>

PAGE 01   MOSCOW 12385   292026Z

11
ACTION EUR-12

INFO   OCT-01   ISO-00   CU-02   CIAE-00   DODE-00   INR-07   NSAE-00

    PA-01   USIA-06   PRS-01   SP-02   /032 W
    ---------------------   017112

R 291456Z AUG 75
FM AMEMBASSY MOSCOW
TO SECSTATE WASHDC 3941
INFO AMEMBASSY BELGRADE
AMEMBASSY BERLIN
USMISSION USBERLIN
AMEMBASSY BUCHAREST
AMEMBASSY BUDAPEST
AMCONSUL LENINGRAD
AMCONSUL MUNICH
AMEMBASSY PRAGUE
AMEMBASSY SOFIA
AMEMBASSY WARSAW

 MOSCOW 12385

E.O. 11652 GDS
TAGS: PINT, UR
SUBJECT: UNOFFICIAL ARTISTS ANNIVERSARY EXHIBITION BANNED

1.   UNOFFICIAL ARTISTS ARE NOW ON A COLLISION COURSE WITH SOVIET
AUTHORITIES OVER AN ART EXHIBITION TO BE HELD ON THE FIRST
ANNIVERSARY OF THE NOTORIUS "ART MASSACRE" OF SEPTEMBER 15,
1974.   MEMBERS OF THE "INITIATIVE GROUP" HAVE HELD DISCUSSIONS IN
A A POSITIVE SPIRIT OVER THE LAST TWO MONTHS WITH THE MOSCOW CITY
CULTURAL ADMINISTRATION BUT WERE RECENTLY SENT TO THE MINISTRY
OF CULTURE USSR ONCE IT WAS ESTABLISHED THAT THE PUTATIVE EXHIBITORS
WOULD INCLUDE ARTISTS FROMOUTSIDE MOSCOW. MINCULT OFFICIALS IN
CHARGE OF EXHIBITION HALLS, FNU FEDEYEVA, TEMPORIZED ON THE GROUNDS
THAT QUARTERS WERE IN SHORT SUPPLY. ARTISTS SPOKESMEN SET FRIDAY,
AUGUST 22, AS DEADLINE FOR THE MINCULT RESPONESE, BUT MINCULT
PROMISED AN ANSWER BY AUGUST 25.

2.   MINCULT DECISION WAS FLAT REFUSAL TO FURNISH EXHIBITION

Two-page cabled report from US Embassy in Moscow to Secretary of State in Washington and select American embassies, August 29, 1975. Archives of the US State Department

Date Printed:
18 Jan 2002   DOC_NBR: 1975MOSCOW12385

CHANNEL: n/a
HANDLING: n/a

1

PAGE 02   MOSCOW 12385   292026Z

QUARTERS OR TO GRANT PERMISSION FOR AN EXHIBITION. DURING
EARLIER DISCUSSIONS, MINCULT OFFICIALS HAD BEEN EAGER TO AVOID
AN OPEN-AIR EXHIBITION, BEARING IN MIND MASSIVE NEGATIVE
PUBLICITY IN WORLD PRESS AFTER FRACAS AT BELYAYEVO SITE LAST
SEPTEMBER.

3.   UNOFFICIAL ARTISTS WERE DETERMINED TO MARK THE ANNIVERSARY
BY AN EXHIBIT BEFORE THE REFUSAL. THEY MUST NOW DECIDE WHETHER
TO STAGE UNAUTORIZED ART SHOW AND FACE UNPLEAANT CONSEQUENCES OR
TO PULL BACK. EITHER COURSE IS DIFFICULT FOR THEM, BUT THEY
CONSIDER THAT FOREIGN PUBLICITY IS THEIR ONY HOPE AT THIS TIME.

4.   EMBASSY WILL KEEP DEPARTMENT INFORMED ON THIS MATTER TO BEST
OF ITS ABILITY IN VIEW OF POSSIBLE CONFLICT WHICH COULD AGAIN
GENERATE MUCH PUBLICITY UNFAVORABLE TO THE SOVIETS, ESPECIALLY IN
THE CONTEXT OF THE HELSINKI FINAL ACT. EMBASSY OPINION IS THAT
SOVIET REGIME IS FULLY AWARE OF THE POSSIBILITIES AND WILL MOVE
TO FORESTALL AN OPEN-AIR EXHIBITION.
WESTERN PRESS IS FULLY INFORMED ON DEVELPMENTS AND IS PRIMED
BOTH FOR PLANNED EXHIBITION OR FAILURE.

5.   EMBOFF WAS TOLD AUGUST 23 BY UNOFFICIAL ARTISTS THAT LEADING
UNOFFICIAL PAINTER OSKAR RABIN HAD BEEN ARBITRARILY DEPRIVED OF
HIS RURAL DACHA NEAR YAROSLAVL' BY LOCAL OFFICIALS WHO INSTRUCTED
HIM TO REMOVE HIS DACHA FROM KOLKHOZ LAND OR DACHA WOULD BE
DEMOLISHED. ARTISTS ALSO REPORTED HOSTILITY TOWARD THEMSELVES
BY ORDINARY KOLKHOZNIKS WHO ALLEGEDLY BELIEVED THAT ARTISTS
WERE SPIES FOR AMERICANS AND FOR THAT REASON WERE SUBJECT TO
SUSPICION AND HARASSMENT.
STOESSEL

NNN

Interviews with Russian artists in the mid-1990s documenting their responses to the 1974 Bulldozer and Izmailovsky Park exhibitions

Lydia Masterkova

I showed works in both places [Bulldozer and Izmailovsky shows in 1974]. Both were incredible events. I will tell you that had Nemukhin not gone to the first show, it would not have taken place because Rabin would not have dared to go alone. The initial group was [Oscar] Rabin, [Vladimir] Nemukhin, me, Evgenii Rukhin, and Nadia Elskaia. The idea for the show was an old one and dates back to when we lived in the country. It was Rabin's idea, originally, to have a show somewhere, anywhere, since we couldn't exhibit our work at all. That is how the idea of an open-air exhibition took root. When we decided to show, I was the first to get up the slight hill where the exhibition took place. I was covered by a tripod. Suddenly I saw a lot of people there who turned out to be artists, and they remained in the area overnight, sleeping in the bushes. We dispersed in two groups, in case the police decided to come after us. In the morning we all went to the field. I felt no fear at all at that point. Then, suddenly, I saw the authorities taking down the paintings. I continued to walk toward them without stumbling. I didn't understand how this could happen. God must have been watching over me because I spoke up and did what I wanted to do and nobody bothered me. About the show at Izmailovsky Park, more than fifteen thousand people came. The police were afraid to touch us at that point. The Russian people have an enormous interest in art and asked us many questions. We had to explain just what we were doing since they hadn't seen anything like that before. People in the West live without art, but Russians are receptive even to new art. They enjoyed the show so much and were so curious.

Ernst Neizvestny

I will tell you why [I did not take part in the Bulldozer exhibition]. It is my belief, and not only mine, that when I had the confrontation with Khrushchev at the Manezh exhibition in 1962, it was the result of a provocation. We were used for some other purpose—not just to argue art with Khrushchev. The provocation did not succeed, thanks to the fact that I found the strength to tell Khrushchev the truth. The Bulldozer exhibition was also a political provocation. I saw it this way. There were tensions between the militia and the KGB. The KGB wanted to organize an exhibition to show the militia as well as the Moscow bureaucrats to be barbarians. So they invited artists to show their works, knowing that these would be cut to shreds by bulldozers. It was a setup, the whole thing. I was invited but did not want to participate. But I will say that the artists were heroes and so were the organizers, Oscar Rabin and Aleksandr Glezer. Others who were very young were less involved.

Vitaly Komar and Alexander Melamid

I'll tell you what happened. Oscar Rabin was a very brave and daring person. He was the only one capable of organizing the artists. For instance, when Rabin asked [Ilya] Kabakov to participate in the exhibition [Bulldozer show], Kabakov said, "All my life I have crawled on all fours. I stand up on four feet. And you are trying to stand like a normal person on two legs." And he said that we should stand on our hands as if upside-down with our legs in the air. He said that he had become used to being on all fours, like a dog. Rabin truly was brave and, unlike Kabakov, was not scared. They were two old men, but Rabin was the only person we, of a different generation, could unite with and gather around. He played the part of an organizer and a speaker. He spoke to the authorities in the name of the artists. After the exhibition he appeared, when everybody was afraid and shook with fear and did not know what would happen. We were afraid of being arrested. He *was* arrested and held for two days. When he was let out he figured that there was some trouble inside the government. The BBC radio station—we all listened to its Russian program every evening—announced that a debate had taken place in the Kremlin between Andropov, who was head of the KGB, and Shelkovsky, from the police. It was about who chased the artists away. Andropov claimed that the police action was an error after he became worried about the amount of publicity the show had received in the West. Andropov called Shelkovsky's conduct despicable and said that it would cause a loss in international prestige.

Excerpts from interviews originally published in Renée and Matthew Baigell, eds., *Soviet Dissident Artists: Interviews after Perestroika* (New Brunswick, NJ: Rutgers University Press, 1995). Reprinted with permission.

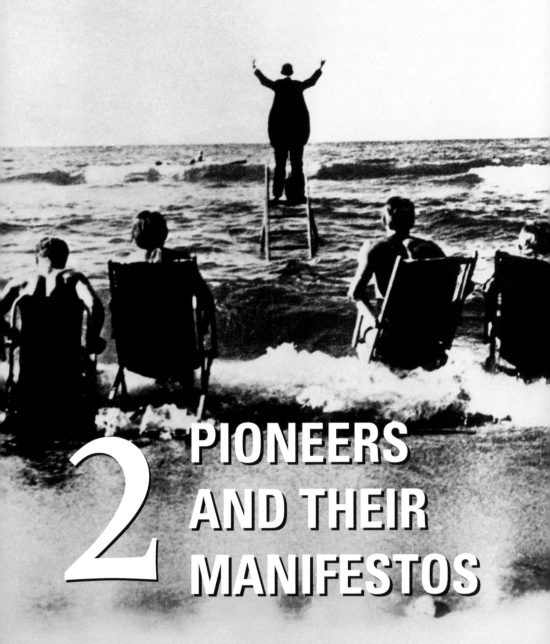

2 PIONEERS AND THEIR MANIFESTOS

Artists themselves are responsible for much of the best writing on the visual arts that has come from Central and Eastern Europe. Their proclamations are frequently more open and uncompromising than those of critics or theoreticians, who consciously or unconsciously self-censor their writing in order to be published in official journals.

Many artists from the 1950s to the present have adopted the manifesto—a classic avant-garde literary form that flourished in particular in Europe during the first half of the twentieth century. The difference between avant-garde manifestos and later manifestos is the way in which recent ones use humor and irony to create texts that are as much independent artistic creations as they are literature. In environments lacking unexpurgated art criticism, manifestos were often the preferred way to theorize contemporary art practice. These manifestos were not only programmatic proclamations; they also acted as the realization of these programs. The numerous short manifestos by the Croatian artist working under the moniker Mangelos are exemplary. Neither lectures nor poetry in the traditional sense, they are works of art in their own right, albeit ones that describe the impossibility of creating art in the modern world.

The MANIFEST "HAPPSOC," written by Slovakian artists Alex Mlynárčik and Stano Filko and theoretician Zita Kostrová, employs text and photography to appropriate the entire city of Bratislava and everything happening within it as a work of art, echoing the Italian artist Piero Manzoni's creation of a sculptural base for the entire world, and the French artist Ben's signing of the sky. In an absurdist gesture that matched Manzoni and Ben in its grandiosity, the Happsoc authors even contacted the city's Institute of Statistics to get the correct number of individually listed components that make up the city, including the number of apartments, balconies, dogs, and tulips.

"An Introduction to a General Theory of Place" was created in close connection with the activities of the Foksal Gallery in Warsaw, one of the few independent galleries in Eastern Europe with a program that, to this day, includes contemporary Western art along with the work of Polish artists. The text is particularly significant in the way in which it deals with theories of Minimalism and the origins of institutional critique, both of which are commonly thought of as exclusively Western topics of discourse.

The "OHO Manifesto" proposes the notion of taking art even farther from its traditional forms and offers us at the same time a joyful mental exercise, a Happening for readers' minds. Similarly, the Hungarian artist Miklós Erdély weaves together, in his writings, the aleatory aesthetics of John Cage with performance theory. Erdély is skeptical of the possibility of understanding art and the world around us, yet he attempts to establish some basic methods to do so. "The Milano Lessons" by the Polish artist and avant-garde theater director Tadeusz Kantor is a symbolic "last manifesto" in which the artist reinterprets the art and culture of the entire twentieth century. Though originally delivered to a master class in stage direction, all of the "Lessons" were written with art in all mediums in mind, from performance art to painting, and were meant to join all artistic disciplines under its common theoretical banner. —*Tomáš Pospiszyl*

DIMITRIJE BAŠIČEVIĆ MANGELOS

Dimitrije Bašičević (1921–1987) was an art historian, critic, and curator at museums in Zagreb, Croatia. Concurrently and less publicly, he was an artist who worked under the invented pseudonym Mangelos, the name of a village near his birthplace of Šid. He was a member of the Gorgona group, an anti-art collective active in Zagreb between 1959 and 1966 (see p. 124). During that period, Mangelos worked primarily on literary-visual creations, writing texts, "no-stories," and manifestos, some of which he painted on wooden boards and on globes in a style reminiscent of writing exercises of children.

Mangelos questioned every field he studied, from philosophy and art to psychoanalysis and biology, and from these polemics sprang his numerous manifestos. These manifestos wittily affirmed his theses on the development of society and the lack of development of art, explaining this discrepancy as a gap between two cultures, one "machine" the other "manual." According to Mangelos, the advent of the machine caused the dying out of disciplines based on "naive metaphorical thinking," most significantly of philosophy and art, and of notions such as genius, truth, intuition, and the subconscious.

—Branka Stipančić

Manifestos

manifesto of manifesto

dear friends
dear fiends

this is not a manifest claim that the experiments
carried out over the years were entirely successful
because they were not
but that another route has been discovered.
instead of following the line of meaning
the thinking process proceeds
along the line of function
corresponding to other processes of life.
this is the framework for my manifestos.

the world is not only changing
it has changed.
we are in the second century
of the second civilization. the machine one.
the social use of the machine
has put an end to the civilization of manual work
and to all the social phenomena
rooted in manual work.

by changing the character of work
the world changes its way of thinking.
the revolution of thinking has the character
of a long-term evolution.

in the course of this process
the previous artistic or naive thought
has integrated itself in the process of application
with another one based on
the principles of mechanical work.

civilization is practically evolving
into a cultural organization of the interplanetary kind
with uniform mechanical production.
and consequently
with uniform types of social superstructure
based on the principle of social functionality.
instead of emotionally structured units
a type of social unit is formed
which thinks functionally.

"altamira" — manifesto

a comparison of picasso's "guernica"
supposedly one of the summits
of human thought
with the product of his ancestor from altamira
the lack of whose signature allows us
hypothetically to call him a country bumpkin
results in the following conclusions.
products of both artists were obtained
by manual technology using identical "psychical" instruments.
so that it shall not be clear in the 30th century
which of these products originated in the twentieth
and which in the minus thousandth century.
picasso and his rustic predecessor
belong to the same evolutional segment
of the same civilization.
from the above it is impossible to decide
that the emotional life of the bumpkin was richer
than that of picasso.
or the other way round.
there is no difference.

manifesto
on memory

memory is older than thinking.
chronologically it is older than man.
It is a replicative characteristic
of reproductive energy.

manifesto
on photography no. 9

photography is not a phenomenon of art
nor a phenomenon of the civilization of manual labor
a photograph does not function as a painting
nor does the lens function as the eye of the artist.
painting and photography
are two different phenomena
of two different civilizations.
and of two different ways of thinking.
the naive and the functional.

manifesto
on aesthetic

aesthetic feelings were never relevant,
let alone decisive, in the production of art.
relevant were primary feelings.
an aesthetic approach to a work of art
is therefore only one of many possible
wrong approaches.

manifesto
on evolution no. 9

it is a known fact that in the course of evolution
emotions die out in inverse proportion
to the development of the brain.
it is less known that it is in this process
that we must look to the reasons
for the extinction of art.
if it is known that berlioz was looking
for inspiration in weber
offenbach in beethoven,
ravel in mussorgsky
rachmaninoff in paganini, etc.
a conclusion must follow
that sources for inspiration
in art are drying up.

manifesto
on gap no. 2

starting with the 19th century
music and painting
have gradually been losing emotion. as raw material.
they make up for this loss with ideas
which cannot function
as either ideas or emotions.

manifesto
on gap no. 3

looking from the 19th century marx still saw
art within society.
in the 20th century a gap could still be seen
between them.
from the 21st century society is seen
but not art.

šid[1] manifesto

we often speak of "two" marxes
"three" van goghs "several" picassos etc.
thus stressing the differences
between early and late periods of artists.
early and late periods differ considerably,
to the point of being diametrically opposed
as if they were made by different individuals.
the explanation is simple.
there are different persons in a single individual.

the material framework
for different persons
is the transformation of the cells in the organism.
cells renew themselves every seven years.

assuming the physiological data
i was taught at school in šid are accurate
there should be 9 and a half mangelos.

mangelos no. 1 1921–1928
mangelos no. 2 1928–1935
mangelos no. 3 1935–1942
mangelos no. 4 1942–1949
mangelos no. 5 1949–1956
mangelos no. 6 1956–1963
mangelos no. 7 1963–1970
mangelos no. 8 1970–1977
mangelos no. 9 1977–1984
mangelos no. 9½ . . . 1984–1987

(assuming my calculations are correct)
1921, šid–1987, les champs du dernier goulag[2]

Notes:
1. Šid is where Mangelos was born in 1921. He formulated his theory on cell transformation in 1933, at the age of twelve.
2. Mangelos predicted that he would die in 1987 (in fact, he was right). As the place of his death, he listed les champs du dernier goulag, a complex wordplay on Les Champs-Elysées (Elysian fields), which stand for heaven. Mangelos, on the contrary, predicted he would die in hell, in the fields of the last gulag (Soviet death camp).

Dimitrije Bašičevič Mangelos. *Post-Gorgonian Moscow Manifest*. 1976–77. Acrylic on board, 25⅝ × 19¹¹⁄₁₆" (65 x 50 cm). The Museum of Contemporary Art, Zagreb

post-gorgonian moscow manifest

kogorgonstvujuščem poslanija
from mangelos

meine libe muzikanten gorgonauts
we are preparing for our posthumous exhibition but ART IS DEAD and so is the old naive way of thinking. there are no profound thoughts only functional ones. the sense is also DEAD and the meaning is losing its function. only that stays alive which functions biologically or socially. art lost its social function with the advent of the machine. remaining on the level of manual production art according to marx and contra marx still functions only as a prop of history. in museums. this and similar functions of art are pseudo-social. these are also the real causes of the historical gap between the society and its quasi-art. the dimensions of this gap have been definitely determined. the world has changed while art is stuck at the beginning of the nineteenth century. despite

its efforts in two directions. to impose itself on society as an avant-garde and to adapt to the machine civilization. the time of gorgonauting is over. and the epoch of the naive way of thinking too. the revolution of consciousness is taking place. a functional one. moscow 26 november 76–zagreb 9 march 1977

Written in 1978 (except *Post-Gorgonian Moscow Manifest*. 1976–77. Acrylic on board). Originally published in *Mangelos, Manifesti* (Zagreb: Atelje Tošo Dabac, 1978). Selection of manifestos by Branka Stipančić; translated by Micheline Popović.

••

STANO FILKO, ZITA KOSTROVÁ, AND ALEX MLYNÁRČIK

The members of HAPPSOC—the name is a combination of the words "Happening" and "Society"—were the Slovak artists Alex Mlynárčik and Stano Filko, and the theoretician Zita Kostrová. During the 1960s, Mlynárčik developed a relationship with the French critic Pierre Restany, who founded the Nouveau Réalisme *(New Realism) movement. Influenced by the lyricism and humanity that Restany claimed was innate in the products of industrial urban centers, Mlynárčik, with his fellow HAPPSOC members, announced a series of "realities" to take place in Bratislava each day during the week of May 2, 1965. (Parenthetically, the week was enclosed by two monumental holidays—May 1 [May Day] and May 9 [Liberation Day]). These "realities" declared the entire city to be a work of art, thus characterizing it as a Duchampian readymade. Along with the eponymous manifesto, also known as "Theory of Anonymity," the HAPPSOC artists drew up an itemized list of the innumerable components that made up the city, which served as an invitation to the "realities."*

Documentary photo of May Day celebrations, Bratislava, May 1, 1965. Courtesy Alex Mlynárčik

• 85

STANO FILKO • ALEX MLYNÁRČIK

DOVOĽUJÚ SI VÁS POZVAŤ K ÚČASTI NA

prennent la liberté de inviter à participer à

HAPPSOC I.

BRATISLAVA, 2.—8. V. 1965

REALIZÁCIA:

1. prvá skutočnosť BRATISLAVA 2. mája 1965
2. druhá skutočnosť BRATISLAVA 3. mája 1965
3. tretia skutočnosť BRATISLAVA 4. mája 1965
4. štvrtá skutočnosť BRATISLAVA 5. mája 1965
5. piata skutočnosť BRATISLAVA 6. mája 1965
6. šiesta skutočnosť BRATISLAVA 7. mája 1965
7. siedma skutočnosť BRATISLAVA 8. mája 1965

RÉALISATION:

1. première réalité à Bratislava, le 2 mai 1935
2. deuxième réalité à Bratislava, le 3 mai 1965
3. troisème réalité à Bratislava, le 4 mai 1965
4. quatrième réalité à Bratislava, le 5 mai 1965
5. cinquième réalité à Bratislava, le 6 mai 1965
6. sixième réalité à Bratislava, le 7 mai 1965
7. septième réalité à Bratislava, le 8 mai 1935

TRVANIE: 1.—9. V. 1965
Durée:

Stano Filko and Alex Mlynárčik. Invitation to HAPPSOC I. 1965. Courtesy Alex Mlynárčik

Stano Filko and Alex Mlynárčik
take the liberty of inviting you
to participate in HAPPSOC 1.
Bratislava, 2.–8. May 1965

REALIZATION:
1. First Reality, BRATISLAVA, May 2, 1965
2. Second Reality, BRATISLAVA, May 3, 1965
3. Third Reality, BRATISLAVA, May 4, 1965
4. Fourth Reality, BRATISLAVA, May 5, 1965
5. Fifth Reality, BRATISLAVA, May 6, 1965
6. Sixth Reality, BRATISLAVA, May 7, 1965
7. Seventh Reality, BRATISLAVA, May 8, 1965

DURATION: May 1–9, 1965

OBJECTS:

1.	Women	137,936
2.	Men	128,727
3.	Dogs	48,991
4.	Houses (including temporary housing)	18,000
5.	Balconies	103,236
6.	Agricultural farms	22
7.	Industrial buildings	525
8.	Apartments	64,729
9.	Water supplies in the apartments	40,870
10.	Water supplies outside the apartments	544
11.	Electric stoves	3,505
12.	Gas stoves	37,804
13.	Washing machines	35,001
14.	Refrigerators	17,934
15.	The whole city of Bratislava	1
16.	The Castle	1
17.	Danube (in Bratislava)	1
18.	Street lights	142,090
19.	TV antennas	128,726
20.	Cemeteries	6
21.	Tulips	1,000,001
22.	Theaters (including nonprofessional)	9
23.	Movie theaters, chimneys, trams, cars, tram cars, typewriters, radios,shops, libraries, hospitals, etc.	

MANIFEST "HAPPSOC"

What is HAPPSOC?

It is an action stimulating the receptiveness and multifaceted enjoyment of reality, released from the stream of everyday existence.

Reality, thus encountered and limited in time and space, acts by means of the potency of its relations and tensions.

Bringing this reality into the open as a new concept ushers in the recognition of the immensity and breadth of mutually dependent relationships.

It stands for gentle and all-inclusive commitment.

It is a process that uses objectivity to stimulate a subjective way of looking at things and elevating their perception to a higher level.

It is, therefore, a generally valid way of dealing with life on the basis of an "as found" reality, thus making it possible to bring into full play its scope in its entirety.

It allows for the possibility of investing a chosen reality with the superreal, that is, a new reality enriched by its own charge.

It is a synthetic manifestation of social existence as such and therefore, by necessity, a shared property of all.

It links up with a whole range of happenings and processes of change and shocks by its very existence.

In contrast to happenings, it manifests itself as a singular, unvarnished reality, which remains unaffected by any immediate encroachment upon its primordial form.

For those who share this concept [of reality], the immediate environment does not merely reveal itself as a thing, but, in addition, includes as well all the relationships and chains of events that grow out of such cognition.

Its realization is not accidental, but intentional and stimulating.

It was realized for the first time between May 1 and 9, 1965, in Bratislava and thus became a manifesto of its own consummation.

Written in 1965 and distributed as an invitation. Later published in *Stano Filko—1965/69* (Bratislava: A-Press, 1970). Translated by Eric Dluhosch.

WIESŁAW BOROWSKI, HANNA PTASZKOWSKA, AND MARIUSZ TCHOREK

The following text was written as a mission statement for the seminal Foksal Gallery in Warsaw, which was established as a noncommercial space in 1966 by art critics Wiesław Borowski, Hanna Ptaszkowska, and Mariusz Tchorek in conjunction with several artists. The premise of the gallery was not a preconceived exhibition program, but close collaboration and discussions with artists who were given creative control over their exhibitions, and the desire to question basic assumptions about art and its presentation. The result was the only Polish gallery of its time that presented radical contemporary works, performances, and Happenings by Polish and international artists, among them Tadeusz Kantor, Henryk Stażewski, Robert Barry, Daniel Buren, Krzysztof Wodiczko, Mirosław Bałka, and countless others.

This declaration of purpose signaled the changes taking place in the Polish art world and was directed against the structural unity and the traditionally understood autonomy of an artwork. While one of the goals of the gallery was to undermine the time-honored methods of exhibiting art, in another document entitled "What We Do Not Like About the Foksal PSP Gallery," the founders essentially conceded the limited possibilities of change, since Foksal, with its clean white walls, was, and is, basically a traditional gallery space.

An Introduction to a General Theory of Place

Many times in its history, art declared itself liberated. By doing this, however, it did not convey what it actually was but what it wanted to become. In reality it has always been self-liberating. As it has often been stated under similar circumstances, art liberates itself of its own inherited features. It casts them off and leaves them behind.

Let us ignore all the self-loathing that art experienced in the past when it reflected on itself. We must now reveal that which art is liberating itself from. First of all, though, we should admit that it is a purely internal affair, for what is at stake is the hatred of art toward itself, and only insiders have the right to feel it. At least one aspect of the object of hatred is to be found right under our noses. It is so close that in order to notice it we must introduce a far-reaching change — that of viewpoint. Let's not look at artworks themselves; instead, let's stop before the space which they occupy. Let's not enter the exhibition, but remain at its threshold. This is what we are going to find:

I. The nature of the exhibition is its transparency. It has been conceived as non-existent. It must not interact with a work of art. Actually, the following is true: The exhibition acquires its own identity, it becomes autonomous. It is the exhibition and not an artwork that becomes a fact. A particular work of art conforms to the already autonomous reality of the exhibition. From then on, it functions as its element. A work of art conceived as unique becomes one of many. Has any work of art been intended to coexist with others? With a multitude of other works?

II. The exhibition is a post-factum operation. The fact of artistic realization has been fulfilled within the four walls of the studio. When exhibited, the finished, ultimately completed work acquires a totally new kind of existence. It communicates what has already happened. What it makes available are only the traces of decisive actions. The exhibition is only a message about something that has occurred somewhere else at some other time. Its reality has nothing to do with the reality of the creative act.

III. SPECTATOR. The spectator comes to the exhibition just to complete the final formalities related to its reception. His or her presence has only a purely ceremonial meaning. Actually, he or she has been given too much freedom, which in most cases cannot even be used. This freedom does not foster any activity which could be stimulated by the simplest ban. As a result, all who come to the exhibition choose one kind of behavior: the convention of contemplation. For the spectator, the contemplative attitude is a guarantee of detachment from a work of art; thus, he or she is given some space at the exhibition to compare, judge, purchase, etc.

IV. ARTIST. At the exhibition, the artist has nothing to do but hold a bunch of flowers. Now, as a spectator, he or she is either bored or galvanized by secondary impressions; he or she can also be an ambassador of future actions, a servant who, having completed a task, for some reason has not been dismissed.

The artist's personality, which is supposed to manifest itself in its truest form, reveals itself at the exhibition in piecemeal, artificial doses, dispensed according to a rhythm that does not reflect his or her real development. The artist hangs at the exhibition as a quartered ox while we make vain efforts to re-create from the carcass the actual animal. Moreover, the artist, who has been persuaded by the connoisseurs that the fundamental virtue is sincerity, is deeply embarrassed by the results of his or her sincerity under the festive circumstances of a public show. Why shouldn't this embarrassment — the most authentic feature of the exhibition — be turned into its object?

PLACE. Well, then, the PLACE. The PLACE for sure.

The PLACE is an area which comes into being as a result of suspending all the laws that are in force in the world.

The PLACE is not a spatial category; it is not an arena, circus, screen, pedestal, and, above all, it is not an exhibition.

The PLACE is isolated, but at the same time exteriorized. Its existence is not just subjective and cannot be brought about by means of purely private efforts. The PLACE as an artistic fact must be conspicuous and significantly objective. It exists only insofar as it can protect itself from the world's pressure; inasmuch as it fails to become identical with the world.

The PLACE is a sudden gap in the utilitarian approach to the world. At the PLACE all the external standards by which it is measured cease to hold true. Its space is stripped of its utilitarian character and leaves behind all criteria, arguments, Euclidean and non-Euclidean interpretations. All the events that happen to occur in it are deprived of any meaning that comes from the outside. Within the PLACE there is no vacillation since there is no difference between right and wrong, between valuable and valueless — everything just *is* there. The PLACE is neither strange nor common; neither refined nor vulgar; neither wise nor stupid. It is neither a dream nor the state of being awake.

The PLACE is not transparent. The PLACE is presence. There are no criteria for judging the better or more valuable filling of the PLACE. It can be empty but its emptiness must be conspicuous.

The PLACE is one and only. The PLACE cannot be divided. The PLACE does not multiply. The PLACE is where we are. It can be conceived as one of many, compared with other places only when we are out of it. Only outside its limits the PLACE

We See You (Galeria Foksal window with Tadeusz Kantor, Anka Ptaszkowska, Zbigniew Gostomski, Henryk Stażewski, Maria Stangret, Edward Krasiński, and Wiesław Borowski). 1968/69. Courtesy Galeria Foksal Archives

can become an object of hatred.

The PLACE possesses any area in the world. From the point of view of the world, it is not any special area. The PLACE cannot be recognized by its external features. Since the PLACE remains in no relation to the laws of the world, it is not their modification either. In fact, the PLACE can look just like any other segment of reality. Still, there are areas in the world that are considered to be more predestined to become the PLACE than others.

The PLACE is neither a construction nor a destruction. The PLACE comes into being as a result of an unchastened decision. In the world there is no rationale for the PLACE. This rationale is in the artist. He or she brings the PLACE into being. Whoever enters it, creates it. Only at the PLACE, not outside it, "everyone creates art."

The PLACE cannot be mechanically fixed, it must be continually perpetuated. A brief moment of inattention is enough for it to be absorbed by its surroundings. There are many anonymous forces whose profession it is to destroy the PLACE or produce substitutes. These forces take advantage of the authority of the dead sphere bearing the trace of the PLACE, and manipulate the material elements which they take from it — the elements which regain their actual measures and proportions.

The PLACE cannot be purchased or collected. The PLACE cannot be put under arrest. One cannot be an expert on the PLACE.

Protection of the PLACE is not just one more initiative with an established authorship, nor is it a product of the present. It has always been there in art history, but it reveals itself only at moments of breakthrough.

Such a moment was a transformation of the painting into the PLACE. In the temple, the painting was not, or had no right to be, the PLACE. Its presence was justified only insofar as it served the temple, insofar as it contributed to the effort of incessant perpetuation and maintenance of that unique area which, after the expulsion of the peddlers, itself met all the conditions of being the PLACE. However, the painting had become independent and for a moment remained alone. The frame persisted as witness of the event. The frame — a naive embodiment of the barrier protecting the painting from the pressure of the world. Thus began the tendency of the painting to generate its own inner bondage — sufficient to protect it as a PLACE without any additional shields. That was how the composition came into being. But the composition — at last a perfect realization of enclosure — remained on its own side, while we are left on the side of the world. At best, the composition can be understood in terms of PLACE, yet we will always remain outside it. Since it is finite and closed; since it is indestructible but also defenseless; since nothing more can ever happen to it, the composition has been subjected to manipulation from the outside. It has been hung in the architectural interior, an inspiration for the use of space. It has been variously adopted and adjusted. It has been defined as an indispensable element of the human environment and absorbed by the world. In its relatively purest, initial form it has been exhibited. Thus, however, it lost its uniqueness and began to be grouped with others.

Therefore, at an exhibition we pass from PLACE to PLACE, indulging in "illegitimate" procedures: we judge, compare, enter, exit, carry out, purchase, etc. In vain, we try to be somewhere, while we are nowhere.

Here, in reference to each other, PLACES came to represent a different, i.e., the outside, world with all its characteristic force of aggression. PLACES destroy themselves. On this grows that entirely new being, the exhibition. The exhibition, which was supposed to be transparent — a natural reservation for PLACES — becomes an unlawful, autonomous product. A quasi-PLACE. A fraud-PLACE. A heresy-PLACE. A treason-PLACE.

The PLACE is a sudden gap in the utilitarian approach to the world. The PLACE results from the suspension of all the laws binding in the world. The PLACE is one and indivisible. The PLACE.

Written in 1966. Originally published in *Program Gallerii Foksal PSP* (Warsaw: Gallery Foksal, 1966). Translated by Marek Wilczynski.

MARKO POGAČNIK AND I. G. PLAMEN

OHO was the most important Slovenian neo-avant-garde group of the 1960s and 1970s. The name is a combination of oko *(eye) and* uho *(ear) and is also an expression of aston-ishment. Its activity can be divided into roughly three periods. In the first period (1966–68), OHO functioned as a multi- and inter-media movement with a broad range of members and collaborators. Its central idea was the so-called Reism—an attempt to reach a non-anthropocentric world of "things," which could be perceived not according to their function and meaning for people but for themselves alone. To avoid ascribing a human meaning and content to things, OHO adherents used impersonal techniques (printing, casting, etc.), mathematical programs, games, and paradox as the basis for their works. In the second period (1969–70), OHO was organized as an art group whose activities included contem-porary and avant-garde art, from Arte Povera and Process art, to Land art, Performance art, Body art, and Conceptual art. In its third and final period (1970–71), OHO was trans-formed into a community and developed a specific type of Conceptual art that aimed at establishing spiritual connections between the members of the group and between the group and the world. In 1971 OHO—on the threshold of international success—decided to aban-don art as a separate field and tried to find a synthesis of art and life by establishing a community in the village of Šempas. The leading members of OHO in its different periods were Srečo Dragan, Naško Križnar, David Nez, I. G. Plamen [Iztok Geister], Marko Pogačnik, Andraž Šalamun, Tomaž Šalamun, and Milenko Matanović. This so-called OHO Mani-festo was written on the occasion of the publication of Plamen's and Pogačnik's book* OHO *(1966), which gave the name to the whole movement.*

OHO Manifesto

What is this on newspaper in printer's ink in a trace that falls and rises in a curve, then falls past three dots and runs a part of the length in a straight line and falls steeply and turns back sharply, curving, falls sharply and levels out lengthwise and curves up to the corner, whence it falls and rises in a curve, then falls past three dots.

This is not a body, rounded along the volume of a foot, with a hole in the form of a split mouth, sutured with three arches of thread, punctured with three holes twice, which are encircled by six-sided, inwardly curved metal rings, while the tongue lolls out of the mouth, tipped with twelve little arches, opposite the belt that hugs the back, bordered by two columns of stitches, turns inward at the edge under the layer of leather that lines the interior, and is then sewn into the material which stretches to the end of the interior and touches the very bot-tom, etched on the sole with the gold letters E, X, P, O, R, and T, and with rub-ber on the outer side with striated parallel ribs which line up from the rough plain on both sides of the center, which is full of hooked teeth appearing from the right and disappearing to the right, emerges the inscription EURASIA, a sharp ridge rises to an arched wall which raises the heel with hooked teeth ap-pearing from the left and disappearing to the right, with a row of parallel teeth on the sides between the striated threshold and the rough plain cut into the sole, which lies tightly against the thick leather line, which lies tightly against the leather belt, which wraps it, sewn with cord with a hundred stitches tightly hugging the body, rounded along the volume of a foot, with a hole in the form of a split mouth, sutured with three arches of thread, punctured with three holes twice, which are encircled by six-sided, inwardly curved metal rings.

OHO

When does prostor ("space") break down into prosti zor ("free vision"). When I write this, therefore immediately or simultaneously. When I sprostim ("release," "relax") prostor ("space") into "prosti zor" ("free vision"), therefore immediately or simultaneously. In the predstava ("representation," 'before-position') ob-staja ("exists," 'near-position') prostor ("space") which is empty, which is prost ("free") in the sense that (n)aught is there. If it is true that (n)aught is there, then what is. Therefore the definition or claiming of space is not possible because of the presence of nothing, that will be there (parts), if anything is already there since the time when (n)aught was.

And truly, prosti zor ("free vision") is liberty-filled vision, such a vision as is its own master. In the same way as a book is not thrown into (societal) space, as there is no space for the book there, rather the book itself is space, where again there is no space for anything else. Where there is space, there is no space.

Is this kind of engagement possible in space? It is not, as prostor ("space") itself is engaged in its prostost ("freeness"). And what is it doing in its prostost ("freeness")? Looking. To look at oneself means being at liberty. To look elsewhere, away from oneself, means being in od-nosu ("relationship," 'from-carry,' 'from-nose') or in dichotomy. Absolutely and relatively these two have nothing in common. As they each preclude the other. Prosti zor ("free vision") is absolute vision. The claimers of space are in odnosu ("relationship") with space. Thus they are not in themselves and not in the claimed space.

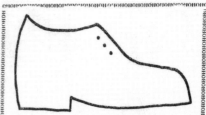

Marko Pogačnik and I. G. Plamen. OHO Manifesto, printed in *Tribuna* newspaper, November 23, 1966–67. Courtesy the artists

OHO

What is this, the absurd. We cannot know how misel ("thought") misli ("thinks"). We can, however, misliti ("think") brez misli ("without thought") of it. To think means to not understand thought. (To understand thought means to know.) Misliti ("to think") z misljio ("with thought") of something, that is to be z misljio ("with thought"), means to think smiselno ("sensefully," "wisely"). Misliti ("to think") of something brez misli ("without thought") of it, that is to be v misljenju ("in thought"), to think precisely, means to think nesmiselno ("senselessly," "unwisely").

We can misliti ("think") brez misli ("without thought") of it because we cannot predstaviti ("imagine") thought and because we cannot understand thought.

The criteria for whether something is pred-stavljivo ("imaginable," 'before-position') or not predstavlja ("is represented by," 'before-position') obstojnost ("quality of lasting," 'near-position-ness'). For human thought, reality ob-staja ("exists," 'near-position') in the manner of predstave ("representation"). Thought which is predstavljiva ("imaginable") is obstojna ("lasting," "existent," 'near-position'). What is the nature of thought that is not predstavljiva ("imaginable"). We shall say that such misel ("thought") is miselna ("of thought"). Is there anyone anywhere who thinks in the manner of misli ("thought") and not in the manner of predstave ("representation"). Children (infants) think in the manner of thought. Child's thought thinks in a fantastic manner. In its pure purpose, therefore, thought which is not predstavljiva ("imaginable") is fantastic.

The criteria for whether something is understandable or not predstavlja ("is represented") by the circumstances, that the stvar ("thing") misli ("thought") which is zamisljena ("in thought," "thought up") has forced upon it the logos of the razumen ("reasonable," "understanding") viewing of the thing (thought), this is videnja ("seeing") or vedenja ("knowing," "behaviour"). When the logos of the stvar ("thing") misli ("thought") is discovered in the stvar ("thing") misli ("thought"), this stvar ("thing") is found in its stvarnost ("reality") (mentality). Reason is found only in vedenju ("knowing," "behaviour"), and for this reason vedenje ("knowing," "behaviour") is the stvarnost ("reality") of reason. We can, therefore, think (not understand) thought in a fantastic manner (this is not in the manner of representation). Ununderstood and unimagined thought which occupies its reality in a fantastic manner is absurd thought.

Now it is clear that thought should be (when it is the issue at hand) fantastic reality or real fantasy. Is not thus thought absurd thought the only thought?

OHO

A MAN A PLAN A CANAL PANAMA: se-stavljene ("composed," 'self-position') words are in a sestavu ("composition") or a skupnosti ("cluster") of stavov ("positions") stalisc ("standpoints"). The stalisca ("standpoints") are the following: A, MAN, A, PLAN, A, CANAL and PANAMA. But, these stalisca ("standpoints") not only se-stavljajo ("compose," 'self-position') the sestav ("composition"), they also se rukajo ("shove themselves"). The right roka ("hand") ruka ("shoves") them, as this composition is left-handed. The standpoints of the right-handed composition are the following: ANAMAP, LANAC, A, NALP, A, NAM and A. A two-handed composition is also possible: AMANAPLANACANALPANAMA. But this kind of two-handedness in the composition of conceptual standpoints is rare. However, the conceptual standpoint is occasionally more lax than that of words, as in the case of the two-handed composition, shut out by one eye and looked at by the other. LEWDDIDILIVEEVILIDIDDWEL. We obviously made up this word, but the concept has remained the same as if we had written dwell. The conceptual standpoint izhaja iz (za za) misljene besede ("stems from [for] the words thought," "stems from behind the word thought up"). Thus we extracted the word from thought for this word. Or is it possible to think up a word at all?

Stvari ("things") are stvarne ("real"). We draw close to the stvarnost stvari ("reality of things") by accepting a thing as it is. And what is a thing as? A thing, we notice first, is silent. But the thing has something to offer!

With a word we entice the unheard voice from a thing. Only the word hears this voice. The word registers or marks this voice of the thing. This voice, marked with a word, speech utters. Here speech meets with music, which is the heard voice of a thing.

Now we would like to know whether we can entice with a word the unheard voice from thought. Is thought also ever silent, although it has something to offer? These are thoughts yet to be wakened, arising from the "subconscious." Words which these thoughts mark are not concepts as long as they are not thought. Only the thought-up word dewL is therefore a word which helps a thing do besede ("to reach expression," 'to the word').

OHO

A book has been published; its name is OHO. The bookstores are selling it at present. I. G. Plamen [Iztok Geister], Marko Pogačnik.

Written in 1966. Originally published in *Tribuna* (Ljubljana), no. 6 (November 23, 1966–67). Translated by Moderna Galerija Ljubljana.

•●

MIKLÓS ERDÉLY

Miklós Erdély (1928–1986) was trained in sculpture and architecture, but as an artist he was a renaissance man of sorts, working in mediums as diverse as painting, filmmaking, performance, criticism, and poetry. His oeuvre can be characterized as uniformly radical as he sought to explore new and unknown directions in art. He is considered one of the foremost pioneers who introduced Fluxus, Conceptual art, installation, and semiotics, among other things, to artists in Hungary. During the revolution in 1956, Erdély staged his first manifestation entitled "Money Left Unguarded in the Street" in which he collected money in a shop window for the families of "martyrs" who died in the revolution. The first official Happening in Hungary took place at Erdély's residence, and although these activities were officially proscribed, his home became a legendary venue for radical art. While Erdély's greatest affinity was perhaps for Conceptual art, his work as a filmmaker, which combined experimental visual language with taboo subject matter was particularly significant.

The statements included here reflect his understanding of history as inherently indeterminate, especially in the first text entitled "A History of Chance," which was released only posthumously. The second text, "Art as an Empty Sign," was his poetic preamble to the third, "Theses for the Marly Conference of 1980," which derived from semiological phraseology and was publicly delivered by him at the Marly Conference that year.

Miklós Erdély. *Time Travel*. 1975. Photograph (from a series of five), 18 ¹⁵⁄₁₆ × 19⅜" (48 x 49 cm).
István Király Múzeum

A History of Chance

Nothing existed by chance. There was no reason whatsoever for anything to exist. Nor was there any reason for anything not to exist. There was no reason whatsoever for a reason to exist, for anything to cause or to prevent the existence of anything else. Since nothing prevented the existence of something, something by chance came into existence. By chance, that something turned out to be something that was capable of changing into something else. More precisely, it just so happened that not all of nothing was the same; some kinds of nothing were incapable of change; these stayed that way and remained nothing, but by chance there was some kind of nothing in the infinitude of nothingness that, accidentally, was not so utterly nothing as to be incapable of accidentally becoming something. By chance, this nothing became something that was capable of further change. In all likelihood there must have been many somethings that were incapable of further change and remained what they had accidentally become. Among those somethings that were capable of changing, by chance there were some that were capable of interacting with each other as well as with those that were unable to change by themselves. By chance they were capable of exerting a certain effect on other types of something that possessed certain other accidental properties; thus certain forms of interaction became dominant, while other forms of interaction dwindled away or never manifested them-selves, not even by accident. We cannot account for the forms of interaction that have dwindled away or have never been manifested, since these do not exist. As for those forms of interaction that survived because of their accidental exclusiveness, they became manifested in the form of laws of nature, although since they came into existence by accident they could also change accidentally, or even disappear by accident. Something that was created by chance cannot protect itself against the effects of chance, unless it accidentally comes to pos-sess a quality that, by chance, enables it to protect itself against accidents. Such an eventuality could be regarded as a lucky coincidence by something or some-one that or who accidentally assigned greater value to the eventuality where something exists than to the eventuality where nothing exists at all. And just as a large enough number of accidents lead to the formation of a law of nature, so the prevalence of a large enough number of laws restores the rule of chance.

Written about 1980. Originally published in *A '84-es kijárat* (Budapest), 1989. Translated by John Bátki.

●●

Art as an Empty Sign

These past days [the time is 1980] we have been looking at the peculiar fate of art in a changing world. During the last hundred years, the arts have un-dergone turbulent transformations comparable only to those in the field of technology. These upheavals enable us to formulate, vis-à-vis art, certain ba-sic laws that possess ever higher levels of universality, while the specific na-ture of artistic activity becomes ever more sharply defined. In the so-called Marly Theses (see following text) I am about to set forth, I have attempted to draw certain radical conclusions made inevitable by the continuous and ac-celerating changes in the arts. However, before formulating general principles, I would like to attempt a brief analysis of the cultural background in Hungary, and to summarize the characteristics that combined to render the strange his-tory of the arts in this country over the past decades even stranger. All the more so since an analysis of Hungary's cultural borderline status may prove instructive in other ways as well. In a country where clinging to the old is en-dowed with the moral force of a proud loyalty and is consequently honor-bound to constantly resist change, it is not only possible but imperative to thoroughly examine phenomena whose assessment may elsewhere be neg-lected, for lack of resistance. It goes without saying that in societies isolated from intellectual change, problems of this sort never arise.

The majority of people in Hungary, caught unprepared by the social changes, expected the arts to take a stand in defense of tradition, to represent stability in a changing world. Since the vast majority of artists would not and could not refuse to meet these expectations, backwardness came to acquire an aura of heroism. To this day, resistance to change and reverence for tradi-tional genres and artistic ideals have been seen as evidence of strength of character. To complicate matters, the political forces responsible for social change had decided to support such resistance, probably on the rationale that any illusion of permanence and stability merited special nurturing in view of the changed social circumstances. As a result artists who have embraced new developments and helped to shape them found themselves relegated to highly disadvantaged existential and moral positions in our country. The press has given ample coverage to statements condemning these artists (us), articles and reviews describing us as superficial, spineless epigones aping the latest fads in the West, or as outright charlatans. Indeed, it would be quite instructive to compile a collection of such texts.

Calmly viewing these violent sallies, based as they are on mistaken notions or regrettable self-deception, one must note the undeniable authenticity of their moral outrage. Such manifestations are obviously rooted in deep conviction, and transcend underlying vested interests. Disloyalty to a praiseworthy cause is indeed repulsive, and true art has forever been a good cause.

Compared to established art—highly wrought and perfected—the new has always appeared to be frivolous and thoughtless. Over the past century, rejection of the new has proved wrong, time and time again, but has persisted nonetheless. At a time of accelerating change, the crisis has become more acute. In the past, artistic movements maintained their validity for at least a generation, at least in the case of the pioneers who had introduced new ideas and fought for their recognition. In recent decades, however, events have taken a different turn: one after another the leading artists of the 1960s stopped producing the kinds of art they were known for, primarily because they lost faith in the continuation of their previous artistic activities. This is the predominant lesson in the arts of the 1970s. That process marked the beginning of an all-out self-examination within the arts and, paralleling this, within artists themselves. To have arrived at this stage, however, is not tantamount to having reached an impasse, as many would have us believe. The road from here does not necessarily lead backward. For artists today there are no lasting established disciplines, and for this reason they must question themselves each day to clarify what exactly they are doing. Such questioning must of necessity stir up the artist's entire being.

For a soldier, this particular sort of self-questioning is inconceivable: the commanders designate the enemy and the action to be taken against it. The assigned task is then executed in a more or less satisfactory manner. Yet even in this sphere, moments may arise such as on the warship *Potemkin,* when those facing the firing squad shout to the marines aiming their guns at them, "WHO ARE YOU SHOOTING AT?" Whereupon the marines lower their weapons; the task has lost its self-evidentiality. In today's parlance, the task had become problematic on some metalevel. Today's artist must acknowledge that his or her mission has become problematic on a metalevel, and from now on the works must reflect this fact.

A variety of artistic activities that are seen by many as opportunistic jockeying amid the shifting trends of the contemporary art world are, in fact, investigations into the very nature of art, and the works I thus produced may be viewed as unbiased propositions for the future mission of art. It is not easy to accept this point of view, and activities of this sort will for a long time to come be accompanied by murmurs of disapproval and shouts of condemnation.

Nonetheless, given this moral pressure, we must, at least for ourselves, categorically formulate our ideas about art based upon our own experience and the available information.

Written in 1980. Originally presented at the conference "Art in a Changing World" in Buda-pest in 1980. Published in *Hommage für Miklós Erdély* (Berlin: Künstlerhaus Bethanien, 1992). Translated by John Bátki.

•●

Theses for the Marly Conference of 1980

• What we regard as art is a matter of decision, not of definitions.

•• It makes sense to regard as art, or the essence of art, everything that the various accepted forms of art have in common.

•• Conversely, we may regard the various forms of art as art because they all share the same essential quality.

••• The greater the diversity of activities and objects we regard as art, the narrower the sphere of their shared qualities.

••• The greater the diversity of activities and individuals performing them whom we regard as artists, the less chance there is that we can find a quality they all share.

• If we decide to regard as artists every significant figure of every art form from prehistory to our days, then it is impossible to find any quality they all have in common.

•• Just because an exhibition is a matter of decisions, it does not mean that it must be arbitrary.

•• Which artists we consider to be significant is naturally also a matter of decisions.

• I consider those artists to be significant whose work demonstrates that the various activities regarded as art should have as little in common as possible.

• That is precisely what the greatest figures in any respectable art history have accomplished.

•• In other words, respectable art history has stripped the concept of "art" of any meaning.

••• Since it is unacceptable that a concept (in this case that of "art") should have different meanings to suit different occasions, and since I do not wish to exclude any artists I consider to be significant merely to rescue the concept of "art" (for I consider them to be significant precisely because their activities make the concept of "art" so diverse), I declare that, thanks to the artists, the concept of "art" has been emptied of meaning, it has no *significatum,* no signification.

• Clearly, the meaning of arbitrary and conventional signs narrows in proportion to the domain of *significata* expanding.

•• There must be consensus about the *significatum* if the significator is to function properly.

• The signification of nonarbitrary (iconic or indexical) signs based on analogy and/or communication expands on the other hand, as their *significata* increase.

• A work of art, insofar as it is a sign, is of this type.

•• Whereas in the case of an arbitrary, conventional sign the *significata* must have something in common, in the case of the other type the sign embodies within itself all—possibly radically different—features.

••• Thus it [the non-arbitrary sign] has the capability of becoming a "super sign" carrying many meanings, potentially infinite in number.

• The meaning of a work of art does not derive from the sum total of its diverse references; rather it makes these possible, virtually containing them, as it were.

•• Because of its analog and communicative aspects a work of art can vary at different points of space and time—or it can have several meanings simultaneously.

••• While in the case of conventional signs meaning narrows down with an increase in *significata,* in the case of iconic, indexical signs polysemy leads to attenuation and devaluation of meaning, and ultimately, as in the case of the work of art, to the loss of all meaning.

•••• Therefore a work of art may be considered to be a sign that amplifies and multiplies the various meanings at the expense of each, and causes them to extinguish each other, thus making it impossible for the work of art as a whole to have any meaning.

••••• A sign of this kind may be distinguished from an algebraic "x" since the latter can carry any value, whereas a work of art can assume a meaning only through misinterpretation.

- Roughly speaking, the various meanings appear on four different levels:
  — Thematic level (what)
  — Technical level (how)
  — In an art-historical context (with reference to all preceding and contemporary works), further distinguished as to
  — what
  — how
  — On a social, historical level (in relation to the broader or narrower social and cultural context, depending on the artist's stature), further distinguished as to
  — what
  — how

•• The destruction of the various meanings follows chiefly from the vertical interpenetration of these four levels.

••• On any one level the relationships of mutually extinguishing meanings is represented by a montage effect (along with inevitable modulations of meaning on other levels).

• The work of art is, as it were, saturated with extinguished meanings and as such acts as a "meaning-repellent."

• The message of a work of art is its inherent emptiness.

•• The receptive mind receives this emptiness.

••• The work of art creates a space within the recipient's mind when the latter "understands" its message.

•••• Then the recipient says, "beautiful" — which is another empty statement.

••••• This is followed by a feeling of freedom, which is nothing else than emptiness, a break in the chain of "recognized necessity": a place.

•••••• A place for the not-yet-realized.

• By speaking of the things of this world, a work of art makes them disappear.

• By speaking of the things of this world, a work of art makes discourse about these things disappear.

Written in 1980 and presented that year at the Marly conference as well as at the Budapest conference, "Art in a Changing World." Published in *Magyar Mûhely* (Paris), 60–61 (1980). Translated by John Bátki.

TADEUSZ KANTOR

The Polish artist and theater director Tadeusz Kantor (1915–1990) is known internationally for the experimental plays he created and produced for the avant-garde theater Cricot 2, which he co-founded in Kraków in 1955. He was also an immensely influential figure in the Polish art scene, introducing Surrealist and Expressionist ideas through his early metaphorical and informel paintings; organizer of the First Exhibition of Modern Art in Kraków in 1948; *a member of the* Krakow Group of Young Artists; *and co-founder of* Foksal Gallery *(see p. 88), where he staged his first Happenings. In paintings as well as theater, he experimented with themes of reality in art, alienation, and the meaning of human existence.*

The following text is the last of the twelve "Milano Lessons" that Kantor delivered to a class at the Civica Scuola d'Arte Drammatica in Milan in 1986. The students had been instructed to create a play based on Surrealist and Constructivist principles, and the "Lessons" presented his commentaries to the explorations of his students, as well as setting forth Kantor's ideas on theater and art. This final lecture presents the art of the avant-garde as experienced by Kantor himself and his thoughts on its function in a society he perceived as endangered by mediocrity and excess. The lecture reveals the depth of his desire for the guiding principles of movements like Surrealism to find new relevance in contemporary art and theater.

The Milano Lessons: 12 — Before the End of the Twentieth Century

Before the End of the Twentieth Century

This lesson will be about surrealism.
But there is time to address only the highlights of surrealism.
We will travel not only to the regions of aesthetics but also to the regions
of civilization, that is, of spiritual and intellectual transformations
of a human being and society.
By so doing, we will stay faithful to the spirit of surrealism, which
refused to be merely an aesthetic movement.
Surrealism defined the function of art in broad terms.
[Art's] influence, according to surrealism, should not be limited merely
to the regions of aesthetic exaltation but should spill over and form
human desires and actions,
revolutionize them
so they in turn would mould a social system
that would be grounded in ABSOLUTE FREEDOM,
the highest human value.
Surrealism proclaimed that
THE FREEDOM
OF A HUMAN BEING
IS THE HIGHEST GOAL OF ART!
This freedom is not freedom that functions exclusively within the
boundaries of a system whose aim is to revolutionize artistic

Tadeusz Kantor. *Panoramic Sea Happening*. Osieki, July 1967. Courtesy Galeria Foksal Archives

conventions;
nor is it freedom
that functions exclusively within the boundaries of a social system
created by communism—that is, a system of equality and justice for all;
but
it is FREEDOM
that embraces A TOTAL HUMAN CONDITION
in its most profound meaning,
that embraces a side of human nature
that has never been taken into account by any of the social
movements—that is,
PSYCHIC REGIONS OF A HUMAN BEING,
their depth,
their immeasurable strength, which up till now has intuitively been felt
by the poets and has been probed only by the intellect (science) and the
imagination (art).
This discovery is indubitably the most significant discovery of the
twentieth century. It cannot be effaced or replaced by anything else.
We are its inheritors.
Yes, since the time of surrealism,
the sciences and, more important, the arts
have joined the ranks of all social movements.
Surrealism as a movement was
so fascinating and obviously necessary
for the natural development of human civilization
that f i n a l l y it had to submit
to the laws of integration and

instant availability.
At the same time, this movement was so sophisticated
and refined
that any attempt to convert it [into something] "easily available" and
"accessible" would make it common and vulgar,
especially today, in a period of total MECHANIZATION.
This is why
I must begin this lesson about surrealism
with a general description and evaluation
of the situation in which
I live and create,
in which you live
and will create.
Before I get to the crucial part of the lesson,
which is shaping into a manifesto,
I would like to share with you
some of my observations and comments.
I do not feel my calling is to reform and save the world.
On the contrary,
*I am carefully taking notes about its mistakes, which stimulate my creative
process.*
What you are about to hear are not the words of a fierce prophet from
the Old Testament.
I hate to preach, command, and forbid,
especially in art.
I have a feeling, or maybe it is a (tragic) premonition,
that in this nightmarish epoch of
mundanity, holy consumerism,
production,
communication, and
all-powerful technical advances and politics,
the world is spinning at its own velocity and will continue to do so,
notwithstanding the calling of ART,
or maybe even against it;
that the power today is in the hands of MATERIALISM,
which is the enemy of art and the human spirit.
These words do not express my frustration or pessimism.
Instead, they are the voice of my deep conviction,
my subconscious; thus they are t r u e .
I cannot be ashamed of or hide them.
I want to explain their meaning and consequences
to describe my own attitude.
These words do not carry
a revolutionary faith in a "bright" and "perfect"
future;
nor do they express
revolutionary slogans of ordering the world according to the laws of
reason and justice.

Despite the fact that these ideas are filled with enthusiasm, I see the shadow of a dangerous MEGA-AGGRANDIZEMENT following
them and claiming its right to rule the world.
Today we know that we cannot let that happen.
At the same time, I am far removed from apocalyptic visions in philosophy and art
that are filled with eulogized suffering and indifferent pathos.
Scepticism does not appeal to me either. It cannot do much for the arts.
In the quest for the essence of this attitude, I prefer to evoke the feeling
of c o n t e m p t for the forces of this world and to appeal
to the spiritual condition, which, I believe, has high intellectual and artistic standards and allows us to accept THE EXISTENCE OF
E V I L when we have earlier consciously rejected the concept of GOODNESS, which was too easy, and BEAUTY, which was too conventional.
EVIL is real and material and is seen all around us.
Actually, it is worse than that: we get used to it.
To go back to my pessimistic "credo" and almost biblical judgement of the twentieth century, I do not despair.
On the contrary, I believe that this pessimistic awareness has paradoxically a certain significance for me (and for many other people). As in the past, it creates
THE NEED TO R E S I S T
and TO ACCUSE.
Well known is a strong FORCE that is contained in these reactions:
THE FORCE OF THE WORK OF ART.

I belong to the generation that witnessed genocide
and terrorist attacks on art and culture.
I do not desire to save the world with my art.
I do not believe in "THE EASY ACCESSIBILITY OF ART."
The experiences of our century have taught me where it will lead to; I have learned who and what benefits from this "ACCESSIBILITY,"
which has dangerously spread all over the world.
I want to SAVE MYSELF;
not selfishly, on my own,
but together with a belief in
THE VALUE OF AN INDIVIDUAL.
I am locking myself in my little room of imagination,
WHERE
I CREATE THE WORLD
AS I USED TO WHEN I WAS A CHILD.
I STRONGLY BELIEVE THAT TRUTH LIVES
INSIDE THIS ROOM OF MY CHILDHOOD.
AND IT IS TRUTH THAT IS AT STAKE TODAY AS NEVER BEFORE!
While writing these words, I realize how far I have removed myself

from the spirit of surrealism.
I do feel, however, that I am its heir.
This is not an act of regression.
I am constantly GOING FORWARD.
I PROTEST.

I refuse to assent to conformity and adaptability.
I destroy obsolete laws of the Past.
And this is an essential feature of surrealism.

THIS IS MY FIRST "REVISION" OF SURREALISM.

There will be more.
To make my point clear, I will read here "A LITTLE MANIFESTO,"
which was presented when I received the PRIX REMBRANDT,
8 April 1978.

A LITTLE MANIFESTO

I wish to read to you, Ladies and Gentlemen, my Little Manifesto (I am still writing manifestos), which was written especially for this occasion.

Before I read it, however, to make it clearer I will take the liberty to remind you that the fundamental (if I could use this pathetic word) idea behind my creative work has been and is the idea of reality, which I labeled the Reality of the Lowest Rank.

It can be used to explain my paintings, emballages, poor objects, and equally poor characters, who, like the Prodigal Son, return home after a long journey. Today I would like to use the same metaphor to describe myself.

It is not true that MODERN man has conquered fear. This is a lie! Fear exists. There is fear of the external world, of what the future will bring, of death, of the unknown, of nothingness, and of emptiness.

It is not true that artists are heroes and fearless victors, as we are led to believe by old legends and myths.

Believe me, they are poor and defenseless beings who chose to take their place opposite fear. It was a conscious act. It is in consciousness that fear is born. I am standing in front of you. I, the accused who is standing in front of harsh but just judges. And this is the difference between the dadaists, whose heir I am, and me.

"Please, get up!" cried the Grand Scoffer, Francis Picabia. "You are indicted." And today I will correct this once impressive invocation: I am standing in front of you. I am the one who is accused and indicted.

I am supposed to justify myself and find evidence of, I do not know which, my innocence or my guilt.

I am standing in front of you, as I used to stand at the class desk in the past, and I am saying, "I forgot I knew, I assure you, ladies and gentlemen."

In the period of the modem Apocalypse,
when the powerful deities of our epoch appropriate the arts
within the regions in which their power is brutally enforced

(it does not matter whether they are in the West or the East);
when it seems that art is dying, there appear suddenly,
I am sure of it (it has always been the case in the past),
as if from nowhere,
people who resemble the old saints, hermits, ascetics,
artists, whose weapon will be
POVERTY
and RIDICULOUSNESS,
poverty and ridiculousness of their means.
They are the descendants of THOSE
who started the twentieth century
in POVERTY
and RIDICULOUSNESS.

Their works will become a stake for those seemingly triumphant and
APOCALYPTIC symptoms of our times.
I wish to collect them and pile them
into one heap.
When isolated from life, they do not threaten or trigger alarming thoughts.
They can be burnt at the stake.
At least this can be accomplished in the work of art.
The following are
diverse kinds of SYMPTOMS of our times:

ALL-POWERFUL CONSUMPTION.
Everything has become a commodity.
Commodification has become a bloodthirsty deity.
Overwhelming piles of food
that could feed the whole world;
but half the population is starving.
Piles of books that will never be read.
People devour other people,
their thoughts, their rights, their customs,
their solitude,
and their individuality.
Grand-scale slave markets
where people are sold,
bought,
bargained for,
corrupted.
Creativity —
this word has ceased to
carry any meaning.
What impact could those who will come, or who maybe have already
arrived — whose names repeat the names of the GREAT:
Pablo, Chaim, Paul, Marc, Henri , , ,
and their POVERTY and RIDICULOUSNESS when they started —
have

on the all-powerful PRODUCTION
of Giant Corporations,
on mile-long MARKETS,
museum-markets,
theatre-markets,
festival-markets,
gallery-markets.
And this is yet another SYMPTOM of our end of the century:

ALL-POWERFUL COMMUNICATION.

There is no place anymore
for the eccentrics who walk on foot
(they say that walking helps thinking).
The rivers of cars float through our houses and apartments.
There is a shortage of water, air, plants, and forests.
The number of living creatures, people, increases with a shocking
speed. Let us go further:

COMMUNICATION,

which we are quick to connect with
trains, trams, and buses,
was perceived as the most appropriate and redemptive concept
for human THOUGHT
and the ARTS.
ALL-POWERFUL COMMUNICATION!
and its principal attribute:

SPEED,

which in no time was turned into a war slogan of
primitive tribes.
The slogan became the ORDER.
The whole world,
all humankind,
all human thought,
and all ART
were to abide by it.
The world rushes headlong with a wild scream.
Why? Is it to catch up with the speed of light and thought?
Not at all!
There is no place for thought in this frightful race.
Light? Possibly "light eternal." After the fall!
COMMUNICATION is supported by the strength and power of

DEMOCRACY

and its soulless mechanisms;
COMMUNICATION has altered the SPACES reserved for human
thought and art (I do not want to refer to them as temples or shrines)
into COMMUNICATION OFFICES

and POSTS OF COMMUNICATION NETWORKS.
The old names were kept to mask the change.
There are no secrets,
unknown lands, or deserted nooks any more;
everything is encoded and transferred
simultaneously to all corners of the world
with an ultra s p e e d
by telephone lines,
by airwaves
by the most sophisticated apparatuses,
which erase all the differences.
Everything becomes dutifully uniform,
equal in importance,
and . . . WITHOUT ANY MEANING!

                    ALL-POWERFUL HOLY TECHNOLOGY.
No. I am not against technology.
I am not a firm believer in
a naive idea of a return to nature
or in a simplified lifestyle.
I do not have any confidence in attempts at resurrecting
artificially conceived,
seriously celebrated,
pretentious, and empty
rituals
that try to indicate to us, people,
a lost bond between a human being and
earth,
water,
air, and
matter.
It is high time we tore the mask from the faces of
those gloomy and limited
shamans and "gurus" of all kinds,
sorcerers,
spell charmers,
witch doctors,
ritual striptease dancers,
pseudo-biblical Abrahams who
bleed
hogs that were rented from
slaughterhouses;
who splash in and wrench their entrails and guts;
who sacrifice them, not to a biblical,
but to a cruel deity
bereft of a Human Mind, that is,
to the All-Powerful Free Market of Art
and Holy Commerce.

Those con-priests of Commerce and Free Market,
those self-aggrandizing crooks,
those thoughtless opportunists,
cleverly procure the false images of greatness
by using
nature,
mountain ranges,
and sands of the desert,
which they cover up with paint,
sculpture them with a bulldozer,
only so they are noticed
in the landscape of the world.
Behind these manifestations of
the SENSATIONALISM of our times,
one can sense
a dangerous anti-intellectualism
and a brutal elimination of thought processes.
I am all for the slogan
"Power to the intelligentsia";
for technology and knowledge
that enhance
the intellectual development of
a human being;
for metaphysics,
whose human side is manifested in
irony, a sense of humour,
and imagination;
for, heaven forbid,
human emotions.
And it is here that one can find
my opposition,
my protest against TECHNOLOGY.
Today surrealism is
uniformly vulgarized;
what is more, this is done on purpose;
it is used in a primitive manner
by anyone who wants to
SURPRISE,
COMMERCIALLY TERRORIZE,
MESMERIZE,
and finally . . . SELL a product.

It is used everywhere where
impressive and profit-making
HALLUCINATORY AND DELIRIOUS EFFECTS
ARE SIMULATED
as a substitute for vision and thought.
Well known to us are those SELF-CONFIDENT PERFORMANCE
ARTISTS,

SELF-INDULGENT CON-POETS,
QUACKS TRYING TO BEWITCH US WITH THEIR FITS OF
HYSTERIA,
WHOSE LACK OF IMAGINATION IS COVERED UP WITH
TECHNOLOGY AND ITS
SOPHISTICATED MACHINES,
WHICH EXTERMINATE ALL
THOUGHT AND EMOTION.
Well known to us are those
PAINTERS AND PRINTMAKERS WHO DISPLAY NOTHING
BUT THE EMPTY
TECHNIQUES OF THEIR PROFESSION,
WHO TRY TO CONVINCE US THAT THEY HAVE JUST GONE
THROUGH
THE MIRROR TO ALICE'S WONDERLAND;
WHEREAS IF THE TRUTH BE TOLD, THEY ARE STANDING
IN FRONT OF IT
with a painted expression of *bouche bée,* as the French would say,
on their faces.

HOLY TECHNOLOGY rules everywhere today
in THEATRES, MASS MEDIA, and
TELEVISION.
It produces this surrealistic "enchantment" mechanically by the
thousands.
In visually oriented musical production,
those powerful but soulless MECHANISMS
reproduce pseudo-surrealistic effects
that are void of
the POWER OF FEELINGS
and the POWER OF EMOTIONS.
Performers run wild and make use of
those devices that were once discovered by the GRAND
REVOLUTION OF SURREALISM only to reduce them to the level
of strategies used in a football game.
There are exceptions to the rule that have a powerful spiritual strength.
But the general trend, like a powerful wave, is the portent of
A DELUGE AND . . .
DESTRUCTION!
    Because of the significance of the topic of surrealism, I have called this
lesson "The Twelfth Milano Lesson." I would like you to get to know the
"commandments of surrealism," to absorb their content and take them as
guiding principles in your creative work.
    This is not a traditional "school" topic; nor is it a lecture. It is something
more than just an act of learning.
    I want you to *discover your heritage!*
    Surrealism was born at the beginning of the twentieth century, our century.
Those were the years of its a d o l e s c e n c e.

We belong to this century.
Its adolescence is our adolescence.
We share the same genes with it.
And these are the very roots of the dynamic and the strength of our
creativity!
We cannot free ourselves from our adolescence.
We cannot betray it.
We cannot trivialize it.
You do not have to study it.
You do not even know that you belong to the same family.
All I can tell you is that you have to
become fully aware of
your heritage and your lineage
to be able to discern the true spirit
of surrealism from
poor mutations of it,
seductive elegance,
comfortable opportunism,
career pursuits,
and gradual entropy.
And that was the last of my warnings.
Thousands of essays and books have been written about surrealism.
Keep reading them. Learn about the lives of your ancestors,
about their victories and downfalls,
about their stormy adventures,
sins, crimes, loves, perils.
Learn about everything: about their ecstasies and passions,
their poverty, extravagance, and pride . . .
It is crucial that you do this. It should not matter that you gain this
knowledge from "books" in a school-like manner. You do not have a
choice. Read these books the way one reads family letters that children
discover shamefully hidden in family scrapbooks.
To have a clear conscience about my responsibility to you and this
Milano Lesson,
I shall play the part of a chronicler . . .
But do not expect from me a lecture about the history of surrealism.
When I encountered it in Paris in 1947,
I studied surrealism at exhibitions, from books, and from manifestos;
absorbed it from the air and the climate, which were full of it.
I can say that my own "path" of youth
led me directly towards the wide road
well trodden by the revolutionary army.

   It is my conviction that surrealism has left deep marks in the genes of
our century as well as in our own. Try to learn about it in a manner similar to
mine, via an apprenticeship with the "masters of surrealism." This way I shall
be freed from the function of a teacher, which is not my function here.

   What you will hear will instead be a confrontation between surrealism
and my personal thoughts, ideas, and "discoveries," which were moulded
by our

t i m e, which is removing us further and further away from, I would say, a maternal "bond" to surrealism.

I would ask you to accept this as my personal "revision" of surrealism and, to be more precise, a revision of our t i m e. We have the right to do it because we live in the eighth decade of our closing century.
In my personal "journey" (and life),
certain "dogmas" of surrealism have lost their power
and effectiveness.

We could ask, What have we today inherited from surrealism? What elements of this inheritance can we take, keep, and use as weapons in our battle?

While discussing surrealism and the surrealists, I am also constantly thinking about dadaism and the dadaists because these two MOVEMENTS were ONE TREND at the very beginning.

When I saw the works of the dadaists for the first time after World War II, circa the 1960s, they had already acquired their collector's value and were museum pieces. The dadaists themselves either were old or had died. But I had the feeling that the spirit of their protests, scandals, and actions was still in the air.
They were the World War I generation; I (we) carried on my shoulders the burden of the calamities of World War II.
It was then that I first saw and understood that there were similarities between their attitude towards art and my own.
This attitude was defined by me and in me during the war.
Knowing nothing about the dadaists, I had created a similar pattern of artistic "conduct" and had described my attitude towards the world and art in a similar way.

I will try to compare these two EPOCHS, these two ATTITUDES, find DIFFERENCES between them due to the distance of time, and, finally, make a "REVISION" in my and your revision made at the end of the CENTURY, that is, a revision of the MOVEMENT that started this CENTURY and, one could even say, that gave life to this CENTURY.

1 9 1 4

World War I.
Millions of corpses
in the absurd hecatomb.
After the war,
old powers were abolished;
generals' ranks, medals, and epaulets,
monarchs' crowns,
were thrown into the garbage cans;
fatherlands went bankrupt;
nationalism turned out to be nothing more than
a base primitive instinct.
In the context of such a colossal ignominy in the world, which up till that time forced us to acknowledge its existence as the only judicially permissible one, the attitude of the dadaists was a healthy action and

reaction:
DERISION,
DISREGARD,
MUTINY,
PROTEST,
NEGATION,
BLASPHEMY,
SACRILEGE of all the SHRINES,
QUESTIONING of all social values.
A holy concept of art was mocked.
CONSCIENCE, which according to the old order should have
conditioned the work of art, was replaced by COINCIDENCE.
FORM and its perfection, which ought to have EXPRESSED important
content, were replaced by crude REALNESS, which expresses
nothing and simply IS.

A quarter-century passed.
World War II.
Genocide,
Concentration Camps,
Crematories,
Human Beasts,
Death,
Tortures,
Humankind turned into mud, soap, and ashes,
Debasement,
The time of contempt. . . .

And this is my (and our) answer:
THERE IS NO WORK OF ART
(later this statement would get a more intellectual label: disavowal of
the work of art).
THERE IS NO "HOLY" ILLUSION.
THERE IS NO "HOLY" PERFORMANCE.
THERE IS ONLY AN OBJECT THAT IS TORN OUT OF LIFE AND REALITY
  (the history of art has given it a more sophisticated name:
  l'objet prêt).
A CARTWHEEL SMEARED WITH MUD became a work of art.
THERE IS NO ARTISTIC SPACE
  (such as the museum or the theatre).
THERE IS ONLY REAL SPACE   (Odysseus returns from Troy to a
                                     room destroyed by the war,
                                     a railway station, a staircase).

SUBLIME AESTHETIC VALUES ARE REPLACED WITH
POVERTY!
POOR OBJECT   (a cartwheel smeared with mud,
                                     decayed wooden board, a kitchen
                                     chair on which Penelope would
                                     sit).

ARTISTIC ATTITUDE IS DESCRIBED BY
PROTEST,
MUTINY,
BLASPHEMY, AND SACRILEGE OF SANCTIONED
SHRINES.
SLOGAN: AGAINST PATHOS, FESTIVITIES, AND CELEBRATION!
Today I will revise my ATTITUDE from 1944.
In the 1960s, having come across dadaism, which had already become a
museum piece, I realized that my protest of 1944 was the protest of dada
in 1914.
I felt that I was dada's descendant, and, as often is the case, I did not
know the name of my "father."
To make a distinction between a theatre EVENT and a performance of
The Return of Odysseus, I will refer to my artistic ATTITUDE as THE
TIME OF ODYSSEUS.
A feeling of an inescapable death, which was the mark of the war
and a premonition in my THEATRE OF DEATH thirty years later,
covered my attitude and that time with a veil of metaphysics that was
alien to the spirit of DADA.
The concept of POORNESS, which was fully explored in my IDEA
OF REALITY OF THE LOWEST RANK, contained in itself a dose
of LYRICAL tone and (heaven forbid!) EMOTIONS,
which were foreign to dada.
These are the differences that make THE TIME OF ODYSSEUS
mine.

1944 to the present.
This attitude, whose shocking, but precious to me, symptoms I have
just enumerated, ought to have disappeared at the end of the war.
The 1940s . . . 50s . . . 60s . . . 70s. . . . have passed.
Artistic ideas have been breaking the surface,
but all the time, as if from far beyond — maybe it was my inner voice —
I have been perceiving warning signals that ordered me and dictated
that I choose one action over the other —
PROTEST,
REVOLT
AGAINST THE OFFICIALLY RECOGNIZED SACRED SITES,
AGAINST EVERYTHING THAT HAD A STAMP OF "APPROVAL,"
FOR REALNESS,
FOR "POVERTY." . . .

Is it possible that the time of contempt,
of bloody and wild instincts,
of absurd actions by authorities that refuse to become "civilized,"
has never left us since the dawn of history?
The answer to this question is indubitably given by the art of the
discussed decades.
"Listen" carefully and you will hear the answer.
In 1948, the authority in power

attempts to put an end to the freedom of art.
In my little and confined room of imagination,
I begin to hear clearly in my art the liberating
"ORDERS" of those times.
They become a part of me, my own.
The only true ones.
Fascinating.
I begin to realize that I have to make them clearer, increase their energy
level, and give them the power of aggression!
At the same time, I have to make quite an important "REVISION" for
the spirit of DADA and the TIME OF ODYSSEUS to stay alive.

With the passing of time, other perilous symptoms of our epoch
emerged and grew in strength. Those were
NARROW-MINDED BUREAUCRACY,
OMNIPRESENT TECHNOLOGY,
CANNIBALISTIC CONSUMPTION,
COMMON AND MANDATORY MATERIALISM OF LIFE
THAT DEVOURS HUMAN MIND AND SPIRIT.
Nightmarish malls have become the temples of a new deity of consumption
and materialism.
I am listening carefully to that "Inner Voice."
ONE HAS TO STAY UNFAITHFUL TO THIS NEW TEMPLE
AND THIS NEW GOD AT ALL COSTS!
My creative work, whose roots are grounded in the subconscious,
"understood" this inner voice and command much earlier and quicker.
The intellect goes through and becomes aware of a different and NEW
STAGE of cognizance:
SPIRITUALISM,
SPIRITUAL IMPERATIVE,
PREMONITION OF THE OTHER WORLD,
THE MEANING OF DEATH,
THE MEANING OF THE "IMPOSSIBLE,"
"AN IMPATIENT WAITING AT THE DOORS," BEHIND
WHICH THERE ARE REGIONS THAT ARE INACCESSIBLE
TO OUR MINDS AND CONCEPTS. . . .
I do not have the time to speculate whether this mysterious assemblage
has been rooted in my subconscious and my character for a long time.
This "revision" seems to be antidada. But it seems so only at the first
glance. The dadaists were against their time and their world; This
"revision" is also done to our present time. A big one! It is a correction of
our world, whose strength has grown to an uncontrollable degree.
At the same time, the madness of the material world leads to other types
of madness: hyperbaroque conventions in art, an unrestrained spread of
ILLUSION, and a delirium of eccentricity. Surrealism and its means are
used indiscriminately in impotent actions void of any intellectual power.
The only purpose in art is to show and demonstrate their eccentricity.
Imagination, that dangerous and blasphemous region of the human
psyche excavated by the surrealists, is turned into a mechanism

producing fireworks.

Charlatans and mediocrity pretend to be the high priests of
MAGNIFICENCE.

In a period of terror caused by the trend for MAKING EVERYTHING
STRANGE (which has nothing to do with "magnificence" in
surrealism),

one needs courage to suggest
EVERYDAY,
BANAL,
POOR,
AND UNADORNED
REALITY

Today, it is only REALITY that can give birth to true
MAGNIFICENCE,
"IMPOSSIBLE,"
SUPERSENSUOUS.
IT IS ENOUGH TO TAKE CAUSE AND EFFECT FROM IT!
REALITY WILL BE AUTONOMOUS AND NAKED.
AND THIS IS ALSO A KIND OF "REVISION."

After many years, the war slogans of dada and surrealism are mixed
together.

New forms emerge.

New forces appear that threaten human freedom.

If we want to stay faithful to the spirit of nonconformity, we must find
in ourselves a NEW SPIRIT OF REVOLT, even if it is foreign to the
old slogans.

This is the reason we have to "revise" constantly.

The surrealists differed from the dadaists in that they added positive,
scientific, and cognitive values to the destructive slogans of dada.

They believed that the function of art is not only to provide intellectual
and aesthetic stimulation but also to REVOLUTIONIZE human
awareness, which was in the grip of stereotypes and the patterns of a
practical mind; to destroy a pragmatic, practical experience of the real
world; to expand awareness to include new regions of the psyche
previously dismissed;

and, finally, to reach a higher level of human existence.

In the context of this logical argument and this perfect train of thought,
today we are distrustful, almost feeling guilty: we do not believe any
more in rational arguments.

THE EXPERIENCES OF THE TWENTIETH CENTURY HAVE
TAUGHT US THAT
LIFE DOES NOT RECOGNIZE RATIONAL
ARGUMENTS.

By so saying, we are more irrational than
irrational surrealism.

And this is the first revision.

Today we also know how PERILOUS ARE SOCIETY'S MOTIVATIONS
FOR THE ARTS.

And this is the second revision.
Art's didactic purpose and its utilitarian tendencies no longer provide a
convincing argument.
Utilitarian arguments concerning the accessibility of art and creativity
based on the principle "and you too can be an artist" advocate
MEDIOCRITY!
And this is the third revision.
It is only one's world that is of any importance, that is,
the world that is created in isolation and separation,
the world that is so strong and suggestive
that it has enough power to occupy and maintain
a predominant part of the space
within the space of life!
In this sense,
"THE SPACE OF LIFE," AND EVERYTHING THAT IS
CONTAINED IN THIS PHRASE,
EXISTS PARALLEL TO
THIS OTHER SPACE,
THE SPACE OF ART.
THE TWO OF THEM CONVERGE, OVERLAP,
AND COALESCE,
SHARING THEIR FATE AND DESTINY. . . .

AND THIS IS ENOUGH!
And this is the last comment. I do not know whether these comments
are connected with or disconnected from surrealism. But this is irrelevant.
These are my own thoughts, which are to serve me. I do not intend
to impose them on anyone. What attracted me (us) to surrealism
in the postwar period was an attempt to GO BEYOND THE MATERIAL,
PRAGMATIC, AND LIMITED
REALITY.
To "go beyond," surrealists tried to appropriate the regions of
DREAMS, deep layers of the human p s y c h e wherein real
elements of life merge with the products of blind and uncurbed forces.
The ability to draw from this experience is labelled
"i m a g i n a t i o n."
So much for the surrealists.
Today I have certain doubts about the validity of these statements. I
must try, however, to get beyond the first impression because they will
shape and mould my life now.
The first heresy:
I DO NOT BELIEVE IN THE POWER OF DREAMS,
where, according to the surrealists, imagination is born.
I am sure that INCREASED PSYCHIC ACTIVITIES AND
THE INTENSITY OF THE THOUGHT PROCESS PRODUCE A
FREE NETWORK OF IMAGES, ASSOCIATIONS, ALLOW US
TO MOVE AWAY FROM RATIONAL UTILITARIAN CONNECTIONS
BETWEEN REAL ELEMENTS.
A sewing machine, an umbrella, and a dissection table could not
possibly have been merged together in the Count de Lautréamont's dream.

Of this I am sure. It must have been done by a newly liberated freedom
of thought.
The surrealists maintained that the PSYCHE IS A STATE
THAT SHOULD BE RESEARCHED AND THAT THE RESULTS
SHOULD BE USED IN THE DEVELOPMENT OF
CONSCIOUSNESS.
I am full of doubts here.
These doubts, however, allow us to hear clearly
"the i n n e r v o i c e."
ART IS NOT PSYCHOLOGY. THE CREATIVE PROCESS HAS
NOTHING TO DO WITH SCIENTIFIC RESEARCH.
THE PSYCHE SHOULD BE ACCEPTED, RATHER THAN
RESEARCHED, IN ART!
IT SHOULD BE ACCEPTED AS A SUPERSENSUOUS
CONCEPT.
THE PSYCHE — THIS IMMATERIAL " O R G A N "
THAT WAS "PLANTED" IN A PHYSICAL BODY,
NATURE'S OR GOD'S GIFT —
INDICATES ITS OWN DESIRE NOT TO GO
"BEYOND MATERIAL REALITY"
BUT TO
S E P A R A T E ITSELF FROM IT.
THE PSYCHE CONTRADICTS MATERIAL REALITY.
IT ONLY TOUCHES IT.
IT CREATES ITS OWN CLOSED REALITY, WHICH MAKES
ONE FEEL THE PRESENCE OF
THE OTHER WORLD.
IT IS THE PSYCHE THAT EMANATES THE FORCE CALLED
" I M A G I N A T I O N . "
IT IS THE PSYCHE THAT GAVE BIRTH TO GODS
                         ANGELS
                         HEAVEN AND
                         HELL,
                         FEARS. . . .
And now I can enter my little
room of irnagination and say,
"IT IS THE PSYCHE THAT CREATES AND EXHIBITS
R E A L I T Y
AS IF WE WERE SEEING IT FOR THE FIRST TIME."

And I think this is all.
My last advice:
"Remember everything
and forget everything. . . ."

Written in 1986. Originally published in *The Drama Review,* T132 (winter 1991). Translated by
Michal Kobialka.

A CASE STUDY: ARTISTS INTERVENE IN EVERYDAY LIFE

Milan Knížák (born 1940) is a Czech artist, writer, composer, and designer. Starting in the early 1960s he created assemblages and installations, which he placed in public spaces in Mariánské Lázně and Prague. He was one of the founders of the Aktual movement, a group of young people trying to "live in a different way" by producing radical art and Mail art, and by staging performances and other activities demanding a maximum of personal engagement from its participants. Knížák organized the first Happenings in Czechoslovakia in 1964 and, through the critic Jindřich Chalupecký, was in contact with members of the Fluxus movement in Western Europe and the United States and later became Director of Fluxus East. In 1990 Knížák was appointed Director of the Academy of Fine Arts in Prague, and since 1999 has been Director of the National Gallery in Prague.

The following text describes the response to an action Knížák and his friend Jan Mach staged in 1966 in which a randomly chosen apartment building—its inhabitants strangers to the artists—became the target of the artists' intervention. Knížák and Mach created installations in the hallways of the building and mailed various unmarked packages to the residents. Some of the residents were perplexed and angry and sought police assistance. As a result, the artists were obligated to explain their actions at a meeting with the concerned residents.

An Event for the Post Office, the Police, and the Occupants of No. 26 Václavkova Street, Prague 6, and for all Their Neighbors, Relatives, and Friends

Milan Knížák, with Jan Maria Mach

Inhabitants of a house selected at random were sent many packages with various things in them; things were left illegally in halls:
books spread around,
coats hung on the walls,
calendars and flocks of paper gliders,
and goldfish flopping around the floor
and beds and chairs, etc.

The inhabitants of the house also received free tickets to a movie in the mail, so that they were all sitting in reserved seats.

Police investigated this for over two months. Finally, they came to my apartment. There was supposed to be a house meeting at that building and with me (under supervision of a police lieutenant) explaining the whole thing.

A house meeting in Václavkova Street 26, Prague 6, March 6, 1966
It begins at 11 o'clock. We meet a police lieutenant outside. *It'll probably be a little thin*, he says. *There's a hockey game on TV.* Even so, in the meeting room with the slogan "For Socialist Coexistence" over the door, there are about twenty people, ranging from fifteen to eighty years old. A baldheaded pensioner, obviously the house confidant, opens the meeting. The police officer reads excerpts from a letter from the Union of Artists (by Jindřich Chalupecký) that the police had asked for. Then a clumsily-dyed blonde of about forty in a sweat suit, obviously a die-hard house-meeting debater, says: *What was all that supposed to mean? What are*

you anyway? Where do you get the time and the money for this kind of thing? WHERE DO YOU GET THE TIME AND THE MONEY? A respectable-looking man, between forty and fifty (they address him, in the Middle European fashion, as "Mr. Engineer"), talks about how they (he and a few others like him) had wanted to take it all as a bit of fun, that they understand, and so on and so forth, *but more and more of it kept coming, and then those tickets to the movies . . . it all made our flesh kind of crawl* (quote).

It looks as if half the people are not too much against us, and the rest are totally against us. *And what about the mess? I had to clean it all up* (an elderly lady, a pensioner). *We were afraid to open up those parcels, afraid to accept them from the postman. There could have been bombs or explosives in them. And then those tickets to the movies. Someone wanted to lure us away from home and then rob our flats, that's what we thought. When did you find out our names? At night? We'll be a lot more careful now! Think of the money it must have cost! How did you know we have a tomcat?* (an elderly lady teacher). *We didn't know. You see I received a leaflet saying, "Get a cat" (among other things, of course). I had so much to do that day, but I was so excited that I didn't do a thing. So as a matter of fact I had a good rest.* She laughs. *The whole school was on tenterhooks wondering how it would turn out.* She's a hundred percent for. *And what do you do, in fact?* No one understood, wanted to understand, could understand that *this is what I do.* A man in a green nylon raincoat speaks up; he's about fifty, has a powerful voice, and we learn he's an army major. He shouts angrily: *Just explain it to me, just explain what all this meant for you, for society, for art.* I reply quietly, in words of one syllable. The peroxide debater butts in once more: she uses logic. *So you want to create a disturbance? The greatest disturbance of all is war. Who wages wars? The fascists. So what are you?* I'm a fascist, then. But the major comes back, insistent. I give him a rapid survey of the most basic facts about art to the present, but he doesn't understand anyway and keeps on shouting as before. I refuse to talk to him. I don't feel like competing with his powerful voice. The others are probably afraid of him. He wants to take it out on Honza Mach, who is in the army, but in doing so he loses face. Two young fellows sitting opposite, probably just out of the army, yawn. *They're always on your back in the army, and now this.* But the major goes on shouting angrily; he wants revenge at all cost, and it bothers him a great deal that there are no laws against what we did. I think he'd ejaculate if he were able to give us each twenty-one days in solitary. But his behavior has lost him any position he might have had, while the others remain silent, more from fear and caution than consent. The meeting ends inconclusively. The two young men leave with us, and the lady teacher. *It was because of him that I didn't get into university,* said one of them, referring to the major. The others nod. *He's an idiot.* They bid us farewell cordially. Even the police lieutenant.

Written in 1966. Originally distributed as a samizdat wall newspaper by Aktual (1966). Translated by Alex Zucker.

3 CONCEPTUAL ART AND TIMES OF TRANSITION

onceptual art is one of the most fluid of current international art movements: it flows easily across borders, in all directions, including the nations of the former Eastern Bloc. In fact, although often unrecognized or forgotten, Eastern Europe has proven to be an important point of origin for the development of many different types of Conceptualism, beginning in the late 1950s and continuing until today. More than forty years ago, artists in the region began to realize that by shifting their focus away from the object, they could free themselves not only from traditional artistic mediums like painting and sculpture, but also from state-controlled galleries and museums, while at the same time reaching an audience on a much-less-mediated and more-personal level.

The availability of Western magazines, the proliferation of art schools and informal artists groups, and the seeming dead end of the modernist movement, together brought radical consequences for the development of Conceptual art in certain regional centers of Poland, Yugoslavia, and elsewhere. A unique brand of Conceptualism based on Neo-Dada concepts of anti-art appeared in Croatia at the same time that similar movements took hold in New York, Milan, and Paris. In the case of Krzysztof Wodiczko, the Zagreb-based group Gorgona, and others, art in the form of traditional objects was abandoned in favor of texts, photographs, mobile sculptures, or private performances and actions.

The situation in the Soviet Union was altogether distinct. In his essay "Moscow Romantic Conceptualism," Boris Groys coined the term "romantic conceptualism," giving a name to a new wave of Russian artists who came to prominence in the 1970s and 1980s. A wide spectrum of these artists employed different artistic mediums, including actions and texts, but more traditional drawings and paintings were also made. Groys argues that these artists' products are, in fact, not only art objects, but also specific conditions of reception under which the art is perceived. In his opinion, Conceptual art in the West can be compared to scientific experiments, but Russian art, with its long tradition of spirituality, is ultimately a romantic and lyrical enterprise. Soviet Conceptual artists created a metaworld, a world of magic, which can only be related indirectly to the material world.

With the rise of Conceptualism in Eastern Europe, the inevitable problems with documentation of time-based actions and events began to appear. Written, photographic, and film documentation remained imperfect substitutes for actions and events, adding extra layers of meaning and creating autonomous works of art that bore only a tangential relationship to the original event. "Seven Photographs" by Andrei Monastyrski chronicles the documentation of the activities of the group Collective Actions in the Soviet Union and provides an interesting record of the relationship between a Conceptual work of art and its photographic afterlife.

Suzana Milevska's "The Readymade and the Question of the Fabrication of Objects and Subjects" illustrates the specificity of the Eastern European milieu in relation to the creation and understanding of Conceptual art. The concept of the readymade is understood quite differently in art cultures where this notion has not been established for as long as it has in other places. In these regions, the readymade object placed in an art gallery has different connotations, ranging from reminders of war to commentaries on poor economic conditions.

—*Tomáš Pospiszyl*

< Braco Dimitrijević. *This Could Be a Work of Braco Dimitrijević* (detail). Photograph. Courtesy the artist

• 123

NENA DIMITRIJEVIĆ

Gorgona is one of the most elusive art groups associated with Conceptual art in Croatia. It existed for only a short time, from 1959 to 1966, and produced little materially. The loose-knit group functioned as a forum for radical Conceptual ideas and proposals, many of which were not executed; others materialized into mailings, the publication Gorgona, *and installations at the self-funded Studio G. In general, production of artwork per se or the publicizing of the group's activities was of no interest to the members, all of whom were individually recognized artists and curators in Zagreb. It was not until the 1970s when an understanding of and interest in Conceptual art had been forged by other Croatian artists, that the ideas surrounding Gorgona found a receptive audience, and that the art historian and curator Nena Dimitrijević started reconstructing the history of the group and its multiple forms of existence. Her research resulted in the Gorgona retrospective at the Museum of Contemporary Art in Zagreb in 1977. The following text, written for the exhibition's catalogue, asserts the group's importance and places it firmly within the international avant-garde of its time.*

Gorgona: Art as a Way of Existence

From 1959 to 1966, there was a group of artists in Zagreb about which little has remained in the written art history of this area. Gorgona was not an art group in the usual sense of those whose goal was to promote a certain ideological-aesthetic concept and recruit protagonists among the elite of the local art scene. It was a group of artists who shared common affinities in a much broader sense than that implied by the framework of any stylistic program. The fact that Gorgona's activities were of a very discrete and unspectacular nature is one of the reasons why it went unregistered in the written tradition, and was rarely mentioned in the oral, cultural tradition of these places. The members of Gorgona were painters Marijan Jevšovar, Julije Knifer, Đuro Seder, and Josip Vaništa, sculptor Ivan Kožarić, architect Miljenko Horvat, and art historians Dimitrije Bašičević (see Mangelos, p. 80), Matko Meštrović, and Radoslav Putar. In its professional structure and, even more, in the absence of a program that acted as a cohesive force and stimulated group activities, Gorgona was not an art group in the usual sense of the word. The fact that five of the group's members were artists does not fully explain the principles on which the group was founded. The "gorgonic spirit" only indirectly determined their individual works, and all of them retained and continued to develop their own creative autonomy. Furthermore, Gorgona was made up of those few rare artistic personalities who, by their own creative contributions, anticipated events on the international art scene, not content like the majority of others with the eclecticism of long-since-expended art concepts. If Gorgona wasn't an art group in the usual sense of the word, based on a common art ideology, and had no strategic reasons for introducing and promoting an ideology in the current art scene, what then was it? In 1961 Vaništa wrote, "Gorgona seeks neither work nor result in art," and a few years later, when asked, "What is Gorgona for you?" he replied, "Result." These two statements suggest one possible definition: Gorgona was a process of searching for artistic and intellectual freedom, the achievement of which was in itself the aim and purpose. Freed from the professional responsibilities of promoting itself in the hierarchy of the local art scene, the group met and exchanged ideas, motivated solely by spiritual and creative affinities. Despite differences in their individual artistic concepts, the members of Gorgona all had one thing in common: the spirit of modernism to which they belonged, i.e., recognition of the absurd, of emptiness, and monotonous aesthetic categories, a tendency toward nihilism and metaphysical irony. Since such affinities are no longer uncommon, it may seem from today's point of view [1977] that this definition does not indicate precisely enough the spiritual coordinates of an art group. However, at the time Gorgona was being formed, quite different ideas dominated the scene in Yugoslav art.

What was happening on the international and local art scene at the time of Gorgona? In Zagreb, at the end of the 1950s, an entire pleiad of young painters was accepting the aesthetic concepts of Art Informel, and owing to this fact, the period of the early 1960s in Croatian art is characterized by various manifestations of Abstract Expressionism, Action painting, Tachism, and lyric abstraction. However, art production at that time lacked the qualities to raise it above the level of provincial, manneristic replicas of [Jackson] Pollock, [Mark] Tobey, [Alberto] Burri. It lacked force, rawness, spontaneity, the uncontrolled explosiveness of color that made Action painting the first American movement that succeeded in threatening the domination of the Paris school. On the other hand, at the same time as the beginning and rise of Art Informel, the early 1960s saw in Croatian art the still-active and notable presence of the one-time founders of Exat 51.[1] The creative interest of Ivan Picelj and Aleksandar Srnec evolves from the geometric abstraction inherited from Russian Constructivism and Suprematism to contemporary optical and kinetic art. The year 1961 is also the time of the first *Nove Tendencije (New Tendencies),* an exhibition which, together with subsequent ones, was to have long-range effects on the art climate of this milieu. It is significant that the first *Tendencies* was not conceived as a puristic manifestation of a strictly stipulated stylistic orientation, but as an attempt to review the international art situation, including discoveries being made in the new fields of art expression. Hence, at the first *Tendencies,* which later grew into a review of canonized optical-kinetic art, we find artists like Piero Manzoni, whose work and behavior were a reincarnation of the principles of Dadaism. And because of the inclusion of Piero Manzoni and Otto Piene, the exhibition in Zagreb registered certain vital and extremely significant (though, at that time, still undiscerned) tendencies in contemporary art. At the turn of the decade, a few solitary individuals re-echo the Dadaist view of the world and art, and accept Duchamp's implicit definition of art as tautology. The achievement of the Dadaists in equalizing the sphere of art and everyday life also marks the end of the imperative to produce a final work of art, which confers artistic status on all procedural, ephemeral, and non-materialized manifestations and works.

In addition, the end of the 1960s is the time when the Western spirit begins to discover oriental philosophical thought, and the experiences of Zen Buddhism which [John] Cage, [Yves] Klein, and La Monte Young introduced into the art of the Western hemisphere provide a vital new stimulus to all fields of creativity. One of the first to introduce the products of the Eastern intellect into European art was the French painter Yves Klein. In 1950 he created the first monochrome, a canvas uniformly painted with a color he called International Klein Blue (IKB).

The monochromes were an attempt to present in painting transcendental and metaphysical categories such as "emptiness," "immateriality," and "eternity." The comment that Klein "was more important for what he did—the symbolic value of his actions—than for what he made,"[2] can be applied equally to Piero Manzoni, as well as to the protagonists of the Happenings and Fluxus movements.

The protagonists of the American European group Fluxus—[George] Brecht, [Robert] Watts, [Wolf] Vostell, [Dieter] Roth, [Robert] Filliou—radically abolished the traditional character of the art act and object. The Fluxus event—a simple occurrence without dramatic tension and metaphorical implications—paved the way to the aesthetics of silence and monotony characteristic of the art in the next period.

In Macunias's manifest, a new aesthetic-ethical stand is formulated: the imperative to produce art objects-goods is replaced by gesture, process, irony, the expression of free will and personal opinion as art forms in their own right. Awareness of the social responsibility of the art act is once again established and turns against the demands of the commercial system, the market which treats the art object as goods. In 1958 Klein sells his exhibition *Void* in the Iris Clert Gallery literally for pure gold, which he subsequently ritually throws into the Seine. *Merde d'artista,* by Piero Manzoni, is a similar protest against the syndrome of "painting as investment." (Manzoni was an extraordinary anticipator whose influence on the art of the next period can be compared with that of Duchamp, and it is not an exaggeration to say that entire art concepts later arose as a result of certain of Manzoni's works and gestures.) Artists of a similar mentality were also members of the Group Zero, founded in 1957 in Düsseldorf— [Otto] Piene, [Heinz] Mack, [Günther] Uecker—whose actions on the streets of the city and along the banks of the Rhine manifest similar attitudes.

Yet, however different these individual manifestations may have been, all the art phenomena we have discussed share a common origin with Gorgona in the interaction of the Dadaistic tradition and newly discovered Eastern philosophical thought. This attempt to define the spirit of avant-garde art at the end of the 1950s should serve to place and objectively evaluate Gorgona in the international art situation of that period. Although in 1959, when Gorgona was being formed, the phenomena and individuals who were to characterize the international art scene in the years to come were not a part of some underground cultural scene, they were still very far from the historically recognized prophetic position attributed to them today. At that time, Gorgona was one of the sources of this new artistic sensibility and outlook on the world, which, as a continuity of the Dadaistic spirit, would achieve full affirmation only at the end of the next decade. Together with Fluxus and Zero, Manzoni, Klein, Fontana, and Reinhardt, Gorgona anticipated and announced the torrent of phenomena which under different names (Conceptual art, Art as Idea, Post-Object art) still dominate the current art scene. Exploring all the discrete, yet nevertheless significant forms in which the "gorgonic spirit" was expressed is both an archaeological and a detective job, since it must reconstruct on the basis of fragmentary recollections, correspondence, and documents, the activities of a group of artists who, from the very beginning, rejected as its goal the materialization of aesthetic-ideological principles in durable art products. On the other hand, this was a discrete and introverted group that was not interested in forcing itself through militant-manifest forms on the cultural scene, and, consequently, it left little influence on its environment. This aposterior classification of the group's various activities is accomplished, in part, with the aid of a vocabulary of recent art history, and is an attempt at subsequent systematization of the works, ideas, and propositions that arose spontaneously as the result of a unique ethical and spiritual relationship toward the entity of art. Gorgona's activities can be classified into three groups:

1. Exhibition in Studio G
2. Publication of *Gorgona*
3. Concepts, projects, various forms of art communication

Exhibitions Organized by Gorgona

The most public, and by its character, least "gorgonic" form of activity was the exhibitions that the members of the group organized in Studio G, also known as Salon Šira. The space, which was and still is a picture-framing shop on Preradovićeva ulica, was rented by the group so that it could function independently of the policies of the exhibition institutions. All the costs of organizing the exhibitions (fixing up the space, posters, a catalogue) were covered by the joint funds of the group, from membership dues that were collected in a rather bizarre way: Gorgona's treasury was managed by a sales woman in the Naprijed bookstore, to whom each member paid a certain amount depending on his [or her] current financial situation, and at the same time could withdraw from the treasury whatever sum he [or she] needed. In addition to exhibition costs, the fund covered the printing of a publication and all other eventual expenses. Because of the financial instability of most of the members, the fund was often in crisis, and the constant lack of resources seriously jeopardized the activity and very existence of Gorgona. This is witnessed by many letters written in the archaic language used by the group's members in their personal correspondence, urging the members to fulfill their financial responsibilities to the society.

A recapitulation of the exhibitions held from 1961 to 1963 in Studio G shows that many important artists of that period were concentrated in and around Gorgona. Seen from the time distance of fifteen years, in the light of later experience—hard edge, Minimal art, and Primary painting—the works of Jevšovar, Knifer, Kožarić, Seder, and Vaništa appear to be the most relevant products of postwar Yugoslav art. This means that besides looking for alternative forms and means of artistic expression, the artists in Gorgona also made valuable contributions within the framework of traditional art mediums.

In 1959 Julije Knifer integrated geometric elements arranged in a zigzag fashion to form a meander. Since then, meander has remained constant in his painting system, a synonym of his artistic identity. By this, Knifer gained two historical advantages: one comes from the nonrepresentational, illusion-free character of his paintings, which makes him a forerunner of the cool primary painting of recent years. With regard to the aesthetics of hard edge, which appeared at the same time as his discovery of meander, and with which he is associated very strongly, Knifer's painting is characterized by consistent and more complete reduction of the choice of motifs to one exclusive symbol. While [Frank] Stella or [Kenneth] Noland maintains a greater freedom in varying colors and motifs, Knifer conceptualizes his method by limiting himself to black-white meander, and his painting is reduced to the infinite repetition of a symbol, to the sublimation of the "radical will." This method of semantically identifying painting with a chosen symbol, that is, not painting as a single pictorial solution but as a part of an a priori adopted system, foreshadowed many later decisions.[3] The consequences and dimensions of such a decision can only be seen today after the experience of Conceptual art, which does away with the importance of the art object in favor of emphasizing the artist's motivations.

Another member of Gorgona whose painting, viewed in retrospect, achieves real significance is Marijan Jevšovar. Like the majority of art phenomena that are ahead of their time, Jevšovar's painting was considered in the early 1960s marginal to the main art current of the period, in this case, Informel. During an epoch of color explosion, he chose dirty colors, lifeless pigments that he spread across the canvas several times until he achieved the desired dirty gray surface. These gray paintings, deliberately marred by blobs of oozing paint, are proof of a very contemporary antiaesthetic attitude: the characteristics, which at the same time rendered them anonymous and unrecognizable, are today exceptionally rare and valued qualities. It is a conscious and deliberate degradation of the painting, a negative composition, with the intention that the painting not be "beautiful" by the traditional criteria of order, balance, and harmony of color. Jevšovar painstakingly selects the place on which to squeeze color and, in so doing, destroys, "disfigures the painting." The sentence, "You would never believe how hard it is not to make a painting beautiful" expresses the basic generic principle of his work. "My painting is a negation of form, dirtying the white surface of the canvas." We are confronted with artwork as destruction, not with the ironic, spectacular destruction of the Dadaists, but a quiet, yet no less effective, process of destroying the surface, a programmed attack on the problem of pictorial structure.

Jevšovar's approach to the problem of a painting's negative organization is best defined by some of Vaništa's statements formulated amazingly early (1961): "The basis of all European painting lies in balance. The factor of balance is not important. Avoid the effects of composition which reflect traditional values in European art. In European art, from [Nicolas] Poussin to [Victor] Vasarely, the details are more important than the whole. Preserve the whole." The painting of Đuro Seder from this period is the product, in certain measure, of a kindred sensibility alike in his intention to question the traditional conventions of composition, and in his seemingly casual, deliberately clumsy, and unsightly manner of execution. The paintings he did after 1959 were, in the words of the author, an attempt "to depict subjectless meditation": a circular or semicircular form of irregular contours is centrally composed on a gray background.

In the fall of 1961, Vaništa began his series of monochrome works. A uniform surface painted in gray, white, or silver is cut in the center by a single horizontal line, which the author describes as "the only remnant of content, of theme in this kind of painting without illusion." In a previously quoted tractate from 1961, which coincides with Reinhardt's maxim "less is more," Vaništa not only summarized the principles of his own painting, but he also anticipated painting trends in the period to come:

Aim for simplicity in painting.
Aim for sparseness.
Avoid illusion.

A very finished look: the negation of the painting approach. School not necessary.
Drawing or drawing experience included. The ways and means of traditional
painting are insufficient. Do not change the paint in the can while painting.
A signature is not necessary.

Several years later, having become fully aware of the conceptual principle of his paintings, Vaništa exchanges factual execution for the verbal equivalent, that is, substitutes the process of painting for precise verbal description.

However different the creative concepts of Jevšovar, Knifer, Seder, and Vaništa were, certain common characteristics tie them with New York post-painterly abstraction: the question is of two-dimensional painting which does away with all illusion of space and reduces all planes to one impenetrable surface, and "tries to clarify the surface of the painting as a 'field,' and not as a composition."[4] However, despite possible analogies with Reinhardt, Stella, Newman, and Noland, the painting of each of the members of Gorgona clearly shows its European origin. Contrary to the preoccupation of Americans with formal and technical problems which is reflected in their exact execution and imposing formats, the members of Gorgona emphasize the spiritual character of their painting. The definitions of "degrading the surface," "subjectless meditation," and "interest in sparseness," which they associate with their work, demonstrate the European intellectual heritage: choice of unpretentious materials and small formats are the expression of a certain nihilism, of an ironic distance with regard to the piety of the painting act.

Especially worthy of attention is the painting of Dimitrije Bašičević.[5] Its spirit and character are very close to contemporary art. For example, as early as 1959, he makes the painting *Hommage à Pythagora,* a black square on a black background under which a dedication is written in red calligraphy. This is also the time when he started using blackboards, writing words or verse on them with chalk. The same pattern will later be translated into the medium of painting. Based on the idea of imitating the blackboards during the period between 1950 and 1960 are several series of paintings: Tabula rasa, Paysages, and Abeceda. For the series Nonstories, Bašičević used old publications and catalogues as material. He painted the pages black, leaving only a word visible here and there, thereby creating a certain kind of illogical narration, a nonstory.

Even though the painting of the members of Gorgona coincides in some of its premises with the current avant-garde trends in monochrome and monotony as a compositional formula, in each individual case it is the product of a complete autochthonous creative concept. The painting of Bašičević, Jevšovar, Knifer, Seder, and Vaništa foils every attempt to classify them within a school or movement; whereas today some of the qualities of their work can be more easily recognized owing to the evolution of taste and sensibility. Each of them, seen as a whole, remains unique, beyond all known stylistic categories.

In addition to the members of Gorgona, other artists exhibited in Studio G. Their work, according to Gorgona, reached a certain level of quality and contemporaneity. Among them was Eugen Feller, certainly one of the most interesting protagonists of Informel in this country [Croatia], the creator of *Malampije* — paintings with cement deposits, tar applications, sand, and other similar found materials. Besides Ivo Gattin's *Zasjenčene površine (Cutup Surfaces),* Feller's *Malampije* are the only successful exceptions from the Informelist production. They possess a robustness, an aggressiveness, and a tactile provocativeness of substances which, in general, were missing in the rationalized Croatian Informel. Another guest at Studio G was the young Belgrade painter Radomir Damnjanović, who exhibited several of his paintings from the series Pješčane obale (Sandy Beaches). At the beginning of the early 1960s, Damnjanović won the sympathy of both the art public and critics in Belgrade owing to the fact that he introduced condensed rudiments of organic forms into a flat, uniform background, which resulted in a free field for association and metaphors. In this way he successfully integrated the Surrealist tradition of the area with the tendencies toward nonillusional, depthless articulation of surface.

Several guests from outside of Yugoslavia also exhibited in Studio G. In 1962, thanks to Matko Meštrović, François Morellet, who first came to Zagreb the year before to participate in the *New Tendencies,* was among them. In the introduction in the catalogue, Meštrović wrote about Morellet: "He was able to see that each of the sixteen squares was an equally important element of the whole, of a given structure. Each square, by clearly showing its place and position, its loyalty, candid and free subordination to pure order, also demonstrates the permanence of the law according to which it is organized." The Museum of Arts and Crafts purchased one painting from the show, and Morellet gave the money to Gorgona to support further activity of the group.

The watercolors of Piero Dorazio, protagonist of Italian Op art, were also shown in Studio G. It is worth noting that the one-man shows of Dorazio, Morellet, and Vasarely in Studio G were more the result of certain circumstances (the participation of these artists in the *New Tendencies* exhibition, private contacts made by Meštrović with them, and the current trends in kinetic and optical art) than any shared ideas or sensibilities, as was the case with certain other personalities of the international art scene with whom Gorgona was associated. The retinal doctrine of optical art and the positivism of the Constructivists that completely dominated the second and later exhibitions of *New Tendencies* was foreign to the ironical, nihilistic spirit of Gorgona.

At first glance, one modestly important exhibition in Studio G illustrates the sensitivity of Putar and Vaništa to the oscillation of tastes and aesthetic judgments, that is, their surprising capability for anticipating the coming style. I am referring here to *Modern Style,* an exhibition of Art Nouveau objects, partially collected from various apartments in Zagreb and partially borrowed from the Museum of Arts and Crafts. This exhibition of the choicest examples from the Secession group of artists anticipated the renaissance of style at the end of the decade, the rage for sinuous form, which will culminate in popular graphic design, fashion, and interior design by the end of the 1960s.

That contemporary taste had still not demonstrated any affinity for the style that characterized architecture and art at the turn of the century is best illustrated by the tone of Putar's introduction in the catalogue: "This is a heritage that for decades we have spit upon, laughed at, hidden as a disgrace, and explained as delusion. Yet, time shows us that in the ground in which we have buried an entire flora of forms, even against our will a similar cluster of forms can sprout again. He who listens carefully and condescends to lower his head will see that in these modest works not all poetry of form has perished. He will see that its truth still lives and resists kitsch."

Exhibition activities terminated in Studio G in 1963. The reasons were mostly of a financial nature, and it left several exhibitions unrealized, among them exhibitions by Antonio Calderara, Marko Šuštarčić, Ivo Gattin, Bruno Mascarelli, Dimitrije Bašičević, and Slobodan Vuličević. By leasing the shop on Preradovićeva ulica, Gorgona was able to make its exhibition program independent of cultural institutions. By inviting colleagues whose work reflected recent tendencies to exhibit in Studio G, the group acted as a kind of corrective of the policies of other galleries. Of this Igor Zidić writes: "It is in no way subjective to say that Studio G was one of the most joyful discoveries of the cultural scene. In a situation in which generations, trends, and ideas are bought and sold, it is a real experience to meet a group of people who, in an intimate, modest way, live their lives without any ulterior motives, base feelings, or spiteful vindictiveness, and with refined sensibilities foster their independence."[6]

Still, the most significant manifestations of Gorgona took place outside of the galleries, and the forms they took were very different from the traditional way of presenting art via exhibitions and catalogues.

Antireview: Forerunner of "Book as Artwork" Phenomenon

From today's point of view, in light of recent events in art, the most significant manifestation of the group's activities was the publication entitled *Gorgona.* From 1961 to 1966, eleven issues were published and two more prepared, which unfortunately were never printed. *Gorgona* was not conceived as an art magazine. Every issue was an artwork in its own right. In other words, it belonged to that kind of art product that appeared as the result of the increasing use of everyday media in art, and which at the end of the 1960s was classified under the designation "book as artwork." The wave of Neo-Dadaism which appeared in early 1960 also brought with it an interest in new media: artists like Cage, La Monte Young, Manzoni, Klein, Rauschenberg, and Kaprow used biological and technological material equally. What Celant called "cool informel"[7] is an art practice that implies the significance of media as media, with no attempt to feed them moral or allegorical content. However, the use of new media does not deny an individual and natural approach in favor of technology. On the contrary, it intensifies the awareness of the possibilities offered by media. The result is that less importance is put on the sensory aspect and more on the uniform, cool, analytical and philosophical aspect of an artwork.

In light of [Walter] Benjamin's distinction between the "cult value" and the "exhibition value" of art, the latter of which, in time, owing to new methods in technical reproduction, will completely predominate over the former, "book as artwork" is just one step further in the process of eliminating artwork as an original fetish object.

With the antireview *Gorgona,* the aesthetic principles of an entire generation are anticipated, and precisely through some of the ideas it presented the future issue of Conceptual art is predicted and defined. We can apply to *Gorgona* much later theoretical thinking in which the phenomenon of the Conceptual work alters the traditional relationship of original work/printed reproduction. In the opinion of Seth Sigelaub, in the case of painting/sculpture, printed reproduction is always secondary information about the work, a more or less successful illusion of the original which is impossible to reproduce faithfully. On the contrary, in the case of Conceptual work, printed information is primary because it contains the same amount of information, as does the oeuvre itself.

A full decade before Sigelaub makes a distinction between primary and secondary information, and Celant places "book as artwork" under the category of "cool informer," the first issue of *Gorgona* is published and, in my opinion, foresees many recent ideas and definitions. Vaništa made the first issue of *Gorgona.* It consisted of the same cool, low-key photographic image of an empty display window in a shop for commissioned goods on Vlaška ulica reproduced on each of its nine pages. Two functions define the work: one is the choice of a neutral, in no way picturesque, motif, without emotional or associative charge; the other is repetition which, through the effect of monotony, destroys all possible metaphors.

Knifer conceived the second issue of *Gorgona* as an endless meander done in such a way that the pages are joined together to form an endless loop. It should be noted that what was accomplished was not the reproduction of a painting, but identification of the publication with Knifer's sign.

Kožarić's issue number 5 of *Gorgona* presents a portrait/sculpture: on one side of the page is a photograph of the face, and on the other side the same head but seen from the back. The work explores the possibilities of the reproductive media offering a sufficient amount of information about a three-dimensional piece.

Vaništa's issue number 6 of *Gorgona* also analyzes the relationship of original/reproduction in an "age of mechanical reproduction." The point in this case is Leonardo da Vinci's *Mona Lisa,* surely the most frequently exploited myth in the history of art, which Vaništa selects by negative criteria: "I chose what I considered to be the most absurd thing to print in the magazine since reproducing the *Mona Lisa* is tantamount to leaving the page empty." Yet, contrary to the empty page, the *Mona Lisa* is a symbol, an element in the myth of genius and virtuosity: By his choice, Vaništa follows in the footsteps of all those artists who saw in the Gioconda the challenge for ironic intellectual intervention, but compared with Duchamp, for instance, he reduces intervention to the tautological act of reproducing.

In general, Vaništa was the first of the members of Gorgona to apply the tautology principle in art. Proof of this are issues 10 and 11 of *Gorgona,* as well as several of his ideas which were never realized. In issue number 10, the pages are completely blank — all information (title, publisher, issue no., year) is printed on a separate piece of paper the size of a calling card, inserted among the empty white sheets. The logical matrix A = A is also applied in issue number 11 of *Gorgona.* The whole issue consists of a photograph of the front page inserted between the two covers.

Gorgona number 3 comes from the series called Perfect Drawings in which Jevšovar tries to draw freehand correct geometrical figures — a circle, parallel lines, a curved line. *Exercises-Perfect Drawings* are a demonstration of the individual creative relationship to geometric axioms: "The triangle is, for me, a terrible shape, primitive, and while the square and circle are definitive, perfect shapes, in their exact geometric form, they are too readable and inartistic."[8] Jevšovar tries to overcome the impersonality of geometric facts and makes them individual by the imperfectness of free strokes. However, on the other hand, he tries to discipline the lines in an asymptomatic approach toward the ideal form. The shapes which result are "perfect"; their perfection is not of a geometric but

Miljenko Horvat. *Gorgona* 7. 1965. Photograph. Courtesy the artist

of an artistic nature, and it comes from the inevitable aberration of form drawn freehand from technically executed geometric figures.

Vasarely's *Gorgona* includes several drawings from that period and the author's text, while Dieter Roth's issue synthesizes reproduction and original technique. The basic comma pattern was printed, but the connecting line was hand-executed for each copy so that every copy of the magazine became an original drawing.

Two issues of *Gorgona* are of a literary origin. Issue number 8 is a translation of Harold Pinter's play *The Tea Party*. Miljenko Horvat's idea for *Gorgona* is indirectly literary, as the idea came from a travelogue about Denmark written by Miloš Crnjanski. It is an interesting issue because instead of being printed, it contained two actual photographs. The origin of the photographs has to do with Vaništa's trip to Skagen, a place on the Danish coast, which Crnjanski mentions in his travelogue, where dead seagulls can be frequently seen. Vaništa wrote about it to Horvat, who went to Skagen, and, hence the photograph with a melancholy motif of a dead seagull on a sandy beach; repeated in two versions, a lighter and a darker print, which served in the realization of issue number 7.

The unreserved acclamation and interest that *Gorgona* encountered in the circle of the then international avant-garde confirms the timeliness of Vaništa's idea about starting such an edition. The magazine was well distributed and artists like Manzoni, Rauschenberg, Fontana, Roth, Piene, and others whose polemic intellect significantly characterized the art period that followed recognized in these issues the product of a kindred artistic mentality. In his letter of March 4, 1961, Fontana compliments *Gorgona* as one of the most lively contemporary reviews, and Rauschenberg expresses the wish to design an issue of *Gorgona* himself. In a letter to Matko Meštrović dated December 9, 1961, Manzoni says, "I think the idea behind *Gorgona* is fantastic, and I immediately put together three projects from which the best and simplest for realization can be chosen. All three projects carry the title *Tavole di accertamento.*"

One of Manzoni's ideas was to draw a horizontal line in the middle of every page, and another proposed rows of letters of the alphabet. The third project, which was chosen for the magazine but because of financial reasons was never printed, proposed that on all ten pages of the publication one of the author's fingerprints be printed. Again, it is a variation of the theme of the mythology of the individual: the artist's identity is literally imprinted on the work. Signature and fingerprints are symbols and proof of identity, and it is precisely the authenticity of identity on which rests the entire commercial mechanism of art which Manzoni wishes to question. (In the meantime, through the example of *Merde d'artista*, the discouraging adaptability of the art market was shown, which successfully absorbs even those "attacks" which try to question it.) It is interesting that Daniela Palazzoli, at that time editor of the Milan art magazine *ARC/do,* wrote in 1966 to Vaništa with the intention of helping to publish Manzoni's *Gorgona,* but for some reason this cooperation never materialized. Another artist whose issue of *Gorgona* never came out was Enzo Mari, an Italian designer whose interests later turned in the direction of radical politicizing and ethical reexamination of the role of industrial design in contemporary society. Two other artists whose issues were never published are Ivo Gattin and Josip Meštrović.

Miljenko Horvat. *Gorgona* 7. 1965. Photograph. Courtesy the artist

In this country, Gorgona was known among a small group of people. One person who was in close contact with the group, although never became a member, was Mihovil Pansini, a physician and filmmaker and later the founder of GEEF, an avant-garde, experimental film festival organized partially under the influence of Gorgona. About this, Pansini says, "During these discussions,[9] the idea of antifilm was born and was roughly defined for the first time at the end of the third discussion in May of 1962. Actually the texts of *New Tendencies* and *Gorgona* were paraphrased, and in that way their influence on antifilm was confirmed. When the discussions ended, we had an idea of the direction in which experimental film could go."[10] In close contact with Gorgona were three painters—Josip Zanetti, Mišo Mikac, and Jakov Bratanić. From correspondence we can see that others who were familiar with the existence and activity of Gorgona included Gabrijel Stupica, Georgij Paro, Slobodan Mašić, and Boris Vižintin. However, aside from personal affinities, no one at that time was fully aware of or correctly appraised the real significance and seriousness of this art phenomenon, and Gorgona has remained practically anonymous, an esoteric phenomenon overlooked in the art history of its milieu.

Language as Art Material in Gorgona's Practice

From today's perspective, the most interesting of Gorgona's activities is that which remains outside the category of visual art, and which inaugurates new ways and means of art communication. This includes all the forms of "gorgonic" activity that never "materialized" in any of the productive or reproductive art media, and the traces of which exist only in the memory and correspondence of its members.

The following classification of this "dematerialized" art is done with the aid of a vocabulary based on art practice and theory developed over the course of the past decade. Classifying these activities under the terminological designation of recent art is merely an attempt at a posteriori orientation in the phenomena that announced, and in many cases directly anticipated, current art practice. The projects, walks as artwork, realization of artwork via mail, were various manifestations of the same creative outlook, the character of which can be best seen in Vaništa's 1961–62 definition of Gorgona:

> *Gorgona is serious and simple.*
> *Gorgona is for absolute transience in art.*
> *Gorgona seeks neither work nor result in art.*
> *It judges according to the situation.*
> *Gorgona is contradictory.*
> *It defines itself as the sum of all its possible*
> *definitions.*
> *Gorgona is constantly in doubt. . . .*
> *Valuing most that which is dead.*
> *Gorgona speaks of nothing.*
> *Undefined and undetermined.*

Concepts and Projects

Gorgona's meetings were a kind of creative and spiritual outlet, motivated solely by intellectual and spiritual affinities, similar leanings and interests, without the obligation to create an art product of any type whatsoever. The meetings were often held in the form of a walk somewhere around Zagreb, and the occasion for them might be to watch the sun set or what they called "an inspection of the beginning of spring (fall)." In the course of these meetings, ideas and proposals arose which we would characterize today as artworks, as a spontaneous intellectual game. These ideas ranged from very concrete ones which, because of technical and financial impossibilities, were never realized in the form of objects or exhibitions, to very analytical and critical works, which in their very conception never presumed to be realized materially. Ivan Kožarić's proposal to place a globe in Studio G that would fill up the gallery completely is one of the ideas that belongs to the first group. By showing an interest in primary geometric form and accentuated interaction between the space and object in it, Kožarić's idea approaches the sculptural premises of primary structures and environmental art. Another one of his projects within the "Collective Work" (1963) reads: "To make casts of the insides of automobiles, apartments, stables, of the interior of a park, in general, of all important hollows in town." The expression which implies an unlimited series — "all hollows in town" — gives the proposal a fantastic, poetic tone, yet if we take just a few examples — the inside of a stable, the inside of a car — we see that it is based on 1) perception of visual values in everyday environment and 2) transforming hollows (negative volume) into sculpture (positive volume). This is also the time when many of Kožarić's projects that aimed at natural and urban ambiences originated.

Kožarić's *Unusual Project* from 1960 seems, at first glance, to be a very ordinary piece of sculpture based on the problem of cutting off certain sections from the mass. However, it soon becomes clear that this is not an ordinary piece of sculpture when we learn that what he has made is a "model" for an undertaking of gigantic proportions which was never realized — cutting off a piece of Sljeme, a mountain near Zagreb. Similar sculptural problems are encountered in *A Piece of the River,* a sculpture done in stone which suggests a "piece of water" cut from the river's course. Ripples on the surface of the water are turned to stone, and the form achieved is a portrait of the flow itself. Both examples introduce us to a complex game of reality and illusion: in appearance the abstract sculpture is very realistic if we are aware of its unusual origin. The Conceptual principle of these sculptures lies in the transformation of material: turning earth and water to bronze or stone, i.e., turning powdery or liquid natural substances into solid sculptural material is similar to the Pop art method of "translating into other materials." Johns's Ballantine Ale cans cast in bronze and Oldenburg's canvas cabinets cause similar confusion because of the discrepancy in the usual material makeup of an object and its artistic interpretation. However, the singularity of Kožarić's approach is that he is looking for motifs in natural, not cultural environments. Instead of glorifying or criticizing the consumer attitudes of contemporary civilization, inherent in the work of Johns and Oldenburg, Kožarić is primarily interested in sculptural problems. Before us is a work of Land art, but cast in bronze! The difference in iconography causes a difference in morphology. A piece of river, a cut hill, are not recognizable and we experience them as abstract forms. Awakened interest in the insignificant phenomena of the everyday is seen in Julije Knifer's proposal to make an exhibition of banality. Somewhat more complex is Seder's idea for making an exhibition in Jevšovar's studio: everyone would bring an object which he feels best expresses the subject of the last meeting's conversation. Several of Vaništa's projects are structured on the juxtaposition of reality and illusion, objects and photography. He proposes photographing the contents of a suitcase and then sticking the snapshot on the top of the suitcase. Based on the same logical matrix is his proposal to take a photograph through the window of Studio G of part of the studio's interior, and then to blow it up and put the lifesize photograph in the studio window, so that seen from the proper angle outside, the real architecture overlaps with the photographic illusion.

Vaništa's *Exhibition without Exhibiting* is one of the most radical of Gorgona's work. Instead of an exhibition, a precise description of each painting was to be made—the dimensions, the chemical composition of paint, the width of the horizontal line—and the work completed with an introduction by Zvonimir Mrkonjić, who was supposed to make a formal analysis of the "paintings." Substitution of artwork with language equivalents as an equally indicative code shows that Vaništa had already understood that the logical structure of work is more important than the manually executed form. "I stopped painting paintings when I realized that it was sufficient to formulate them by means of language."

The proposal to make the color Gorgona's Black coincides with Klein's IKB: in both cases, painting as the combination of a finite number of colors is opposed by the individual act of creating a new color which is no longer a means of pictorial mimicry or metaphor, but becomes an absolute trademark of a particular artist or art group.

One more idea from this period announced later recognition of the fact that the aura surrounding the personality of an artist is an indistinguishable element in judging the quality of his [or her] work, which in recent art has resulted in the building of personality myths, as an exclusive art practice. Vaništa proposed that an exhibition be organized in the window of Salon Šira entitled *In Honor of Manet,* which would consist of object-symbols of the painter's personality: a top hat, white gloves, and a cane. (In order to acquire all these things, Gorgona advertised in the want-ad section of the daily newspaper and, surprisingly, received many replies.) The intention to present the classics of modern painting, not through the work the artist left but by means of objects/attributes of personality and fashion of the times, shows that even then thinking had begun about the function of personal mythology[11] in the mechanism of art history.

New Means of Art Communication

In addition to the proposals, projects, and ideas that resulted from or were reported at their meetings, an important source for discovering the spiritual coordinates of Gorgona is the *Gorgona's Post*. Namely, the group made use of institutionalized systems of communication, like the post and press, to communicate their art messages. It is particularly interesting that with several works intended solely for the postal media, Gorgona announced the much later phenomena of Mail art, as well as the trend to use official means of communication for art purposes. Thus in 1961 an invitation was sent to several addresses with the text "You are invited," the idea behind this incomplete invitation being the parody of comprehending cultural events only as an occasion for social gatherings.

It was the practice of the group that once a month one of the members collects and sends to the others a selection of quotations from philosophical, literary, and aesthetic texts which he [or she] considered best expressed the state of mind and current mood of Gorgona.[12] Consequently, "Thoughts for the Month," as they referred to this selection, is the most important key to understanding the aesthetic-ideological principles and mentality of a group that created its place of spiritual freedom in almost complete anonymity and seclusion. "Thoughts for the Month" are a laconic and indirect form of self-definition. Gorgona defined itself by way of reflection, recognizing itself in distant mirrors of time and space. Still, these various corresponding planes crossed each other in a common line, which is the recognition of nihilism as an aesthetic category. For example, "Thoughts for February" (1961) consist of the following quotes:

> *"Abstract painting is the picturesque literature of psychological states. That's sad. I'm glad I'm not an abstract painter." — Yves Klein*
> *"Only in emptiness does the essential abide." — Lao-tzu*
> *"Earlier I liked prose for its richness of emotion, profound music, and hot colors; weaknesses which surely deserve to be punished; now after a quarter of a century, I am led to the kingdom of pure and esthetic line." — Tin Ujević*
> *"Heidegger remains alone in his stand on a particular kind of nihilism, which, by reducing man's existence to an existence destined for death, sees man's greatest task in the acceptance of this fact and living without illusions in a conscious and apprehensive freedom doomed to death."*
> *"For man, speech hides, rather than reveals singularity." — M. H.*
> *"Thoughts for June, July, August: Buddhist priests live alone in the summer, and come together in the winter." — H. de M. Carnets, années 1930–44*

At times "Thoughts for the Month" contained fragments of texts from art periodicals which recorded kindred phenomena. In one word, this selection reflected the essence of the group's theoretical and philosophical points of view, and was the recognition of kindred sensibilities — of the gorgonic *modus essere* in the art phenomena of other places. Another interesting form of the group's internal activities was the "Gorgona Choice." Compared to "Thoughts for the Month," which condensed their attitudes on literature, philosophy, and art, "Gorgonic Choice" was searching for material and nourishment in everyday life. From newspapers, magazines, and events from their own lives, they chose those phenomena and occurrences which distinguished themselves through certain qualities from the sphere of the ordinary, rational, logical, and predictable. The work functioned partly on the principle of a "readymade." The whole intervention consisted of discerning, choosing, and "appropriating" the phenomena and situations which satisfied the gorgonic criterium. Compared to Duchamp, who was looking for neutral, cool objects to add to art products, Gorgona used different criteria. They were searching for events which distinguished themselves through their absurd, grotesque, and bizarre qualities. This "choice" offers one more possibility of defining Gorgona, which Putar formulated as: "We are not Gorgona — we are only searching for Gorgona in the world around us."

After 1966 Gorgona's activities reached a crisis. However, its death was not literal; it refers more to the end of those few media by which Gorgona communicated with the external world than any real end of the group's existence. In 1966 the last issue of the antireview was published, while the last exhibition activities in Studio G had ceased three years earlier, mainly because of financial reasons. However, in its most essential form the group never ceased to exist. Through their meetings, exchange of ideas, and intellectual and spiritual ties, it still lives today. Not acknowledging the significance and achievements of Gorgona during the time of its greatest activity was a lost opportunity to perceive and assess a progressive art phenomenon which brought with it the destruction of many myths of bourgeois aesthetics. Gorgona's practice implicitly criticized the traditional concept of art as class institutions which by attributing eternal, precious, monumental, decorative, and divine qualities to art, insures it the privileged status in bourgeois society. Gorgona's practice jeopardized the sacrosanct position of art in all these aspects because it used everyday, nonart materials and means of communication (press, mail, speech). It destroyed the notion of painting as decoration and pleasant illusion, and finally by emphasizing the conception of a work over its craftsmanship, it tended to destroy the Christian myth of the artist's hand being led by divine genius. The failure to acknowledge Gorgona signified a lost opportunity for the art history of this area to record one of the most significant phenomena to occur here, and to permit the continuity of progressive art ideas in the period to follow. This has been an attempt to correct that.

Notes

1. Exat 51 is a Croatian group of artists, designers, and architects who were active from 1950 to 1956. They worked in geometric abstraction, kinetic art, and Op art and were influential in promoting modernist art.
2. Edward Lucie-Smith, *Movements in Art since 1945* (London: Thames and Hudson, 1969).
3. Buren's much later choice of striped fabric as his personal trademark is only a more radical form of the same concept.
4. Barbara Rose, *American Art since 1900* (London: Thames and Hudson, 1967).
5. Bašičević also suggested the name for the group, which comes from the title of one of his poems.
6. Igor Zidić, "A Few Lines about Gorgona," Studentski list, Zagreb, 1966.
7. Germano Celant, *Book as Artwork 1960–72* (London: Nigel Greenwood, 1972).
8. From an interview with Nena Dimitrijević, catalogue of a solo show at Galerija Nova, Zagreb, 1976.
9. He is referring to the discussions held by filmmakers in the Kino-Club, Zagreb, in connection with founding a festival of avant-garde and experimental films.
10. "Book of GEEF, 1963," GEEF Organization Committee, Zagreb, 1967.
11. A phenomenon referred to by Johannes Cladders as "die individuelle Mythologie," catalogue of Documenta 5, Kassel, 1972.
12. The author of this choice was mainly Vaništa.

Written in 1977. Published in *Gorgona,* exhibition catalogue, Galerije grada zagreba (Galleries of the City of Zagreb), 1977. Translated by Ann Borčić.

•●

BRACO DIMITRIJEVIĆ

Born in Sarajevo in 1948, Braco Dimitrijević studied at the Academy of Fine Arts in Zagreb and at St. Martin's College of Art in London. His art comments on the arbitrary result of narrative history, its omissions, and the prejudicial conditions of fame versus anonymity. The Casual Passerby *series, started in 1968 and realized internationally, represents images of randomly met people in large photo portraits, busts, and memorial plaques that are displayed prominently in places typically reserved for people of cultural significance. Often Dimitrijević's works legitimately dupe the public, as on the occasion when photos that were hung on the facade of the Republic Square in Zagreb led people to believe that there had been an overnight change of government.*

Dimitrijević is a prolific theorist as well as an artist, and his artistic projects serve to exemplify his concept of "post-history, " which is informed by a belief in the simultaneous coexistence of multiple histories and forms of art. In the following selection from his publication Tractatus Post Historicus, *Dimitrijević rejects formalism and teleologically driven art history for its prescription of a dominant style.*

The Ethics of Form or Aesthetics of Logic

Art History as the History of Formal Evolution

Art as it is shown through the history of art exists as a succession of styles. It is presented as a series of pure and uniform formal units in which the later one is always better than the previous one. According to this theory, art is presented as ever bettering itself. This concept of art history is based on the following idealistic presumptions: 1) The idea of continuous amelioration of forms, change of one art form for another supposedly better one, presupposing the Hegelian idea that there exists a certain model into which the whole process leads. In other words if Baroque is more perfect than Renaissance, or Color Field than Abstract Expressionism, then there is supposed to exist one absolute ideal style to which the whole process of perfection aims; 2) The whole process occurs by merit of genius, or by creators of style who, independently of the socio-historical circumstances in which they live, infuse their masterpieces with divine inspiration. It is easy to see that the concept of art history as amelioration results in oppressive consequences. Primarily it justifies, even implies, the existence of exclusive criteria within each epoch which eliminate everything that differs from the dominant style. This idea justifies the existence of "totalitarian taste." After the geniuses establish the domination of a certain style, there is no longer any need for creative and independent individuals, only for an army of mannerists who have to confirm the dominant style by using the newest art technology and by creating multiplicity of variations of the same stylistic nature.

The idea of art history as consequent and linear evolution is only possible if all cases that don't fit in line with the dominating style cliché are overlooked and eliminated. (For instance, I'm sure that in Rococo there was at least one artist applying aesthetic principles close to Minimal art, but he remained unknown because the collective taste and sensibility weren't ready to accept his ideas.) This model of art history is only a reflection of general history because it reflects the ideas of Western man about his own history as a series of changes which through conflicts and struggles nevertheless result in so-called progress.

Style as a Form of Racism in Art

Style is made from numerous variations of the same conceptual formula. Style is the accumulation of the signs with different signifiers and the same signifieds. If, according to [Roland] Barthes, language consists of the Plane of Expression and the Plane of Content, then we can say that in the language of art, numerous variations of the Plane of Expression correspond to the same Plane of Content. In other words, there is a great discrepancy between the production of new forms and new substances. If art is a cognitive process realized through the creation of new logical relationships, then the period in which style proliferates is a period of cognitive stagnation because the same conceptual formula is filled with numerous different, but generically identical, elements. For instance, once the principle of monochrome (the surface of the painting is entirely covered with one homogeneous color) is defined, then all later variations (use of different colors, change of format) are without any cognitive value. Art activity that occupies itself with formal variations of the same conceptual formula is analogous to the work of "cosmetic" industrial designers who every season invent new forms for technically unchanged products. The purpose of both activities is to stimulate the consumer's appetite. The surplus of monochromatic paintings on the contemporary art market could be compared with production of the newest models of an electric blender which is always basically the same, but it comes out every year with a new look and more speeds. Artworks of this kind have a two-fold function: 1) They satisfy an increasing demand from the art market; (The resistance to which the pioneering works of the same kind were confronted with at the beginning, in the meantime, has given way to increasing acceptance.) 2) In the periods of cognitive stagnation in art production, they give the illusion of change. Variations of the same principle are presented with the help of the art-support systems under the guise of progress in the process of evolution. Giving an illusion of freedom of expression, this practice leaves only the possibility of formal change while eliminating almost any chance for consideration of new signifying systems. In this way the purity of style is assured. Style, in fact, is illustrative of the oppressive mentality of an epoch, i.e., it is a kind of aggression, a mental impotence which eliminates differences. Style is lack of tolerance, aggression against the plurality of art concepts in a given moment.

"Myth is the Best Investment"[1]

Formal Innovation: Macro and Micro Style

The theory of formal evolution based on the chronological homogeneity of styles imposes formal innovation as the supreme critical criterion while disregarding the essential concern of art—its role and place within the given socio-historical structure. According to the demand of the production of new forms, particular artworks are evaluated on the basis of identifying the artist's personal handwriting. Within the value system of art that we have today, stylistic uniqueness is the accepted trademark of a top-quality product. The form of this trademark has evolved through the course of art history, from artist to artist, but its significance in our value system has remained unchanged since the Renaissance. The fact that the criteria of visual recognition of an artist's handwriting, i.e., criterion of formal novelty, survived numerous changes of aesthetics and art technologies, which happened in the last five hundred years, shows that in that period the social interpretation of art has not basically changed.

The idea of art as a series of formal innovations encourages aesthetic excess. But the aesthetic excess or the divergence from established style is not really as revolutionary an act as we used to think. It only feeds the myth of the evolution of art, leaving untouched all essential questions about the position and function of art. This claim is best proved by the rapid integration of recent avant-garde movements in the cultural establishment. For instance, the recurring mistake of the twentieth-century avant-garde is that, although they proclaimed to be anti-esthetic in their manifestos, it became clear later they were in fact only introducing new visual statements. That attempt to free themselves of aesthetic failed because the new criterion of beauty was quickly adapted and that which was not thought to be retinal became a model for new art production, an optical measure of an art epoch. This shows that these anti-aesthetic attempts carried within themselves antitheses that could later be easily manipulated for commodity purposes. They remain only as a symptom of a situation which was mature enough to take this problem into consideration, but fell short of successfully solving it.

The process of assimilation of a new art occurs more or less always in the same way. The conceptual contents of it are often forgotten, and formal/decorative aspects are emphasized instead. The examples known to us from previous art movements are only the vestiges of their philosophical standpoints. That which is recorded and glorified as art of the past is no more than a remnant of past art ideologies. The conceptual content of an artwork is reduced or completely ignored by the metalanguage of art (art history and art criticism): only decorative and formal components of the work are considered. This is actually a process of eliminating the revolutionary potential of art in favor of its peripheral and easily manipulated characteristics—decorativeness. The tendency to present art history as a formal evolution alienates art from its potential for ideological clarity and turns it into a means for ideological manipulation. The critical/analytical potential of art producers is weakened and made ineffective by irrelevant criteria, namely, by insistence on personal handwriting. When an artist is identified with a particular visual formula, he is expected to adhere to it. Such an adherence to a particular expression might be said to produce a micro, or personal constriction that reflects a larger cultural oppression through style. The myth of formal evolution is structured on a series of easily recognizable signs, and the artist is expected to confine his production to this clear image. On the other hand, the critical and selective capacity of the recipients of art messages (consumers of art) is disturbed by their assumptions: 1) that art is sacred activity; and 2) that the art object is a precious thing in itself. The support system and metalanguage of art in its present form has the exclusive role of promoting the art object as fetish, i.e., to insure its magical status. Viewed this way the art object is justified solely as an end in itself, whereas it could be thought of as a means of transferring new models of consciousness through its catalytic power.[2]

Two Logical Spaces

The following analysis refers to analogies and the differences between 1) the language of this work—$E_1R_1C_1$; and 2) the language which is used by the power structure for communicating messages of special significance—ERC. By using examples of analogous signs from ERC and $E_1R_1C_1$ systems, the mechanism of this work will be shown.

Sign A (from ERC system): Monument to Alfred Nobel
Signifier A—Bust cast in bronze on a marble pedestal
Signified A—A person of special social importance

Sign A_1 (from $E_1R_1C_1$ system): Monument to Alberto Vieri
Signifier A_1—Bust cast in bronze on a marble pedestal
Signified A_1—Casual passerby

ERC is a language of primarily repressive nature because it attempts to impose and perpetuate a particular system of values. $E_1R_1C_1$ is the language of this work that attempts to "defunctionalize" the signs from the ERC system.

ERC System

Two groups of signs can be distinguished here:

> *1) Signs which promote contemporary subjects because their signifieds are present-day personalities/ideas.*
> *2) Signs which verify history because their signifieds are certain selected individuals from the past.*

The function of the signs from both groups is repressive with regard to the recipient of the message, who is expected to accept it in a certain way, not questioning its credibility and source, i.e., the motives of the groups that are sending it. Starting from the premise that individual creativity is directly limited by the amount of data available, the reduction of data by a selective mechanism of both history and the power structure in turn restricts the creative development of the individual. Criteria are passed on by means of the educational system, which does not give the individual the opportunity and freedom to make his own judgments. The whole concept of education and culture is based on the obedience to authority and hierarchy of values. One of the liabilities of that cultural concept is that it says that the evolution of art took place through the divine attributes and contributions of certain geniuses and epoch heroes. This linear and reductive version of the history of culture is built on personal mythologies which are fostered by isolating elements from the artists' private lives. Monuments and memorial plaques ("lived here," "worked here," etc.) are only the means by which the status of genius is created, and their function is to instill a passive awe in the masses. The result is that the consciousness of those for whom the message is intended is dulled into passive acceptance of the cultural authorities of the past. All figures presented via the historical media are accepted a priori as genuinely relevant. "In fact, what allows the reader to consume myth innocently is that he does not see it as a semiological system but as an inductive one. Where there is only equivalence, he sees a kind of casual process: the signifier and signified have, in his eyes, a natural relationship. This confusion can be expressed otherwise: any semiological system is a system of facts; myth is read as factual system, whereas it is but a semiological system."[3] The complete dulling of the individual's critical judgment is achieved by an entire system of repressive signs: Monument and memorial plaques are not innocent reminders of cultural values of the past, but a carefully constructed mythical system which conceals the chaotic reality of the past. Its function is to do away with the contradiction between this reality and the ordered image of the past; the differences, conflicts, and contradictions which characterize a period are disregarded in this system, in which only clear, pure signs are presented, which constitute a harmonious record of the past.

The repressiveness of the signs from group 2 is indirect compared with the effect of the signs from group 1: whereas in the case of contemporary persuasive messages, the recipient offers resistance, in the case of historical means of persuasion, not even the minimum of critical reserve remains due to the complete lack of interest and access on the part of the victim.

For instance, there are few people who would understand that the memorial plaque on [Hector] Berlioz's house is an attack on free thought and judgment, while most of us would be skeptical toward overly commercial or political messages. However, this in no way means that signs from the second group are less repressive. Take, for instance, the already mentioned example of the marble plaque on Berlioz's house on which the sentence "Berlioz lived here" is written. The basic system is linguistic, but substituting the linguistic code for the message of its presentation gives us the statement: "Genius lived here." It means that the implied message of all places without a memorial plaque is "A genius never lived here."

$E_1R_1C_1$ System
Method
A person chosen by chance, because of an accidental meeting on the street, becomes the subject/content of the following stereotyped models of presentation which, in our civilization, are recognized as the transmitters of especially significant messages.

> *Large photo-portrait hung in a public place*
> *Monument erected in a public place*
> *Poster displayed on a billboard*
> *Banner carried on the street*
> *Memorial plaque on a facade*
> *A cocktail party in honor of Mr. X*
> *A dinner party in honor of Mr. Y*
> *Poster on the bus*
> *Street sign*
> *Historical group photograph*

Chance
Chance is taken as the basic principle of choice, as an alternative to the selective mechanism of the power structure. The intention of the work is not to make the accidentally chosen people famous; the casual passerby only embodies the principle of chance, one choice from a broad spectrum of possibilities. This is not a pseudo-humanistic story about the glorification of the "little man" (the notion "little man" is already discriminating and comes from class-alienated consciousness), but the casually chosen subjects of these works represent undefined possibilities. This method, in its opposition to so-called historical ways of imparting value, is used to provoke doubt in existing criteria. Chance as a characteristic of disorder can shake the image of the established order of things.

Formal Nonoriginality
Principle of Ready Aesthetics
In a formal sense, this work is completely nonoriginal. There is not one element on the basis of which the artist's personal handwriting could be identified. This work does not wish to contribute, in any sense, to the formal evolution of art. It takes already existing forms *from* and *outside* the context of art and gives them new content.

This is in no way the principle of the readymade, which is based on the change of context. (For instance, a portrait cast in bronze existed for centuries as an art form and as a means of glorification.) This means that the technological spectrum of this work is several thousand years old, from a bust in bronze to photography on canvas and therefore cannot be identified with particular media/technology. Contrary to the art in an era of technological boom (from the beginning of the twentieth century up to now) which based its originality on introducing new materials/technologies in art, this work uses already existing art materials and forms. This principle could be defined as a juxtaposition of ready aesthetics. This work does not exist as a formal novelty, but exclusively as a new semantic structure, and consequently is not noticeable. Furthermore, it is almost invisible at first glance. Since it faithfully imitates the real forms of historical glorification, it can't be noticed without additional information. All this demonstrates that the work deals exclusively with problems not connected with formal novelty and visual appearance. This reduction of the formal is not to narrow the spectrum of creativity, but rather to call attention to the polysemic nature of the image.

Artificial Myth or Aesthetic of Logic

As it has been shown, the signifiers of the signs in the system ERC and $E_1R_1C_1$ are analogous: the signifieds are essentially different. And it is precisely on the similarity of forms that this work functions. When the person is confronted with the signs from the system $E_1R_1C_1$ he would react in the same way because he is used to passively and automatically accepting the messages of the similar signs from the system ERC. It is just this conditioned reflex, this passive acceptance, that forms one of the basic elements of the work, i.e., the first phase. The next phase is correction of this intentionally provoked incorrect conclusion, which is achieved through additional information provided by galleries, museums, the press, etc. The effect is that every subsequent encounter with the signs from the system ERC results in a questioning of their signifieds. When the conventional relation of the signifier and signified is once shaken, the sign ceases to function "normally." The actual purpose of the work is to defunctionalize the signs from the system ERC by means of their "mistaken" replicas from system $E_1R_1C_1$. In this way suspicion regarding the intentions of the myth is cast by means of the myth itself, and the one-way communication on which it is based (from myth-makers to consumers) is exchanged for a reversible, two-way communication. Instead of only one way of reading the signs from system ERC, this work intends to provoke doubt regarding the value system they are based on. Instead of passive acceptance of uniform values offered by tradition and history, the work aims to create a new situation: the establishment of very open and flexible individual criteria which could permit the coexistence of different and often contradictory values.

This text is written in collaboration with Nena Dimitrijević.

Notes

1. Braco Dimitrijević, lecture given at University College, Slade School of Art, London, November 1974.
2. Braco Dimitrijević, "Just as a piano is not music, a painting is not art" (catalogue of the Museum of Contemporary Art, Zagreb, February 1973).
3. Roland Barthes, *Mythologies* (New York: Hill and Wang, 1972), p. 131.

Written in 1976. Originally published in *Tractatus Post Historicus* (Tubingen: Edition Dacić, 1977).

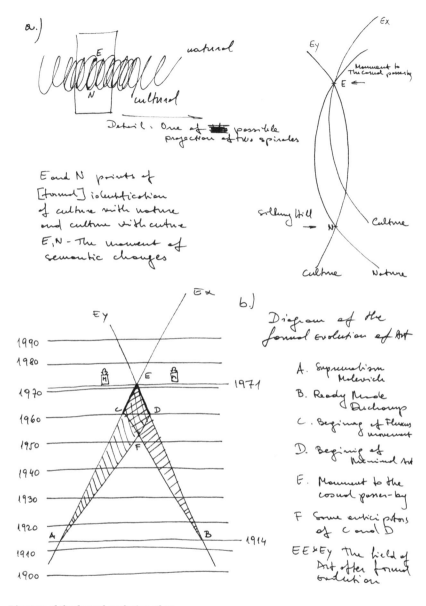

Diagram of the formal evolution of art

A—Suprematism: Malevich

B—Readymade: Duchamp

C—The beginning of the Fluxus movement

D—The beginning of Minimal art

E—Monument to the casual passerby

F—Some anticipators of C and D

CEDF—Overlapping BCE (the spirit of Conceptualism) with ADE (cold Minimalist presentation), we get the field of so-called Conceptual art.

CE—Development of Conceptual art

DE—Development of Minimal art

ABF—Movements of relative importance for Conceptual art. Left from AEEy, and right from BEEx: activity which imitates art.

EExEy—The field of art after formal evolution.

Braco Dimitrijević. *The Casual Passerby I Met at 11:28 A.M., London*. 1972. Poster displayed on bus, 32 × 24" (81.3 x 61 cm). Tate Gallery, London

Braco Dimitrijević. *This Could Be a Work of Braco Dimitrijević.* Photograph. Courtesy the artist

Braco Dimitrijević. *The Casual Passerby I Met at 1:49 P.M., Venice*, 1976. Photograph on canvas, 15 × 12' (4.6 × 3.6 m). Courtesy Sperone Gallery, New York

Braco Dimitrijević. *This Could Be a Work of Braco Dimitrijević.* Photograph. Courtesy the artist

Braco Dimitrijević. *The Casual Passerby I Met at 4:15 P.M., Turin*. 1973. Bronze head on marble pedestal, height 8' (2.4 m).
Gian Enzo Sperone, Rome-New York

Braco Dimitrijević. *This Could Be a Work of Braco Dimitrijević*. Photograph. Courtesy the artist

ANDRZEJ TUROWSKI

Andrzej Turowski is currently a professor of contemporary art at the Université de Bourgogne. He is a leading specialist on Constructivist art in Poland and Eastern Europe, and he frequently writes about Polish contemporary art as well.

In this essay, Turowski concentrates on the artist Krzysztof Wodiczko, who was born in 1943 in Warsaw and graduated from the Academy of Fine Arts there in 1968 with a degree in industrial design. Among Wodiczko's early work was Vehicle *(1973), which consists of a platform with wheels that were set in motion by someone walking back and forth on top of it. Some of his best-known productions include his* Public Projections, *which began in the 1980s and consist of large-scale slide and video projections of politically charged imagery on the facades of public buildings and monuments. Wodiczko is currently head of the Interrogative Design Group at the Media Lab at MIT in Cambridge, Massachusetts.*

Turowski's essay demonstrates how Polish art intersected with political reality from the 1950s through the 1980s. Wodiczko's work epitomizes such a confluence since it abandons formalism and modernist utopias in favor of ideologically informed art.

Krzysztof Wodiczko and Polish Art of the 1970s

In a 1977 interview, Krzysztof Wodiczko stated his conviction that "artists are concerned with the exploration of reality, [and] they even attempt to transform it." They are not producers of beauty, he continued. If they were, they would just be "narcotizing society by means of art."[1] His position was closely related to the tradition of revolutionary Constructivism, with which he was becoming acquainted at the time through exposure to work by the Soviet artists Vladimir Tatlin and Aleksandr Rodchenko and the Polish artists Katarzyna Kobro, Władysław Strzeminski, and Mieczysław Szczuka. A standpoint such as this situated his investigations squarely within the realm of social reality. As Strzeminski had written in the 1930s: "Instead of decorating life with pictures, contemporary art can become an organization of the processes of collective life."[2] Today it may seem simplistic to attempt a search for deeper structural affinities between revolution in the arts and in politics. Still, one must concede that when an artist's functioning is based on a critical analysis of reality, it may be viewed as an intervention in public life; and thus it bears all the characteristics of revolutionary activity. In this sense, it is not aesthetic structures but artistic and political strategies that vie with each other to establish a critical or an affirmative judgment and appropriation of reality. Avant-garde utopias and ideologies of power may be seen as the modernist precursors of this state of affairs. With these considerations in mind, I would say that it was a process of historical reflection, undertaken in the context of Poland in the 1970s, that introduced Krzysztof Wodiczko to his present mode of work.

I once defined *ideosis* as the space in which dominant political options hold sway over individual choices.[3] It really does not matter whether this dominance is justified by "historical necessity," by "reasons of state," by a "common understanding," or by a "proper goal." What is important is that these justifications are formulated from the position of a political power that aims to subsume the decisions of individuals.

Krzysztof Wodiczko. *Vehicle* (1971–73). Warsaw, 1972. Courtesy the artist and Galerie Lelong, New York

From the end of World War II until the upheavals of the 1980s, Polish art was subject to the constant pressure of just such an ideosis. Thus a correct appreciation of the attitudes that the art of this era produced and the values it represented cannot be limited to reflections concerning the Polish, or even to a universal, artistic tradition. Even assuming that full cultural independence can only be an illusion, the essential question is the extent to which political power seeks, and manages, to subordinate culture to its own aims. In postwar Poland, political power held culture in its monopolistic sway for many years, but the means implemented to uphold this monopoly varied over time.

In the so-called culture of Socialist Realism in Poland during the 1950s, the position assigned to the artist was that of an object. The aim was the total degradation of his social role. The artist was compelled to choose between nega-tive options — to abandon his artistic position or dissimulate it. The only posi-tive alternative that remained was to take on the role of the political activist who accepted the idea and form of realism, as defined by the authorities. Artists thus were either turned into political agitators merely carrying out decisions made by the political ideologues, or they were led to abandon all public activity.

The end of Stalinism and the political evolution of Poland in the second half of the 1950s put the political condition of the artist into a new light. A public dis-cussion on culture was generated by Władyslaw Gomułka (who had just been named first secretary of the Communist party),[4] but it was a discussion that had its roots entirely in the Stalinist period and that, significantly, focused on the tra-ditional Marxist opposition between realistic and abstract pictorial styles. The first steps were to restore to the artist the right to manifest his position openly, and to outline the boundaries within which the artistic consciousness might intersect with political tactics. This was not always an easy task for the authorities, who had no intention of disclosing their real motivations. For that reason, the debate was quite soon reduced to art itself and the formal limits of abstraction. This debate obviously enlivened artistic life, and certain individual works went beyond purely Polish problems to enter the realm of the universal problems of art. From that point on, official policy in the cultural sphere was based on limiting, stimulating, or appropriating already existing or emerging means of representation and containing them within the orbit of sanctioned ideologies. It no longer imposed definite artistic formulas.

In Polish artistic life of the 1960s the discussion of modernism reached full maturity, a development that manifested itself in a universalization of artistic attitudes. In the realm of painting this led to the consolidation of the formalism of abstract art in all its variations. Although initially tied in with the post-Stalinist breakthrough, by the beginning of the 1960s abstraction had become a mass convention, undergoing a process of stereotyping. From a political standpoint, it could be justified on the basis of the aesthetic theory of "a realism without bounds,"[5] a philosophically inspired attempt to find existentialist elements in Marxist doctrine. Among other things, this theory vindicated the concept of "creative individuality" and initially enabled the political authorities to use abstract art as a means to legitimize their own role. On the one hand, the geometricism of abstractionism was assimilated by industrial design. On the other hand, the painterly base of the *Informel* made it possible to launch the "Polish school" of the poster, which had its roots in expressionist pictorialism.

In Poland, the negative impact of Socialist Realism was (and continues to be) so immense that the only response on a major scale to the model of culture imposed in the 1950s was refusal. Consequently, all vestiges of realist doctrine were erased, without any critical revision, from the collective social memory by the formalism of abstract art and, later, by the self-referentiality of Conceptual art — a development that greatly suited the authorities. The events of 1968 in Poland brought no fundamental change in this respect.[6] Considered by society as having been manipulated by the government, these events brought about a superficial critique in the field of culture, but opposition was limited to the interference of censorship in the national heritage. The revolt, initially aimed against the rule of the Communist party bureaucracy, gave rise instead to a campaign of anti-Semitism (a campaign that had been planned as an element in the factional struggle for power within the Party) along with a governmentally manipulated wave of resentment against the intelligentsia. There had been no fundamental questioning of cultural institutions and policies or of the social functions of art. The role of the bourgeois tradition, of the avant-garde, of ideology, and of artistic utopias had not been contested. Thus, after 1968, artists continued to think in terms of the antinomy of realism and formalism (although realism already had suffered a total defeat) in the sense defined by Györgi Lukács.[7]

The late 1960s and early 1970s was a period of turmoil in the arts, the result of the confused political situation surrounding the ouster in 1970 of the Gomułka regime. During the first half of the 1970s, the reform government of Edward Gierek attempted to take advantage of this situation in the arts.[8] Using an official art critic as a mouthpiece, the Party expressed its tactical doubts concerning the opposition between "realism and the avant-garde, which — as we have read in a programmatic statement — need not necessarily be a radical one."[9] While proposing an "open" point of view of all cultural phenomena, this rhetoric in fact advocated administrative control of the "social tasks of realism" and claimed the right to judge "the avant-garde's capacity to reassess the tasks it set for itself."[10] This fundamental encroachment upon creative freedom was due to characteristics of the Polish art scene at the time. The new figurative movement in painting, drawing, and the graphic arts was developing a narrative form of art. In light of the political tensions of the early 1970s, the verism of this art form could all too easily have taken a critical form, directed against the Party as well. For this reason, the attempt was made to encourage the Polish version of Pop art (after first fallaciously identifying it with the avant-garde), to the extent that it could be institutionally controlled. What is more, the new Gierek government, with its "consumer society" policy, was in need of a "modern" aesthetic wrap — and all forms of art that were related to mass culture could be useful in this context. From a political point of view, it was quite unimportant that a form of art that was born of a critique of mass culture became, in Poland, its decorative surrogate. Of course artists responded to this attempt to realign the entire avant-garde under a realist banner with increased "anti-realistic" attitudes. Thus Conceptual art, which was just developing in the early 1970s and had come out decisively on the side of the avant-garde by appealing to the well-known opposition between realism and formalism, turned out to be not so much a critique of formalism as a rationalized version of it. This turn of events led the Party to modify its strategy again, although the use of the old blueprint greatly facilitated that task.

To understand this process in full it is necessary to return for a moment to the 1960s and outline another trend in Polish art. By this I mean the extra-pictorial radicalization of the avant-garde, grounded in artistic tradition and so significant for the 1960s — the entire realm of Happenings, events, and environments. This trend presented the Party with a difficult political problem. For these manifestations did not fall within the theoretical definition of realism. Instead, they often took place outside the gallery-and-exhibition structure and were therefore not always easy to control. From the very start, then, the authorities, unable to dominate this form of art, attempted to limit its influence. A social motivation also was found for certain of these manifestations, which might take place under the sponsorship of large industrial enterprises (in the name of worker patronage) in the course of state-organized artists' seminars and retreats. Other events, those that could be circumscribed by the official formula "shaping the environment aesthetically" (i.e., that could be defined within an already controlled urban space), also met with a certain measure of approval. I mention this because the first generation of Polish Conceptualists was recruited from this circle of artists, a fact that does not cast doubt upon the theory of the formalist roots of Polish Conceptualism but that somewhat complicates its definition. I would like to emphasize that it was precisely this formalism that made it so easy for many artists who were supposedly working "beyond the realm of art" to pass to the level of a purely tautological quest within the framework of art itself.

While the government, through its new policy of the 1970s, loudly proclaimed "artistic pluralism," it was giving silent support to purely formalist works — in spite of the doctrine of realism, which was still officially defended at the time. All of this fit in perfectly well with the slogans about the modernity of the state and its politics, a further legitimation of the government's cultural liberalism. This liberalism also differentiated Polish cultural policy from that of other countries in the Eastern bloc. One should, however, not assume that the Party had abandoned its claim to ideosis. Conceptual art could be of use to the Party only if it gave up its acuity of expression. Consequently, when dealing with this tendency, it was never the Party's aim to limit its meanings (since these referred to art itself) but to deprive them of their conceptual values and their inherent analytical potential. It is indeed no paradox that, in their cultural policies, Polish political authorities tended to maintain the formalist status with which the artists themselves had endowed Conceptual art.

In this context, a significant trait of the new policy was its acceptance of the avant-garde's "differentiated modernity." This acceptance took the form of sponsorship of numerous exhibitions and debates, usually conducted under the patronage of state-controlled socio-political organizations. Conditions for apparently independent artistic choices were created, with a preference given to those of a commercial nature. One could say that what most characterized these years was the political acceptance of "modernist" art that made use of avant-garde devices, formulas, and categories but that already had been tamed and deprived of its analytical and critical artistic value.

Although behind the times ideologically, the cultural policy of the Party was, in practice, effective. It confirmed the theses of the philosophers of revolt of the 1960s, such as Herbert Marcuse, who claimed that the annihilation of the autonomy of art (and thereby of its utopia) and the basing of autonomy within strictly formal categories leads to a paralysis of the oppositional power of art. The effect of this paralysis is that works of art may finally be assimilated within the bounds of utilitarian values and transformed to serve the ends of mass propaganda and commerce. In Poland, where there had been no true revolt in the 1960s, few artists were aware of the authorities' intentions. Moreover, the opposition between realism and formalism there had never been reconciled. This opposition turned into a long-lasting component of the negative tradition of Socialist Realism in Polish culture—and was shrewdly exploited by the authorities. Taking these two facts into consideration, one must conclude that official policy in the 1970s succeeded in implementing the cultural policy of the first post-Stalinist years to a notable degree. Works of art were almost totally deprived of their artistic and social identity, yet the social role of artists was not called into question. For this reason, the emergence of Solidarity in 1980 and the imposition of martial law the next year by the government under General Wojciech Jaruzelski left Polish art totally disarmed.[11] It took several years, under conditions in which political opposition was widespread, to elaborate, in Neo-Dadaist form, possible responses to the situation of martial law.

This is the context in which Krzysztof Wodiczko's work in Poland in the 1970s must be viewed. One might suggest that his first artistic questions concerned the creative subject and the problem related to it: "How is one to create?" Within the general ideological mystification surrounding him, along with his everyday experience of urban space, the question fairly imposed itself. The metaphysical dimension—the artistic "I" ("he who creates")—was a subsequent stage of the artist's interest in the environment. Where are the boundaries of the artist's intervention in the world to be found? Which fragment of the world is accessible to the cognition of the artist? Two of his earliest exhibitions, *Personal Instrument* (1971) (stemming from a work of 1969) and *Self-Portrait* (1973), can be seen as the expression of his dealing with further problems. The instrument that Wodiczko constructed with the help of the technologies available to him was exclusively intended to enable the artist to "capture sounds and light" from the environment. The ultimate and ambiguous achievement of this performance work was virtuosity — a questionable goal from the creative point of view. This is why in *Self-Portrait,* a photographic representation of the artist as Narcissus the Creator, seen gazing at his own reflection in a mirror placed on the floor beneath the photograph, Wodiczko questioned the sphere of private creation by the artist engrossed with himself and caught within his own aestheticism. He concluded that the attempt must be made to abandon the egoistic position of the artist situated at the center of creation. Genuine creativity is public dialogue, and the shaky balance between the interlocutors in this dialogue is the result of the play of arguments, rhetorical modes, positions, and strategies.

This attempt to comprehend the laws that govern dialogue led Wodiczko to analyze the structure of artistic language, whose form has always defined itself through illusion. *Drawing of a Stool* (1974), an analytical drawing of a few lines creating the illusion of an object; *Ladder* (1975), an attempt to construct the object itself according to the laws of illusion; and finally, *Line* (1976), a minimalist reduction of a line to its concept, were works that moved Wodiczko to dispute the value of all arguments about illusion in art that ignore the concept of reality as a historically and an ideologically defined phenomenon. From this point of view, there was a breakthrough in *References* (1977), an exhibition in which the illusionistic "law of vision" exploited in art was replaced by an ideological discourse. In the exhibition, horizontal, vertical, and diagonal lines were superimposed on images from a slide projector: stock political photographs, fragments of official architecture, and works of art defined the message within categories of domination and rule.

To understand better the importance of this exhibition and its relationship to other works by the artist, let us turn to the first *Vehicle,* constructed in 1972. Although built with an almost engineer-like precision, it was not characterized by technological perfection. In fact, it bore greater kinship to Vladimir Tatlin's fantastic *Letatlin* (1929–32) — the impractical, human-powered "air bicycle" Tatlin hoped would become an object of daily use by the masses — than to the shining surfaces and aerodynamic shapes of present-day high-speed vehicles. Tested on the streets of Warsaw — "perfectly functional," one might say — it fulfilled its function in that the "stationary movement" of its author, who walked up and down in the vehicle, produced the "forward movement" of the entire vehicle. Through its allusion to function and progress, *Vehicle* was a caricatured version of both the grounded Icarus of Tatlin's utopia and the socially useful machines produced by the Bauhaus. One may well see in this work the origin of what was to become Wodiczko's primary ongoing focus: the critical project as artistic action. Of course, *Vehicle* should not be viewed in isolation, any more than his other work should. Understood as a whole, his output elucidates a whole series of problems. In the 1970s his work was typified by a process of reflection on the structure of language and on history. As he made clear in statements at the time, Wodiczko did not seek any essentialist dimension in history, but he strove to disclose through his work (although he did not reduce it to) the history of subordination, expropriation, and domination. Although he did so openly only in the 1980s, he was, in the 1970s, already aware of this manipulation and attempted to make use of the "language of culture" that depicts the history of victories to reveal instead the history of barbarism. Wodiczko's vehicles, including his latest ones for homeless people, contribute to a general historical discourse from a critical point of view, a critique of history in which the concepts of function, progress, altruism, "the Other," security, and so on are seen as ideological components of the social vision of political power. In both his art and his historical and theoretical investigations, Wodiczko's attitude has enabled him to reject the game of appearances (illusion) by consistently disclosing the underlying fallacy (ideology).

At this point, the ideas apparent in the realized vehicles encountered the problems seen in Wodiczko's *References* and, from 1981 onward, in his public projections. Specifically, he situates the latter in that historical sphere in which construction and negation form a dialectical identity. "Universal history should be constructed and negated," the late German philosopher Theodor Adorno wrote. "In the face of past and future catastrophes it would be cynical to maintain that a blueprint of the world, aiming at improvement, manifests itself in history and organizes it. On the other hand, one cannot for this reason negate the unity which binds the discontinuous, chaotic moments and phases of history and which since the subjection of nature has passed to the rule over people and finally to the subjugation of their inner nature. There is no universal history that leads from savagery to humanism. But there is one which leads from the sling to the megaton bomb. It ends with a total threat to organized people by organized humanity, that is with the very essence of discontinuity."[12] In this sense Wodiczko's work, seen as a whole (with its roots in the 1970s), is not, strictly speaking, a political statement. He has never abandoned the social role of artist and accepted the characteristics that define it. He is not afraid of being ideological, which in essence today means the abandoning of utopias and a concurrent penetrating intervention into the "historicity" of such concepts as power, freedom, coercion, and poverty.

In the Poland of the 1970s, Wodiczko was one of a handful of artists who viewed historic and artistic problems in the critical perspective described here. In the 1977 interview quoted at the outset of this essay, he expressed disagreement with the professors at Polish art schools, stressing that, by situating their reflections outside the contemporary world, they were unconsciously situating themselves outside history. "Suspended in 'extra-temporal art' they claim to have contact with its 'spirit,' and they have power and position — which always have magic. But the issue here is not art but position and consequently the preservation of current institutional structures."[13] It is therefore no wonder that in his work of that decade Wodiczko sought a different tradition than the formalist one for Polish art. To a certain extent, he found what he was looking for in the writings of Władysław Strzeminski. That highly influential Polish Constructivist defined the history of visuality as the point where art (formalism) and reality (realism) intersect. This, in its most general outline, is the thesis one can draw from Strzeminski's 1948 book *The Theory of Vision*. A consequence of the modernist "zero degree" of Unistic painting, his theory attempted to capture history through the prism of the "rationalized view" of reality, by means of which successive social strata strove to gain power or maintain it. Seeing, the "post-Unistic" Strzeminski would have said, is the history of domination and deception. "There is no one absolute realism," he wrote, "no realism as such. But there is such a thing as concrete realism, conditioned by given historical relations. Under different historical conditions, this very same realism ceases to be a method of disclosing reality and becomes a means of falsifying and masking it."[14]

Krzysztof Wodiczko finds the roots of his present work in his questioning of the Polish cultural ideology of the 1970s and, in a wider context, in the ethos of the Left, which is itself deeply rooted in the intellectual thought and social and artistic activity of the twentieth-century avant-garde.

Notes

1. The interview, entitled "Jestem za Akademia" ("I Am for the Academy"), appeared in the newspaper *Sztandar Młodych (The Young People's Banner)* 184 (8487), August 4, 1977, unpaginated.
2. Władysław Strzeminski, "Sztuka nowoczesna w Polsce" ("Modern Art in Poland"), in Jan Brzekowski et al., *O sztuce nowoczesnej (On Modern Art)* (Łodz: Wyd; Tow: Bibliofilow, 1934), p. 92.
3. Andrzej Turowski, "L'Idéose polonaise: La Politique culturelle du pouvoir communiste en Pologne, 1945–1981" ("Polish Ideosis: The Cultural Politics of Communist Power in Poland, 1945–1981"), *Ligeia* (Paris), no. 1 (1988), p. 30.
4. Gomułka was head of the Polish Communist Party (PZPR) from 1956 to 1970. Under one-party rule, which lasted until mid-1989, the government was subordinated to the Central Committee of the Communist party and its first secretary.
5. Roger Garaudy, *D'un réalisme sans rivages (Of a Realism without Shores)* (Paris: Libraire Pion, 1963) and (Warsaw: Czytelnik, 1967; Polish edition).
6. In March 1968 students at Warsaw University, and then at universities throughout Poland, stood up to defend political and artistic freedom and to oppose censorship. Strikes and violent demonstrations lasted for several months. As a result, brutally repressive measures were taken against both students and the intelligentsia.
7. Lukács put forward this definition in his essay "The Ideological Foundations of Avant-Gardism," the Polish translation of which first appeared in the Communist party publication *Zeszyty teoretyczno-polityczne (Theoretical-Political Notes)*, nos. 9 and 10 (1957), pp. 41–46.
8. Gierek utilized the mass discontent stemming from a stagnant economy and from Gomułka's bloody repression of the Gdańsk shipyard strikes of 1970 to rise to the position of first secretary of the Polish Communist Party in 1971. Aided by Western credits, the new government was able for a short time to raise the standard of living. This period was followed by a deep economic crisis, which led to another wave of strikes, to the formation of Solidarity in 1980, and to Gierek's removal from power the next year.
9. Krzysztof Kostyrko, "Realizm i awangarda" ("Realism and the Avant-Garde"), *Sztuka,* no. 1 (1974), p. 2.
10. Ibid.
11. Jaruzelski, long Poland's minister of defense, was named Party First Secretary early in 1981. He introduced martial law in December of that year in an effort to break up political opposition and Solidarity. In 1989, by agreement between Solidarity and the Communist party, he was made president of the country. He resigned in 1991, clearing the way for postwar Poland's first free and universal election, in which Lech Wałesa was chosen president.
12. Theodor Adorno, *Negative Dialectics* (Frankfurt am Main: Suhrkamp, 1966), p. 440.
13. See note 1.
14. Władysław Strzeminski, "Realism w malarstwie" ("Realism in Painting"), *Wieś,* no. 47 (1948), p. 6.

Written in 1992. Originally published as "Wodiczko and Poland in the 1970s" in the exhibition catalogue *Public Address: Krzysztof Wodiczko* (Minneapolis: Walker Art Center, 1992).

BORIS GROYS

Boris Groys was born in 1947 in East Berlin and studied mathematics and philosophy at the University of Leningrad. He became an important member of unofficial art circles in Moscow and was one of the first interpreters of Ilya Kabakov's work. He emigrated to Germany in 1981 and is currently professor of aesthetics, art history, and media theory at the Zentrum für Kunst und Medientechnologie in Karlsruhe, Germany, and rector of the Akademie der Bildenden Künste in Vienna. His 1988 book The Total Art of Stalinism *caused great controversy by linking Socialist Realism to the heritage of avant-garde artists in the Soviet Union.*

In this essay, Groys defines a distinctly Russian brand of Conceptual art and focuses on three artists—Lev Rubinstein, Ivan Chuikov, and Francisco Infante—and on the artist group Collective Actions. Although each of these artists approaches Conceptualism in a different manner, Groys argues that they all share a belief in probing a spiritual world that they access through the process of artmaking.

Moscow Romantic Conceptualism

However odd the juxtaposition of these two words may sound, I know of no better term than romantic conceptualism to describe the present development in the Moscow art field.

The word "conceptualism" may be understood in the narrower sense as designating a specific artistic movement clearly limited to place, time, and origin. Or, it may be interpreted more broadly by referring to any attempt to withdraw from considering artworks as material objects intended for contemplation and aesthetic evaluation. Instead, it should encourage solicitation and formation of the conditions that determine the viewer's perception of the work of art, the process of its inception by the artist, its relation to factors in the environment, and its temporal status. The rise of modernism or avant-garde art did away with direct cognitive reception of works of art as objects. At the end of the nineteenth century, artists and spectators alike began to doubt whether there was such a faculty as an inborn gift. The artist was creating things resembling other things. The very principle of resemblance was challenged. As it turned out, resemblance between objects mirrored analogous aspects in the lives of artists and their audiences. And it was a function of a general prereflective ground for judgment, shared by the artist and the viewer as members of one and the same community. But as soon as this was recognized, the unity fell apart. Artists became analysts: their analytic efforts were now aimed not at finding a similarity between the artwork as representation and the subject represented, but rather the distinction between artworks as extant objects and other objects existing in the world on an equal footing. The resemblance was perceived as a "contingency," and when the resemblance exceeded the realm of contingency it was always regarded as an experiment showing how far one might depart from similarity while yet remaining within the confines of art. Each successful experiment extended the boundaries of art and, or so it seemed, sharpened the demarcation between art and nonart. Previously, if the audience was enthusiastic, that meant the artists were on the right track; now, public disapproval was seen as proof that the approach was valid!

The crisis came to the fore when public indignation waned, and it was discovered that contingency didn't reach far. The contingency of resemblance became contingency of difference. That is to say, the contingency of resemblance between works of figurative art (and all arts are figurative) and the object depicted, based on a "natural" identity of artist and viewer, was transformed into a contingency of the distinction between artist and layman. The fact remains that, once this recognition has taken place everything else falls into line: the artist is capable of turning any object into a work of art.

And so it would appear that all was going well. Each artist did what he wanted, thereby expressing his personality, and everything was fine. But there are two objections to this view: Firstly, if pictorial truth had previously resided in resemblance, where was it now to be found? If it had passed over, along with contingency, into the artist's existence, then the question arises: what kind of existence is a true one? This very question casts doubt upon the artist's individuality. Secondly, while individuality is supposed to predominate, and does indeed predominate in works viewed synchronically, there is a logic that can be seen plainly in a succession of trends.

It was natural, in seeking a solution to this contradiction, to look at the question of how artworks function by comparison with other types of objects. Clearly, if art possesses some kind of truth, it is precisely at this point that it should be discovered. Here, however, as Hegel might say, Art comes into its concept; that is, it becomes "conceptual." True, Hegel himself held that, with attainment of Absolute Spirit (or the sphere of ideas or concepts), art disappears, because of its very nature, which is that of the actualization of the immediate. Yet if art subsists while having ceased to be direct, it is only for the reason that it has become a "concept." Again the question arises as to what happens to the immediate. Has it really been left behind once and for all? I think this is hardly the case, but the scope of the present essay will not allow for a detailed examination of the problem.

From what has been said so far, it is evident that Conceptual art by its very nature must be absolutely explicit. It should contain within itself the clear criteria of its existence as art. It must not imply any immediacy. The projected intent of such art must reach the mind of the viewer in a way that he could repeat it as if it were a scientific experiment. Though the knowledge and equipment may be lacking, it is always possible to do this in principle. A work of Conceptual art must embody the explicit prerequisites and principles of its origin, its communicability, and it must be able to convey these to the audience.

An artwork possesses that capability as far as it does not exclude the possibility of criticism. For a fairly long time, it was recognized that contemporary works of art were "incomprehensible" without a guiding hand from the critics. This meant that criticism had lost its original role as a meta-language and had taken over some of the functions of the language of proper art. Conceptual art is now reclaiming these functions.

There are different forms of transparency. In England and America, where Conceptual art originated, transparency meant the explicitness of a scientific experiment, clearly exposing the limits and the unique characteristics of our cognitive faculties. In Russia, however, it is impossible to paint a decent abstract picture without reference to the Holy light. The unity of collective spirit is still so very much alive in our country that mystical experience here appears quite as comprehensible and lucid as does scientific experience. And even more so. Unless it culminates in a mystical experience, creative activity seems to be of inferior worth. And this is essentially true to the extent that, where a certain level of understanding has been attained, it must be traversed. Along with religious mysticism, and related to it, we also find a definite sort of "lyrical" and "human" quality in art—an element assigned even to those artists who have happily left such things far behind.

The general tenor of emotional life in Moscow, thus forming a lyrical and romantic blend, still stands opposed to the dryness of officialdom. And this climate is propitious to the phenomenon of romantic and lyrical conceptualism—a phenomenon rather clearly discernible in the emotional atmosphere of the capital. I do not hesitate to call it conceptualism, notwithstanding the lyrical aspect, bearing in mind the basic essentials and remembering that the term has been applied to Yves Klein, a French artist who distinguished in the French manner between a world of pure dream and a world governed by earthly laws.

There are even more important reasons for using this term. During the 1970s, Western artists drew a line between conceptualism and the "analytical approach," on the one hand, and the rebellious mood of the 1960s on the other. In those days, art was regarded as the last forward-defense position held by the individual human being in his battle against a depersonalizing existence within the society. Belief in the unique status of the artist as a privileged person, and in his ability to rebuild life in keeping with the dictates of creative freedom, proved illusory. In the 1970s the collapse of this belief prompted conceptualists to cling to a notion of artistic creativity as belonging to a specific profession, possessing its own techniques, purposes and confines alongside other professions. Art acquired an operational definition: What art is will be evident when you can see what the artist does, how he does it, and how the results of his work interrelate with other objects in the world.

Nonetheless, this kind of positive-transparency approach to art presupposes a new form of academism. For it confronts the artist in his creative work with a certain extra-historical norm that is identified with the clearly demarcated boundaries of the profession or, as they say, of the media within which the artist operates. Romantic meta-physicism and other trends in art likewise have their ways of doing things. Furthermore, to each school belongs its particular usages in the field of perception, or interpretation. That is, the "romantic" view of art has its own facticity: reducing it to illusion amounts, above all, to closing one's eyes to the facts. Even if art of this type loses its immediate appeal, it still preserves its significance, which is to say, its relationships with the realms of action and cognition. It is important to clarify these relationships, without stressing as before, on totality and immediacy of perception, and to free ourselves from the evocation inherent in attempts to present a work of art as a revelation that speaks for itself.

The positivist view on art as an autonomous sphere of activity determined solely by an available historical tradition has always been alien to the Russian mind. We can hardly reconcile ourselves with the idea that art should be regarded as being simply the total sum of its techniques, and that its purpose has been lost sight of. Therefore, romantic conceptualism in Moscow not only testifies to the continued unity of the "Russian soul"; it also tries to bring to light the conditions under which art can extend beyond its own borders. It makes a conscious effort to recover and to preserve all that constitutes art as an event in the History of Spirit and which renders its own history uncompleted.

I shall now examine the work of several artists and poets who may be numbered — somewhat arbitrarily, to be sure — among the romantic conceptualists.

1. Lev Rubinstein

At first encounter, what strikes us about the texts of Lev Rubinstein is their resemblance to machine algorithms. And this is not only because they are written on perforated cards. The texts themselves are performatory. They shower the reader with stern instructions and they register irreversible events. They also contain descriptions. As in the case of real working algorithms, the texts are structured into descriptions and instructions. Generally speaking, descriptions in algorithms have no autonomous significance. No one expects them to do anything more than to provide information for continuing action. And they contain nothing more than that. Actions predominate over description, and the structure of the actions is determined by their sequence. This is how the algorithm-like texts of Lev Rubinstein look at first glance. The unity of the text is ascertained not by the unity of description or of the object being described, but rather by the unity of action — unverbalized and confined to working pauses. We get the impression that, from card to card, something is going on: something is blinking, unfolding, making a dull grinding noise, and altering the world around us.

As we go on reading, however, it dawns on us that something is not quite right with those stern instructions. And in the attempt to find out what exactly is wrong with them, we also down our reading somewhat and turn our attention to the description of those situations which the instructions are designed to act upon.

And now it becomes clear that they are not precise enough to serve as a basis for machine activity and at the same time they are too precise to serve as a basis for human action. They are not so much precise as they are subtle, refined and just plain romantic. Yes, romantic.

For example, in the "Catalogue of Innovations in Comedy" (September 1976) we read: "It is possible to discern the causes of various phenomena and not to tell anyone." "It is possible to look at one another with such keen watchfulness that this can become a rather exciting kind of game."

Yes, that is possible. That is indeed the way romantic heroes behave. They conceal their knowledge and they play exalted games with each other. Yet we know very well the price of that "possible." It exudes the horror of the impossible. If this romantic "possibility of being impossible" is broken up into isolated instructions, it loses the possibility of using the halo of the romantic hero's personality to inspire direct confidence as a desirable and indeterminate model for emulation. The performatory "it is possible," replacing description of the "hero who can" and with whom the reader unconsciously and in an illusory manner identifies, leads the reader to a knowledge of his own possibilities. Here we see a revelation of the inner mechanistic nature of romantic discourse as well as a challenge hurled at the reader: to take cognizance of the true measure of his participation in the romantic dream. The distance between "able to do it" and "able to read it" becomes evident.

In the text "That is All," the subjectivity that ascertains the world discovers its own romantic origins. This text is a sort of "Anti-Husserl." The description is given inside that space of language which is formed, as it were, by the language's own possibilities and to which no experience corresponds.

"That is All—an avalanche of forebodings, crashing down for no reason at all . . .

—the voice of longed-for repose, drowned out by other voices" and so on.

When we read a rarity of this type, the ease with which we can understand what is being said is in proportion to our utter bewilderment when we try to relate it to our own extra-literary experience. These descriptions are possible only in a world where literature exists as an autonomous sphere of linguistic development and functioning. Whereas Husserl sought to give a foundation to the word in purely subjective experience, here the subject faces a task that is transparent on the literary plane but cannot be carried out empirically.

We may say that here Lev Rubinstein, in the way he builds his definitions, is coming close to René Char. But René Char believed it possible to live in the world as defined by him. Rubinstein, on the other hand, leaves the question open: whether it is possible to live in that world or merely to read in it. Surely we cannot seriously suppose that we are capable of participating in "All of That" which

gets built
gets bound
analyzes
signifies
gets explained
originates
relates
gets more involved etcetera

Here, for all to see, there is an infinitude of findings, flagrantly contrasted with the finitude of existence and yet open to being read and understood. An infinitude of findings is romantic to begin with. And the internal infinitude of descriptive literary stereotypes grasped at a glance by the reader is likewise romantic, but an operator researcher cannot break it down into elementary components.

So what about those stern instructions? They have turned out to have no basis. They have not gained so much as a square inch of ground for justifiable action from the conquest of literary language-space. The only action forming an exception to this is that of reading. All of the instructions boil down to an order to read.

Thus, we find the following text ("New Entracte," 1975):
Read, beginning with the words
"At certain moments many resort to silence," etc. up to the words
"The author excels in silence."

So the reader reads and the author is silent. And further on in the same text we read:

"Turn the page"
or
"See below," written at the end of the page
or

— read the following:
"Things which have invaded the sphere of poetical perception become signs in a poetic sequence."

We now know the kind of algorithms we are dealing with. They are reading algorithms. The only activity in which we are given "all that" and in which the that-is-all becomes "it is possible" is reading: life is reading, life as existence in the impossible space of literary language. The pages are written out with effort, amid loud interjections by the author. "Read, turn the pages, read, turn the pages . . . " and the things become signs in a poetic sequence.

Performatory verbal acts reveal their illusory character and return to the text as pure literature, making nothing evident but the despair and the torment of reading. The literary text itself is impenetrable and transparent: it requires no interpretation. Hermeneutics has been replaced by an algorithm of reading. Understanding is attained by means of the effort it takes to turn the page. What is reading? It is turning the pages. The rest is obvious on its own terms. In the writing of Lev Rubinstein, the reading process uncovers its own active substratum, its nature as vital effort. The effort of reading is disclosed to be a principle of textual structure. The text is that which is performed in the reading of it: you turn the pages, you move your eyes, and you "imagine." While the romantic imagination occupies its rightful place at this point, in the pose of the person reading, it then begins once again to beckon in the endless distance of the reading effort that registers the text.

As the reading is, so is the writing. In the *Program of Works* (1975), no descriptions are offered, yet at the same time no instructions are issued on what to do. The *Program* sketches out the emptiness occupied by pure spontaneity, that is, by romantic subjectivity as such. And in this text we read:

> In the event that the realization of this or that point in the Program should be factually impossible, the verbal expression of these points is to be regarded as a special case of realization or as a fact of literary creation.

Actually, two imperatives are being equated here: to read and to write. Literature is endowed with being, with its own reality and with "realization" when another form of realization is "factually impossible" — in other words, always.

A text by Lev Rubinstein is both the syntax and the practice of the romantic, given in unity. The effort of reading and the effort of writing here appear as autonomous work engendering and organizing an independent reality. As cognizance of the practice of the romantic, these texts likewise lead beyond the boundaries of romantic conscience. And they return it to the finitude of its existence, to the state of being doomed to labor and to die, while at the same time they soberly set up the landmarks of those possibilities for its existence which are attainable through the factitious language of literature and are not attainable by any other road.

2. Ivan Chuikov

Ivan Chuikov is an artist who centers his attention on the problem of the correlation between illusion and reality. A picture, in the traditional sense of the term, is a thing which is not self-identical. It presents us with the spectacle of something different from itself; and so distinct is that presentation that the picture dissolves its own subjective being, as it were, in the object represented. This,

Ivan Chuikov. Untitled. 1977.
Oil on fiberboard, 41¾ × 44¹¹⁄₁₆"
(106 × 113.5 cm). Jane Voorhees
Zimmerli Art Museum, Rut-
gers, The State University of
New Jersey, The Norton and
Nancy Dodge Collection of
Nonconformist Art from the
Soviet Union

precisely, is the illusory nature of the picture as a work of fine art. The attempt to perceive things in their external aspect has always been tied to the attempt to know them by discovering their identities and differences. Modern science, however, has cut the ground under such attempts.

Behind the apparent external aspect of things, science has uncovered some-thing else — atoms, vacuum, energy, and, last but not least, the mathematical formula. The primordial contemplative perception of things has itself become an illusion, an illusion moreover that leads astray. The identical and the non-identical have lost their old connection to the similar and the dissimilar. The world of appearances has become the deceptive shroud of Maya, cast across the void or over matter as the case may be.

Under these circumstances, art has veered away from illusion, which it re-gards as a lie. Art has become analytical. The work of art has disclosed its own structure and its material presence in the world. Attention is now focused on what distinguishes the artwork from other things, rather than on the resem-blance to other things that it acquires by means of illusion — which is to say, at-tention has been directed to the constructive basis of the picture as an object that is simply there. This process gave rise to what we call avant-garde art.

Nonetheless, representation continued to be representation, and this means that art did not lose its links with illusion. Discovering the laws of an empirical world, science destroyed the visible world and accomplished its disintegration, only to assert thereafter the identity of its findings with the primordial form. Ex-perience, trying to find the law of the visible, moves ever farther away into the invisible. But art does not extend beyond the sphere of representation. A painting, containing the depiction of the structure of some other paintings that existed before, hangs alongside that one on the walls of a gallery. Its privileged status can be proven only historically. It passes judgment by itself on the art before, just as it is judged by that art. A stone smashed into bits and reduced to atoms is still the same stone; but a picture torn to shreds is either annihilated as a work of art or is transformed into a different picture. Experimentation in art does not penetrate into representation or destroy illusion: it merely engenders a new representation and reestablishes the illusion. As long as society protects art from outright destruction, art retains the fundamental character of an insurmountable illusion that no experience is able to transgress.

Ivan Chuikov's work is a thematic treatment of this aspect of art as a conserving force. He stretches a film of landscape over parallelepipeds and airtight windows. This way of handling the landscape is in keeping with its function as a membranous encasement that conceals the thing-in-itself from the solitary romantic rapt in contemplation. To a classical landscape painter, the landscape was a view to be understood as a stage in the cognitive process. The next stage in that process is the next view—the one opening up to the wanderer who travels to the interior of nature and gains knowledge through observation. Contemporary man finds landscape overcome at the very first step on the cognitive road. Landscape is an illusion that makes up the world of romantic subjectivity; or else it is a collective illusion shared by those who dwell within it: the illusion of art.

The insurmountability of art is the same thing as the insurmountability of landscape. Chuikov exposes the material substratum of romantic subjectivity. A thin layer of paint is applied to the surface of a nameless object without a distinct form of its own. The social definition of art, by its very essence, renders that object unattainable and invisible alike. The parallelepiped wrapped in a landscape emerges in all its coarse materiality to the viewer's gaze. It is "right at hand," as Heidegger might put it. The void behind the film of a "real" landscape, surrounding the observer on all sides, has taken on the vulgar form of a box, which now passes into the ownership of the viewer. However, as the material carrier of the film of "art" this box is no more accessible than is the thing-in-itself—the Kantian *Ding an sich*. The box is under guard, and in its banal materiality it remains an eternal secret. Its discovery would be equivalent to the demise of art; this would be sacrilege, not experimentation.

Here we see the role played by illusion, institutionalized in art as defense and protection. In this context, the anonymity of style in which the illusion is reproduced ensures collective recognition of its protective character.

The works mentioned above retain a certain degree of ambiguity. The question arises as to whether the artist is trying to make a gesture of guardianship and defense, as being the purpose of art. Or is he demonstrating a condition for the existence of a romantic painting? One may suspect that his box-landscape demonstration was inspired less by a desire to conceptualize the romantic experience than by an aspiration toward nostalgic and ironically innocuous elaboration of the romantic picture itself. The transcendental conditions for that gesture would thereby be shown.

All reasonable considerations lead us to favor the second of these alternatives. Indeed: in itself, the parallelepiped and the completely anonymous window are such negligible objects that the artist can hardly be seriously interested in their preservation. Hence the parallelepiped is taken here to serve, rather, as a tangible example. And it could be replaced by any other object. So what we see is the sheer possibility of protection, rather than the actuality, insofar as it leaves the viewer emotionally indifferent. The pathos of involvement as authentic interestedness is not aroused in his soul. On the other hand, the landscape depicted on the box is itself so trivial and easy to grasp that its reproduction by the artist would perhaps appear to have been occasioned solely by the problem of conceptualizing the object portrayed.

An interpretation based on this kind of reasoning nevertheless is still nothing more than an interpretation. It stands in opposing contrast to the artist's work by presupposing an external vantage point. Conceptualization is not carried out in the work itself. The individual work is not placed within any kind of series, nor is it supplied with any attributes which might unequivocally impose a reading. An artwork as such must possess an expository force and a compulsive quality directed at the viewer. That is what distinguishes it from natural objects revealing themselves passively to man. If a concept takes form only in the mind of the observer, that means that in the artwork it exists only as a potentiality, without having acquired genuine actuality. Thus it is only natural to suspect that, in the case at hand, we are shown the box-landscape not so much because of an attempt to conceptualize the romantic experience, but as in the sense of still another nostalgic elaboration of the romantic picture itself.

Ivan Chuikov proposes to define art as illusion — a definition that unquestionably narrows the field of art already in existence, an art that is already there. In essence, art is always an exit, an avenue of access to the things themselves. Not of course in the sense that the art becomes a thing itself, but that it affords us an insight into the true nature of the things. By presenting us with an image of art as an illusion, and that in all seriousness, Ivan Chuikov is saying something true to us. Further, by creating a work of art in which art displays its illusory nature, it is clear at any rate that the artwork he himself has produced is a true one.

At this point we must inquire whether that work still belongs to the realm of art, or whether it goes beyond it. One way or the other, we arrive at a paradox. Maybe this very paradox gave the artist pause, preventing him from using the resources of art to complete his exposition of the artistic truth revealed to him. One gets the impression that Chuikov assumes the existential status of art to be revealed not in itself but in the discourse of which it is the object. However, it is contemplation and not illusion that is insurmountable in art. To suppose that contemplation is always illusion, or that genuine contemplation is impossible, and that all contemplation must be founded on the unseen (in other words, on reasoning) is to remain within the romantic framework and to deprive oneself of the right to truth. Yet in practice a perceptive grasp of existing art, that is, of art as illusion, has always been for the artist a motivating occasion to overcome illusion and to go out toward the things themselves in true contemplation. Artistic truth is historical and, like history itself, it is irremovable.

Ivan Chuikov does accomplish the journey beyond the confines of the conditional, but not by way of conceptualizing the romantic (as earlier suspected) but rather via its further expansion. In the works entitled *Corners and Zones* he opts conclusively for the direct gesture, eschewing self-analytical reflection. In these works he restores to an enclosed space — the room — its spiritual and mystical significance. (Let us recall: *Red Corner, Happy and Unhappy Walls, Place for Household Gods*, etc.) *Corners and Zones* organizes space in such a manner that it acquires an individual hallowed character and loses the impersonality of mere living space. At the same time there is a risk of nonrecognition and of nonartistry, which signifies a genuine departure beyond the confines of reflection.

Unlike the box, the room calls for protection, and this appeal arouses an immediate reaction in the viewer. The authenticity of the interest thus stimulated guarantees that involvement in the happening, which transforms one or two features on the ceiling and in the corners of the room into a work of art. A few elegant and reliable tracings confer to the room the status of an indestructible object of contemplation, unrelated to any stereotype; its illusory character is thereby transcended and it becomes rooted in authentic emotional experience. The characteristics of these tracings (the effect of play when the viewer moves, for instance) are not very important and in fact superfluous. What is important is that Ivan Chuikov, in denying to art the right of true contemplation, is directly continuing the tradition of incantatory gesture and chivalrous defense which he singled out and perceived as one possibility for intelligent artistic activity in our time — for art understood as insurmountable yet genuinely experienced illusion.

3. Francisco Infante

At the beginning of our century, art became aware of its autonomy with respect to "life," or the depiction of life, and at the same time it grew inflated with an attitude of arrogant superiority toward it. If art has its laws, then life, too, can be understood as art; and life perceived in this way may be quickly recognized as an ugly art. An artist familiar with the law of creative freedom has a duty to transform life in accordance with that law — to make life beautiful. Futurism and the Bauhaus are well-known examples of artistic projectionism. In the 1950s and 1960s a desire to subordinate life to art found expression in the Happening and in utopian visions of the future. But from the very outset the aggressiveness of art was met with resistance. Indeed, can an artist really lay claim to a position outside of the society in which he lives? In his activity the artist is defined by the limits of his vision and by the way he relates what he sees to reality.

But the limits of his vision are narrow ones, owing to the finitude of his existence. The process of knowing the mechanism by which the visible and the knowledgeable are interrelated becomes an adventure without end. This mechanism is above all anonymous and historical. It holds the artist prisoner. To discover and to grasp it he has to overstep the bounds of art and rely on other procedures having little or nothing to do with it. Thus he falls into renewed dependence on "life" as it realizes itself here and now. Extension of art into the social domain, or the attempt to force a particular aesthetic ideal onto society, is always a diachronic undertaking, for that ideal is itself nothing more than that same society, albeit in its historically transcended form.

Art in our day is more than ever disinclined to put its faith in aesthetic platitudes. It turns to the common and vulgar categories as a way out. The old arrogance toward life's drab and humdrum aspects is gone forever. And yet the dream and the ritual have not died out, not by any means, as the work of Francisco Infante so eloquently testifies.

Stylistically, his art lies within that traditional tendency of the European and the Russian avant-garde, which took upon itself the mission of remaking the world. Infante's pictures are projects for another kind of life in another sphere of living. Of late he has begun photographing the modifications introduced into

Francisco Infante-Arana,
Artifact from the series Play of
Gestures. 1977. Photograph,
16⅛ × 16″ (41.1 × 40.6 cm).
Jane Voorhees Zimmerli Art
Museum, Rutgers, The State
University of New Jersey,
The Norton and Nancy Dodge
Collection of Nonconformist Art
from the Soviet Union

the natural environment by superimposition of artifacts, as well as by organizing actions in natural settings that take on a ritual character. But the actions organized by Infante are performances rather than happenings. They are not aimed
at inciting the audience to direct participation or to changes in customary ways
of life: the artist wants a pure visual show. It is not the action itself that is so important as the photographs taken with the artist's camera.

For a long time, painting was looked upon as the antithesis of photography.
It disclosed a world arranged by the artist's imagination, while photography presented "things as they are." The myth of the dispassionate photographer, however, vanished quite a while ago, and the artist's imagination seems no longer
so much like a law itself; but in performance photography both of these illusions
spring to life afresh. The artist forms the *signifié*, the meaning or the content-
plan, and not the *signifiant* — the name or the expression plan: the photograph
reveals itself to us as a faithful document testifying the authenticity of another
life. Instead of aggression, what predominates here is the nostalgic dream.

The performance in Infante's version is quite different from the Western one.
In the West, attention is centered on individual, social, and biological definitions
of the human body and on the limits of human existential possibility; Infante gives
us a world of technological reverie reminiscent of faraway childhood. By their grace
and elegance, their clarity and wit, his photographs stand distinctly apart from the
science-fiction designs that became a boredom for everyone. Infante's world is a
world of trust, whereas the real technological world is a world of distrust, for technology is control, and you cannot exercise control without suspicion. What makes
the reality underlying Infante's photographs attractive is their purity of formal representation. This reality is free from suspicion inasmuch as it does not demand
penetration beyond the form. Consequently, there are only the photographs that
are real. The subject photographed is merely art, containing reality only to the degree to which art is real at all. Infante modifies the concept of a picture in such a
way as to preserve that concept: deception lies at its basis, but it is precisely that

deception that constitutes art. By his modification, Infante's art is finally recognized; an achievement which was not easy.

4. The Group Collective Actions
Nikita Alekseev, Andrei Monastyrski, and others

Performance art is represented in Moscow by the group known as Collective Actions. The artists in the group have assigned themselves serious tasks, in an attempt to decompose the visual effect produced by events into its primordial elements — such as space, time, sound, or a number of figures. A characteristic common to all these works is their pure "lyricism," or their dependence upon the viewer's emotional predisposition.

Their performances are all somewhat ephemeral. They set up no law as to how they should be approached and judged; they give themselves over to the observer's perceptive whim. The viewer's encounter with these works is often intentionally left to chance. The artist, for example, may leave a ringing bell under the snow, or a painted tent in the woods. The effect brought by this kind of accidental encounter opens up a world of unexpected forebodings and amazing discoveries — the sort of world in which mankind was actually living not so very long ago. There was a time when people came across inexplicable traces of some indefinite presence, signaling the existence of active and purposive forces that lead beyond the limits of common-sense explanations. These indications pointing to the presence of magic forces can be regarded as facts of art opposed to facts of reality that cannot be explained but only interpreted. The artists of the group Collective Actions endeavor to nudge the contemporary observer into some such fortuitous encounter or discovery as will compel him to engage in interpretation.

In the foregoing we have undertaken to analyze the creative work of several contemporary Moscow artists. This naturally leads us to a further inquiry into the typical characteristics of contemporary Russian art as a whole. What is it that makes this art unique, if indeed it is unique? Can we relate it antithetically to Western art to see what the two have in common?

It is certain that such an antithesis does in fact exist. Perhaps the differences are not so plainly evident in the works of Moscow artists today compared with their counterparts in the West; but the contrast is clear beyond all doubt in the way the public and the artists themselves understand their work. Consequently these works bear the stamp of distinguishable difference, though unfortunately to an only half-recognized extent so that interpretation is required in order to see them in a proper light.

In one way or another, Western art says something about the world. Even when concerned with faith it speaks of faith as incarnate in the world. It may turn its attention inward onto itself, but what it says has to do with its own process of realization in the world. Russian art, from the age of icons to our time, seeks to speak of another world. Russians of today like to point out that the term "culture" is derived from "cult," whereby culture is understood as the totality of the arts. Culture comes out as the guardian of primordial revelation and also as the mediator for new revelations. The language of art differs from everyday language not because it speaks of the world in a more elegant and beautiful way or discloses the "internal world of the artist." What makes it different is the message it has to convey about the other world—something that only art can say. The inner structure of artistic language empowers it to convey the structure of that other world, just as the inner structure of our everyday language discloses the world of here and now. Each discovery of the power of artistic language to communicate something new is accordingly a discovery of something new, something never known before, about the structure of the other world. We may love the artist for showing us a region we long for; we may hate and fear him for revealing a world we do not want. In Russia, art is magic.

What is the other world? It is the world opened up to us by religion. It is the world that opens itself to us only through the medium of art. It is also the world that is situated at the point where those two worlds intersect. This is the reason why there is so much tension in the relationship between art and faith in Russia. In any event, the other world is neither the past nor the future. It is rather the presence in the present into which we may withdraw without reserve. No waiting around and no wheeling or dealing is needed in order to live in the church or in art. All you need to do is to take one sideward step and you find yourself in another place. This is quite as simple as dying, and essentially it is the same thing as dying. You perish for the world and you are resurrected alongside the world.

Magic subsists in space but not in time. The cosmos is constituted in such a way that it contains adequate space for different worlds.

The artists whose works have been discussed here are not religious persons; yet they are able to comprehend art in terms of belief. Whether as merely potential existence or as straightforward portrayal (revelation or absence of concealment) or as a sign from above that calls for interpretation, art—as they see it—involves impingement of that other world on our own. We must make an effort to understand what this invasion signifies. The intervention has occurred with the artists' complicity and we cannot be ungrateful to them on that account. By invading our History the other world gives us the power to make statements about it that it could not make itself. And what may we finally conclude? Precisely this: that other world is not another world at all; but it is our own historicity, revealed to us here and now.

Written in 1979. First published in the samizdat magazine «37» (Leningrad); also published in A-Ya magazine (Paris), 1979.

●●

ANDREI MONASTYRSKI

The artist and writer Andrei Monastyrski (born 1947) belongs to the second generation of Moscow Conceptual artists, having been influenced by the work of Ilya Kabakov while taking a decidedly more radical approach. He was a poet before forming the artists group Collective Actions in 1976 together with Georgii Kizevalter and Nikita Alekseev (later joined by Nikolai Panitkov, Igor Makarevich, Elena Elagina, Sergei Romashko, and Sabine Hansgen). Together they organized events in remote areas of the countryside. A typical work by

Collective Actions would involve a group of invited participants traveling long distances to reach a designated place, where they would witness or take part in an action, performance, or work of Land art, at times suggestive of physics or philosophy experiments. The event was later presented through detailed documentation, including analysis, photograph, and testimonials from participants.

The group's intention was to create a continuum from life to art, adjoining the passage to the art and the action itself, while also collapsing the distinction between artist and spectator. In 1998 Collective Actions published the book Trips to the Countryside, *which until now remains their major oeuvre and source of information about them. In the following text, Monastyrski provides an intellectual context for the development of Conceptual art in Russia and speaks about the problematic nature of secondary sources in representing the essence of firsthand experience.*

Seven Photographs

These notes assume that the reader was either present at the actions described here or, better yet, is familiar with our book *Trips to the Countryside*. I will attempt here to briefly analyze the connection between the actions themselves and the secondary materials which document the event.

It is quite evident that the secondary material engenders a completely different aesthetic reality. The laws governing structure and perception during the process of carrying out the action differ fundamentally from the structural unity of the secondary material, which includes not only photographs, but also descriptive texts such as the participants' narratives.

It is generally assumed that the secondary material reflects the essence of the work. In examining it we can discern the intent of the artist and understand and evaluate his work. None of this, however, applies to our work. At most, an examination of our photographs and texts can produce a feeling of positive uncertainty. What remains unclear is which symbol in the material (it may be a symbol of its totality) points to the essence of the event. Let us attempt to find this symbol. In order to do that we have to make clear the concept of the "essence of the event." At first glance—approaching this problem superficially—it may seem that there are three categories or levels of this essence: the demonstrational, the existential, and the intentional. For the sake of brevity let us assume that in our actions the existential and intentional essences coincide. As far as existential essence is concerned, the actions are realized on the basis of real experience and not on the basis of a representation of this experience. It therefore makes no sense to look for a direct correlation between the secondary material and the existential essence. It is also impossible to relive this experience by examining the secondary material.

Let us now turn to the demonstrational essence which develops in "parallel" with the existential essence during the realization of the action. The symbolism of this essence is determined by the fact that it belongs to the system of demonstrational relationships and, consequently, there should be a symbol in the secondary material pointing to this essence which must be searched for in the many photographs included in the secondary material.

In the artists' commentaries to the actions, we assumed this demonstrational essence to be in the so-called empty action, when an extra-demonstrational

Collective Actions Group. *Comedy.* 1977. Photograph. Courtesy Andrei Monastyrski

element is introduced into the structure of the action. The mechanism of the empty action can be followed very clearly in "Comedy." The figure in the shapeless garment is moving in the direction of the spectators. With his hands he imitates the space in which, as far as the spectators are concerned, the second participant is located. In reality, however, there is no second participant, and the participant in the garment seems to be carrying a "hidden emptiness." Later, when he removes the garment, the "hidden emptiness" is revealed and he retreats into the woods. The spectators are left with the empty field. But now the emptiness of the field is not the same emptiness which existed before the beginning of the action. The emptiness is not "random." The entire point of the action was to create this "nonrandom emptiness," *to return the "nonrandomness" of the emptiness to space which is always "randomly" empty.* On the empty field which "hid" the second participant at a certain undefined moment, there occurred something close to the "nihilation of Nothingness" of which Martin Heidegger says: "Nihilation is not some fortuitous incident. Rather, as the repellent gesture toward the retreating whole of beings, it discloses these beings in their full but heretofore concealed strangeness as what is the radically other—with respect to the nothing. . . . [It] brings our human Dasein for the time before being as such."[1]

While the participant in the garment did not lift or reveal "the hidden emptiness," everything that had hitherto occurred in the field was only a preparation, with the spectators in a state of usual expectation. But after the emptiness was liberated and "filled" the demonstration field, the expectation turned into an event, which we refer to in our commentaries as a "completed expectation." The experience of the "completed expectation" is the real experience we spoke of in connection with the existential essence of the event. However, this process takes place in the consciousness of the spectators and cannot be depicted. What can be depicted though is that which accompanies this internal process—that which occurs on the field of action at that time. However, nothing happens on the field of action, as it is empty, and the participants have left it. But as a result of the fact that one of the participants who "liberated" the emptiness and went into the woods and the other one disappeared into the field already metaphorized as "hidden," the spectators were left with a "nonfortuitous" emptiness, which differs from an always fortuitously empty space. This nonfortuitous emptiness is in fact the demonstrational essence of the event. The photograph of the empty field, taken at that moment, is the symbol pointing to this essence. All of the other photographs of "Comedy" are only the documentation of the preparatory work, including those photographs which show the man in the bulky garment moving across the field—what was directly observed by the spectators during the action.

Thus the photograph of the empty field, taken out of the series of documentary photographs which narrate the events on the field of October 2, 1977, ceases to be documentary. Instead it becomes a higher symbol of the "nonfortuitous" emptiness and can be interpreted as follows: "Nothing is depicted [in the photograph] not because nothing occurred at a given moment, but because what occurred cannot be depicted in principle." The demonstrational essence of the event—the empty action—is depicted through the absence of an image. In my opinion, this "nondepiction" works independently and positively (within the framework of this discourse) in the suggested sequence of the seven "empty" photographs of our seven actions.

In addition to the photographs of "Comedy" described above, there are three more photographs in this series in which an empty field is also depicted. All of these empty fields are symbols of "nonfortuitous emptiness." Upon leaving the place of the action of "Lieblich," the participants knew that the bell, invisible under the snow, would continue to ring. In "Comedy," after the participant in the garment entered the woods, the spectators, as they stood at the edge of the woods in front of the empty field, knew—albeit with a less certain sense of localization than in "Lieblich"—that the invisible, disappeared participant was lying somewhere in the field. They also understood that in the action "Third Variant," the headless double of the participant who entered the woods is also somewhere in the field. In "Action Location," the replacement of one participant by another was also invisible from the initial position from which the photographs were taken and the action observed for its entire duration. All of these "empty" photographs reflect the constructive and essential moment of the action. They depict "invisibility" as a demonstrable relationship. This was done by using two methods. In "Lieblich," "Comedy," and "Third Variant" this was achieved through "concealment," whereas in "Action Location" it was achieved through distance. In these photographs invisibility points to concealment, which is the opposite of "discernible appearance," an area of concrete meaning where "being as a whole" disappears in a concrete appearance of an infinitely multiplicitous world. Between the "invisibility" and "discernible appearance"—in the demonstrational structure—there is a transitional stage which may be called "indiscernibility," where "being as a whole" appears and disappears. Breaking through the disappearing veil of "concealment," it changes into the visibility of the visible world.

In my opinion, the borderline nature of "indiscernibility" justifies the inclusion in this series of three more "empty" photographs of three actions. They are "Appearance," "Paintings," and "Slogan (To Kizevalter)."

In the photographs of the actions "Appearance" and "Paintings," two barely discernible participants can be seen at the point of the intersection of the field and the woods. In the photograph of "Appearance" one sees an emptiness which has just ceased to be empty. The participants have not yet emerged, but are just emerging from "concealment." (This is a purely discursive "concealment." At the level of the event and the secondary material, the participants emerge from the woods, which have not been metaphorized as "concealment" either in "Appearance" or "Paintings.") Perhaps they have already emerged from "concealment" but have not entered the "visibility of the visible world." They still have not differentiated themselves as "having appeared." They are still marked by the stamp of fortuitous coincidence. The expectation of the spectators has not yet been destroyed by the banality of the situation. At this stage of the action, the semantic space has not yet formed. It is still lagging behind and not developing simultaneously with the physical space of the "appearance." This time lag of several seconds between the beginning of the action and the beginning of its comprehension is the demonstrational essence of the event — the "empty event" — whose symbol is this photograph.

The situation depicted in the photograph of "Paintings" is different. Here the participants, unnoticed by the spectators, have already passed through the "demonstration zone" of "discernible visibility" and are about to disappear into "concealment." The action is built in such a way that the participants appear before the spectators right away in "indiscernibility," as "people disappearing in the distance." However, the photograph is not about the people disappearing in the distance. There is already too much empty space in the photograph. It relentlessly fills the photograph, blurring the figures of the participants into "invisibility." The empty space is ready to appear in all its fullness, and meaning dominates all other meanings.

In all of these six photographs, "concealment," depending on the way in which "invisibility" or "indiscernibility" is formed, is expressed either through the distant line of the black woods ("concealment") or through perspective space ("remoteness") or the field ("concealment").

The photograph "Slogan" is also a symbol of perspective space. The distance from the object (the white stripe on the distant black forest) forms the "indiscernibility" — the thin barrier of the vanishing objectiveness beyond which begins the emptiness of "invisibility." In the photographs "Appearance" and "Paintings," this barrier is movable, and in one case is ready to disappear ("Paintings") and in the other to turn into the differentiated concreteness of visibility. In the photograph "Slogan," on the other hand, it is static. Acting as a dam, it prevents emptiness from filling the perspective space of the photograph. "Indiscernibility" does not turn into "invisibility," and "concealment" is not expressed here by the perspective space. It is obvious that a sense of emptiness pervades this photograph. Just as in the photographs "Appearance" and "Paintings," there is a depiction of "invisibility" pointing to "concealment" which is not the forest, nor the field, nor the perspective space.

Let us now turn to the only participant and photographer of this action. Where is he and what is happening to him? The mechanism of the functioning of "Slogan" is similar to that of "Comedy." The participant of "Slogan" (he is also the photographer) combines the roles of the "participant in the loose-fitting garment"

Collective Actions Group. *Appearance*. 1976. Photograph. Courtesy Andrei Monastyrski

Collective Actions Group. *Paintings with Three Figures*. 1979. Photograph. Courtesy Andrei Monastyrski

Collective Actions Group. *To Kizevalter (Slogan 1980)*. 1980. Photograph. Courtesy Andrei Monastyrski

Collective Actions Group. *Lieblich*. 1976. Photograph. Courtesy Andrei Monastyrski

Collective Actions Group. *Third Variant*. 1978. Photograph. Courtesy Andrei Monastyrski

Collective Actions Group. *Action Location*. 1979. Photograph. Courtesy Andrei Monastyrski

and the spectator. The participant in this garment in the action "Comedy" knows that he is carrying "hidden emptiness," something the participant of "Slogan" does not. However, the latter, while manipulating the slogans, also carried and strung up "concealed emptiness" — in this case hidden "indiscernibility." The participant discovers the indiscernible text (having removed the cover of the slogan with thin string) and at once finds himself on the boundary of the prohibition put in place by the scheme of the work. The space between himself and the slogan has become forbidden to him. He is left with only one direction in which he can move — away from the slogan. "Indiscernibility" strives toward "invisibility" and requires empty space. The emptiness fans out and chases the photographer, who disappears in the multiplicity of the visible world. The "concealment" of this photograph is expressed by nonphotographic space, where the "hidden" photographer and the spectator looking at the photograph are. The "nonfortuitousness" of the potential emptiness of this photograph is conditional upon the invisibility of the photographer "hidden" in the nonphotographic space. In contrast to the photograph "Paintings," the emptiness in this photograph, stopped by the dam of the slogan, unfolds toward us, whereas there it unfolded away from us. There the participants disappear into the forest, which becomes the symbol of "concealment." In this photograph the photographer (and we) are "hidden" in the nonphotographic space, in the "real" world which becomes the symbol of "concealment" in this photograph. The "nonfortuitousness" of the potential emptiness appears here through the special character of the space which has "hidden" us and which does not permit us to read the unclear letters of the text on the slogan banner.

We began our discussion by stating that "nondepictability" is the demonstrational essence of our actions and can be correlated with their existential essence. We then saw that this "nondepictability" is constructed through various means, and in the present sequence of photographs it depicts either a forest, a field, a perspective space, or a nonphotographic space pointing to the "nonfortuitousness" of the emptiness of these photographs. The seven "empty" photographs which were analyzed here have a higher symbolic significance than simply being documents. The independent metaphoric nature of the photographs corresponds to the aesthetic reality which appears during the process of the realization of the action. The aesthetic reality of the photographs follows its own laws of construction and perception, which differ from that of the event itself. This aesthetic reality is on the same symbolic level as the aesthetic reality of the event. Any other photographs of actions or texts, including all of the secondary material, do not reflect the demonstrational essence of the event and do not adequately reflect its existential essence. The ordinal nature of the symbolic levels is the necessary condition for the correspondence between the secondary material and the event which it reflects. I believe that the most important quality that this series of seven "empty photographs" possesses is its metaphorical independence.

Note
1. Martin Heidegger, "What is Metaphysics?" in *Basic Writings* (New York: Harper Collins, 1993), p. 103.

Written in 1980. Self-published in "Poezdki i vosproizvedenije" ("Trips and Reproduction"), Moscow, 1983; officially published in *Kollektivnye deistviya: Poezdki za gorod (Collective Actions: Trips to the Countryside)*. (Moscow: Ad Marginem, 1998). Translated by Daniel Rishik.

SUZANA MILEVSKA

Born in 1961, Suzana Milevska currently works as an art theorist and curator at the Museum of the City of Skopje, Macedonia. In this essay, she evaluates how the concept and the physical manifestation of readymades in the Balkans differ from those in Western cultures. Milevska argues that in Central and Eastern European countries, with their transitional economies and lack of high-quality production, readymades represent a different type of art object than in the West. However, art-appropriated technological or industrial products can effectively express the reality of economic and cultural development in a highly conceptual way. She uses as her examples the work of three artists: Igor Tosevski, Zaneta Vangeli, and Zoran Naskovski. Tosevski addresses the discrepancies between efficiency and quality in art production in the new market economies of the Balkans; Vangeli confronts the need to legitimize new cultural symbols to represent the ideological break with the past; and Naskovski records the bizarre and tragic intermingling of media and reality in war.

The Readymade and the Question of the Fabrication of Objects and Subjects

> *Whether Mr. Mutt with his own hands made the fountain or not has no importance. He CHOSE it.* — Marcel Duchamp[1]

> *I want to be a machine.* — Andy Warhol[2]

The phenomenon of the readymade and its usage as an art object (and possibly later as an installation) is proximal to the abandonment of the art craft. If painting signifies art, skill, and craftsmanship, then, with the onset of industrialism, craftsmanship was rendered useless, and thereby, so was painting. Nevertheless, new technical achievements have continued to emerge from within the realm of painting. Today, the international art scene is moving dramatically in a new direction. When it comes to participation in large international exhibitions, the growing tendency has been to rely on the use of new technologies, and new and serious obstacles have been placed in front of artists coming from the East. The possible frustration of such artists is derived from the usage of objects that are completely industrially produced or even ordered to be produced. In the case of exhibiting readymade objects, the painter has been replaced by a machine. This proves that the motivation for readymade objects was closely related to production and fabrication,[3] although, Marcel Duchamp, for one, did not have in mind any obsession or glorification of the perfection and beauty of the readymade: "When I discovered the readymades I thought to discourage aesthetics."[4]

Differing visual and conceptual results are a consequence of the acceptance and presentation of the readymade object as part of artistic activity, specifically in the context of the Balkan region — a region in which industrial production, following World War II, has never been applied in a complete capitalist free market economy.[5] In fact, in all socialist countries, there existed a kind of "simulation of production" in which ideological emphasis was put on the fulfillment of a social policy of full employment and on the quantity of production, while the quality of the manufactured objects was of secondary importance. Of course, this was possible only under special circumstances wherein industrialization and the market functioned under State supervision and control — a system that survived until the period of transition following the break-up of the Yugoslav federation and the fall of the Berlin Wall in 1989. From this point a series of complex political and economic transitions began that continues to evolve today.

According to Adorno's aesthetic theory, there is a relationship between the level of development in a given society and the art produced in that society.[6] If we accept this, then there must be a difference between the art produced by these societies and their production development. The nature of the situation today can only be explained by the ongoing process of globalization and the will to simulate that they are equal participants in it. During the transition from one mode of production to another, and from one model of ownership to another, a whole range of relationships has changed. The invisible patterns that rule Western society (long suppressed in the East) have started emerging as "desiring machines"[7] — unconscious mechanisms latent in the individual but also in social and historical structures.

The usage of high technology for art purposes poses a question about development in the arts — an unsolvable problem that creates many paradoxes, not only in countries with underdeveloped technological capacities. Although this article aims to give an overview of some of the different applications of readymade objects by artists living in unstable political and economic regions in times of transition, another aim is to examine the limits of the readymade object as a medium. Artists using readymade objects usually exhibit perfectly produced and iterated forms in order to give installations a look of unification and repetition, with no difference among the repeated objects — an effect possible only if the objects in question are industrially produced. As mentioned before, the problem here is that different visual effects and meanings are produced when the readymade object is faulty in its original production or montage. Furthermore, the term "perfection," as used in its high-technological context, is problematic when used in the context of art. Issues of technicality, materiality, tools, and media have always been important, although not the only consideration in art-making; the discovery of certain rules has always been connected with certain technical means. Therefore, an artist today who avoids the latest high-tech wonders must still confront the question of means.

What, then, makes the readymade different when it is made and represented as artwork in the region of the Balkans — a region where socialism has been intermixed with inefficient productive means? It never looks as perfect as the objects made in Western countries since the tools and means of production are not perfect themselves (similarly, this argument can also be taken into account when it comes to the installations presented in the wider Eastern European context). How the management context, the free market economy, or strong competition affect the perfection of products is not more important than readymade objects being beautiful or imperfect. Should the form of the readymade object not be essential to its own existence as a way of revolting against the act of skillful art-making?

The examination of the readymade object in the context of Eastern European art, and the question of its difference in meaning between Eastern and Western art communities, are particularly called to mind by one very unique project, *Dossier '96* (1996), by the artist Igor Tosevski from Macedonia, one of the former Yugoslav republics.[8] The project refers to one of the most talked-about issues in the formerly socialist countries of Eastern Europe. It specifically questions the necessity of the perfect readymade object in the context of the widespread bankruptcy of noncompetitive factories and their subsequent privatization.

Dossier '96 derived from a one-year research project by the artist, along with four exhibitions, that placed the artist in a new role as he discovered new paradoxes. Tosevski re-examined the problem of the extensive "production" of faulty objects by bankrupt factories as well as the process of privatization in various stages. First, he visited the factories that were declared insolvent, and with permission (not always easily obtained) he took photos of the buildings and the piles of rejected objects. He observed tons of decaying material on the premises of factories awaiting privatization. Some managers declined to assist in the export and use of this material because they hoped instead that they would be able to purchase the firms more cheaply if these firms appeared to be less productive.[9]

It is worth noting the "desiring machines" concept, in which there is no distinction between the product and the production—the desiring production has become the continuum: Machines are connected to other machines in an endless chain, and in such a context, *Dossier '96* could be treated in a way similar to that in which desiring machines function—with ruptures, cracks, and fissures. Distances and fragmentations, in this schema, function best when they produce nothing at all except the art itself.[10] To adopt the terms of Maurice Merleau-Ponty, the invisible power of capital is that it forces the system of managers and politicians to abuse their positions and act as "wild beings."[11]

The conversations with the workers and managers presented real adventures. Tosevski needed to explain readymade and Conceptual art to them, a challenge in itself, especially when the workers were reluctant to talk for fear of losing their jobs and the managers were reticent because they suspected their work was being investigated for purposes beyond art. During 1996 the artist realized three exhibitions in different cities where he found similar factories and received permission to relocate a certain amount of waste material, although he was obliged to pay for some of it. Galleries that usually display local artists were now being used to expose local factory installations. For example, in Titov Veles, while Tosevski was exhibiting broken plates from the local ceramics and porcelain factory, he projected a slide made of the original enormous pile of abandoned material over the small pile of objects in the gallery and thus simulated the actual situation in the factory yard. In addition, the destiny of the gallery itself furthered the concept since it was otherwise vacant.

In March 1997, Tosevski opened his large exhibition at the Museum of the City of Skopje, displaying faulty textiles, granite blocks, and porcelain from the three previous exhibitions and adding a fourth—irregular bottles from a glass factory in Skopje. In addition to the rejected factory material he projected slides of words taken from an economics dictionary, defining terms such as "transition," "transformation," "privatization," "solvency," and "bankruptcy." The paradoxes that Tosevski dealt with may be interpreted by applying a theory of linguistic discourse to the given aesthetic context. To be sure, the polemics surrounding the issue of whether performative artistic acts still fall within the realm of the aesthetic can reach radical extremes, from Duchamp's assertion that art is separate from aesthetics to [Clement] Greenberg's claim that the aesthetic is identical with the artistic. Regardless of one's critical stance, it is obvious that the performative work of art re-examines the relationship between the artistic, the aesthetic and the real.

The approach underlying the entire *Dossier '96* project can be called a performative act, since it exemplifies J. L. Austin's definition that performative exhibits produce meaning even when they are themselves rhetorically empty.[12] That is, the very demonstration, articulation and proclamation of the performative utterance carries out the act. The separation of rejected objects from their original real context and their transposition into gallery spaces is in fact similar to Duchamp's first performative artistic act: the displaying of the urinal with the signature "R. Mutt," in conjunction with its proclamation as a work of art.[13] If a work of art is a work of art because the artist designates and proclaims it to be such, then what becomes of the original manufacturer of the object that has now become art? In this case, Tosevski takes heaps of rejects from bankrupt factories and exhibits them as works of art; are not the producers of these objects — the workers and the managers — deprived of their original function? Do they now become artists themselves?

According to the theory of speech acts, there are certain criteria by which to judge the success of a performative act. These utterances/acts are outside the consideration of truth or falsehood; they are semantically empty — they can produce only meanings. These are, above all, the intention, and the awareness of the intention of the performance, the competence and legitimacy of the performer, and the institutional setting in which the act is performed. According to these criteria, the "producers," whose "products" have been proclaimed as works of art, can by no means be considered the artists. However, because of their metaphorical association with unusable objects, once they are labeled "technological surplus" — the term used in Macedonia for workers dismissed from their work — their status approaches that of the art objects in question, and not subjects with control over their products.[14]

If we pursue the analysis of this paradox further, starting from the same premise, we can pose a question as to the status of the insolvency official. If the manager, rather then trying to use discarded material by recycling or modifying, proclaims the material unusable for no obvious reason, has the official become an artist? Is not this act similar to that of an artist carrying out a performative act? Of course, the answer is no. If we take into account the circumstances of this official's involvement then the criteria of the institutional theory prevents us from regarding these two acts as identical. That is, the manager's motivation is not artistic. He is concerned more with rendering production sites insolvent so that they can be purchased more cheaply.

In contrast, the artist's awareness throughout the process — the relocation of the rejects to the gallery, the organization of exhibitions, the preparation of a catalogue, and the intention itself — has met the necessary preconditions for the illocutionary power and success of the performative act. By fully exercising his right to judge and confirm the universal validity of his act, he remains subjective. In this way, according to institutional theory, theories of taste and aesthetic views are surmounted and the skeptical observer who believes that something has been deemed artistic merely because it has been placed in a museum cannot develop alternative criteria, as even the act of naming is validation.

In linguistics there has always been a dichotomy between speech and action,

Igor Tosevski. Installation view of *Dossier '96.* 1997. Multimedia installation. Courtesy the artist

language and body, and their association has been in place since the appearance of the first readymade in the case of Duchamp, through the Conceptual art of the 1960s and 1970s, to postconceptualism and the most recent media: installation, electronic art, and the reemergence of body and performance art. The current practice of exhibiting accumulations of readymade objects and material leads us to another paradox arising from the *Dossier '96* project — its ambivalence on the plane of visual perception. Sometimes the appearance and form of Tosevski's installations are highly reminiscent of some works by Man Ray (e.g., the hangers displayed in *Kumanovo,* the third of four exhibitions that complete the series of the *Dossier '96* project), Tony Cragg or Richard Wentworth (e.g., the installation with broken plates in *Titov Veles,* the first exhibition in the series) or Richard Long (e.g., the granite blocks in *Prilep,* the second exhibition) or other internationally known artists. Even though the material — being readymade — is identical (this is not surprising, simply because they are readymade objects and therefore can be produced anywhere with the same quality) Tosevski's works are utterly different in content, precisely due to their performative character and production of meaning.[15]

Tosevski uses a medium much in vogue in Western art today (installation and readymade) but manages to create a project originating from his everyday life. Not only does it offer information or knowledge of reality; it also touches upon that reality, carrying out its performative act within it, so that the very act itself becomes a part of the reality within which it is performed. And so we come to the most sensitive question posed by Tosevski: the possibilities of engagement in art and whether art can change reality. According to Adorno, art is always both inside and outside reality, and its status and autonomy are dependent on the level of social freedom in a given society. Taking into account institutional theoreticians such as Arthur Danto and George Dickie, the institution dictates the conditions and decides what art is and what it is not.[16] Tosevski questions the problem of the appropriate position of the artist in relation to art institutions and the adequate medium in these circumstances. For this purpose he has also deemed it necessary to re-examine the social, economic, and political context within which he creates. The marginal role assigned to art and artistic institutions, in a society preoccupied with a myriad of more important problems, is another significant point illustrated in this project. The first three exhibitions in particular, which were held in galleries or cultural centers in provincial Macedonian cities, emphasized the similarity of these spaces to the factories themselves: the spaces were dirty, almost abandoned, turned into storage rooms.

Therefore, the artist's personal engagement takes place in the realms of reality and its portrayal as art. The art is a study of reality itself, as well as a part of everyday life, thereby blurring the lines of an artistic act and a real life case study. The relationship between reality and art is usually set up in a hierarchical sense — reality having the dominant role, one expecting an engaged artist to pursue his battles on the barricades instead of through artistic and conceptual means.

The latest project that Tosevski exhibited was during the group exhibition *Words, Objects, Acts* in 2000 at the Museum of the City of Skopje. In this piece, titled *Perfect Balance or* 23 *Kilos Human Rights,* Tosevski used 23 kilos of original documents from the UN (United Nations) Committee for Human Rights.[17] Many old files full of typed or printed declarations, conference résumés and letters were placed on seven scales suspended from the ceiling. Tosevski was targeting the bureaucracy and hypocrisy of the international institution for human rights, questioning its efficacy and commitment. By turning these official human rights documents into art, the artist created art out of human tragedies depicting ironies even in the highest political establishments and art institutions, while declaring these documents of numbers and names "art."

The usage of readymade art by Zaneta Vangeli, another young artist from Macedonia, relates the problem of the readymade to the problems of subjectivization and national identity and other unresolved political problems in the Former Yugoslav Republic of Macedonia. In particular, her project "Social Plastic of Macedonia" (1996) — created for the group exhibition *Liquor Amnii I* that was held in a fifteenth-century Turkish bath in Skopje — exemplifies the metaphorical way in which the artist juxtaposes objects that are either industrial readymades or objects found in nature. Although the exhibition itself was imagined and based on the theme of amniotic fluid as the border between the body of the mother and child, Vangeli focused on the problems of national identity in Macedonia.

The project consisted of three installations in different rooms of the main venue. In the first room, Vangeli placed six black-and-white photographs; three on one wall and three identical, blurred ones on the opposing wall. These were life-sized photographs of the Minister of Foreign Affairs, the Archbishop of the Macedonian Orthodox Church, and Baskim Ademi, a well-known local underground figure. The composition of the three standing, blurred figures in the photographs was an ironic reference to the Holy Trinity and was meant to emphasize a major problem of the government, namely its alleged involvement in illegal drug activity. While one would have expected to see the archbishop at the center of the composition, as it is the usual position reserved for the omnipotent figure of God, it was in fact the drug addict, Ademi, who was placed in that position, alluding to a more contemporary "religion."

The exhibit in the second room displayed an even greater reference to the connection between the local government and the drug underworld. This part of the installation titled *Spiritual Macedonia, or Anything Goes,* included ten Macedonian flags, two plates of gold and lead, and framed objects with poppies, the source of most drug use in Macedonia, an obvious reference to the chaotic situation in the country where neither the State nor the Church is recognized in the wider international context. The well-known problem with the recognition of the constitutional name of the Former Yugoslav Republic of Macedonia — it was replaced by the acronym FYROM — went so far that even the design of the flag was changed due to the intervention of the Greek government. Thus, the placement of the new flags opposite the opium poppies was a deliberate metaphor referencing the state and government not being organized and completely legitimate (another kind of imperfect readymade) and its blurred, uncertain future. The third part of the project included a video installation showing a drugged Ademi watching the Fluxus artist Al Hanson recite a poem so that the whole scene signified a hallucination, even though each of the two video scenes was documentary and realistic — ordinary readymade images from everyday life.

In *Culturalism or About the Ontological Failure of Tragedy* (1999), Vangeli deepens her interest for the relationship between local and global cultural problems with national and religious identity. Vangeli's exhibit was part of the group project, *Always Already Apocalypse,* which was held in both Skopje and Istanbul. The work itself consisted of a large ink-jet printout of a photograph of the interior of the Hagia Sofia Church in Istanbul, the title of the work inscribed over it while a slide projection of the inverted image acted as its own reflection; the Byzantine frescoes and the Islamic calligraphy written over them were seen both as real and ghostly transparent hallucination — false presence of the religious object with lost function as either a church or a mosque. There were also four separate glass cases that contained small objects (Macedonian bank notes of 1000 and 500 denars and four neckties put in the shape of a cross), and photographs of the small models of objects tested for seismological resistance found in the venue of the exhibition in Skopje — The Institute for Earthquake Engineering and Engineering Seismology.

The investing of Hagia Sofia's Christian interior with frescoes and Islamic writings became a metaphor for cultural misunderstanding in this piece. A similar unexpected conclusion about the absurd relationship between the important institutions of the State and Church can be seen in the display of denar notes. While the government tries to simulate historic continuation with the cultural and religious heritage, it insists on using the religious symbols. On the surface of the 1000 denar note there is a reproduction of an icon of the Mother of God. From the religious point of view this is an act of blasphemy. Inscribing the most sacred symbol on something profane and worldly, such as money, works against the religious canons. The icon is taken as an object symbolizing the presence of God; the money thus gains the significance of a sacral object as well. On the other hand, the engraving of a poppy flower on the surface of the 500 denar note was intended to be a symbol of the natural resources of the country, although its association with opium is inevitable.

Zaneta Vangeli, *The Inner Circle*. Detail from "Social Plastic of Macedonia." 1996. Six photographs, wood, each panel 39⅜ × 6'10¹¹⁄₁₆" (100 × 210 cm). Courtesy the artist

Such clashes of meaning place strong emphasis on the many absurdities in social, cultural, and political life in Macedonia. According to Vangeli, the only way to find meaning is through the mystical belief in redemption that does not depend on ephemeral or profane concepts of tragedy. While criticizing the social and cultural conflicts (the example of turning the church first into a mosque and then into a tourist attraction), Vangeli negates the relevance of tragedy even when caused by postcolonial cultural domination. In this context, Vangeli's artistic concepts are influenced by Orthodox Christian theology. Tragedy and suffering in earthly life are not recognized as relevant due to the sacral concepts of redemption and salvation obtained only through the Apocalypse.

The money fetish is embraced as strongly as the image of the Mother of God, an icon that is a phantasm—immaterial and powerful although still as vulnerable as any other material object.[18] On the other hand, the fetish of the poppy is also a very old and strong phantasmatic image that can serve for manipulation with the fragile national consciousness, and by taking into account Lenin's famous quote that "religion is the opium of the masses," religion and drugs are already closing the vicious circle.

Vangeli's usage of Macedonian flags and money should be understood metaphorically. Instead of questioning the possibility of a perfect readymade within the Balkan context, Vangeli has posed the question of fabricating. In establishing legitimate State, Church, money, and subject-identities as widely recognizable symbols, she posed questions of identity rather than fabricating perfect objects.

Interestingly enough, for the second phase of the *Liquor Amnii 2* (a project that took place during the 1997 Convergence X Summer Festival in Providence, Rhode Island) Vangeli created another site-specific installation also dealing with issues of identity, this time using the latest model of life vests—produced in the United States—as readymade objects. She floated the bright orange objects on the dark surface of the Providence River in order to represent the optimistic concept proclaimed by the title of the work itself: *The Constant Desire for Eternity.* Thus, she also avoided any kind of possible national exoticism that could be taken as an argument against the imperfect readymade. They can be replaced with perfect readymades that can be ordered and found even in the Balkans under special conditions. However, then the question arises of context and content becoming underestimated and neglected in favor of formal appearance.

In terms of the proliferation and consumption of images and the continuous flourishing of new media, one project by Yugoslav artist Zoran Naskovski gives a strange and tragic example. His project *War Frames* (1999) is a radical example of using TV programming as readymade images in extraordinary circumstances. After he was selected as a participant in *Always Already Apocalypse,* he found himself imprisoned in his home during the NATO bombardment over Belgrade. Not having access to any other materials, nor the freedom to produce any other work, he made the only possible choice—he recorded the images from the local TV stations including the strong media campaign of Slobodan Milosevic, the leader of the ruling government at that time.

The question of the perfection of the medium and the living standard became unexpectedly intertwined; the barest life styles were followed by a perfect political and blinding usage of the medium of television. By using this medium, the everyday suspense of the sirens announcing the war mingled with the suspense of Hollywood movies. The TV programs recorded for the project included everything from the local news to music entertainment to religious documentaries to cockfights. In the top left of the screen the words "war danger" were written, reminding us of the absurdity of the animal and human fights appearing in miniature on the television. The presentation of the work, with an interactive CD-ROM, can be interpreted as a simulation of what an average TV viewer was watching during the bombardment. The viewer in the exhibition space could also represent the experience by clicking the mouse in order to change the channel.

The consequential outcome of the war, the tide of about 200,000 refugees who emigrated to Macedonia during the NATO intervention, provoked the artist Ismet Ramicevic to create the work *Pain + Food = Souvenir* (1999). Ramicevic's work was shown in the context of the group exhibition *Artists and Refugees* that was organized by the Center for Contemporary Arts (appearing at the Museum of the City of Skopje). Ramicevic displayed the plates of several refugee families that he had previously photographed. These objects were their only belongings after they left the refugee camps—signifying their short, yet tragic, experience. The destiny of those subjects was strongly connected with the simple aluminum plates—the only remaining evidence of the harshness of life during that period. On each empty plate's inner surface the artist had placed a photograph of some of the refugees just before they left the camps.

The readymade might be not the most appropriate medium for the art activities in the Balkans in the technological sense, but it is appropriate in terms of the content. It can express the specific reality of countries affected by continuous economic and political instability, especially if the industrial shapes and their difference from perfection are used within profoundly conceptualized artistic projects. Focusing on the readymade as an artistic mode of expression was expressed in Tosevski's *Dossier '96.* Its method of investigating the possibilities for a perfect mode of production, along with other problems initiated by the switch to a market economy, implies there are other ways of using and interpreting the ready-made: e.g., the treating of State symbols as "unready" readymade products. Or, in the conditions of establishing a new state with unclear strategies, as in the case of Vangeli's projects. Naskovski used these images as a strong critical context of the bombardment of Serbia, emphasizing the possibilities for manipulation via television—the most powerful readymade of all—during a time when the whole population was forced into a "home TV prison." The absurdities and paradoxes of life and art in the Balkans are emphasized by the medium of readymade. The tendency toward a society of high-tech objects and the not-so-perfect everyday life of their consumers are inevitably in conflict so that partial information about globalization and its technological advantages often sounds unconvincing and hollow in such social, economic, and political conditions.

Notes

1. Marcel Duchamp, "The Richard Mutt Case," in *The Blind Man,* no. 1, April 10, 1917. (*The Blind Man* was a magazine published on the occasion of the first exhibition of the Society of Independent Artists, at the Grand Central Palace in New York City.)
2. Gene Swenson, "What is Pop Art?" *Art News* 62 (November 1963), p. 26, quoted according to Hal Foster, *The Return of the Real* (Cambridge: MIT Press, 1996), p. 130.
3. Thierry De Duve, *Kant after Duchamp* (Cambridge: MIT Press, 1999), p. 413.
4. Ibid., p. 295. The statement, "I threw a bottle rack and urinal in their faces as a challenge and now they admire them for their beauty," once attributed to Duchamp, now, according to De Duve, is reattributed to Hans Richter.
5. Trajko Slavevski, *Makedonska ekonomija vo tranzicija* (Eko Press: Skopje, 1955), pp. 83–87. In this book, a professor from the faculty of Economics at Skopje University investigates different models of privatization in Western and Eastern countries, arguing with the local government and solvency officials that the fast model of privatization employed in the Czech Republic would be more appropriate than the slower approach already employed in Macedonia.
6. Of course, Adorno's thesis should be applied from the appropriate distance, taking into account his theory of negative dialectics and eternal tension between art and society.
7. Gilles Deleuze and Felix Guattari, *The Anti-Oedipus* (New York: Viking, 1977), p. 19.
8. The last presentation of a new version of this project took place within the *After the Wall* exhibition in 1999 that Bojana Pejić curated for Moderna Museet in Stockholm. (It also traveled to Budapest and Berlin.)
9. This situation inevitably reminds us of the desiring machine concept from Gilles Deleuze and Felix Guattari, *A Thousand Plateaus: Capitalism and Schizophrenia,* Brian Massumi, trans. (Minneapolis: University of Minnesota Press, 1987), p. 161.
10. Ibid., pp. 100 and 501–14.
11. Wilhelm S. Wurzer, "wild being/écart/capital" in M. C. Dillon, ed., *Écart & Différence: Merleau-Ponty and Derrida on Seeing and Writing* (Atlantic Highlands, NJ: Humanities Press, 1997), p. 235.
12. J. L. Austin, *How to Do Things with Words* (Cambridge: Harvard University Press, 1975), pp. 106–108.
13. De Duve, pp. 89–142.
14. This relationship calls to mind the Dialectic of Enlightenment by Adorno and Horkheimer: "the single relation between the subject who bestows meaning and the meaningless object."
15. Argument given during a round table discussion at the European Biennial *Manifesta 2* in Luxembourg in 1998 as an answer to Joseph Bakhstein, art theorist from Moscow.
16. George Dickie, *Art and Aesthetic* (Ithaca: Cornell University Press, 1974), p. 34.
17. The documents belong to the personal collection of Ivan Tosevski, the artist's father, who was employed for many years as an expert in the UN Committee for Human Rights.
18. Slavoj Žižek, "How Did Marx Invent the Symptom?" in *Mapping Ideology* (London: Verso, 1999), p. 314.

Written in 2000. Originally published in *Afterimage* (Rochester, NY) 28, no. 4 (Jan./Feb. 2001).

A CASE STUDY

"Weekend Art: Hallelujah the Hill"

Aleksandar Battista Ilić (in collaboration with Ivana Keser and Tomislav Gotovac)

In 1996 three Croatian artists—Aleksandar Battista Ilić, Ivana Keser, and Tomislav Gotovac—embarked on a joint project, a work-in-progress called *"Weekend Art: Hallelujah the Hill."* The originator of the project, which is a "performance without audience," is Battista Ilić (b. 1965), who is also the project photographer, performer, director, producer, and promoter. Ilić had previously worked with Ivana Keser (b. 1967) in the informal art group EgoEast (1992–95). In contrast, this project marked the first time that Tomislav Gotovac, who is almost twice the age of Ilić and Keser, collaborated with other artists. Gotovac is a legend in contemporary Croatian art, a pronounced individualist, and the most radical and consistent Croatian performer and experimental filmmaker.

Ilić's idea was extremely simple: to transform what is traditionally considered a day of rest into an artist's workday. With Keser and Gotovac, he decided that their walks and Sunday hikes to the hill of Medvednica, in the vicinity of Zagreb, should be an art performance documented by photography, i.e., a camera with a self-timer. All three of the artists are film buffs, and the project therefore draws inspiration from and is dedicated to the avant-garde director Adolfas Mekas and his cult movie *Hallelujah the Hills*. Originally just an innocent walk in nature, this ongoing project gradually grew into a complex artwork, which implicitly functions as a social criticism of the time and place of its origin. Ilić himself has said: "The superfluity of beauty, calm, and peace [of the setting] did little to hide the clamor and violence still resounding through the region at the time the work was started (between the war in Bosnia-Croatia and the war in Kosovo). 'Hallelujah the Hill' is not only a hymn to nature, the body, and a simple life, but also an aesthetic repression of horror. Here the weekend is not a time for communing with nature and meeting friends, but a time for artistic expression of the dramas tearing the region apart." *Weekend Art*'s deliberate mixture of divergent artistic procedures and strategies, with elements of Behavior art, Body art, Land art, Conceptual art, and Mail art, focused on human relations as an artwork *per se,* sharing the spirit of the art at the end of the century.

The dissemination of the project through slides, photographs, and performances at shows, the publication of a series of postcards traditionally mailed to art professionals and friends, billboards, as well as Internet presentations and the production of special publications all demonstrate a change of sensibility in the 1990s, with art projects often appearing in the form of modern commercial enterprises.

—Nada Beroš

Weekend Art, Hallelujah the Hill, 1996 – ongoing. Photographs. Courtesy the artists

4 BODY UNBOUND

Experimental sculpture and performance art in Eastern Europe in the 1970s, as in the United States, led to a renewed interest in the body as subject and site, especially among an increasingly visible number of women artists. In the poem and sculptural work "One Sunday . . . ," by the Polish artist Alina Szapocznikow, the body is present only as an imprint, but in the film scenarios of the Romanian artist Geta Bratescu it has a more immediate and visceral presence. Although body art was sometimes performed in the public arena or recorded for exhibition using film and video technology, in Eastern Europe it had very little or no institutional support and survived mostly through private efforts. The risk of these activities typically deepened the intensity of the works, but sometimes also obscured their message. Czech philosopher Petr Rezek was one of the first theoreticians to attempt theoretical reflection on these modes of expression.

Working with the artist's body signified more than just the elevation of intimacies or a new tool of feminist critique; the body was also now being used as a general and radical expression of subjectivity. In this sense, Piotr Piotrowski's engaging analysis of the body of the male artist in Eastern Europe argues that issues of the body can address subjects of both the male and female gender.

In the mid-1970s, the Croatian artist Sanja Iveković worked with images found in magazine advertisements, juxtaposing each found image with a photograph of herself taken in very different circumstances, but with an appearance that was similar or even identical. This photo essay, which Iveković pointedly titled "Double Life," exposes stereotypes of women living in a commercial culture. These images of the artist, raw and vulnerable in comparison to the slick advertising images, offer a strong and somewhat surprising emotional punch. Iveković's pioneering efforts, similar to the principles and explorations of early works by the American Cindy Sherman, are echoed more than a decade later in the work of younger artists, including the cross-dressing Russian performance artist Vladislav Mamyshev, whose essay "Where the Heck Am I? Where Are My Things?" clarifies the artist's bipolar attachment to the identities of Marilyn Monroe and Adolf Hitler.

The chapter concludes with a contemporary case study of a scandal caused by Polish artist Katarzyna Kozyra's controversial thesis project for the Warsaw Academy of Fine Arts. The artist presented a pyramid of taxidermied animals that she had arranged to have killed and stuffed. The work, a protest against the hidden cruelties of a carnivorous society, set off a heated debate on the ethics, violence, and propriety of sacrifice in the name of art that raged in the national press for more than a year and conferred both celebrity and notoriety on the young artist. It also paved the way for a veritable school of Polish video and film artists whose stock in trade consists of more and more daring transgressive gestures.

—*Tomáš Pospiszyl*

Alina Szapocznikow. *Multiple Portrait* (quadruple). 1967. Black granite, bronze, and colored polyester resin, height 43¼" (110 cm). Muzeum Sztuki, Łódź

ALINA SZAPOCZNIKOW

Alina Szapocznikow (1926–1973) was born in Kalisz, Poland. She studied for one year at the School of Applied Arts in Prague, and then at the Ecole Nationale Supérieure des Beaux-Arts in Paris. Early in her career, her sculptures were primarily figurative, executed in bronze, marble, resin, and plaster. Her work explored the amorphous and erotic shapes of the human form and its biological functions. Facing illness at the end of her life, she increasingly cast her own body, leaving an enduring record of her own existence and showing a conscious awareness of her own mortality.

In the following poem, written two years before her death, Szapocznikow refers to a Rolls-Royce that she sculpted in Carrara and pink Portuguese marble while in Italy during the summer of 1970. These sculptures reveal an artist's desire for sumptuously tactile materials, which are both timeless and permanent. In counterpoint, the second part of the poem captures the fleeting moment of creation which, like pliant chewing gum, is both transient and quotidian.

One Sunday . . .

One Sunday, in full sunshine
tired of hours of polishing
my Rolls-Royce
in pink Portuguese marble,
I sat, deep in thought
chewing absent-mindedly my chewing gum.
Pulling out of my mouth the strangest forms
I suddenly realized
the existence of an extraordinary collection of abstract sculptures,
passing between my teeth.

It would be enough to photograph and enlarge
my chewed-up discoveries,
to face the fact of sculptural creation.
Chew well, look around you.
Creation is contained between dreams
and ordinariness.

Written in 1971. Originally published in *Alina Szapocznikow: Fotorzeźby 1971* (Wrocław: Wrocławska Galeria Fotografii, 1978). Minor corrections to the spelling and grammar have been made, with the permission of the copyright holder

•●

GETA BRATESCU

The Romanian artist Geta Bratescu was born in Ploiesti in 1926 and studied at Bucharest University and at the Academy of Fine Arts in Bucharest. She works in many mediums, from graphic art and sculpture to installation and video. She was one of the first artists in Romania to experiment with Happenings, recorded on film and video, and with concepts like the morphing of her own body and face on film.

Bratescu's film script "Sleep—Awakening—the Game" is part of a larger film project from 1978 entitled The Studio. *In the following excerpt the focus is on the relationship between the artist and the camera "eye," which is described as recording each scene with irony and humor, expressions intended to be perceived independently, and yet inextricably, from those of the actual cameraman, Ion Grigorescu. In the first part, the camera, as if a curious intruder, visually explores the space and content of the artist's studio, including the body of the artist who lies sleeping. It is followed by a passive observation of the artist at work in the studio. Finally, in the third part, "The Game," the artist, evidently aware of the gaze of the camera, performs for it in a comical and absurd manner. The scene ends with the camera, seemingly grown bored, letting its gaze wander off.*

Sleep—Awakening—The Game

Sleep

The studio door opens slowly. The Eye (movie camera) infiltrates, not directly toward the center of the studio but, faltering and curious in equal measure, to the left, leisurely, along the wall. The bulky fireplace, the cardboard cylinders, two crates with piles of paper on top and a large satchel of translucent plastic, inside of which you discern pieces of canvas, motley leftovers, skeins of wool. When it is about to cross over to the other wall, the Eye detects me, spies me in a sudden perspective as I sleep on the bunk bed, sprawled out, my skull in the foreground (bristly, twining hair strands), monumental forehead and nose, then the body, diminishing progressively as the Eye moves to the distant toe tips. Once captured in the Eye's memory, sleep coalesces all that the Eye has seen and continues to see. Objects become heavier, heave, secrete filament for the cocoon whose larva I am.

The Eye advances along the walls: frames, boxes, paper, felt, canvas, other bags larger and smaller, all on a metal shelf; the cabinet with the etching tools, flat wooden boxes, metal boxes, tubes, paper rolls; crates for shipping figs (read label) placed on top of one another to mimic shelves; on top of them: the hot plate, the coffeepot, cups, glasses, coffee in a glass jar; from the upper rafter, fastened on tiny nails, hang numerous tea bags, dried up after use. The window, open. The Eye glides over the windowsill, beyond the balcony's grating, creeps toward the poplars across the way, verging on their tops and veers to the right, where it brushes against the corner of the St. Joseph Cathedral, bedecked by aluminum scaffolding.

Then the Eye retracts and continues on its path in the studio, along the walls. The sink; below, the dustpan, the broom, an unidentified object belonging to a mechanical device; the floor, worn, its scratches; once again, the wall, the other one, this one entirely empty all the way to the corner by the door; there, panels and frames; above, in a swing strapped to the pipes, numerous paper rolls. The door is closed, the studio space is now completely encompassed. The Eye aims its attention at me, from the opposite side now, the soles; these, in the foreground, are acutely amplified; above them, as if suspended, the chin and the nostrils. The Eye becomes hazy; then, refocusing, shoots up over the drawing board: traces, lines, a row of jars of tempera paint on a tray, paint tubes, some barely used, others well-squeezed, water glasses; crucibles, pencils, ruler, compass, stained rags, paintbrushes in a jar, another jar for bamboo sticks, goose feathers, air brush, a spatula, a shoemaker's knife; a bulky volume of *Max Ernst: Collages;* the edge of the drawing board connected by a vise to the foot of the jointed, high arm of the lamp; the chair with the bulging seat, with the austere back and arms. Beneath the drawing board, the same scratched floor, full of holes; pieces of paper, the straw wastebasket; inside it, crumpled paper, a box of glue, peach pits, a bottle of kefir, broken. Behind the chair, on the floor, a metal rod, wire, wood planks. The Eye swivels. I sleep. Above, suspended on a hook from the beam next to the fireplace, two folding chairs (tools of the landscape painter); folded, they interweave their curved legs, their circular seats stacked over one another, one of them sporting on its back two burn spots that give it the aspect of a face. The Eye (movie camera) roams, retraces its steps in a haze.

Suddenly lucid, it encounters on the ground a large, unfolded sheet of paper. On it, a peremptory sketch, squares, and in each square the symbol of a person (five lines, torso, arms, legs) each time in a different position, surrounded by arrows, words dispersed everywhere, numbers. The Eye lingers on the word PLAY, then glides toward the white wall; white.

Awakening

A space articulated by two white panels, one vertical, the other horizontal, both white; I find myself in this amorphous space. Standing, gluing my spinal column to the vertical panel, I mark the level above the top of my head, my height. From there I trace downward a perpendicular line on the horizontal plane; parallel to this, starting also from the mark of my height, I trace an upper horizontal line. I sprawl out at the intersection of the two panels, careful that my sole matches the level of the vertical line; once again I mark the level above my head; from this point I trace upward a second vertical line, and when it meets with the upper horizontal line, the perimeter of the square of the vertical plane is now enclosed. In the same manner I sketch its projection on the horizontal plane; the two squares dictate the image of a cube the same dimension as my height. (Once, during the summer, I swam in a glacial lake between two mountains; emerging out of the water, my skin's weft proclaimed itself autonomous, a cool wrapping studded with bubbly beads of water; this event, I recall, awakened at the level of sensation, a full conscience of existence: I am!)
I act within this cube of awakening

The first action: I trace the diagonals of the two squares, on a vertical plane and on a horizontal plane. (The diagonal line, though part of the economy of the square, contradicts its character, its stability: restricted by angles opposite to one another, the diagonal desires to surpass them; it is movement; in the pictographic system it describes ascent and descent.) I attempt numerous times to give my entire body the ascendant direction along the diagonal of the vertical square; I am not

Geta Bratescu. *The Studio*. 1978. Still photographs from 8mm film. Courtesy the artist

successful. I recline across the diagonal of the horizontal square; I rest there for a long time. (This extended time period castigates earthly indolence and inertia and thus valorizes the discomfort and the risk-taking of the first attempt, the temptation's irrepressible force, as well as, each time, its failure.) I crawl along the diagonal until my outstretched hands can grab hold of things on the floor, in the vicinity of my spatial grasp; I draw them to myself. I sit up on my knees, examine attentively: seven wooden boards wrapped in black felt, identical in shape and size, rectangles the size of a hand, rounded corners; a box with a lid.

The second action: I sit cross-legged in the center of the square, I organize the wooden boards wrapped in felt in a circle; I pick one up and strike the surface of the other six with it; at first the strikes follow one another at random; then they gain their own rhythm, and this order of felt, neither noise nor sound, responds to the elementary symmetry I enjoy inside the cube.

The third action: Pafnutie's box (An edition of *Who's Who* that is not yet published should keep a record of Pafnutie; a monk situated on the lowest rung of the monastic hierarchy, mimicking the fate of his patron, St. Pafnutie, situated on the lowest rung of Heaven; the monk Pafnutie incarnates a limit: in him Nasrudin, the keeper of Aesop's last breath, breathes his last. Pafnutie doesn't know how to pray; he is filthy and a mute; all the thankless labor at the monastery is passed on to him, work is like breathing to him. At night he gathers his thoughts through another kind of labor: out of a heap of old cassocks, he sorts, cuts, sews, fastens, crimps, twists, braids. In other words, he tailors sorts of toys for no one. He organizes them in wooden boxes, but not before he whittles at the bottom of the box a hollow to fit the form that will occupy it.) I open Pafnutie's box and extract a long, thin strip of cloth compressed like a little ball; freed from its hollow, the spiral unfurls; I compress it again and stand; I drop it from this new height; in its fall, the ball begins to unfurl; on impact, the unfurling combines with a forward motion: a wild beast, an odd reptile. I redo the experiment, but do not obtain the same result; the cloth spiral manifests its personality in a different manner each time.

The Game

As from a crypt the Eye (movie camera) watches; everything takes place at its own level and in front of it, in a section of the studio already recorded by it. The two zoo-anthropomorphic chairs have descended from the beam next to the fireplace and can now be viewed in an open position. I sit on a chair and play "patty-cake" with the invisible occupant in front of me. I stand, I execute a reverent bow, I stare into the glass window of the cabinet with the etching tools; the window transmutes to mirror, I stare at the overlong and large man's shirt I wear, I unfasten the buttons at the neck, raise the collar, I pull the shirt over my head, I button it back again; the collar is supported by the top of my head, my head has disappeared. My arms motion in a wayward manner, my hands flail at the air, they grab hold of all that gets in their way, they grab hold of each other, duel with one another with metal bars, wooden bars, ransack stacks of paper, wave I don't know what sort of striped-canvas sheets, rummage through and scatter tubes, pencils; the palette vibrates under the swat from my fingers, my arms vibrate too, my torso, the stiff collar flutters to one side, then the other; the palette flies off; the printing press, caught by its handle, the body spins faster and faster around its spiraling axis; flung off, the body loses its balance; falls; rests in its curled-up position. Then, abruptly, rises to its knees, and as the arms open they form, together with the torso, the shape of a gigantic Y; only the clenched palms betray the nature of this artifice. To the right and left of this figure, enhancing its symmetry, the two chairs delineate a more removed plane, the background. The Eye (movie camera) lingers upon this tableau, "like a connoisseur"; then, as though disillusioned, rises to the ceiling; descends along the electric wire and, under the metallic shade of the lamp, attempts to decipher the generic label on the bulb which condenses the studio within itself. Spherical, concentric, anamorphic, globular image-object, ornament, the studio thus mirrored flashes with the irony of present magic, to be encompassed in what you encompass, to wear what wears you.

Written in 1977. Originally published in *Atelier Continuu* (Bucharest: Cartea Romanesca, 1985). Translated by Julian Semilian.

•●

SANJA IVEKOVIĆ

A graduate of the Zagreb Academy of Fine Arts, Sanja Iveković (born 1949) is a media and performance artist who, in the late 1960s, chose the area of public space as the venue for her activity. To her the concept of public art did not only involve acting in that space, it was also aimed at questioning the socio-political context of the work and its functions and supporting mechanisms. By the early 1970s she had become one of the most prominent feminist artists in Eastern Europe.

Iveković's work Double Life *from 1975 is a series of photographic collages composed in pairs, a selection of which is shown here. On one side are photographs of the artist at various stages in her life and on the other are ads from popular women's magazines. The original edition of* Double Life, *which was issued as an artist's book, included sixty-two pairs of photographs and was printed in 1976 by the Museum of Contemporary Art, Zagreb. The ads were reproduced in color and Iveković's photographs were in black and white. The artist added captions, much as in a family album, indicating when and where each image was taken. For the ads, she cited the primarily Western European magazines that served as her sources. With strikingly minimal intervention, Iveković transformed these personal photographs into narratives of the invented double life of the artist.*

The juxtaposition of public and private images, advertisements and intimate snapshots, politics and aesthetics, illuminate the long-term goal of Iveković's subversive tactics: to turn these seeming opposites into works of fiction. —Nada Beroš

Double Life: Documents for Autobiography 1959–75

Originally published in *Dvostruki Život-Double Life 1959–1975,* Galeriji suvremene umjetnosti u Zagrebu (The Gallery of Contemporary Art in Zagreb), 1976. Courtesy of the Generali Foundation, Vienna.

Klorane non vi promette una pelle da bambina.
Perché anche una bambina ha bisogno di Klorane.

Di solito si cita la pelle di una bambina come esempio di pelle perfetta.

Certo, è una pelle tesa, compatta, elastica. Non presenta rughe né imperfezioni rilevanti.

Ma già a dieci anni, la nostra pelle è una pelle grassa o tendente al grasso, oppure è una pelle secca o tendente al secco.

Ha bisogno, cioè, di un trattamento specifico che garantisca l'igiene, la pulizia, la protezione, in perfetta armonia con le funzioni naturali dell'epidermide.

I ricercatori dei Laboratoires Klorane hanno individuato la risposta a questi problemi in alcuni estratti vegetali, che sono alla base delle quattro linee dei fitocosmetici Klorane.

Si tratta, naturalmente, di prodotti che vantano un'origine naturale, si sono sempre dimostrati ipoallergici.

Sfruttando l'azione emolliente, idratante dell'Althea, una pianta che appartiene alla famiglia delle Malvacee, e quella astringente dell'Aubépine, un arbusto comune nelle campagne, la Klorane ha messo a punto la Linea à l'Aubépine naturelle per pelli decisamente grasse, la Linea à l'Aubépine enrichie per pelli miste tendenti al grasso, la Linea à l'Althea naturelle per pelli miste tendenti al secco, la Linea à l'Althea enrichie per pelli secche e sensibili.

Vendita esclusiva in farmacia.

Sono trattamenti completi, con latte, tonico e base protettrice.

Non usare anche uno solo dei prodotti della propria linea significherebbe diminuire i benefici di tutto il trattamento.

Latte, tonico e base devono agire in associazione per rafforzare l'azione dei rispettivi principi attivi.

Parlatene con il vostro farmacista.

E' lui che, pur non vantando i prodotti Klorane proprietà terapeutiche, li vende in esclusiva, e vi potrà consigliare il trattamento più adatto al vostro tipo di pelle. Per rendere la pelle più sana. Cioè, più bella.

Klorane tratta ogni pelle secondo natura. E' solo in farmacia.

144

Italia

"GRAZIA," June 1974

Summer 1959

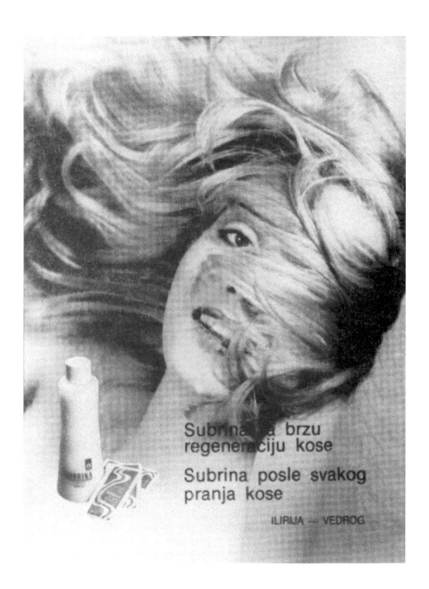

Subrina za brzu
regeneraciju kose

Subrina posle svakog
pranja kose

ILIRIJA — VEDROG

"DUGA," 1975

1962

Ladyzeta Relax
il Collant elastico alla moda.
(Perché rende ancora piú belle le tue gambe, mentre le fa riposare).

Quando indossi Ladyzeta Relax, ti accorgi subito che è diverso dagli altri collant elastici per la sua eccezionale trasparenza, proprio come un collant alla moda.
Cosi le tue gambe diventano ancora piú belle, mentre la speciale maglia ad elasticità differenziata di Ladyzeta, le mantiene riposate per tutto il giorno.

Collant elastico
Ladyzeta Relax L. 3.900
è un prodotto Zambeletti,
venduto solo in farmacia.

in **Lycra*** Du Pont

"GRAZIA," June 1975

1961. In the fifth class of the High School of Dance

Estée Lauders feuchtigkeits-konservierende

Performance Creme

Pflege-Hochleistung für Ihre Haut –

vielleicht zum ersten Mal in Ihrem Leben.

Verbessern Sie die Leistungsfähigkeit der Haut – und Sie verbessern Ihr
Aussehen. Die im Gewebe festgehaltene Feuchtigkeit ist entscheidend für
die frische, glatte Hautoberfläche. Estée Lauders Performance Creme
versorgt die Haut nicht nur mit Feuchtigkeit, sondern erhöht auch ihre
Fähigkeit, Feuchtigkeit zu binden.

Ein antibakterieller Wirkstoff in Performance Creme schützt die Haut
vor den negativen Einflüssen unserer stress- und schmutzbelasteten Umwelt.
Vitamine aus natürlichen vegetarischen Ölen, kombiniert mit aktiven
Depot-Feuchtigkeitsspendern, machen die Haut bereiter zur Aufnahme des
nachfolgenden Estée Lauder-Nährpräparats. Das Resultat: ein frischer,
lebendiger, funktionsfähiger Teint.

Estée Lauder

Exclusiv-Depotnachweis:Estée Lauder Cosmetics GmbH, 5 Köln 1. Brabanter Str. 53. Tel. 02 21/52 60 74-79

"BRIGITTE," May 1974

1966. In the first class of the Academy of Fine Arts

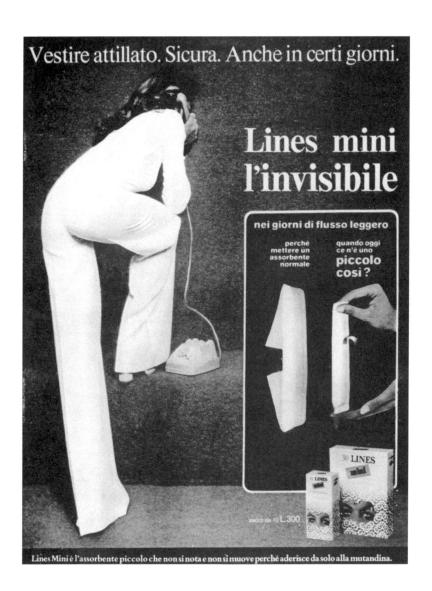

"ANNA BELLA," August 1975

October 1974. Speaking with Vojan

November 1975. On the way to Seurre-Beaune, Bourgogne

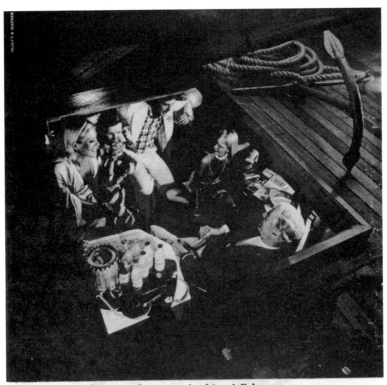

Spia cosa bevono nei cabinati d'alto mare.
Schweppes Bitter Lemon, per esempio.

Schweppes ha molte buone conoscenze.

"AMICA," December 1975

August 1975. Sailing. Breakfast aboard with Henri and Dubravko

"ELLE," December 1975

November 1975. Trying on a skirt, made by myself

PETR REZEK

Petr Rezek (born 1948) is a Czech phenomenological philosopher and enfant terrible among Czech intellectuals. He has lectured extensively on subjects ranging from classical philosophy to contemporary art. Rezek taught briefly at the Academy of Fine Arts in Prague and also spent several years as a teacher of philosophy at Charles University in Prague. He is head of his own publishing house, which specializes in classical and contemporary philosophy.

In the 1970s Rezek worked as a psychologist, and the following essay, from 1977, was one of the first attempts to reflect theoretically on the activities of Action artists in Czechoslovakia. A group of these artists gave Rezek short accounts of their dreams, which he analyzed. After doing so, however, he was informed that he had been tricked and that these accounts were not dreams but descriptions of their Action art pieces. Rezek then became interested in the unique conditions through which such artworks were perceived, especially the difference between the conditions of viewers present during the action and viewers perceiving the action only through photography and written text. In this sense it is interesting to compare Rezek's text with that of another writer in this anthology, Andrei Monastyrski, from the group Collective Actions (pp. 174–75).

Encounters with Action Artists

I.

I have known Karel Miler since 1970 and have followed his attempts at Action art for the last three years (this being 1977). Similarly, I have known Jan Mlčoch and Petr Štembera for two years. I made their acquaintance one evening, an event that will be discussed at some length later.

From the very beginning, I decided not to ask these authors certain types of questions such as: "What is it that you are really doing?" or "What is the meaning of your work?" Any answer coming from somebody else, i.e., from the outside, did not satisfy me either. Instead, I tried to find the answers myself.

It is for these reasons that I made it my first priority to find out the manner in which they conceived and presented their work. Usually I received comments that went somewhat like this: "I got this and that from here and there to be made into this and that." (After some time I was given a chance to view the photographic documentation of their work.) In general terms, this sort of report may not be considered very different from, say, an account by a friend telling me that during a visit to his girlfriend, they roasted some meat and subsequently ate it. Everything in my friend's story seems obvious to me, since it is easy to imagine their actions as a contingent feature of their relationship, even though I may have been somewhat puzzled by my friend's decision to visit his girlfriend on that particular evening because I knew they had been quarreling the day before. Nevertheless, this too puts my puzzlement squarely in the context of everyday life. Perhaps I may have been somewhat surprised, but that is all. At most, my curiosity may have gotten the better of me and prompted me to ask him for an explanation.

It is quite a different matter if an author tells me that he has wrapped some garbage in paper or buttered a slice of bread. Neither am I sure that I would want to bother to tell someone that I happened to climb a mountain during foul weather, period. The only reason for mentioning the bare facts of this activity would be to offer them as a necessary introduction to something more important to follow, or, to use the previous example, to emphasize that what I did was leading toward something out of the ordinary, namely, "While I was buttering my bread. . . ." Thus, if I had ventured to climb the mountain only scantily dressed during cold weather, I could be using this "experience" as an introduction to reveal my "ignorance" with respect to sudden weather changes in the mountains, or as part of a story concerning a wager, or in connection with an attempt to rescue somebody in distress.

In general, any story will either directly or indirectly try to answer the question **WHY**? In part, this is in order to provide an answer to the **WHY** of telling a story, and in part, to find out **WHY** this or that was done. However, even though the above-mentioned authors related similar incidents to me, they never provided an answer to the **WHY** of their stories. It is as if the **WHY** had somehow vanished.

This means that I was told stories that could not be made intelligible within the normal range of conventional inter-subjective circumstances. I had a hunch that somehow this reluctance to deal with the **WHY** was also meant to say something about the author himself. I further felt that they did not want to reveal their private self to some outside observer, and that I had no real justification in pursuing this line of questioning. It also meant that as long as I stuck to the **WHAT** of the story, I should avoid asking for its **WHY**.

A written version, typical of this kind of storytelling that does not offer explanations but only a narrative, would read something like the following:

> Jan Mlčoch
> Climbed Kotel Mountain
> April 26, 1974:
> I climbed the Kotel Mountain by myself during foul weather, in wind and rain.
> I took photographs during my climb.

Clearly the text does not provide any clue as to what the author had in mind. It merely describes what happened, without mentioning the **WHY** or **BECAUSE**. It simply presents the event as **something that happened** (of its own accord), but not what made it happen.

Once a story is **framed in this manner**, the statement "I took a teapot, boiled water, and poured tea" is transformed into an act of puzzlement with respect to its portents. It does not only suggest a break with ordinary circumstances, but at the same time challenges any concept of the "ordinary." For example, the ordinary act of pouring tea is not presented as something "special," but simply as "**pouring**." As an ordinary act, pouring has no significance attached to it. Thus, if Mlčoch told us that he climbed a mountain and took photographs along the way, he differs from an ordinary tourist in the sense that he did that and nothing else. He did not delight in nature, he did not watch the sunset, he did not take part in recreational activities, nor did he try to get fit.

It took me a full two years before I came to understand this peculiar way of storytelling. And, it was also exactly two years ago that I was introduced to Jan Mlčoch by Karel Miler and Petr Štembera during a conference on the interpretation of dreams (*Four Lectures on Phenomenological Psychology and Psychotherapy,* Prague, 1975).

II.

Our first meeting took place soon after the above-mentioned conference. The authors asked me to interpret their activities as if they were a dream. Why they should have advanced such a proposition can only be understood by those who are familiar with the interpretation of dreams, as set forth by Medard Boss (cf., *Der Traum und seine Auslegung [Dreams and Their Interpretation]*, Bern, 1953, and, more recently, *Es träumte mir vergangene Nacht . . . [I Dreamed Last Night . . .]*, Bern, 1975). Boss's interpretation of dreams differs from the generally accepted theories of Sigmund Freud in that it does not interpret dreams as symbols that stand in for something else. Instead, Boss asserts that in his dream interpretations, one thing is not substituted for another. This makes it possible to discern the full range of possibilities constituting the dream world on the basis of its what and how, according to the predispositions of the dreamer. However, in order to reach such a conclusion, one must first come to know what makes the objective content of the dreamer's experience exactly what it is. Boss calls this preparatory unveiling of the interpretation of things an uncovering of the ontological phenomenon, which entails the necessity of discovering objectively substantive hints in a similar manner as revealed in the analytical passages of Martin Heidegger.

During our first meeting, Jan Mlčoch offered me the following dream as a "warm-up" exercise for interpretation:

> I am in the attic of a vast building, possibly a mansion or a castle; I came here of my own free will, accompanied by two other men. We brought along some ropes and a few other items. The attic is covered with dust, and cluttered with all sorts of wires and boxes, probably left there by some repairmen. The two men approach me. They appear to be a few years older than I. One of them blindfolds me while the other ties my wrists and ankles with some sort of bandages. Finally, they plug my ears with wax and I lie down on the floor. The two men tie ropes to my hands and feet and hoist me up into the air. After a few minutes I tell them that my wrists are in pain. They quickly lower me to the floor.

This is how I interpreted the dream: "The attic is a place where the top of a house points directly toward the sky; the roof covering the house is therefore close by, thus bringing the outside close as well. But the attic is also that part of the house which remains uninhabited; it is a space, somewhat secluded from the inhabited parts of the house, representing a realm of secret games. Its seclusion is used by all those who want to hide—lovers, suicides, cats who need a safe place to hide their litters. These peculiar characteristics of the attic are important for the act of suspension to occur as experienced in the dream: It takes place in seclusion, heightened by the fact that all sensory experience is isolated from contact with the outside, including the ground (i.e., the floor). It is an attempt to free oneself from the confinement of "place," to be "in the air," free from any point of spatial reference. All is well as long as the weight of the human "here" does not start registering the sensation of pain. Up to that very moment one succeeds in being "nowhere," which means that any relationship to tangible things is eliminated and that it is possible to feel virtually at one with the totality of the entire world."

Conclusion: an explicit act of opening oneself to the all and a subsequent return to one's corporeal predicament. Not wanting to infringe upon private matters, I ended my interpretation with the above ontological-structural analysis, which should, at least by implication, be considered part of any valid interpretation

Jan Mlčoch. *Suspension—The Great Sleep.* Prague, August 5, 1974. Courtesy the artist

of a dream. Jan accepted my interpretation as deeply perceptive, not of the dream as such, but, to my surprise, because it reminded him of an action performed in Prague in August 1974. The documentation of this event is complemented by the following text: "I allowed myself to be suspended by my hands and feet by means of plastic ropes attached at three points. My eyes were blindfolded with a black scarf, and my ears were plugged with beeswax." I would have found it extremely difficult to produce a similar interpretation as the one cited earlier, based solely on the above short and dry "story," even though it does contain all the essential elements of the more extensive dream account.

My second dream interpretation, attempted during that same evening, was that of an action performed by Petr Štembera. It dealt with some sort of ceremony of self-acceptance, which took place in front of a photograph of the author, which he had placed on an improvised altar lit by candles. After having some of his blood drawn by an assistant, the artist mixed it with his urine, hair and nail clippings, and subsequently swallowed the whole brew. Spectators, standing, surrounded the scene. Apart from its other functions, the photograph was obviously meant to remind everyone of the purpose of the ceremony. Once the ceremony was concluded, it was assumed that the photograph was no longer needed, and the author tried to set it on fire. However, it would not burn. I interpreted this unexpected event as an important factor, contributing to the meaning of the action.

Evidently, the burning of the photograph was also meant to signify that it was no longer necessary to have it present as a focus of attention and as an indicator of the purpose of the ceremony, since by having accepted himself in his own inner self, Petr was now ready to join the others—the surrounding spectators. But the fact that the photograph did not ignite seemed to indicate that anyone who begins by looking at himself (the action was titled "Self-Portrait: Narcissus") will never succeed in finding the path to himself, since understanding oneself is only possible through the understanding of others.

III.

These actions, documented in photographs and texts, conceal the profound link between human experience and the humdrum details of everyday life. But in order to become aware of this relationship, they must not be viewed as if through the eyes of some fact-finding statistician who may have no interest in questioning the meaning of what he is recording. In contrast, these original texts, complemented by documentary photographs, are of an evocative nature, similar to a dream, confronting us with the need for interpretation.

The statement "Mlčoch had himself suspended in the attic" is different from the statement "Yesterday I became the father of a son." The second event is self-evident; only detailed questions remain concerning the baby's weight, name, etc. The fact of the birth itself remains uncontested. In contrast, the first statement obliges us to accept it as a case of the self-constituting evolution of meaning (all our actions have this character, except that we seldom pay attention to it), which we are able to discern only because it has been presented to us as a proposition in the form of a project conceived and planned by the author. Here, the author accepts responsibility for a situation which he has designed himself, but which eventually turns out not to be a situation exclusively of his own making. Even in cases where we plan to have a child and a child is actually born, we accept the responsibility for the consequences of a situation that is essentially not entirely of our own creation. However, what is missing in the latter case is an explicit orientation toward constitutive meaning.

What is it then that we are confronting in the first example? For one, it is an account that refers to something that happened. For another, the interpretation of any dream that somebody has related to us must include a reference to the existential world of the dreamer. In contrast, the documentary evidence of an action does not point toward a dream, which is, in fact, experienced "involuntarily," but toward something that in its very makeup comes very close to a celebration.

Both the temporal nature and the meaning of a celebration are similar in their fundamental makeup to that of these actions—the temporal structure remains the same, even if the celebration itself is always different. The meaning of a celebration resides in its relationship to the whole, in the reenactment of a historical event and the representation of one's place within a totality. Life proceeds from celebration to celebration, for celebration endows it with meaning and thus provides a foil for everyday existence, but otherwise leaves behind nothing of concrete substance. A celebratory act only becomes possible by confronting the commonplace with the festive.

In a similar manner, life proceeds from one action to the next, each phase being the preparation for what is about to happen within another time frame. The above-mentioned actions differ from a common celebration in the sense that they are primarily the acts of an individual and also because they do not recognize any other tradition than that accumulated by the life experiences of their author. The meaning of these experiments is best captured by the answer of the pond to the question of the animals of the forest about what Narcissus looked like. The pond replied that it did not know, but added that it adored Narcissus simply because it discovered in his eyes the reflection of its own beauty (Oscar Wilde).

Just as the pond was unable to bear witness directly, the Action artist is unable to leave behind a fixed pictorial representation of his work. If asked what he is actually doing, he will answer: "I merely see myself in what I am doing." It is in this sense that his every action turns into a nonpictorial self-portrait, a celebration of the self-exploration of the territory of his own self-awareness — physical, spiritual, in action, and in thought. Action becomes a celebration, adding significance to the ordinary. Just as the pond was unable to "see" Narcissus, the Action artist does not "see" the mirror reflecting his image. And just as the pond hinted with its answer to the forest animals at what Narcissus expected to hear, thus indirectly exposing the underlying meaning of Narcissus' situation, documented "storytelling" indirectly exposes (documents) the possibility of life situating itself within a special moment of time in time, thus acting within its own special time frame, not subject to external happenstance, but consciously planned. The contents of an action are thus just as elusive for the author as the countenance of Narcissus proved elusive to the pond. This shift away from image toward action creates a situation in which it seems impossible to get hold of anything and where nothing seems to be at hand to guide us. The document merely tells us that there has been a celebration and what it was about. A celebration cannot be faced with its own image; it can only be celebrated.

IV.

Analyzing the "narration" of an action may also enable us to understand [Donald] Judd's statement: "If someone says his work is art, it's art." Only somebody who knows that something like this is possible can say this. But if something like this needs to be said, it also follows that art ceases to be a self-evident proposition. To say that what I am doing is art represents not merely a new attitude toward action, but also means that it has to be executed differently — simply executed and nothing more. There is a challenge as well as an urgent appeal contained in these statements, declaring that this is art. For obvious reasons this urgency gets easily lost in magazines, where such "stories" appear next to each other by the dozen.

The above-mentioned three authors assert that what they are doing is art. Given the fact that my mind has been engrossed with their actions for two years, their assertion that this is art has the same evocative character as that of a dream that we may have dreamed some years ago, and that we still cannot fully understand to this day. It is a dream that still cries out for interpretation and poses a challenge for a deeper level of understanding.

Written in 1977. Originally published in Petr Rezek, *Tělo věc a skutečnost v současném umění [Body, Object, and Reality in Contemporary Art]*, Prague, 1983. Translated by Eric Dluhosch.

•●

PIOTR PIOTROWSKI

Piotr Piotrowski (born 1952) is an art historian and curator. He has written extensively on the art and theory of the avant-garde, politics, and visual culture with a focus on the history of Central and Eastern European modern and contemporary art. He is Chair of the Institute of Art History and head of the History of Modern Art section at Adam Mickiewicz University in Poznań, Poland. From 1992 to 1997 he was Chief Curator of Contemporary Art at the National Museum in Poznań.

The following essay was written for a symposium organized by the Moderna Galerija in Ljubljana, in response to their 1998 exhibition Body and the East. This survey of performance and body art from fourteen Central and Eastern European countries was presented in Ljubljana and in New York at Exit Art. Piotrowski draws a comparison between the perception of the male and female body in Eastern European and Western cultures and argues that the totalitarian political system in the East perpetuated the traditional notion of the "active" male and the "passive, objectified" female, and in fact relied on its functioning in these social structures. By challenging official doctrine, body art that directly addressed notions of sex and gender thus automatically became an act of subversive resistance to the political system. Piotrowski takes as an example the work of Polish artist Jerzy Bereś and Romanian Ion Grigorescu.

Male Artist's Body: National Identity vs. Identity Politics

As has been convincingly shown by the exhibition *Body and the East,* since the 1960s, in East Central Europe the art of the male body has had quite a number of adherents.[1] There are many relevant examples: Tibor Hajas, Via Lewandowsky, Petr Štembera, and others. Most of them were interested in the problem of physical and mental fitness, that is, the limits of the confrontation between the body and external stimuli. As usual, the body was defined by these artists not just in terms of subjectivity (my body), but also as a universal phenomenon (human body). Sometimes it played a purely instrumental role, functioning as an almost transparent surface that contrasted with the opaque artist's "interior." Ultimately such undertakings reinforced, rather than subverted, the traditional duality of body and soul with its hierarchical order. The recognition of one's own corporeality was often combined with more universal conclusions about corporeality as such or the human condition in general. The process of the corporeal/"psychic" self-recognition was often expressed in action—through popular Happenings and performances which also epitomized the traditional male role of the active subject. Paradoxically, the problem of the sexual definition of the male body was addressed quite rarely, as it was considered predominantly in terms of the traditional parameters of male sexuality. Thus, in many artistic presentations the male body confirmed its traditional functions rather than becoming an instrument of critical practice that would challenge the social foundations of traditional identity politics. Of course, that rule allows for certain exceptions, yet the most interesting works which appeared in this context touched upon the political dimensions of male body art. Every act of self-recognition, every challenge to conventions that defied official ideological doctrine and accepted morals, particularly in those countries where the enclaves of tolerance were either marginalized or eliminated, acquired a political meaning that deserves analysis.

The exposure of the nude male body in the art of the recent past relayed different meanings than that of the female body. In most cases, the latter was approached under the pressures of heterosexual eroticization, the dominance of the male gaze, and the proximity of that gaze to desire and pleasure. Contemporary studies of visual culture, drawing on psychoanalytic theory, have explored this problem quite comprehensively. By contrast, the male body has never been turned into an object of perception. In classical European culture, the male body therefore retained its subjective status, which was related to power and heroism, concepts associated with activity and action rather than with being shown and seen. That order, it is true, was upset by medieval Christian culture in which, according to Mario Perniola, the naked body (not only male) was interpreted in terms of humiliation and degradation, the loss of dignity and the ability to act. Early modern times, however, returned to the classic valorization of the body as either the topos of pleasure/passivity (the female body), or that of power/activity (the male one).[2]

Significant changes in the modern meaning of the male body came only with the rise of the neo-avant-garde and the cultures of sexual minorities. By systematically focusing on the male body as a combination of both elements, artists such as Robert Morris (*Waterman Switch,* 1965), Robert Mapplethorpe, or Andy Warhol reversed the relations that existed among the gaze, desire, and pleasure in classical European culture. The background of these efforts was the gay margins of culture between the world wars, while their immediate context was the sexual revolution after World War II. In East Central Europe, such a revolution did not occur. There, if at all, the male body—particularly in official visual culture of the 1950s—was represented in a heroic manner. Usually, it was not stark naked—the genitals were camouflaged in one way or another. Conservative and prudish societies of that part of the continent (perhaps with the exception of the GDR [German Democratic Republic], where the culture of nudism was quite widespread), rarely allowed for any nudity and preferred the attitude of the male heterosexual voyeur to the search for subversive models of sexual orientation.

The Eastern European male spectator was aroused by naked female bodies in photographs or films. In fact, such an attitude was not exceptional—his Western counterparts often reacted in the same way. Amelia Jones has proven that the postmodern rhetoric of the identity of the female body easily turned toward the tradition of phallocentrism, dominated by the culture of the male gaze combining desire and pleasure, which has—in her opinion—effectively prevented feminists from approaching body art in terms of identity politics. Paradoxically, feminism—particularly in its later incarnations of the 1980s—rejected body art as too vulnerable to the domination of the male gaze. Jones's critique, however, does not turn against the male heterosexual spectator to whom (at least in this case) she is quite indifferent, but against the inconsistency of feminism which, in Jones's view, all too easily falls into the traps of the culture which it rejects, and which is overly cautious in its approach to the truly revolutionary proposals of body art.

This kind of art not only has been radically challenging the Cartesian idea of the subject but, focusing on the thoroughly subversive problematic of the subject and its body, it has deconstructed the metaphysics that has turned the (female) body into an object.[3] Yet in the countries of East Central Europe, where feminist theories and gender identity politics were developing under the Communist regime without much success (if at all), such practices were particularly susceptible to phallocentric recuperation. A good example is the work of the Polish woman artist Natalia LL, who would envelop her visual representations, definitely seen in feminist terms, in a modernist, if not outright formalist, discourse. Her *Consumer's Art* from the early 1970s consists of a series of photographs showing the face of an attractive woman eating a banana or a hot dog in a manner evidently imitating oral sex, suggesting the experience of sexual pleasure without the participation of a man. What is more, contrary to the tradition of sex and gender representation, it is the man whose status is here reduced to that of a fetish. His fetishization and deprivation of sexual activity and initiative (he is the passive provider of sexual pleasure to the woman) — his obvious ironic objectification by means of trivial consumer goods — can be interpreted in the context of feminist theory and politics, largely based on Lacanian psychoanalysis.[4] In its ideological and critical aspect, Natalia LL's work undermines the masculinist representation of woman and man. Yet, paradoxically, her work is accompanied by theoretical texts that have nothing to do with the gendered definition of visual representation or with the subversion of the codes used to represent the female. In fact, these texts have nothing to do with the female at all. Rather than to feminism, Natalia LL refers to the discursive practices of Conceptual art, particularly those which, paradoxically, belong to the formalist tradition of modernist art. This is in fact a wider problem in East Central Europe, where artists routinely combined a postmodern visuality and poetics with a modernist discourse.[5]

Regardless of the specific side of the Iron Curtain, the difference between male and female body art consisted in their starting points — different status of the man and woman in European culture. In the phallocentric culture, the man is associated with action, hence male body art refers to the active body; to the body which creates circumstances itself, while in female body art the reverse is the case. Amelia Jones (following Craig Owens) claims that the female body expresses itself in the "rhetoric of the pose," since because of its conventional social roles it is passive and acquires its meaning from the outside. In other words, the meaning of the male body is created, as it were, immediately; whereas the female body means something only in relation to the images imposed by the masculinist culture, conditioning the "existence" of the female only in the perspective of the "other's" desire. This is the cause of differences both in strategies and in meanings of body art produced by male and female artists respectively.[6]

Yet, the subject matter of my talk is not the female body, but the male one. The former has been mentioned only to indicate the limits of tolerance of East Central European societies or, more precisely, the character of their tolerance, namely, the heterosexual eroticization and objectification of the female body in the male gaze of the voyeur. The appearance of the male body causes other problems, because of an evidently homophobic orientation of these societies (which is still quite widespread). The nude artist, performer, or sitter shown in a photograph, in a film as well as in other means of expression, particularly exposing his genitals, definitely challenged a taboo of visual culture. As I have said, in East Central Europe there were relatively many male artists exploiting their body. Yet, there were only a few who would turn their sex and gender into a medium of expression — who, to coin a somewhat paradoxical term, would "genderize" and "sexualize" their bodies in their artistic practices. In this short paper, I would only like to mention two completely different artists who used two different strategies, frames of reference, and — as we will see — ideologies. One is a Polish artist, Jerzy Bereś: the other a Romanian, Ion Grigorescu.

To begin with, I will give a short description of some performances of Bereś.[7] An extremely significant series of events included his performance *Prophecy I* in the Warsaw Foksal Gallery in 1968, followed by a related *Prophecy II*, performed several times in Kraków in 1968–88, and concluded by *Prophecy II Comes True* shown in 1989 in Cieszyn. During *Prophecy I* the artist, with the help of the audience, dragged a fallen tree from a nearby park to the gallery, and then, wearing only a red and white piece of canvas, assembled a "work" crowned with a bow whose red and white string was made from his "garment." *Prophecy II* was his response to violent attacks in the press, which appeared in a very tense political situation early in March 1968, during mass demonstrations of students and a brutal anti-Semitic campaign of the Communist authorities. Bereś's performance was actually provoked, as it were, by a journalist of an influential Warsaw the weekly, *Kultura,* who, under the pen name "Hamilton," published preposterous and arrogant feuilletons on various aspects of modern culture. In the middle of the Kraków Krzysztofory Gallery, Bereś placed a cartful of timber, and then, once again clad in red and white, helped by the audience, lighted some fires, using the copies of *Kultura.* After a while, he ascended the high pile of timber, made on its top a huge bow with a red and white string, and next, having asked for a burning chip from one of the fires, blew out the flame and signed the whole structure with the word "work," written with the tip of the charcoal. During the final *Prophecy,* also shown at a turning point in Polish history, right after signing the so-called round-table agreement, which put an end to the decades of Communist monopoly of power (April 1989), Bereś, having first repeated some gestures known from the previous performances, finished his presentation by writing on his body the words "comes true" and putting a red and white dot on his penis. Another relevant performance of Bereś's was *A Picture from Poland* shown in London in 1988. Its plot was quite simple, yet, particularly for the foreign (mostly British) audience, it proved very meaningful. On his naked back, the artist painted red stripes which looked like traces of flagellation, and then on his torso he painted a white question mark, completed with a red and white dot on the penis. Thus, Bereś asked a question about the sense of Polish suffering for freedom and national independence, lost after World War II under the Soviet domination.

In the *Prophecies* and *Picture from Poland* the artist called himself (his body) a "monument." The same motif appeared very distinctly in another performance called *Artist's Monument* (1978). The artist, wearing a wooden perizonium with an inscription "the artist's body," with a flag on his arm (with an inscription "the artist's soul"), pulling a tree trunk like a wheelbarrow, walked a few kilometers from Warcino to Kepice in the north of Poland. Getting to the end of his way, he made a circle with his white paint footprints, placed there his wheelbarrow, burned in it his perizonium ("the artist's body"), and put on a long robe (the flag) bearing the inscription "the artist's soul." One may realize that in all his performances (not just the ones which I have mentioned) the nude artist seemed to touch upon two different realms: the politico-historical reality of Poland, and the problem of the artist involved in history and responsible for the shape of reality—the past as well as the future—the artist-prophet.

The national paraphernalia (that is, the colors of the Polish flag) significantly demonstrated his engagement in the history of the country. Their connection with the prominent role of the artist as the one who knows the meaning of history and sacrifice for the sake of future salvation—the restoration of national independence—referred to the Polish romantic tradition. In the nineteenth century, when Poland was occupied by the three neighboring empires (Russia, Prussia, and Austria), the artist (usually the poet) created (discovered) the meaning of history, prophesying that eventually the sacrifice of the people would bring about salvation, just like the sacrifice of Christ resulted in the salvation of humankind. Bereś consciously referred to those grand narratives of Polish culture, using their authority in his confrontation with the usurped authority of the Communists. Hence, the naked body of the artist was a vehicle of authority confirmed not only by the metaphysical sense of history, whose end would be salvation, but also by the phallocentrism of European culture which was referred to in a positive, not a critical sense. The artist's penis, with a red and white dot, would become a phallus — a symbol of the authority of genius and prophet, but also of that of culture in general. It was the source and historical legitimation of resistance against the Communist power.

The body, which was the main medium of the artist's expression and the realm of the constructed ideology, paradoxically underwent a kind of "disembodiment," being at the same time a symbol of authority and, as in the mystical Christian tradition, an expression of the "spirit." Humiliated and mangled, it died for the "spirit," or the soul to be reborn. Thus, under the circumstances, the exposure of genitals had an exclusively symbolic function — it was the phallus, the sign of authority and spiritual power sanctioned by tradition and the metaphysical sense of history, opposed to the par excellence material and usurped authority of the Communists. The Romanian artist Ion Grigorescu, counted by Ileana Pintilie among the "post-Happening generation" and more eager to use photography and film than "live" action, started from quite different premises.[8]

I will focus on his two interrelated works: a 1976 film called *Masculine/Feminine* and a series of photographs from 1977 *(Delivery),* elaborating on the idea of sexual identity. Generally speaking, in both cases the artist exposed masculine genitals in positions imitating childbirth and next to the attributes of womanhood: ovaries and a coiled umbilical cord. No doubt, Grigorescu posed a problem of sexual transgression — of feminization of the male body, open to biologically alien experience. At the same time, however, the sexual difference, highlighted by taking on the role of the female, was defined in his images not in terms of biology, but of culture. If, following Amelia Jones, we assume that in the tradition of European culture the male body has been associated with action, while the female one with exposure, adopting a pose superimposed by the phallocentric culture, then the strategy of the Romanian artist consists precisely in taking over the position assigned to the woman. The most significant are neither the natural attributes of womanhood (ovaries and the umbilical cord), nor the female function (giving birth), but the way the body is exposed to the camera eye. Simply, the artist posed, made poses, which has been traditionally [sic] assigned to the female body. A radically anti-masculinist manifestation of Grigorescu pointed to a conventional character of sex and gender roles, which implied that the authority was conventional just as well.

The phallus — a symbol of power — was degraded because its role turned out changeable and ambiguous, disrupting the functional stability of power. By the same token, the destabilization of the sexual difference became politically subversive, indicating conventional legitimation of every authority, all of a sudden questionable and precarious. In fact, quite important was the historical context of such art. After a short period of liberalization in the late sixties, the Romanian dictator

Nicolae Ceausescu, called also the "Genius of the Carpathians," made a distinct move toward strengthening the grip on social life in the early seventies, while his being "elected" president of the Socialist Republic of Romania in the middle of the decade was interpreted as the beginning of the end of one of the most authoritarian regimes of East Central Europe. The police system of control was parallel to extreme prudery and stabilization of patterns of sexual behavior. Incidentally, until today Romania has one of the most restrictive laws criminalizing homosexuality. Under such circumstances, the art of Grigorescu, revealing sex and gender, their function and meanings, acquired a par excellence political character.

In a conservative society, the very exposure of the naked male body violated the prevailing norm, while the merger of phallic and vaginal representation aimed at questioning the very foundations of the social and political order. What was actually undermined was not just the (phallocentric) legitimation of authority, but the stability of the subject itself which turned out not to be established once and forever as a result of some metaphysical verdict, but negotiable in the context of meanings imposed on sex by various social practices, including those of visual representation. The Cartesian cogito was supplanted by a dynamic construct whose meanings could be defined only by way of constant, endless confrontations. In the traditional order, sex and gender identity is fixed, allegedly determined by the biological functions of the body which constitute the sexual difference and its hierarchical character. In the post-Freudian psychoanalytic theory, and particularly in the works of Jacques Lacan, such naturalistic determinism has been questioned, and — as we know — the sexual difference has been defined in terms of culture. According to Lacan's commentator, Jacqueline Rose, the anatomical difference does not translate directly into the sexual one, but is its "figure," a representative which lets it surface on the level of speech.[9] Thus, the sexual difference is symbolic and cultural, not biological or natural. The stable, necessary, or ultimate character of the construction of subjectivity is questioned, giving way to a collapse of the hierarchy of genders.

The identity politics formulated by various minorities, including feminists, has taken advantage of this chance to develop critical instruments of analysis aimed at authoritarian social and political structures. Ion Grigorescu also situated himself in this context — because of the essentially totalitarian character of the Romanian regime, his art became particularly radical and subversive. Any authoritarian system — or its extreme, totalitarianism — can function safely only with stable and hierarchical social structures whose foundation seems to be phallocentrism. Therefore all the Stalinist and post-Stalinist political regimes adopted definitely anti-female policies, often under the disguise of spectacular gestures: women could have their own organizations (which were, of course, official and fully controlled by the central committee of the Communist party), or "even" become high-ranking party and state officials. Perhaps their paradoxical ally was the traditional conservatism of the societies under the Communist rule — it was paradoxical indeed, since at first sight tradition appeared to be a perfect antidote to the "proletarian revolution." Yet, when we take a closer look at the functioning of the societies of Soviet Europe — reaching beneath the level of class struggle, state control of the economy, and the transformation of institutions — we are quite likely to discover that the conservative models of social behavior, for instance as regards sex, favored the stability of the system. Hence, questioning the social principles was actually aimed at the very basis of the totalitarian regime.

Bereś and Grigorescu adopted two different strategies of resistance — I have put them together somewhat arbitrarily to illustrate a wide range of artistic practices and theories of male body art, as well as to provoke a question about the critical functions of their art under the Communist regime. No doubt, the very use of the male body and the exposure of the genitals must have had, in the context of heterosexual and homophobic societies, a subversive significance. This is, however, the only link between the Polish and Romanian artist. The former made references to tradition, to the grand narratives of Polish culture which is the heritage of romanticism, which became an authority of the strategy of resistance; the latter, on the contrary, questioned the traditional sexual politics — the core of conservative society — suggesting that its destabilization was a radical challenge to the very essence of power. Bereś opposed the totalitarian regime with the authority of tradition — in other words, he pitted one authority and hierarchy against the other. Grigorescu, in his critical identity politics, rejected the principle of authority based invariably on hierarchy; he rejected hierarchy as such, for if it forms the foundation of all authority, the Romanian artist repudiated the very principle of authority, opposing it by means of his critical practice of subversion aimed at its cornerstone. Both the *Prophecies* of Bereś and *Masculine/Feminine* of Grigorescu were determined by history. They were created in specific places and at particular moments in time, although, as it seems, the strategy of the Romanian artist implies a more general perspective, reaching beyond the local frame of the East Central European Communist regimes.

Let us, however, ask a question about their function now, in the present context of both countries and the whole former Soviet bloc. Let us ask about the critical tradition (or traditions) of the present political debates as they have been determined by art, by different artistic practices. The answer does not come easily and simply; to a large extent, it depends on the definition of the present or, more precisely, the present dangers (ideological, rather than economic) faced by the post-Communist societies. Taking the risk of oversimplification, I will point to two apparently different perils haunting not just the post-Soviet, but all Europe: on the one hand, it is nationalism, with its xenophobia and socio-political obscurantism; on the other, globalism, with its totalitarian uniformity. These two dangers are indeed only seemingly contradictory, since one is to a certain extent an effect of the other. Stuart Hall writes that the return to the local is often a response to globalization.[10] The local can, however, be expressed in various forms: through nationalism or through the defense of the identity of margins. Nationalisms can be more or less closed, more or less defensive, surrounded by the walls separating them from all the "others." This way goes straight to an ethnic (or supra-ethnic, religious) fundamentalism. On the contrary, margins function within the global culture; even though they do not make its mainstream, they still remain parts of the whole so that their defense can only take place in the open. One cannot build walls around them but, on the contrary, develop channels of communication, for only in such space, in confrontation with the "mainstream," can the local be successfully defended.

In such a context, identity politics, practiced either for the sake of nationalism or the margins, may take quite different forms. In the former case, subjectivity is stable and well-defined; in the latter, its definition can never be completed, since it is constructed during permanent confrontation in a channel of communication with its round-trip traffic between the center and the periphery. This kind of identity politics is processual and ambivalent, while in the other case it becomes categorical and unambiguous. The margins are always moving, for it is impossible to pin down the essence of the relationship between them and the center. In contrast, national identity is based on a metaphysical "presence" — it is constructed on the basis of a well-defined and stable kernel. Now, to return to our examples, it seems that the art of Bereś would be closer to the national identity. Referring to the grand narratives of Polish culture, the romantic myth of the artist-prophet and the sense of national mission, he did not put tradition into doubt or propose any kind of critical discourse. On the contrary, Bereś explored the national heritage as a source of authority to criticize the reality of Communism. Will this tradition and its related identity politics match the danger of globalization? Will it resist the temptation of nationalism, trying to defend the local against global cultural developments? This is perhaps an open question which, in addition, brings us to another one: how can we defend national (and not marginal) cultures against the process of globalization? Theorizing within the framework of psychoanalysis, one may assume that the defense of identity put in such terms becomes possible only if the collective subject (nation, people) has been defined in confrontation with the outside (international culture), and not on the basis of some metaphysics of history. This is not, of course, the case of Jerzy Bereś. Another open question, however, is whether global culture is indeed international, that is, if it belongs to the same paradigm as national culture. If not it means that any defense of national identity may not be effective, and should be made, if any, in a different paradigm than the opposition of a national/ international. In such a context, let us take a last look at the identity politics founded on the deconstruction of sex and gender, presented in the art of Ion Grigorescu. No doubt, in his case the definition of subjectivity is both dynamic and, in the first place, critical.

It seems, then, that the destabilization of authority favors the margins of the "mainstream." Apparently, permanent tension which constitutes this strategy gives chances to all minorities trying to defend their identity. Yet, does this kind of art not imply the danger of speech which belongs to no one; the threat of dissolving the margin in generalized theoretical discourse? In other words, does it not — paradoxically — suggest the danger of recuperation of critical strategies by globalism? This is, perhaps, the last open question here. However, feminist, gay, and ethnic (not national) minority cultures, which create their identity politics in reference to the deconstruction of the imperial subject, point to distinct places from which they speak and to specific values which they affirm, formulating distinct identity politics. This place seems to be definitely on the margins of global imperialism. Consequently, the tradition inherent in the art of Grigorescu seems to offer a method of criticism which can be used against the threats of global imperialism and nationalism alike.

Notes

1. *Body and the East: From the 1960s to the Present,* ed. Z. Badovinac (Ljubljana: Moderna Galerija, 1998).
2. M. Perniola, "Between Clothing and Nudity," in *Fragments for a History of the Human Body,*

Part II, ed. M. Feher (New York: Zone Books, 1989); cf. also M. Walters, *The Male Nude: A New Perspective* (New York: Peddington Press, 1978).

3. A. Jones, *Body Art/Performing the Subject* (Minneapolis: The University of Minnesota Press, 1998), p. 21 ff.

4. A. Jakubowska, "Kobieta wobec seksualności — podporz dkowana, uwikłana czy wyzwolona? O kilku aspektach twórczości Natalii LL z perspektywy psychoanalizy Lacanowskiej" ["Woman and Sexuality — Submission, Involvement or Liberation? On Some Aspects of the Art of Natalia LL from a Lacanian Psychoanalytic Perspective"], *Artium Quaestiones,* no. VIII (Poznań: Adam Mickiewicz University, 1997).

5. Cf. *Nowe zjawiska w polskiej sztuce lat siedemdziesi tych: teksty, koncepcje [New Developments in the Polish Art of the Seventies: Texts, Conceptions],* ed. J. Robakowski (Sopot, 1981), pp. 60–73.

6. Jones, pp. 121, 149–50.

7. Cf. *Jerzy Bereś: zwidy, wyrocznie, ołtarze [Jerzy Bereś: Phantoms, Oracles, Altars],* ed. A Wêcka (Poznań: Muzeum Narodowe, 1995).

8. I. Pintilie, "The Ulysses Masks. An Introduction to Ion Grigorescu's Visual Mechanics," paper delivered during the Congress of Kultura Czasu Przełomu — Tożsamośći Kulturowa Europy Srodkowo-Wschodniej/Culture of the Time of Transformation — The Cultural Identity of Central/Eastern Europe (typescript). Cf. also documentation of the artist's achievement in Soros Center for Contemporary Art, Bucharest.

9. J. Rose, "Introduction II," in J. Lacan, *Feminine Sexuality,* trans. J. Rose, eds. J. Mitchell and J. Rose (New York: Norton, 1982), p. 42.

10. S. Hall, "The Local and the Global: Globalization and Ethnicity," in *Culture, Globalization, and the World System: Contemporary Conditions for the Representation of Identity,* ed. A. D. King (Binghamton, N.Y.: Macmillan and Dept. of Art and Art History, State University, 1991).

Written in 1998. Originally published in *M´ARS* (Ljubljana: Moderna Galerija, no. 1–2, 1998).

VLADISLAV MAMYSHEV (MONROE-HITLER)

Vladislav Mamyshev (b. 1969) is a photographer and performance artist from Leningrad. He re-invented himself in the artist persona of Monroe-Hitler, a combination of the sexually sincere actress and the repressed despot. In this essay, the Russian collective identity is confronted with Mamyshev's personal identity, comprised of two figures symbolic of world culture. Yet, as he states, his interest in subsuming both into his personality was deeply offensive to Russian society, which, he maintains, is not ready to admit transgressive imagery into its cultural milieu. His actions are representative of an artist's obligation to push the boundaries of decency and morality in order to forge an open and enlightened post-Soviet society.

Where The Heck Am I? Where Are My Things?

The stable mobility and the mobile stability of Vladislav Mamyshev's objective subjectivism

It is difficult to write about oneself in the third person and it is even more difficult to write about oneself in the first or in the second person. But am I writing about myself? "Who am I? Where am I? How the heck did I get here? Where are my things?" — these are the questions which I have had to ask myself since I took on this difficult task — to put the universe in myself. Not the way just anyone does it when he puts the universe into his cerebral cortex. To do it in a different way, through my subjective personality, through all my physical and mental mechanisms to embody mankind in all its variety, experience all these destinies myself, take on myself all these countless sins, neutralize these with countless good deeds, eliminate sexual, national, social, and other differences and remain myself in this singular variety. To not let myself dissolve, but dissolve others. To not fall into the chemical solution, but be that solution myself.

"Don't get excited, excite" — Marilyn Monroe wrote this motto in lipstick on a mirror at the beginning of her star career. "Don't submit, subjugate," held Adolf Hitler. A personal subjectivism regarded to be of tantamount importance led both of them to similar conclusions. And it led them to sad ends. Monroe and Hitler (Hitler and Monroe) maximally occupied humanity's attention. The decade of Adolf Hitler was followed by the decade of Marilyn Monroe. Thus they captured the very middle of the twentieth century. As Man and Woman, Evil and Good, Black and White, Beast and Beauty, Fire and Water, Devil and Angel, Mars and Venus . . . Two extremes that showed the face of mankind at the end of the extant civilization's act. Splitting the consciousness of the planet's population, Hitlerism and Monrology operate to this day. For having so contrastingly split man in half in their vivid pagan subjectivities, Hitler and Monroe cross out and give up for lost the centuries-old Christian myth — the basis of recent human history. On the other hand, by plunging into the thickets of graphic symbolism we might discover that Hitler & Monroe represent a model of man in pure form: H. M.

Thus, it becomes evident that in the persons of our heroes man is discredited and destroyed — but also born again, should one unite these two extremes. And this is just what I did: I united these extremes in myself. I didn't dissolve in the thick, mental-historical, hitler-monrovian dough, but dissolved both of them in myself, thus appearing as a model of the new man. To this I devoted my humble labor of mystificating and manipulating the images of these two heroes; to this I devoted my artistic, actorial, literary, and research work in recent years. I would now like to acquaint the editors and readers of *Kabinet*,[1] with the mechanisms of this work, with my arguments and the results of my experimentation.

In the beginning was "the Case." "The Case of Vladik Mamyshev, a.k.a. Hitler, student of middle school #27, leader of a neofascist youth organization in the St. Basil's Island district of St. Petersburg." That's how it appeared in my "case" file, but that had nothing to do with reality. Just like the activities the officials of the Committee for State Security (KGB) charged me with: organization of fascist rallies, parading on the 9th of May[2] with standards and machine guns down Nevsky Prospect in the company of Goebbel's, Himmler's, Göring's (etc.) "doubles." The food for these insane fantasies on the part of these quite serious people from the Committee was a letter from the parents of one of my classmates, a letter in which were enclosed photographs of me in my Hitler makeup and my drawings — full face and profile portraits of Adolf Hitler. I didn't deny the existence of these photographs and drawings, but as to all the rest . . . The sick imaginations of the KGB officials were only whipped up by my imperturbable peace of mind as regarded the "crimes" I'd committed. This unconscious but single-minded work with a vivid historical image was for me a pure passion full of discoveries and revelations. How could it not be a revelation when as a child you find in your own appearance similarities with an object that interests you and you feel the entire complex of subjective experiences evoked by an immediate perception of what is alien as your own and your own as the alien! To these arguments KGB Major Sobolev reacted rather inadequately and with great feeling he told me how in 1944 on Lake Ladoga the Germans had beaten his grandfather to death with the butts of their rifles. And by blaming me, Vladik Mamyshev, for this sad event he unwittingly confirmed that my experiments — in which I was no longer myself, but Führer of the Third Reich Adolf Hitler — were not without a certain utility. In these experiments I wasn't pursuing any sort of fascistic ends. As far as I understood, German fascism of the 30s and 40s — with its cruelty, inhumanity, and adventurism — served only as a pedestal for the elevation and immortalization in history of the deeply symbolic persona of Adolf Hitler. Just as American cinema of the 50s and 60s became a pedestal which the twentieth century's goddess of love and beauty, Marilyn Monroe, mounted. But back then, being a ninth grader, I didn't understand any of this and was not aware of what I was doing.

Due to the subjective humanist ideology of the times, Hitler was a forbidden topic. Nevertheless, as far as I remember, he seeped in everywhere when I was a child: through Soviet war films and the propaganda leaflets of Kukryniksy;[3] through social realist "exposés," patriotic war literature, periodicals, and anecdotes. Already in the first preschool years, my mates liked to repeat: "Achtung! Achtung! This is Germany speaking: this morning Hitler was captured under a bridge with his tail wagging." And then a bit later: "On June 22 at 4 o'clock sharp Hitler boiled up in a pot and that's how the war did start." This constant stream of information was enough for me to be able to plug into Hitler's personality through those invisible frequencies linking all of us in space and time and to penetrate into his essence. I'm not saying that I wanted this, or that I could have not done this. It didn't depend on my wishes, as if it were an important mission not subject to discussion. A mission given me by God? By Hitler? By schizophrenia? It's not important — the main thing is that I've completed the mission. Now I am able to peacefully and subjectively feel myself to be Adolf Hitler and — thanks to my physical resemblance to him, a resemblance graciously bestowed on me by nature — to be him should my soul or work require it. The "Case" was, in any case, closed within a year. This was the first year of Perestroika. At my mother's request (she was a distinguished Party member), I was expelled from school in order not to be expelled from the Young Communists League.

By that time I had gotten over Hitler and had seriously come down with Marilyn Monroe. A mysterious force dragged me into the cinemas to see *Some Like It Hot,* which suddenly engulfed Soviet cinemas in 1986–87 under the title *There Are Only Girls in Jazz.* It was literally running in all cinemas at the same time and in one after the other during that year. Wherever I found myself due to circumstance or need, in any part of the city or any suburb, I could go to the theater to the detriment of my studies, work, or family responsibilities and gawk at my "passion," Marilyn Monroe. Seeing that I was reaching puberty, many ascribed my passion to the category of powerful sexual upheavals. My mother even took me to a psychiatrist in order to correct my libido. The psychiatrist and my friends asked me whether I was jerking off with her picture. This way of putting the question literally nonplussed me. It was anything but sex that interested me in this woman. Sometimes I thought that she was my mother, sometimes that she was my god. There ceased to be anything more important than Marilyn Monroe. All my time was consumed by showings of *Some Like It Hot* (the only Monroe film in Soviet theaters) or by the infiltration of various libraries in the attempt to find any information (books, photographs, newspaper articles) about Monroe and to steal this material for visual study at home. Nothing and no one could stop me. Even the scandal in the "Publichka" (the Leningrad/Petersburg Public Library) — I was caught there red-handed cutting out newspaper articles and defamed in the local newspaper *Smena* as a vile punk and thief with "a sheepish, senseless expression in his eyes" — did not put an end to my obsession. What didn't I get up to in this flood which carried me away! What principles, what decencies did I not trample! It scares me just to recall it! It was an abyss into which I plunged, burning my bridges.

This behavior was justified by the lack of accessible information on Marilyn Monroe in the Soviet space of my *nomenklatura* childhood. And I began devouring greedily this image, an image which, in fact, like the subject of Hitler, was suppressed in Soviet ideology — due to its appalling and unaccountable sexuality. One might say that I received another "mission" and hastened to carry it out. In 1987 I was drafted into the army. This was an event of much lesser significance than my "mission" and so even at the space center "Baikonur," where I served, I did not meet with any obstacles. So my subjectivism ripened enough to accommodate Marilyn Monroe within myself. And, oh God, once again I discovered my incredible resemblance to both Hitler and Monroe. Not tarrying for a second, soldier Mamyshev found some old rags in his military post as artist and director of a drama circle at a children's club, ripped all the hair from little blonde dolls, and reproduced on himself that unique image. I was Marilyn Monroe! My pal, a photographer, was with me and we shot several photographs. Shortly after that our chief ideologist, Officer Klochkov, found the photographs. Set in motion by this ideological control officer, the weighty tome of my new "case" migrated to the psychiatric clinic. Whence the doctors sent me home around Easter 1989 as unfit for military service.

Fate seemed to reward me for the missions I'd successfully fulfilled. Soon after my return to Leningrad from the army, I became a famous artist, actor, singer, and writer . . . Whereas Hitler's image often depresses fun-seekers, weighs heavily on the psyche and even evokes aggression, and therefore does not suit concert halls, then in such places Monroe's image is like a fish in water. Even more so when a man is dressed as Marilyn Monroe. Such a thing had never been seen before on Soviet stages. The audacity and selflessness with which I carried out my "mission" made my image of Marilyn Monroe quite noticeable in society. On the one hand, this fame was pleasant. But, on the other hand, I was nearly sucked into the dangerous quagmire of transvestism. What goofy broads didn't I have occasion to play in order to please the entertainment-hungry crowd! And only a principled pseudo-laziness and the rejection of "tempting" offers saved me from the fate of Sergei Penkin.[4] But to make up for this, in my independent work, a labor hidden from the philistine, I continued to study the phenomenon of my stable and mobile subjectivism. That is how my "Monrology" department at the Moscow Free Academy appeared. There, through numerous theoretical investigations and practical experiments, I revealed the true significance of Monroe's image as a positive and light-bringing divine subject. These experiments and research resulted in the historo-philosophical work "This is Not the Sun Rising — This is Monrology Coming Over For Coffee," a work written in the genre of eccentric dissertation. The first edition of this work was prepared

Vladislav Mamyshev-Monroe. Untitled, from series Her Story (Unhappy Love). 1993. Hand-colored photograph. Courtesy XL Gallery, Moscow

in haste—in time for my personal exhibition at the Museum of the Revolution.

The world was then being shaken by the thunder of the Iraqi-American war in Kuwait: therefore in this edition one can find many naive stylistic defects and a not lesser quantity of subjective, purely ephemeral connections to the social processes of that time. I hope soon to be able to present this work to "Kabinet," fully revised and supplemented. Oh, whatever I write now, it's all heavenly dew—for thanks to my radical reincarnations I seem to have touched upon the mystery of the universe. And having touched this secret, I have grasped this knowledge and bring forth this truth to the people, to the readers of "Kabinet." I repeat: I did all this involuntarily, for reasons which had nothing to do with my will. Nature programmed that these three subjectivisms—Adolf Hitler's, Marilyn Monroe's and my own (or supplementary, or collective), Vladislav Mamyshev's—should merge in my persona. Or, to be more precise—the subjectivism of Vladislav Mamyshev consists of two parts: the subjectivism of Adolf Hitler and the subjectivism of Marilyn Monroe. Thus, one supplements, amplifies, and neutralizes the other. And all this happens inside of me and I finally learned to cognize, analyze, and use this in my work. The final stimulus to this awareness of my all-encompassing nature was a series which came together spontaneously for "Pirate TV." The series was entitled "The Deaths of Famous People"[5]: in this series I visually recorded the births and deaths of Hitler and Monroe in myself. Consisting of the halves Hitler/Monroe, Vladislav Mamyshev was then liberated from the previous biographical subjectivities of the former—in the end they had become pure symbols, as I noted at the beginning of this article. These symbols are like "two shores of the same river" and having accepted a baton from each of these leaders, I can also become the river and the bridge. This pleasant discovery (a discovery I made in my Free Academy department) is also a serious responsibility. To tell you the truth, this burden is not light, and I enjoy no privileges, neither material nor social. So it turns out that "my address is not a street and house number," but the whole world, a world in which "not under every bush will you find table and shelter waiting for you." Consequently, conditions are not always suitable for creative work.

But maybe that's good, because this way the basic principle of my subjectivism is maintained: stable mobility (or mobile stability). In this interpretation two senses are mixed — the literal and the mental. It is the ordinary fate of man that he objectively evaluates his own qualities and his own work with difficulty. And this is by virtue of a personal subjectivism which directs the personality with its individual peculiarities and pathologies into a particular cell. To reject this cell and dissolve in life's formless ocean is also no big problem and such people sometimes approach closest to true objectivity in their judgements (these are usually "bomzhi,"[6] "clochards," and other tramps). By virtue of the natural historical flow of time I've had the chance to represent a new, unique case of objective subjectivism. I might only compare it to the objective subjectivism of Jesus Christ — my predecessor, one might say — in the end a similar personality phenomenon led him to institute a new mental order on Earth. For the present I do not have these goals in my project, although I do not rule out the possibility of them appearing in the future. At the very least, this necessity is objectively ripening. The obvious ineffectuality of religious practice (as a consequence and confusion of all and sunder in this estrangement) is a glaring fact of the loss of individuality and the representation of civilization in ideological, philosophical, visual, and other aspects. Human life turns into the elementary functioning of biological and rational (well, so what?) beings, into a supplementary and stinking membrane of the Earth, on a level with soil, minerals, flora, and fauna.

Multilingual verbiage on religious topics has, it would seem, completely deprived man of that divine essence with which fate once endowed him. The hidden perfidy and contradictoriness of those democratic ideas which emasculated god from life did their job by simply allowing full freedom of his interpretation. A confused person already has nowhere to turn, except a judge or a cornerstone at least. A thousand other possibilities will be opposed immediately to any such attempt — in modern society man spends his life scurrying from one such possibility to another. The purity and classicity of genres and morals are forgotten and all attempts to adhere to these principles are ascribed to fascism and are completely removed from life. To occupy a clear and optimistic position based on the striving toward ideals is becoming old-fashioned: depressed, pathological, and broken characters are now in fashion. Nowadays we are more likely to encounter a hero who has suffered defeat and been broken by fate than a victorious, godlike hero. And if this is the case, then the idea of idealism itself, the system of ideals of the epoch now coming to a close is imperfect, immobile, and unstable: therefore, its collapse is natural and inevitable. An utterly new image of the human individual, an utterly new mentality will soon become clearer or will appear out of nowhere. Dissolved in the liquid of melted values and ideals, it is impossible to face this news head on. To do this one needs to turn to some kind of Olympus as the basis of the existing civilization — in my view this Olympus was designated by the symbols of Hitler and Monroe. Having discovered this basis, I am trying to reveal the entire spectrum of this "Olympus" with the help of other mystifications and transformations. And many call this work of mine performance.

Performance as a form of contemporary art exists. Critics ascribe part of my work to this genre. But what is performance? It is just another loophole to procure municipal funds and festival money, nothing more. In and of itself, performance is a secondary art, a derivative of the theater and conceptual culture. Moreover, a pathetic mockery of both. Although you might be an Einstein and the most talented man on Earth, given the task of doing a performance you will be forced to forget about your talents or, more precisely, to combine all of them as a condition of the genre and feebly demonstrate that in the boring darkness of the performance one of your talents prevents another talent from revealing itself. The idea itself is good — mockery of a talented person, and many like the word "performance" — mysterious, serious and, at the same time, meaningless. Subject to bureaucratic structures, that is, to an apparatus, contemporary Western art will never refuse the chance to put on a performance: thousands of "art functionaries" earn their living by organizing festivals, seminars, symposia, and so on; they persuade the state or sponsors to allocate millions of dollars for this empty exercise. Having formed utterly snobbish performance structures, bureaucrats have already bred and continue to breed an army of performance artists, for this is a chance for the egotistical artist to present his humble pursuits and often receive remuneration for it. It is without doubt that in some cases this solves unemployment problems in contemporary bourgeois society, especially after Beuys' imprudent war-cry that every person can be an artist. Some Bill or Stephanie hears this and thinks: so, I too am an artist, I also have something to say to mankind as represented by museum and festival clerks, critics and art historians — they also need to eat — that is, discover new names. And so here's the completely contemporary artist: along with the art historian, he sets out in search of adventures at exhibition openings and symposia. Well, sculpture or painting or installation or video art is great, of course, but you need a studio, some sort of material base. Performance is the best thing of all! The democratic and, correspondingly, humanistic approach to the consideration of such art allows one to emasculate once and for all the idea of talent, not to mention genius. But if these criteria no longer exist or are not taken into consideration, no obstacles or end to this performance madness in Western art are in sight. This is only one link in the vicious chain of bourgeois vices.

It is shameful and funny to observe the growth of the performance movement in Russia. Okay, so they have their traditions over there — one fool made a joke, others took it seriously and set the machine in motion. Time and the history of art are, in any case, merciless toward these tricks. But in its craving to imitate the West, Russian culture is insatiable. Communion with this piggy bank and feeding trough of the universal democracy of performance (since we were free of this virus) begins without understanding and without serious analysis. Does life demand this? Do the times demand it? Does mankind need it? Does eternal art need performance? Perhaps as a sign, a symbol of the decay of a civilization rotten to the core and backed into a corner. Only it's not clear where all the noble and ambitious strivings of our contemporary artists toward the beautiful, toward ideals disappeared. Or perhaps the artist and creator has disappeared from our everyday life and was replaced by a bureaucratic artist? Nowadays exhibitions are reports: "We are together, we deserve each other, and together we're not worth a thing." One and the same set of judgments, terms, and emotions in the analysis of contemporary art, inflation of the same ideas, the undetectability of personality in works of art — all this has become a rule, the rare exceptions which only confirm it. The performance is a symbol of the mutation of art from something spiritual and sublime into something faceless, conceptual, and bureaucratic. I would rather not cite specific examples, for what do all these little signs and squiggles which form the names of authors, galleries, museums, and concert halls mean if all of them put together form a homogeneous, viscous, colorless mass of performance which begins to swell like a malignant tumor in the sick organism of Russian art?

At first I did not turn down offers to perform a bit. I even understand that particular delight felt by a performance artist at especially pompous festivals and seminars. The feeling of the unshakable position of one who has been chosen to commune with "the mystery of performance," but also a considerable per diem, favorable press reviews, a good hotel, and various excursions and entertainments. And the most important thing is that atmosphere of the event's mysteriousness. The mystery consists in one's not being able to understand "Whence all these blessings?" It seems that you haven't done anything special. It's all so simple: you just freeloaded off the organizers; understanding the principle of performance, you put together some cliches in an elementary combination, drug it out to make it "longer" and "duller" and washed your hands of it. But everyone around you is satisfied: "You are a brilliant performance artist!" If I've been brilliant since birth, then of course I was brilliant, but what does this have to do with performance? The radical changes in my appearance cause deeper changes in my personality, in my subject. In various guises I stroll along various paths. Every man has his own destiny, a fatal itinerary which is tightly connected with his image. For example, a fair-haired man will never get into those places and secluded spots most sacred and important for a dark-haired man, and vice versa. And there's no need to talk about the different itineraries that men and women have. If you can, moreover, be both Hitler and Marilyn Monroe. Thus, my permanent mutation in a multitude of different images is rather the possibility to walk all paths, to influence destiny and change its influence upon myself — not the actor's craft; even less so, a performance. Why did I choose the cultural milieu, the sphere of contemporary art as the field for my activities?

Firstly, in contemporary art we can trace those processes which later will be found in everyday life. It is a kind of avant-garde of mankind in which all phenomena are concentrated, clearly designated and anticipated. Secondly, contemporary art's viewer and artist — the so-called cultural milieu — are mentally more flexible, are inclined to accept radical ideas to a greater extent than, say, other professionals, whose consciousness is limited to their specialization. In contemporary art no sort of specialization limits anything. By virtue of its avant-gardeness art has — quicker than any other discipline — lost all criteria of decency, morality, sensuality, and beauty. It has become so cynical in its all-consuming indifference to human values, as well as to the object of art, that it is rightly that fertile soil onto which the seed of the "new man" will be cast.

Notes
1. St. Petersburg-based critical art journal in which this essay first appeared.
2. Officially Victory Day in Eastern Bloc countries. It celebrates the anniversary of Nazi Germany's surrender.

3. Kukryniksy: "The most famous (Soviet) wartime cartooning team was Kukryniksy, an acronym for Mikhail Kuprianov, Porfiry Krylov, and Nikolai Sokolov" (Richard Stites, *Russian Popular Culture* [Cambridge, 1992]). One of their most famous propaganda cartoons depicts Hitler as jilted bride. The caption reads: "I lost my ring at Stalingrad."
4. Sergei Penkin is a Russian pop singer who has been described as the Russian Boy George.
5. The title of this series is an allusion to a series of books published in the Soviet Union, *The Lives of Famous People.*
6. *"Bomzh"* (pl. *"bomzhi"*) is the Russian word for a homeless person and, generally, any tramp or bum. Interestingly enough, the word is actually a bureaucratic acronym meaning "without fixed place of residence."

Written in 1993. Originally published in *Kabinet* (St. Petersburg), no. 5 (1993). Translated by Vera Zakharova and Thomas Campbell.

•●

A CASE STUDY: THE LIFE AND DEATH OF A HORSE

The artist Katarzyna Kozyra was born in Warsaw in 1963 and graduated from the Academy of Fine Arts there in 1993. Her videos, installations, and sculptures explore societal notions of death, gender, and otherness, and she is one of the best-known and most controversial Polish artists working today.

Her diploma work, Pyramid of Animals, *caused a public outcry, and the ensuing controversy was extensively reported by the Polish media. The work consists of a sculpture—a taxidermied horse, dog, cat, and rooster placed on top of each other—which, for her graduate thesis, was presented together with a theoretical text "The Symbolics of Animals" and a short text explaining the process and thinking behind the monument. A video documenting the killing and stuffing of the horse was included in a 1996 exhibition of the work. The public debate was initially sparked by a report on the TV program "Animals," broadcast in July 1993, and accusations leveled against the artist ranged from cruelty to animals to immorality and insanity. Rising to her defense was her professor, who sought to clarify the intentions of the artist, as well as the context and facts of the piece. The work has been exhibited extensively and has become an important reference point in discussions about Polish contemporary art. Following the interview between the editor of* Czereja, *Artur Żmijewski, and the artist is a sampling of the responses to* Pyramid of Animals.

Carrying Buckets, Trotting like Pigs

Artur Żmijewski interviews Katarzyna Kozyra, July 10, 1993, Warsaw

Artur Żmijewski: Tell me about *Pyramid of Animals.* It appears that it was quite easy for you to create.

Katarzyna Kozyra: Oh! That depends! It seemed easy at the time when only my mind was engaged in this project. It's one thing to say to yourself that you are going to kill a horse and stuff it, but it's quite another thing when you actually take responsibility for it, when you actually see it, when the emotions start creeping in. I did myself some harm there. I didn't falsify anything. I told no lies. It was very destructive for me, so it wasn't easy.

AZ: I was referring to the involvement of other people . . .

Katarzyna Kozyra. *Pyramid of Animals.* 1993. Taxidermied animals, height 8'7⅞" (260 cm). Zachęta Gallery, Warsaw

KK: Oh that!

AZ: That it was easy to do because you could use all these helpers.

KK: Terribly easy.

AZ: They didn't resist.

KK: Not at all. It rather surprised me even.

AZ: And it was easy to organize everything.

KK: Easy beyond belief. It was quite shocking.

AZ: You used four animals, but how many did you have all together?

KK: There was one horse that was paid for. There was a whole load of dogs; I could choose any one I wanted. They all had the same defect, however—they were all rotting. Eventually I got a dog that had been put to sleep some fifteen minutes earlier at the request of its owner. I had six cats to choose from, and I killed two cocks, as I didn't know which one would be better, the big one or a little one. But I had a problem—in the name of consistency, shouldn't I have bought live dogs and cats and killed them? What stopped me? Emotions. I couldn't have done it. At least not then.

AZ: Tell me about how you looked for the horse.

KK: I went around a lot of horse fairs, not hiding why I wanted the animal. They pushed a few my way, some better, some worse. I had to think not only about whether it was white, or like this or like that, but also about its dimensions. It had to be able to get out of the workshop after being prepared. In any case what was suitable for putting to sleep was not suitable for the sculpture because it had to have a good coat and good coloring. In the end I decided on the red one. It wasn't too big or too small, and its name was KASIA. . . . This is the Monument to Excellent Metabolism. The horse was devoured by cats and dogs; they in turn were turned into meal; the meal into fodder for pigs and cocks. And we have eaten all of it; if not this horse then another one. In this sense it is excellent. In praise of reincarnation. Sometimes I would run to that bunker twice a day. There was a whirling, wolfish, writhing mass, one on top of another. The stench, and here and there some paws sticking out of the heap. That's where they throw the animals they've put to sleep. After Saturday and Sunday the worms came up to your ankles. That's where I looked for my cat and my dog. Every two or three days Bakutil would come and take all this carrion to his factory and turn it into meal. You have to do something with the carcasses. In this closed circle it all comes back to us, so nothing really gets lost, it's all in use, one in the other. Excellent.

AZ: What's the bunker?

KK: It's where you can leave your beloved animal that you've just put to sleep. It is a hymn in praise of reincarnation. It has changed forever my attitude to animals. I have seen everything that moves stuffed and mounted on a horse. A strange approach. Later, when the horse had fallen, and I imagined that the cats and dogs devoured him, I saw corpses everywhere. Everything is part of a total metabolism. I wanted to understand what I was doing, to see where things come from. It drove me into a three-week-long paranoia. Now I can see how terrible emotions are. Intellectually this does not get through to people. You have to see that nothing rational counts. And nobody and nothing can explain it to you. I suffered terribly because of that horse. For three weeks I would go outside, just to slip away and quickly return. The people recognized only a watch strap (because I was subconsciously looking for a guilty party), leather shoes, no faces. Oh God! Where am I living? It's horrible. People just don't understand, they haven't got a clue what is really happening. Now even when I'm buying flowers I do it knowing that it's also a kind of total destruction. And everything is so beautifully arranged, everything, so that you don't feel the blues.

AZ: Secret.

KK: Everything is secret. All of these imaginary philosophies, it's all been thought up to camouflage the obvious, really significant facts—destruction, quite simply. No, I don't think it's a tragedy; it's harmony and I'm playing a good part in it all. . . . The horse was bought so it would have been silly to back out. I got caught up in the turmoil. It wasn't certain to the end if the animals would die.

AZ: You could have backed out?

KK: Of course.

AZ: But it so happened that you did not back out. You paid, so you ate.

KK: Yes, well, I don't know, it pulled me in like a chain reaction. Step by step I had to go on cutting my own throat. . . . It was amazing with that cat in the freezer. One night Agata brought me a cat in a pressure cooker. You see all my friends knew that if their cat or dog died, they had to bring it to me. But I already had one in the freezer so I sent Agata away. Amazing, because everything went as normal. You keep meat in the fridge, except for the fact that this meat was somewhat different. Nothing really changes. Or the fact that this dog was lying at my place for two days, with blood dripping from its head.

AZ: You kept it in the fridge with all its guts?

KK: It was whole, with intestines and all. Anatomically complete.

AZ: Tell me about the film documenting the killing of the horse.

KK: It's a strange film. Full of long and boring bits. It is the documentation of the creative process. Total documentation. The film is terribly sad, no glamour, just as it was. Bloody sad.

AZ: Was it a creative process or a killing?

KK: Difficult to say, I had to accept certain categories for my own use.

AZ: So as not to go mad? A kind of justification?

KK: I was doing my diploma work. People document their creative processes so I documented mine.

AZ: A creative process.

KK: Art cannot simply be a game with building blocks. It's completely senseless then. Doing what I do, I am convinced that I am right. There is no messing about. There's no pretense. With me it really was a death.

AZ: Creating corpses.

KK: Creating corpses—from beginning to end. I was accused of playing around with death. I didn't do it in cold blood. The condition for our being, our existence, is stinking guts. Annihilation is the tool of being. It is the condition for the existence of comfort for the consideration of existential problems, it allows for the luxury of philosophy. That is what I wanted to check, I wanted to see the lowest level—killing. The fact that you have to get your hands dirty, that it stinks, that you're stirring around in the guts. I wanted to separate the levels of reality and to see each one separately.

AZ: And how does this death fit in with you personally?

KK: Do you know, it turned out that a cancerous tumor is growing in me. But as we are living in the kind of world where you can put it off "chemically," I don't have to die—it can be cured. There remains the consciousness that it is only a putting off, despite the galloping destruction. It suddenly turns out that I am seriously ill and what's more my prospects are pretty poor. I suddenly jumped to another level of consciousness. I experienced a feeling of finality. What the hell, I like extreme situations, free from ambiguities. It was these very circumstances —the fact that I didn't have to turn the horse into a shoe and in any case no one would guess that it had once been alive—that awakened in me a sensitivity toward destruction. Because it is total destruction that we have here, all of it.

AZ: On what does it depend?

KK: Let's take the furniture as an example. If I wanted to make it myself I would have to run around the woods with an axe [she taps the kitchen dresser] and kill the plants. It's all destruction. If you had to do it yourself you'd go mad. How lucky that others do it for us. And that is why those shitty hypocritical ladies think they can feel outraged at me. It's absurd.

AZ: During the killing of the horse, did you have the impression that it was the abattoir assistant who was doing the killing, or you?

KK: I just felt that it was all happening as a result of my decision, that it was final. I became hysterical. I screamed.

AZ: A feeling of irreversibility?

KK: From that there was definitely no going back. I appreciate only such things, only they have any weight.

AZ: This was one of the motivations of the holocaust—a nation taking part in such killing . . .

KK: And no turning back?

AZ: Yes. The authorities blackmailed society through irreversibility.

KK: It's a good method, except that it was sick. But people themselves make their own laws.

AZ: Now you have started to make laws.

KK: I just use those that already exist. . . . While the horse was being put to sleep, there was a person there who wanted to see how a horse is killed and stripped of its skin. Afterwards she was ashamed to touch me—because I'm a monster. So a person is able to take part in this with the consciousness that it won't be put down to his karma. And then he is able to look at everything with total acceptance, starting like a stupid monkey. . . . The strangest thing was the juxtaposition of situations—in the dissecting room but with a healthy animal, put to sleep like a sick one, not slaughtered but intended for the butcher's shop, stripped of its skin like a hunted animal, and at the end it's still a horse. A whole collection of people took part in this process, all from different branches of the animal-killing business, and all with the certainty that what they were doing was right. Here everything got mixed up. Even now I don't know how to describe it. Things just weren't right. These people could feel that somehow they had been knocked off their stride, that something had sucked them in and that there was no return. Death had ceased to be useful. The horse had fallen and we had to go forward, because something had to be done with this lump of meat. The vet said that as the animal had been put to sleep, it could not be sold for shop. The butcher thought that he could do a deal and buy the meat more cheaply. They were circling like hyenas. In the end the vet chased them away and said to me, "What about this meat?" That was the end! They didn't let the meat be taken to the butcher's because the assembled company wanted to feed itself! They came with their buckets, four hours they had worked on the killing but in ten minutes there was only the skeleton left. They were pushing me out of the way. I was still taking photographs, but they were there with their knives, climbing all over me with their buckets—slash, slash, slash. They took it apart and left just the skeleton. I was astonished by the pile of meat—here one minute, gone the next.

AZ: Where did they take it?

KK: I don't know. A whole swarm of people came along with their buckets and their knives, took it in pieces and then disappeared. Just the skeleton was left.

AZ: Do you know who these people were?

KK: I suspect they were employees. They must have got the scent from somewhere, like hyenas. They did this with the feeling that although I may be a bad thing, at least they could get some benefit from it. As the horse has fallen, as it has died, then, by the way, I'll just take these guts. A bit here, a bit there, five minutes. Carrying buckets, trotting like pigs. All gone. When one of them was cutting a bit away, the corpse's muscles were still twitching. . . . The intravenous drip-feed that was putting the horse to sleep started to work and the pupils became dilated. Total, bloody deep blue. And the light fell so strangely onto the eyes. Later the pupils became smaller, but at first they opened up in such a way that the whole eye was filled with this intense blue. . . . The bad thing, the horrible thing, is that you die and that's the END. Most religions offer you some kind of immortality, a kind of extended existence. I don't understand why this is so attractive, why people want so much to exist that they jump at every faith, every doctrine which "guarantees" them this. I would like to see this END. . . . So what, if people are incurably ill, maybe they have an advantage. Maybe they live with increased consciousness of the ultimate. It offers incredible freedom.

AZ: On what does this freedom depend?

KK: I would not have been able to do this, to be raped emotionally, if I had not had this feeling of the ultimate, that I am quite simply dying. It's always there, but it's not always in my head. It's always ultimate, and when they tell you that you're dying, nothing changes. Maybe you only have the feeling of a greater psychological burden.

AZ: Did you feel guilty, and if so, when? Was it when you were selecting the animal?

KK: Something like this did appear within me, but I immediately tried to obliterate this feeling, and not allow it to have a voice at all. Because I could see in my mind's eye the finished sculpture, I tried to get rid of anything that could have interrupted the realization. A priority. I tried to fight my emotions, and act by calculation. When? During the week when I had fixed the date, the hour, got the ten people together, and arranged ten different things: transport, who, how much. During that week I used to visit my horse because I wanted them, despite everything, to feed and groom it. And the whole night before the operation in the dissecting-room I didn't sleep at all, total mess. After that everything went quite simply mechanically: the departure, the loading.

AZ: The realization of the plan, yes?

KK: The realization of the plan.

AZ: Did this free you from emotional responsibility?

KK: No, absolutely not. It simply made things easier because I wasn't doing everything myself. The fact that I had to arrange so many people required a plan. If I hadn't had those people then I don't know if I could have stood it emotionally.

AZ: Your emotions became dissolved among these people.

KK: I was dependent on many people, and they on themselves. And this required organizing. The organizational work pushed away problems connected with my emotions.

AZ: The burden shifted.

KK: Yes, the burden shifted to the organization.

AZ: Try to characterize the specific forced situation created among the people during the killing of the horse. You've already said that it would have been "silly to back out."

KK: They delivered the horse to the dissecting-room and in came the expert who was going to put it to sleep. Everything moved with the momentum of some strange machine, people were talking, anything so as not to look. I was screaming, I knew that the horse would fall in a moment. And when it fell, then something strange burst. The first step—the killing—meant that everything had to go forward.

AZ: The killing of the next animals was the result of the killing of the first one? It became necessary?

KK: Obsessive. Since I had killed a horse, such a huge lump of meat, it was so much easier to kill something much smaller, like a cock or a cat.

AZ: And easier to get rid of them.

KK: Oh, a lot easier.

AZ: Was this confined to a sensible solution to a technical problem?

KK: What do you mean?

AZ: You know, delivery, clearing up. It should have been easier with the next one.

KK: What is easier?

AZ: I am interested in what caused the compulsion. Could you name the stages of the situation being created among all those people in the dissecting room?

KK: They felt as if they had been drawn into something, that I had turned everything upside down, and that they had been made fools of.

AZ: With one move, with the killing of the horse, you had made them dependent on you?

KK: I think so. What were they supposed to do—run away?

AZ: Did you take away their will?

KK: They did it. I fitted in; I fitted ideally in with what was allowed. Every field has its own building blocks. From each I took what I needed and built my own little building. I did not hold a gun to their heads. They put to sleep a completely healthy animal. In addition, not how it's normally done. And I had the feeling that this time death became something . . . new? Not as obvious as usual. It was not such an obvious procedure. Maybe because I'm not from any of the killing fields. Maybe that's why. The guy with the drip-feed told me that he wouldn't take money for such services. The laboratory assistant dressed up as a hunter . . . and used a clasp knife. Each of them looked for some kind of support. I, however, did not step outside the accepted moral norms so they were not able to refuse categorically. I spoke to the vet who selected the horse for slaughter. I asked him if we would put a healthy horse or cat to sleep. He said no, it's immoral. He selects horses for slaughter, but in this situation he would not put it to sleep. He looked at me as if I were an idiot. A whole institution stands behind him. He is carrying out his professional duty, just selecting, no emotions, he is a cog in a machine. It was I who made everything move.

AZ: Is this really the need to create a sculpture, or an artistic justification of a risky undertaking?

KK: It is not an artistic justification. I don't see the difference between simply eating the horse and shitting it out, and just killing it and letting it stand preserved for several years, instead of shitting it out straight away. I don't see the difference. I don't know what's wrong with using real animals instead of preserving the image of these animals in clay. It's obviously perverse that I have to destroy in order to create, but I don't see the sense, if something exists, to create it again and make a double.

AZ: They say that instead of preserving the animals, you wanted to install them dead in a kind of construction/frame, real corpses.

KK: Didn't I tell you about this?

AZ: Tell me now.

KK: I got a shock when I was looking for the lab assistant, and I found myself in a place where they told me that preparing the horse was no problem and that, in fact, they were working on one at that time. They said they'd show me, so in

I went and there was a horse. It was all wet with its hair all matted, levitating above the floor. There was a steel barrier all around it and the horse was attached to it on both sides with an iron hook under its spine. So it was raised a bit. It had the skin severed above the artery, rolled back and secured with clips. A trocar tube entered the cut and first the blood was pumped out, then formalin was pumped into the empty bloodstream. The horse was simply suspended in formalin fumes. The amazing thing was that they had closed its eyes. A horse never closes its eyes. Even when it's dead. They had made a human gesture—they had closed the corpse's eyes. It was then that I saw the construction, with the horse, the dog, the cat, and the cock, all with tubes and formalin. I associated this with my own situation—they are also pumping chemicals into my veins, so it's very similar. It was an amazing feeling—it looked asleep, and it was levitating, I had formalin in my lungs, my eyes, and I couldn't see anything. The horse was ready for the operation; one of its flanks was to be stripped away layer by layer in front of a student audience. I even wanted to attend, but somehow I never got around to it.

AZ: Is your illness some kind of tumor? Can you feel with your fingers what is being destroyed?

KK: They are my beloved tumors which do not want to disappear. The doctor examined me recently [she touches herself] and here there is something more lumpy than here. When I started doing the *Pyramid,* I had a great lump on my neck. They took some kind of sample from this lump.

AZ: Oncological juices.

KK: I lost all resistance. I like to overdo it, go for broke, push myself all the way. Several times in various situations I have pushed my resistance to the limit and lost it completely. I would go to the bathroom and I couldn't even have a bath, undo the tap. Extreme lack of resistance. These cancer cells began to eat away at me. I stopped fighting, I lost all will to live, everything. It began to spread within me. I definitely used the illness. It would have been idiotic of me not to have used it. Don't you think so?

AZ: You think it's a good opportunity?

KK: I try to use everything that comes along in life, so yes it's a good opportunity. I'll either come out of it or I won't. Two or three weeks ago I didn't even know if I wanted to get better or not. This gave me a great feeling of freedom and independence. I allowed myself to do things which I had never allowed myself to do before. The illness was an excellent stage in my life. It showed me that I can be here, I can achieve things and that you do care and you do run around me. Who would have gone with me for these horses? I wouldn't have been able to do it myself, I was so pumped full of "chemicals." First they gave me chemicals to make me vomit, then the next batch to stop me vomiting. I felt like a puppet. There were days when I just lay in bed and couldn't even imagine getting up. I exploited my illness one hundred percent.

AZ: You've used it up.

KK: I've used up my illness. I don't need it any more.

AZ: The operations which took place meant that your process was returning to life while that of the animals was leading to death.

KK: "Chemistry," radiation, and at the same time taking part in the deaths of animals. It's all connected but I don't know if I want to draw it out.

AZ: Let's draw it out.

KK: On the same day that the horse was killed, I had my last dose of radiation. All my hair fell out, complete destruction. A bald head, and I had strange blotches from the radiation. . . . The most important thing was what happened during work—revealing the well-trodden paths on which we function. Then when someone comes who knocks us off these paths, not strongly enough to go against the law, there are no arguments in favor of turning down and not doing something. Because you know what interests me the most? Emotions. No one needs to see my stuffed animals any more. It's enough that a rumor is going around Warsaw that someone has killed something and stuffed it. The work itself ceases to be important. It works mentally, fuck it. Everything is fucked up in their heads.

Originally published in *Magazyn Sztuki* (art magazine) (Gdansk), no. 5 (January 1995). Translated by Tadeusz Wolanski.

Nothing Justifies Murdering Animals for Fun, Even If the Pretext Is an Attempt to Be an "Artist"

Maciej Iłowiecki [a well-known publicist]

Recently we were informed by an interesting, much needed, and socially useful TV show "Animals" about an astonishing "graduation work" submitted at the Academy of Fine Arts in Warsaw.

In order to make a unique piece of sculpture, a student at the Academy personally chose a horse, a dog, a cat, and a rooster (the point was that they had to be healthy and beautiful, she confessed, giggling, on TV) and then had them killed.

She supported her "work" with fatuous pseudo-philosophy that killing healthy animals for whim supposedly has some deep meaning.

The student may be a soulless and insensitive person (although it is surprising that she chose art as her field of study—actually, it is perhaps good she didn't choose medicine). Still, one must not remain indifferent to the views of her academic teachers and adviser.

If academic teachers do not think it is immoral to kill animals for fun (despite the best intentions, the product of the student cannot, and even MUST NOT, be called art)—indeed something very wrong must be going on in Poland.

Letter to the editor of *Życie Warszawy,* August 17, 1993. Translated by Marek Wilczynski.

A Sculptor or a Dogcatcher?

Xymena Zaniewska-Chwedczuk [a well-known stage designer]

In the Department of Sculpture at the Warsaw Academy of Fine Arts, the student Katarzyna Kozyra submitted a topic for her graduation work, which was accepted. Then she went out to look for the needed materials. She chose a horse, a dog, a cat, and a rooster. The animals were killed, stuffed, and placed one on top of another. The object was accepted by the graduation committee. The student received her degree.

Since I have become involved in improving the relations between humans and animals, I would like to find out in reference to the above—at this point I am appealing to Professor Ewa Letowska [official ombudsman]—whether the law allows us to kill animals for decorative purposes.

At the most recent Biennale in Venice a Japanese sculptor put some ants into glass containers. Moving, they put into motion compositions of grains of sand. After an intervention of Greenpeace the ants were set free.

The intention of the Charter of Animal Rights is not to kill them without vital need, which is, after all, in our best interest. Fighting for the life of every animal does not imply oversensitivity or sentimentalism. Animals are natural, physical, and spiritual companions of humans, and our biological survival depends on theirs. The fact that they are killed to provide us with food cannot mean that we treat them exclusively as moving meat.

Man who does not recognize in the animal a partner, does not treat it as another sovereign being, will finally flood the world with oil from tankers, fell all the trees, and, sooner or later, dig in this way his own grave. Therefore law specifies, or will have to specify, under what circumstances killing animals is really necessary.

Just a few more words on the graduation of Ms. Katarzyna Kozyra. Substituting technical indolence with a thrill caused by the fact that we face the dead bodies of real animals seems to me particularly hideous. However, even if the artistic effect had been different, I protest against killing for decoration and I will do everything I can to prevent such cases in the future.

Letter to the editor of *Gazeta Wyborcza,* August 18, 1993. Translated by Marek Wilczynski.

Why the Heck Is This Alive?

Aleksandra Jakubowska

In the fourth century B.C., Herostrates, a fame-hungry shoemaker from Ephesus, set fire to the famous local temple of Artemis, for which he was sentenced to death. It was not death, though, that was supposed to be his harshest punishment. In addition, the priests decreed that his name be erased from all the contemporaneous records and from human memory. However, the latter turned out to be impossible, and the name of the shoemaker has been known until today as a synonym of someone who, for the sake of renown, is ready to commit a crime.

I hope that the name of Katarzyna Kozyra, a graduate of the Warsaw Academy of Fine Arts, will not—contrary to that of Herostrates—find its way into the encyclopedia. My knowledge of ancient history is incomparable to the expertise of Professor Krawczuk. Therefore, I cannot claim with absolute certainty that Herostrates burned only the walls of the temple and not some believers who might have been worshipping the goddess inside it. But let's assume there were no casualties and the wretched shoemaker of Ephesus was sentenced just for the annihilation of the edifice. Katarzyna Kozyra annihilated four beings: a horse, a dog, a cat, and a rooster. She chose healthy and beautiful specimens, had them killed and stuffed, and then created a "work of art" in the form of a monument which let her earn a Master's degree and obtain the right to practice an artistic profession. And maybe the only aftermath of that would have been gossip, if not for someone's sensitive conscience, thanks to which the whole affair became known to the makers of the TV show "Animals." After the show [focusing on Kozyra], Maciej Iłowiecki published in *Zyciu Warszawy* a letter full of indignation: "If academic teachers do not think it is immoral to kill animals for fun, indeed something very wrong must be going on in Poland." On the next day, Iłowiecki was followed by Xymena Zaniewska in *Gazeta Wyborcza:* "Substituting technical indolence with a thrill caused by the fact that we face the dead bodies of real animals seems to me particularly hideous. However, even if the artistic effect had been different, I protest against killing for decoration and I will do everything I can to prevent such cases in the future."

Perhaps some of you believe that so much hassle and hysteria about some peccadillo of a student at the Academy of Fine Arts is rather immoral in the context of what is going on all over the world and what we can watch every day at 7:30 P.M. in the national newscast full of images from the former Yugoslavia, interspersed with shots of starving children in Somalia and victims of tragic earthquakes, fires or terrorist attacks. Taking bite after bite and drinking our tea, we eye with a kind of detachment the horror and terror on the screen, thinking with self-complacency: "Oh, this is fortunately far enough . . ." But all of a sudden it turns out that it is not so far—quite the contrary. We stay safely in the castle of our home, and suddenly a Ms. Katarzyna K. comes banging at our door trying to convince us that killing is art. I am not going to condemn the student. For me, she is just mentally ill, a pathological personality who ought to be treated. Such pathological cases occur in every profession and age or ethnic group. There are people who have been deprived by Mother Nature of some feature, be it imagination, pity or—as in the case of Katarzyna K.—conscience and morality. Let psychiatrists take care of someone whose reason is asleep and haunted by demons. I would only like to know who—of all the respectable professors of the Academy of Fine Arts in Warsaw—was Katarzyna K.'s adviser, allowing her to submit a graduation work which required killing. What measures is the rector of the Academy going to take with respect to that person? Will he continue to work with young people? Maybe he will not come across another psychopathic individual of the same kind, but what if he does? Perhaps, then, he should be confined to the four walls of his private studio, since he is unable to tell good from evil and pass the knowledge of the difference to his students. . . .

"Why the heck don't you love a sparrow, girls, why don't you . . . ," appealed the poet, sneering at a ladybug that it has no neck and distracts our attention by crawling on the wall: "Why the heck is this alive?"

"Love thy neighbor," let me appeal to all those who have turned hatred into the object of the eleventh Commandment.

Originally published in *Wprost,* no. 35, August 29, 1993. Translated by Marek Wilczynski.

Why the Heck Is This Alive?

Professor Grzegorz Kowalski

In her feuilleton titled "Why the Heck Is This Alive?" Aleksandra Jakubowska expressed her opinion about the graduation work of Katarzyna Kozyra, whose academic adviser I was. The text implies that Ms. Jakubowska did not bother to actually see the work, and that she based her claims concerning Kozyra's mental derangement on other views published in the press. In this way public opinion has been given another confirmation of an untrue and derogatory version of the course of events: a student of the Academy of Fine Arts allegedly murdered four animals, for which she has been given an academic degree in art. The facts in this case are the following: Katarzyna Kozyra executed a graduation work called *Pyramid of Animals,* composed of stuffed figures of a horse, a dog, a cat, and a rooster. She used the skins of animals that had already been dead (the dog and the cat), or which were about to be slaughtered (the horse and the rooster) and which she purchased before killing and had put to sleep (killed in a different way). All that she did of her own will and on her own responsibility. *Pyramid of Animals* is a work of art devoted to death in its universal sense. Hence the means of artistic expression: a stuffed animal, which is supposed to look "as if it were alive," creates a stronger impression of death than a sculpted one. Kozyra's graduation thesis may be summarized in the following manner: the death of animals killed by industrial methods is invisible and sanctioned by utilitarian purposes so that it has been virtually eliminated from human consciousness. On the contrary, the death of a single animal, visualized in a work of art, is restored to the spectator's consciousness. As Kozyra's adviser, I want to defend her work arranged in this way, together with its articulated message, and not the "killing of animals for artistic purposes." The Graduation Committee accepted the work for the same reasons, with no objections from the audience present. Ms. Jakubowska rather crudely called me to examine my conscience in public. If we assume that the norm is killing animals for "vital needs," my examination will be like this:

> Question: Is it ethical to kill a horse in order to use its skin for ladies' purses and turn its meat into pet food? Answer: Yes, since it is justified by a vital need.
> Question: Is it ethical to kill a horse in order to use its skin to make a sculpture? Answer: No, because no vital need justifies it.
> Is it ethical to kill a rooster to make broth? YES. To make a sculpture? NO.

This examination demonstrates that there is a double moral standard as regards killing animals. Personally I cannot accept a view that a "vital need" means exclusively consumption, while provoking reflection on an important subject means violation of ethical norms.

Letter to the editor of *Wprost,* no. 37, September 12, 1993. Translated by Marek Wilczynski.

A Disciple of . . . Benetton?
Pyramid of Animals—Pyramid of Hatred

D[orota]. H[ill].

The Society for the Protection of Animals in Gdynia has announced, also in *Gazeta Gdanska*, that it will start a protest campaign aiming at a public condemnation of the graduation work submitted by a student at the Warsaw Academy of Fine Arts under the title *Pyramid of Animals*, composed of a stuffed horse, a dog, a cat, and a rooster. Despite the recognition of two outstanding artists—the adviser, Professor Grzegorz Kowalski, and the rector of the Academy, Professor Adam Myjak—the work has provoked an ongoing public debate in the national press and on TV.

The author of the *Pyramid of Animals*, Katarzyna Kozyra, has been both relentlessly criticized for cruelty, spiritual poverty, and psychic deviations, and strongly defended by the artistic circles. Professor Kowalski believes that the *Pyramid* is devoted to death in its universal sense, that the death of animals killed by industrial methods is invisible and sanctioned by utilitarian purposes, while the death of a single animal visualized in a work of art is restored to the spectator's consciousness.

Ryszard Ziarkiewicz, Director of the State Gallery of Art in Sopot: I believe that many conversations on this subject have been fueled by ignorance. The stories about the artist having killed the animals are not true. Besides, the specimens were neither healthy nor beautiful. The horse was about to be slaughtered; it was put to sleep instead—and the dead cat and dog were both taken from a veterinary clinic. In my opinion, the more details we know, the less horrible Kasia Kozyra's deeds become. On the other hand, as an art critic, I think that an artist has the right to do such things. Kozyra's work is not stupid, but deeply rooted in reflection. It has been supplemented with a video film showing the situation in a slaughterhouse where animals are actually killed. I think that it is the film that's horrifying, and not her work.

Witoslaw Czerwonka, Deputy Rector of the Academy of Fine Arts in Gdansk, head of the Intermedia Studio: I also own a few dogs, but I don't think Katarzyna Kozyra has done anything wrong. An artist has the right to tease, although this case is no simple provocation. Kozyra's motivation is profound and sincere. I think that the spontaneous protests of animals' defenders have been misdirected. There are many more cases which should be denounced.

Teresa Szydlowska, artist: I have just returned from an embroidery plein-air meeting at Jastrzebia Gora, and I must say that all the participants, about twenty people from all over the country, expressed their protest against Kozyra's graduation work. I think that its motivation is nothing new—in Bremen there is a similar pyramid composed of the same animals, illustrating a fairy tale by the brothers Grimm. I don't understand why after all the harrowing experiences she has been through, Kozyra did such a banal thing. In my opinion, the rector of the Warsaw Academy, Kozyra's adviser, and she herself are at a loss as artists, unless, of course, she uses the *Pyramid* as an advertisement analogous to the gory posters of Benetton . . .

Originally published in *Gazeta Gdanska*, September 20, 1993. Translated by Marek Wilczynski.

Artist's Response

Katarzyna Kozyra

I am the author of the composition called *Pyramid of Animals*. Together with this piece, which consisted of the stuffed carcasses of a horse, a dog, a cat, and a rooster, there was a commentary in which I presented my motivation, the creative process, and the doubts that accompanied them. I asked the question: is only the sculpture to be evaluated or is it also the process of its creation and the reactions and experience linked to it? With this act I exposed myself to confrontation with people who think differently than I, but from whom I had expected respect for facts.

Meanwhile the various lies have been repeated and publicized, among them that I had raised these animals, subjected them to suffering, and killed them with my own hands. That is not true. During my diploma exam it was publicly stated that the skins of the dog and the cat had been removed from dead animals, whereas the skins of the horse and the rooster from animals that were meant for slaughter, which I bought and then put to sleep. The "killing" was for purposes other than the making of a pair of shoes or the eating of meat, which is a violation of norms that are considered obligatory and humanitarian. The infliction of death on animals in a civilized and industrial manner takes place anonymously and beyond the view of their later consumers. The taking of the life of an animal in an open manner and by an individual is the cause of shock and condemnation. I consciously exposed myself to this test. My observing the death of the horse was a hundred percent more terrible than all of the invectives that have been leveled against me. In an effort to be consistent I also took upon myself the death of dead animals. My composition is about death, generally speaking, and about the deaths of these concrete four animals. I did not do this for any tingling pleasure or because of technical indolence. I did this out of my internal need to ask the question: do we still feel the presence of death eating chops, using cosmetics, or using other animal-based products, or has that been effectively neutralized by the household representatives of animals, which receive our feelings on a day-to-day basis? *Pyramid of Animal* is a violation of norms in treating the death of animals as a phenomenon that has nothing to do with the consumer.

If I decided to use this form in my first totally independent artistic work, it is not because art is treated by society as a game among artists playing in their own backyard, far from important issues or, as Ms. Xymena Zaniewska writes, serves only "decorative purposes."

Unpublished letter to the editor of *Gazeta Wyborcza*, August 20, 1993. Published in *Katarzyna Kozyra—The Men's Bathhouse: XLVIII International Biennale, Venice, 1999* (Warsaw: Galeria Sztuki Współczesnej Zachety, c. 1999).

5 ONWARD TOWARD THE RETRO-AVANT-GARDE!

B eginning in the mid-1980s, and particularly around 1989, when political revolutions in the Eastern Bloc countries erupted, postmodernism and some of its strategies turned out to be among the most effective means by which Eastern European artists could come to terms with their totalitarian heritage. The appropriation of different styles from art history and their usage in different contexts—one of the principal tenets of postmodernism—was a popular strategy, although it had a regional twist. Borrowings from past art were not simply humorous or purely formal exercises: they were also politically charged.

The most well-known practitioner of this kind of appropriation was, and still is, the Slovenian movement NSK (Neue Slowenische Kunst). NSK took symbols and motifs from different totalitarian regimes (not differentiating between Stalinism or Nazism) and combined them with elements of both kitsch and classical avant-garde art. They presented this subversive pastiche via many mediums (related NSK spin-offs include musical and theater groups, as well as an organization of writers) and mimicked the rhetoric of propaganda, not only to shock their audiences, but also to reveal its aesthetic mechanisms. As the case study in this section shows, the multigroup consortium takes liberties with the trappings of totalitarian culture to the limits of political acceptability.

The subversive use of totalitarian symbols was widespread throughout Eastern Europe, even before the rise of NSK. So-called Sots art, which used elements of official propaganda and treated Socialist Realism in a manner that echoed Pop artists' exploitation of mass culture, was pursued by many Russian artists working in the Soviet Union or living in exile. The Russian duo of Vitaly Komar and Alexander Melamid were among the most prominent of these artists. The combination of elements of consumer society and socialist iconography was also present in the work of Czech painter Milan Kunc and in other artists in the former Czechoslovakia as well as in Hungary and Romania. In Poland the ironic actions of the Orange Alternative, in the form of mass demonstrations, took to the extreme the absurdity of the public spectacles orchestrated by the late Communist regimes.

The past, however, was not simply erased after the revolutions of 1989. In some countries, oppression in many forms still prevails. As Călin Dan's article on the situation in Romania in the mid-1990s attests, the use of subversive techniques continues to exist under conditions of general "stupidity and cynicism." With new situations arising, it also becomes necessary to critically examine one's own history, as demonstrated by Nedko Solakov's matter-of-fact confession of his youthful complicity with the Bulgarian secret police.

—*Tomáš Pospiszyl*

< *The Christmas Eve of the Great October Revolution* (detail). Wrocław, 1989. Courtesy Waldemar "Major" Fydrych (see p. 274)

• 257

KOMAR AND MELAMID

*Russian artists Vitaly Komar (born 1943) and Alexander Melamid (born 1945), both origi-
nally from Moscow, attended Moscow Art School and the Stroganov Institute of Art and
Design together, and since 1965 have been working collaboratively. In 1967 they originated
Sots art, the Russian equivalent of Pop art, which appropriated images from Socialist Realism rather than from consumer culture. At that time, they actively involved themselves
in the unofficial art scene in Moscow. In 1978 they emigrated and eventually settled in
New York, where they now live and work. Their paintings, installations, and performances
play with the dialectic between the ideologies of the artists and the expectations of the spectator. A series of paintings entitled People's Choice, which they initiated in 1994, draws its
form and content from public-opinion polls.*

The following essay was written for Artforum *magazine in 1980, shortly after Komar
and Melamid moved to the United States. With the new perspective gained during their
first years abroad, they chronicle the intricate landscape of Russian art, mapped by the
émigré periodical* A-Ya. *They also discuss their feelings about aesthetic innovation and
changing content in Russian art.*

The Barren Flowers of Evil

> *Truly now, isn't it a strange phenomenon? The Petersburg artist! An artist in the
> land of snows, in the land of Finns, where everything is wet, smooth even, grey,
> cloudy. — Nikolai Gogol, "Nevsky Prospect"*

How difficult it is to understand something you know nothing about. Leafing
through the pages of books arrived from afar, it is pure torment to get inside a foreign text, to separate metaphor from reality. In order to form a mental
picture of another world through the comparison of words and images, texts
and illustrations, one must possess a truly iron will and a stubborn belief in the
necessity of such an activity. Besides, such an endeavor requires that the researcher combine the acumen of Sherlock Holmes and the caution of Doctor
Watson, particularly when countries on the other side of the Iron Curtain are
concerned. A detective's work is frequently unglamorous but is always exciting,
at least for mystery lovers.

It is with nostalgia that we, the authors of this article, remember Igor Shelkovsky's small studio which could barely hold our friends: Rimma and Valerii
Gerlovin, Sasha Kosolapov, and several others. Ivan Chuikov was the only one
of us who knew English, and we would gather and listen as he translated for us
from the pages of the very magazine which you, dear reader, now hold in your
hands *[Artforum]*. The articles of an art critic with the Russian name Kozloff,
being structuralist in form and elusive in content, created special difficulties for
the translator. And the others were no easier. However, we were not deterred
by such difficulties. We pored over those glossy pages with reverence, scrutinizing
the colored splashes of the reproductions, the self-expression of distant and unknown American souls, until our eyes blurred. Gogol once described us, Russian
artists, in the epigram at the beginning of this article. While living in Italy, he
wrote of his distant homeland and came to the most pessimistic conclusions

concerning both Russia, and the fate of Russian artists: "They [artists] often possess true talent, and if only the fresh air of Italy could blow upon them, this talent would undoubtedly spill forth as freely, widely and brightly as a plant which has at last been taken out into the fresh air."

Much has changed since Gogol's time; Italy's artistic reputation waned, and the capital of Russia was moved from Petersburg to Moscow. Nevertheless, more and more often, as if on Gogol's advice, Russian artists are leaving their country, sowing themselves about the world in order to blossom in the smog of Paris, Tel Aviv, Munich, and New York. We ourselves settled in New York over a year ago. And what a surprise was in store for us! The participants of the Moscow readings of *Artforum* and still other of our Moscow friends came to lie on our American table in the chic gloss of a Western European magazine: *A-Ya: Contemporary Russian Art—Unofficial Russian Art Revue.* To work once again! Once more we set ourselves the task of divining already thoroughly forgotten secrets.

But how can you, Americans, how can you understand what this all means? Never fear, dear reader, we will help you to pass through the labyrinth of an alien and enigmatic culture.

Of course, it's possible to doubt the necessity of this endeavor. However, mystery fans have been intrigued by this pretty novelty. The press of Europe and America has informed the entire world. A certain excitement is in the air, and not all for Hecuba. The magazine is baffling from the word go: the title is untranslatable in any Western European language (Ya is the last letter of the Russian alphabet as well as the pronoun "I"); the magazine is published in Paris, though it is printed in Russian and English; and subscriptions may be obtained by writing to Switzerland. The front cover is strewn with English and Russian words, incomprehensible signs, and the Russian word DANGEROUS, repeated four times. Are you expecting explanations? Much of the above cannot be explained. Only conjectures are possible, conjectures which might harm those authors living in the Soviet Union, bring down upon our heads the wrath of those who have emigrated, and fail to satisfy the editorial board of *Artforum* by turning from the path of pure art into the wilds of socio-political research. We will confine ourselves to what we do know.

The magazine is published through the selfless efforts of a few artists, recent émigrés from the Soviet Union, in particular Igor Shelkovsky, a sculptor who left Russia several years ago and who currently lives in Paris. It is almost entirely devoted to Moscow artists who began their creative careers or sharply changed their style in the 1970s. The section of the journal entitled "Studio" examines six of them and contains a large number of reproductions and texts in which (for the most part) the artists speak for themselves. In the "Gallery" section, biographical information on nine artists is accompanied by reproductions and, in some cases, short theoretical manifestos. The remaining pages are divided as follows: "Critics on Art"; "Artists on Artists"; and the archival "Sources of the Avant-Garde" (K. Malevich, Diary "A," 1922).

The magazine is devoted to those artists who are called unofficial, dissident, or nonconformist in the world from the Bering Straits to the Baltic Sea. At this point some clarification of these terms is necessary, based upon our not-so-distant experience of such artists. Turning the pages of this respectable

Eric Bulatov. *Danger.* 1972–73. Oil on canvas, 42¾ × 43⅜" (108.6 × 110 cm). Jane Voorhees Zimmerli Art Museum, Rutgers, the State University of New Jersey, The Norton and Nancy Dodge Collection of Nonconformist Art from the Soviet Union

publication, it is truly difficult to imagine in relationship to what these artists constitute an opposition. But wait! In accordance with Leninist dialectics, an action, and likewise its result, cannot be evaluated in and of themselves, but only in the context of their meanings. Whatever helps a good cause — is good; what doesn't help — harms, i.e., it's bad. Whether or not our action is good or bad is a matter to be decided by the plenipotentiaries for the separation of good from evil, who in the everyday parlance of socialist reality are referred to as officials.

Each official has his particular department which deals with a well-defined range of questions. Should something arise which does not fall under the aegis of existing departments, then a new one is created. Officials think and speak in a language of instructions and fulfill the role of censors. Everything produced in the Soviet Union, from buttons to milk cartons, passes through bureaucratic hands. Thus, if an artist has created a work of art and wants to exhibit it, he must approach the proper department and explain to the official, in officialese, what the work of art means, and into which category of existing instructions it fits. The department, which handles art — The Union of Artists — is divided into various sections: sculpture, murals, and monuments; graphics; design; criticism; painting, etc. Therefore, if an artist were to draw something in pencil on canvas, it could not be exhibited, because that would be mixing the Graphics section (pencil) with the Painting Section (canvas), and there would be no appropriate section for the work. The same thing occurs with the artist who does not approach any departments and publicly shows his works. The artist who pursues such a path is eventually transferred to a section in an entirely different department, organized in the bowels of the secret police. Such are the artists represented in this magazine.

The journal *A-Ya* did not pass through bureaucratic hands. The authors of the articles speak freely. But just freely enough so as not to wind up in prison. Their language is at times evasive and it requires an experienced eye to draw meaning from the words. Take, for example, the dialogue of the two major contributors to the magazine, the critic Boris Groys and the artist Eric Bulatov: "You were saying that the space of authentic existence — is the space beyond the visible world, and now it seems the sense arises that this space is inside the painting." Bulatov: "No, that space is on the other side. But how to get there, that's the question." Groys: "So, how do we get there?" Bulatov: "How do we get there? Through the painting. Once we say that the painting is a model of the world, then everything that exists in the world should be in the painting. All of salvation should be in it. It shouldn't take place apart from it but inside it."

As the outstanding contemporary Russian writer Zinovii Zinik noted: "Russians are tormented by the desire to have their say, and the fear of saying too much." The name of this magazine, entirely devoted to the visual arts, consists of letters, and for that matter, of all the letters of the Russian alphabet, from the first (A) to the last (Ya). Apparently the editors have in mind words which remain unspoken, or cannot be pronounced, an important factor in contemporary Soviet art.

The magazine *A-Ya* differs from its Western counterparts in its goals. It is a dispatch, a coded communiqué, the whisper of someone crying in the wilderness, a secret sign to the world, the art critic, the curator, the art dealer. Reading through the magazine, we come to understand that the texts do not explain the works but create their meaning. The exterior is deceptive and frequently a sham. The painting is a covering, clothing which conceals and warms the author's soul, and is linked to the sinful external world and therefore always either ugly or neutral. One could formulate a common rule of thumb for self-evaluation for the majority of these artists: "Everything depends on the content which is poured into the form" (Joseph Stalin).

The Hegelian division of phenomena (including art) into form and content found fertile soil in the Russian consciousness whose duality was also noted by Freud — see Dostoevsky and Parricide. For this reason it is impossible to limit ourselves to an exclusively formal analysis of this strange art which is at the outer reaches of a specific mode of spiritual life. The social consciousness of the country in which we were born possesses a series of secret sore spots or zones which are both erogenous and pathologically hypersensitive. The value of cultural phenomena is defined by the nature of the zone and the manner in which the author touches it.

"I am not interested in problems of style and aesthetics as such," acknowledges Ivan Chuikov, an artist who is profusely reproduced in the journal. When

Warhol makes this sort of statement it's understandable; Andy is making money. But what interests this 45-year-old Russian whose work cannot be exhibited and who has no buyers? With wiliness worthy of a Russian diplomat speaking to Kissinger, the author avoids any direct answer, intimating that there exists a certain "context" which "makes any object placed in it something bigger, something more, invests it with a certain fiction." The clash between this fiction and reality occurs in his work.

As promised, we'll try to make our way through this labyrinth. Let us turn to the artist's biography and art. In early childhood Ivan Chuikov began painting landscapes in the Post-Impressionist manner of Socialist Realism. Gradually this manner became more individual, and finally in the 70s the artist began to seek a way out of the traditional framework of the romantic landscape. He started combining planar elements and volume, laying pictorial and graphic images over objects and constructions.

The cycle "Windows," with its plastic pun worthy of an artist of the proto-renaissance, is particularly interesting. The picture frame is the window frame. But in vain will you search for the illusory depths of a classical landscape within these frames. You'll run up against the flat bottom of a shallow recess, more suitable for the touch than for the eye. The relief of these window views forces us to recall the tactile principle of Braille. The blind window of Chuikov's landscapes is a stage in a tiny theater, a nostalgic fiction of cosmic space, the cynical consolation of a prisoner for whom the sky beyond his prison bars long ago became a geometrical abstraction. Speaking of the "several levels of interpretation of an artist's work," the author admits that "the most important level of exegesis is the silent declaration." In truth we have here a frightening theater, where mute actors perform before a blind audience. Chuikov's trees most closely resemble the mountains of a relief map. What are their leaves rustling about? What is the author's silent statement?

What does concern him, if it is not aesthetics or style? This question can only be answered by an inhabitant of the Russian Empire who is skilled in the Aesopian language of Soviet culture. The author is concerned with a simple question: where is the boundary between falsehood and truth? His Russian audience seeks an answer to this question. Where are the social and ethical truths concealed behind a veneered theatrical setting rudely imitating space which cannot be entered? And the artist, balancing on the edge of silence and revelation, hems and haws, saying that "an artistic object is by its very nature paradox—is ambiguous," reality and fiction simultaneously.

In order to explain to the patient reader just why it is that the Russian intelligentsia is so preoccupied with the search for some abstract truth and the logically hopeless task of its separation from an all-too-concrete lie, we must digress a bit from problems of "pure art" and venture on yet another historical excursion. The problem is that in 1917, no ordinary revolution took place in Russia. In 1917, a secret society rose to power in a huge country. The traditions and cultures of such societies remain remarkably obscure despite their "instinctive antiquity," to which the presence of secret fraternities among pagan tribes and the games played by children of perfectly civilized parents attest.

It is impossible to understand contemporary Russian culture if one does not take into account the fact that the Bolsheviks came to power with no experience governing anything other than a secret society. They had their own laws and traditions. Thus it is not surprising that they gradually transformed the entire country into one enormous, secret society.

This is the key to understanding our homeland with its mania for secrecy, the Party's doubling of governmental administrative functions and other such delightful customs. Having deciphered the pages of the magazine with the help of this key, you will understand that these artists, like all Soviet citizens, are part of a 260-million member secret society. This society contains different "lodges" and its members are involved to varying degrees of complicity. The consciousness of a member of a secret society is a schizophrenic Russian Bloody Mary of the legal and illegal. This is a theatrical psychology—it's fitting to recall here that Lenin and his friends often had to disguise themselves and changed their identities as effectively as the trickster heroes of Russian fairy tales—the psychology of a participant in the social spectacle entitled "Soviet Russia," where each person, from the cradle to the grave, without intermission, identifies with his role to the point that he cannot distinguish the lie from the reality.

He begins to confuse things. Where is the mask? Where is the face? Does the face lie beneath the mask, or the mask beneath the face? Content becomes form, and form content, and everything fuses in a strange carnival which actually resembles the organized boredom of military parades. The participants in this permanent happening perform their roles so sincerely and realistically that they are capable of deceiving such experienced Western spectators as Romain Rolland, Lion Feuchtwanger, and even that old skeptic Bernard Shaw. Of course, people aren't angels in any country anywhere—they are capable of deceit and are not averse to lying. But a ritual culture of lies, worked out down to the smallest details, has been created by this secret society, one in which a theatrical camouflage imitates the superficial impression of a normal state. The artist's mask has also become an aspect of the camouflage in this curious society.

We hope that by now the reader understands why it is that the Russian viewer seeks an answer to this naive question, "Where is truth?" This question is the sore spot behind the inoffensive mask of Chuikov's and [Sergei] Shablavin's landscapes, with their play on conditionality and illusion.

Boris Groys is the most prolific contributor to this magazine. His introductory article, "Moscow's Romantic Conceptualism" on four artists (pp. 162–74), and his interview with Eric Bulatov occupy a third of the entire magazine. In speaking of Chuikov's works, Groys defines quite precisely the belief of his circle that "the visible world has become a deceitful veil of Maya covering alternately the void or matter." In such conditions "the works mentioned remain ambiguous in part," since the picture is transformed into "something not identical to itself."

Calling on artists to "liberate themselves from ambiguity," Groys writes, "the positive view of art as an autonomous sphere of activity has always been alien to the Russian mind. . . . Romantic Conceptualism in Moscow not only testifies to the preservation of the integrity of the 'Russian soul,' but is a positive attempt to make known the conditions under which art may go beyond its borders." Though we do not consider such an approach to art the exclusive property of the "Russian soul," the author is correct in everything else. The work of art, as is the case with every phenomenon in Russia, is fatally unable to disengage itself from its context of social and religious ideas. It becomes an ethically heroic deed on the part of the creator—the visible form of an invisible ideological content, a flat mask which conceals an inexpressible depth.

The dialectical duplicity of Russian culture is a tradition with a much longer beard than those of the founders of dialectical materialism, Marx and Engels, and is vastly longer than Lenin's short little beard. This tradition has its origins in the country's geographical situation, located as it is on the periphery of Western and Eastern civilizations. In the visual arts this duality is reflected in the struggle between two- and three-dimensional treatments of space and color. At the time of the Petrine reforms, the strictly regulated, flat decorativeness of Russian icons came into conflict with proto-renaissance painting which arrived from Western Europe. The interaction of the two continues to this very day to define the development of Russian art, just as the well-known disputes of the Slavophiles and the Westernizers in the last century directed the development of Russian social thought.

Dialectical reminiscences of this conflict can be found on the pages of *A-Ya*. We have already given a sample of the dialogue—worthy of the Theatre of the Absurd—between Groys and Bulatov. We now quote another typical fragment from this interview. Groys: "In your paintings there is always a certain ambivalence for the people living in the painting—it seems that they have either frozen on this plane or that they might expand into space." Bulatov: "I can understand surface to be depth as well. . . . I understand social existence as surface. Everything visible is surface. And if we penetrate beyond that which is hidden, then we only see an inner surface anyway. . . . Space itself, in my understanding, is not distance. The concept of space as such is of course linked with spiritual life —with liberation for me. The absence of space—is prison."

One needn't be a profound thinker to detect that very same duality in this statement. Freedom (space) vs. non-freedom (surface). The West (democracy) vs. the East (Siberia). Bulatov: "Rilke has a definition: the beautiful is the terrifying to a safe degree. So you see, for me, this is not to a safe degree. I constantly perceive this as danger. I feel only a constant terror in relationship to this. And once there is terror, there can be no aesthetic relationship. . . . Perhaps this is also terror in relationship to today."

Look carefully at Bulatov's work on the magazine's cover (p. 260). The optic depth of this serene landscape, created by linear perspective, alternately engulfs and repulses the alien, flat, "red banner" words: DANGER, DANGER, DANGER, DANGER. This very same flat color, now in the guise of a ribbon from some medal or trophy, covers the sea-sky horizon in the painting *Horizon*. This work could serve as an illustration to the biography of the sculptor Sokhanevich. Not content to wait for opportunities made by détente, this artist escaped from the Soviet Union by crossing the Black Sea at the end of the 1960s, in a flight that was full of dangerous exploits. As far as we know, despite the existing possibility, Bulatov does not wish to emigrate into "space."

As if they had come straight off a Soviet political poster, the red letters "No Entry" barricade the sky blue "Entrance" in another of Bulatov's works. We do not wish to reduce the problem of perspective and flatness in the painting exclusively to the problem of crossing the well-guarded borders of the Soviet Union. To do this would be to oversimplify, and to impoverish the complexity of the material we have analyzed.

In the troubled mind of a frightened spirit, the image of the Western "other world" splits and takes on religious overtones of "paradise" and "inferno." The relationship to the West (that "machine for the production of things and ideas") has changed throughout Russia's history, but nevertheless it has remained the cornerstone of the intelligentsia's world view. However, neither those who saw in the West an "earthly paradise," nor their opponents, the Slavophiles, could foresee the paradoxical consequences of the 1917 Revolution, when the idea of socialism, borrowed from the West, transformed Russian culture into one of the most original phenomena in history.

Today Soviet Slavophiles understand that any individual Western phenomenon, when brought into Russia, finds itself in a different context, and begins to shine with some Holy Light, in the way that Edison's electric light bulb became Lenin's light bulb when it crossed into Russia.

Groys is a typical representative of this "neo-patriotism." He has set himself the goal of pouring old vodka into modernist wine skins. Sometimes it seems that a drunken mix-up occurred in the printer's shop where the magazine was typeset, so obvious is the lack of correspondence between Groys' arguments for Russian originality, and the thoroughly ordinary performances of artists such as Francisco Infante and the group "Action." The photographs of these works might have come from the pages of *Avalanche*.

Try as one might, it is difficult to see any mystical national originality in the restrained elegance of Infante's kinetic games. We see how his triangular mirrors, like some unexpected neo-Cubism, decompose the reflected landscape into illusory planes, containing the world in a utopian diamond whose geometrical edges refract tree trunks, grass, a river sandbar and the sky. These artifacts could, with equal success, reflect the skies of Russia or Spain, as well as the skies of any other country or climatic zone.

Unfortunately, the magazine did not print, as they promised, the texts which are an integral part of the performances of Alekseev, Monastyrski (pp. 174–81), and others. This blunder endows the visually most "Western" work in the magazine with a purely Russian air of mystery. Groys manages to see a certain magic innate to Russian art in these works as well. Not afraid of contradictions, he acknowledges that "this group is less concerned with social issues: it is oriented toward problems which face art as such"; i.e., the group possesses a quality which is not inherent in the "Russian mind," if we are to believe the propositions laid forth in another of the critic's articles.

The same absence of Russian dialectics can be seen in Infante. The reality of his artifacts is "free from suspicion insofar as it does not require any penetration beyond its form." But nevertheless (this is dialectics for you!) "Infante's performance differs significantly from Western (performances)," since in the West there's no way on earth you'll find "technological reveries recalling a distant childhood." Note that the erudite author compares the familiar names of Moscow artists, not to concrete Western names, but to no less than the entire West! This global gesture intended to resolve concrete, individual problems is incredibly typical of the apocalyptic mind.

At this point it must be said that we, the authors of this article, also have contradictory feelings. Of course, at a safe distance, it is easy to speak ironically of the judgments of a provincial patriot who isn't here to defend himself. But what if a real surprise is ripening in Russia — one of the many at which the world has not yet ceased to wonder? Groys is not alone in his conviction that Western art "in one way or another speaks about the world," while "Russian art, from the icon to the present, wants to speak of another world." This "other world" lies at the crossroads of religion and art, whose relations "are extremely tense in Russia." Similar ideas are expressed by V. Patsyukov in his article on the landscapes of Sergei Shablavin. Shablavin's "magical" realism is for some reason ascribed to hyperrealism and photorealism.

The sculptor Ernst Neizvestny, a participant in the infamous argument with Khrushchev,[1] once very wittily called Russian counterculture "a catacomb." And who knows, perhaps a new paradox will bear fruit in the third Rome. Religion is beginning to play the role of a "left" opposition, using the avant-garde forms of modernism, an "ism" genetically and spiritually bound with socialist dreams of the destruction of the old world. In this regard, the incomparably bolder experiments of Polish and other Eastern European artists are of great interest!

It's difficult to foresee what the character of the coming cultural revolution will be, not to mention whether or not it will be the result or cause of a social revolution. As we were taught at the Moscow Institute of Art and Design, a revolutionary situation arises when new content, quantitatively growing inside an old form, comes into contradiction with a form and destroys it, resulting in the appearance of a new form, a new quality. Of course, it may be that we confused everything, or have forgotten, and it's possible that Hegel imagined all this not quite as simply as our professors presented it to us. Still, it's an interesting question; can the renewal of modernism from the inside, that is, the search for content, give birth to new phenomena, or more promisingly, continue purely formal searches which have lost their revolutionary content and become fully respectable traditions? This is the question which, at the beginning of the 1980s, concerns not only us.

The husband and wife team Valerii and Rimma Gerlovin began working separately and now work almost exclusively in collaboration. They give us their own solution to this problem, and it differs significantly from that of the rest of the artists in this journal. Their works contain words or are accompanied by texts. In their opinion, conceptualism "is the most topical and fruitful stage of Russian art." Their extensive philosophical treatise is published in the magazine. Numbers in the text refer to separate descriptions and reproductions as if underlining and explaining the authors' ideas. One has the impression the Gerlovins are afraid they will be misunderstood, or not taken seriously. Here we have an opportunity to compare "talking" works with the "speaking" authors, to see how and to what extent desire is transformed into reality. They begin their treatise straight away by separating form and content, proposing, with the help of content (given their "indifference to the formal perfection of the work"), "to resolve moral, religious and social problems on the basis of our philosophical viewpoint." Such an approach is said to be "a characteristic tendency of contemporary art" in general and a fundamental principle of Russian art in particular.

At one point in their treatise, the Gerlovins suggest that we engage in play to solve the above mentioned problems. They refer to Rimma Gerlovin's work,

Rimma Gerlovina. *Cube-Poems*. 1974. Fabric, cardboard, small wooden cubes, and paper, each 3⅜ × 3⅜ × 3⅜" (8.5 × 8.5 × 8.5 cm). Jane Voorhees Zimmerli Art Museum. Rutgers, the State University of New Jersey, The Norton and Nancy Dodge Collection of Nonconformist Art from the Soviet Union

Cubes. The work consists of cardboard cubes which are covered with cloth and open on one side. Inside some of these cubes lies one or more smaller cubes. Some of the large ones are empty. Some of the cubes, large and small, bear labels describing their particular qualities, either from the author's or the cube's point of view. For example: the cube's pronouncement, "This is — me."; "Mongolia"; "This cube is five centimeters closer to the Moon than this one." Still others remain silent, but are accompanied by captions. The first thing that comes to mind when we see the pile of cubes scattered at Rimma Gerlovin's feet is that we could build something with them. But no! For then they wouldn't be able to open and we wouldn't be able to read what's written in and on them, and this clearly was not part of the artist's intent.

Gerlovin's cubes really resemble more precisely the music boxes of our grandmothers' time. Reading the label on the top, we open the box and see a label inside. When the melody is over we close the top. You can't play with music boxes, and you can't put anything in them; Grandmother might get mad. You can only listen, opening and closing them.

What do they say? They speak in ambiguities. Box: "There's a sphere inside me." The inside of the cube: "He's a sphere, I'm a cube." Box: "You think." Small cube inside: "But I am." This is not a dialogue, but a monologue in which the inside plays the role of an inner voice. Here we are face to face with the dichotomy of Homo-Box's consciousness. As the Gerlovins see it "with the aid of play, mastery and accessible knowledge of the world occur; internal and external conflicts of self-orientation are overcome and self-analysis takes place." An indisputable, widely accepted statement.

But what are we supposed to play? Is listening really playing? No. In the case of cubes, we cannot be led to self-analysis. We must employ analysis quoting the Gerlovins once more: "The author is not in opposition to the object." The implication is clear: we have been listening to Gerlovin herself. These are her boxes and her voice. The cubes are covered with beautiful materials, they are clothed alternately in pajamas and in evening dress. The only woman in contemporary Russian modernism exhibits a profound inventiveness in designing a wardrobe for her soul. Rimma Gerlovin's soul, if we are to believe the accompanying texts, yearns for freedom, to go out into society, but her place is on the shelf along with other idle knickknacks.

The Gerlovins have other, more global ideas as well. "In the work, *The Big Dipper,* we see people as astral bodies." Where are people to go? Must they either conceal themselves on a shelf or soar into the heavens? Thus, in resolving world problems, the Gerlovins propose that we leave this world. The logic of their work led them to emigrate from Russia several months ago. It is easy to suppose that their image of another world, which consciously or unconsciously was associated with the real world of Western Europe and America while they were still in Russia, will prove to have been an illusion, as has been the case for the majority of Russian emigrants. For them, the other world will move to Russia, and along with this, the understanding will arise that *every* "other" world (be it social, religious or whatever) is hell. Thus Russian modernism, and world modernism are deprived of yet another fundamental of their illusions — creation in the name of the betterment of mankind. For us, the authors of this article, recent émigrés from Russia, it is obvious that the world is not only monotonously bad, but that changes in it have no meaning.

Likewise, change in art is meaningless. Art ceases to be a movement from and to, and becomes only a reshuffling of what exists. Dragging in ideas from all over the world — Hinduism, Buddhism, Eastern Socialism, African art, etc. — European artists of the last two hundred years have created an illusion of progress. However, the quantity of combinations of the existing, though large indeed, is nevertheless limited. People who have been through two worlds know this.

It is imperative to mention Joseph Beuys's recent show here. Though Beuys has not emigrated, he has experienced life in two worlds. Beuys is an anti-fascist, reared on fascism, just as some Russians are anti-Communists, reared on socialism. They have ideas which they take for convictions. The complex of a "normal" person, who believes in certain truths, torments them, and forces them to put on various masks — of prophets, philosophers, political activists and God knows what else. But in their heart they know that this is all bullshit. They have to lie, dodge, make art — in order to be like everyone else. Their art displays certain common characteristics:

1. *Conscious or unconscious deceit.*
2. *The division of art into form and content, with the latter reigning supreme. (Which on occasion results in a tragi-comic effect.)*
3. *The lack of correspondence between the proclaimed goals and the things created, according to the principle that the end (content) justifies the means (form).*
4. *Anti-aestheticism. The placing of the work of art in a non-artistic context. (The "negative" image of Duchamp's anti-aestheticism where an object from another realm was placed into an artistic context.)*

The artists represented in the magazine *A-Ya,* as we have already mentioned, were creatively formed in the 70s. Their predecessors, the "left-wing" artists of the 60s, struggled with the "remnants of the personality cult" through artistic means: Cézanne's tradition versus the academic formalism of Socialist Realism. Like their Western colleagues of the same period, they believed that to alter form is to change one's world view. There is good style and bad style. But according to a Russian proverb, "the bad is only a step away from the good." Lev Rubinstein takes this step in his brilliant texts. Unfortunately, he is given very little space in the magazine — only small excerpts (and those without English translation). Rubinstein is the author of small, typed books, three of which are mentioned: *The Catalog of Comic Innovations, New Intermission,* and *A Working Program.* To look at, his books are typical samizdat (underground self-published works) — poorly typed pages bound in cardboard. The *Catalog of Comic Innovations* is a masterpiece of spiritual bureaucratese. It consists of numbered aphorisms, each one sentence in length and each beginning with the words, "it is possible to." The range of possibilities is vast, and according to Rubinstein there are 122 of them.

The first possibility: "It is possible to do something." From this starting point — activity — possibilities ascend by overcoming the "pale cast of thought." And the fifth: "It is possible to classify possibilities according to the degree of their comical qualities." The following paragraphs classify comic possibilities.

It is possible to mystify, eliminate, speak about, represent, disregard, consider, and most importantly, as the last, 122nd paragraph declares: "It is possible to not think about the consequences, they will be comic in character." We are hearing the voice of a doubting prophet, who utters indisputable truths. "And further, by these, my son, be admonished: of making many books there is no end; and much study is a weariness of the flesh" (Ecclesiastes 12:12). Read, for example, beginning with the words, "Many take refuge in silence at certain moments," etc., up to "The author thrives in silence" (*New Intermission:* 4). A possessed bureaucrat, a prophet, a silent Moscow prattler, a samizdat author, a candidate for the crazy farm, and a subtle lyric poet — everything is mixed together in Rubinstein's image of the author of his books. Perhaps this is Rubinstein himself. Who knows?

Combining the good and the bad, Rubinstein has the wisdom not to reject anything — that is, to remain himself. Fragments of holy truths, the permissible and the taboo, float about in the head of any intelligent person on either side of the Atlantic. A comic effect results when they come into conflict. This is obvious in the Gerlovins's works and is hinted at in Bulatov's canvases. Frequently, irony as a form of the paradoxical is invisible but is present in many of the works reproduced in the magazine *A-Ya.* The critic Groys says, "There is an entire tradition (in contemporary Russian art) of separating oneself from the world we live in through jest or satire." And truly, there are such artists in Russia today. The work of Vagrich Bakhchanyan, who emigrated a few years ago and now lives in New York, illustrates this trend. The problem of jest and irony in art is much more profound than Groys imagines. We ourselves belong to this group of "ironic" artists.

It is hard to judge all of new Russian art on one 55-page issue of a journal. *A-Ya* is not the "alpha and omega" of Russian art. Russia is large and has many artists. However, in a journal which is "not the mouthpiece of any particular group (and whose) pages are open to everything new, bright and independent," it is pleasing to see such a fully defined and distinct tendency. The magazine deals with postmodernist, or in our terminology, post-totalitarian Russian art. There are no more than about thirty such artists in Russia as far as we know, and what they do is a miracle. The reader must imagine for him or herself the situation in which they live and work. Dreary, boring, terrifying Moscow, whose inhabitants are oppressed by a monstrous fear. We mention this, not to stir pity in the reader, but in order to explain the peculiarities of this new art.

We are linked by friendship with the majority of artists in this magazine. We met some of them when we were only beginning our work in this new direction. We have worked side by side with some of them. For this reason, it's hard to say what part of our review is about them, and what is self-portrait. Many of our accusations in regard to these artists may seem horrifying. But if our philippics are understood, not as a condemnation, but as a statement of stubborn facts, and if they are believed, then this could be regarded as something, like an artistic platform (laid out by points above), a certain original aesthetic. Of course, from the point of view of American aesthetic norms, post-totalitarianism seems hideous, both artistically and morally. But this has been the accusation leveled at every new movement in art.

The most important part of the magazine opens with an article by a contemporary art critic and closes with a version of a 1922 essay by Malevich. Here we can see how far Russian artistic thought has progressed. Groys is undoubtedly an intelligent and penetrating critic whose ignorance of the world around him prevents him from seeing certain things, a fact that becomes particularly evident when you read his article in the West. But it is difficult to say anything serious about Malevich's asinine scribblings. We can only point out that not only was Malevich an illiterate philosopher and the inventor of the artistic movement Suprematism—think about the name a bit: super + mat (mother in Russian)— but he was also an active Commissar, one of the first of the Soviet bureaucrats who concerned themselves with the separation of good from bad in the realm of the arts. His bureaucratic heirs, having exchanged Malevich's bad form for their own good uniforms, left his content untouched, and currently reign supreme in Russia. Recognizing this, Russian artists discovered that Lenin's avant-garde and Stalin's academism are essentially only two different sides of the same socialist utopia. With the failure of this utopia its art too was discredited. Indeed, if stylistic opposites are bad, then there's no point in discussing subtleties.

Having just learned, with great difficulty, the modernist ABC's from the West, Russian post-avant-gardists unexpectedly revealed the full and horrifying power of that which is now called the avant-garde. These artists began their education during Stalin's lifetime and completed it after his death. In the 1970s they realized that it is impossible and unnecessary to struggle against Communist reality, for we ourselves, individuals, citizens, and creators, are both its main ingredients and its leaders. It became apparent that time does not exist in Soviet reality and yet space submits to it.

In contrast to their Western colleagues, who think in terms of color, line, etc., and who can be evaluated in comparison to each other, if only because there are many of them, these new Russians turned out to be much more radical. All their subterfuge, dialectic blather, and stylistic exercises clearly demonstrate the complete and senseless void of dead European culture. Sacred European traditions have been laid to waste, and the scabs of dead forms flake off from the extremities of Europe. Malevich's squares, though they did bring something "new" with them, turned out to be empty in all respects. However, to understand this, Russian artists had to go through Stalin's academism — the last attempt to stop European time.

Note
1. See Erofeev text, pp. 37–53, and Bulldozer show, p. 65.

Written in March 1980. Originally published in *Artforum* magazine (New York) (March 1980). Translated by Jamey Gambrell.

•●

WOJCIECH MARCHLEWSKI

Conceived as an alternative to "red" Communism, the Orange Alternative was a group of Polish artists, art historians, critics, and social activists from Wrocław who staged peaceful and humorously absurd street actions during the 1980s that ridiculed government demonstrations and their ideological monopoly on "truth." Led by the art historian and activist Waldemar Fydrych, known as "major" to his "comrades," the Orange Alternative was a direct response to the imposition of martial law (1981–83). Their actions, which were met with enthusiasm by the public and featured ironic slogans such as "I am sensitive to your problems," often flummoxed the authorities, leaving them bewildered as to how to intervene.

In the following text, Marchlewski recounts the evolution of one of the largest Happenings concocted by the group. On November 6, 1987, on the eve of the anniversary of the October Revolution, the Orange Alternative took to the streets with mock-ups of the battleships "Potemkin" and "Aurora." Participants in the action were asked to wear red and to yell Bolshevik slogans; the Happening ended with the arrest of one hundred fifty people.

Chronicle of the Events

Preparations start a few weeks before the planned Happening. As previously, the happeners from the Orange Alternative meet in a friend's apartment. They agree upon the planned course of action, its time frame, and venues. The meeting changes into a brainstorming session. When one participant presents his vision of the event, others make comments, add new details, and laugh. Their suggestions become more and more hilarious, though less and less implementable. They refer to the experience gained during former actions, recall the reactions of the police, and make various remarks related to what happened in the past. Finally, as the meeting comes to its end, they decide which ideas will be put into practice and who will be responsible for what.

A group of organizers is formed. They agree upon the props that will be used and the slogans that will be shouted. There is also a "propaganda unit," preparing a leaflet to be distributed. After a long debate and much quarreling, they specify its content, including the points that are supposed to stimulate the participants to action. The leaflet reads as follows:

> *Truth will liberate us.*
> *Comrades,*
> *The day when the Great Proletarian October Revolution broke out is a day of a Great Event. At present, the Revolution Day does not have its eve.*
> *Comrades, it is high time we put an end to the apathy of the people. Let us start to observe the Eve of the October Revolution. Let us gather as soon as November 6, on Friday, at 4 p.m., on Swidnicka Street, right under the clock of history.*
> *Comrades, wear your red holiday clothes on that day. Put on red shoes, a red hat, and a red scarf. If you don't have even a red band or any other garment of that color, borrow your neighbor's red purse. If you don't have a red flag, you can at least paint your fingernails red. If you have nothing red at all, you can buy a piece of baguette with ketchup on it. All of us Reds (red hair, red pants, red mouths) will gather on that day under the clock at about 4 p.m. Comrades! Let's meet to commemorate and pay our respect to the Revolution!!!!*
> *THE IDEAS AND PRACTICE OF LENIN AND TROTSKY WILL LIVE FOREVER!*
> *COUNCIL OF THE PEOPLE'S COMMISSARS*
> *Bring your dog — at 4:15 p.m. under the clock, there will be an exhibition of purebreds and mongrels. The motto is "Dogs for the Revolution!" Red ribbons attached to the leash are welcome!*
> *BOW! WOW!*

The holiday celebrations are scheduled to end at the snack bar Barbara, where the participants of the meeting will have a chance to eat from a single bowl the red "eve borscht" [red borscht is a traditional Polish Christmas Eve soup] and other appropriate dishes.

When the content of the leaflet and the manner of its distribution have been determined, the organizers go home.

November 6, 1987. A few days before the planned action, its organizers have moved in with their friends who live near Świdnicka Street. That is because they are afraid of the potential countermeasures of the police. Since the morning they have been completing all the props and making a precise schedule of the events. From the streetcars going along Kazimierza Wielkiego Street leaflets are being thrown out of the windows. People waiting at the stops are at first reluctant to pick them up, but then they do it more and more eagerly; they read them and laugh. Around 11 a.m. a few young people affix leaflets on the walls of the Old Town. Other leaflets fall down on the sidewalk of Świdnicka Street from the top stories of the local apartment buildings.

Around noon the first police patrols show up. They check the IDs of all the young and strange-looking passersby. Particular attention is paid to those who carry backpacks and big bags. They are stopped and taken to the local courtyard gateways to be searched. If the items found in the bags and backpacks are classified as "normal," the policemen let their owners go. A little later the first patrol cars arrive. They block the Old Market and the passageways under the arcades. Some vehicles stop on Ofiar Oświęcimskich Street. Then come the big vans that block Kazimierza Wielkiego Street. Some of them park in front of the snack bar Barbara.

This is a regular business day, and people are shopping in the stores on Świdnicka Street. They are surprised to see the police. They ask why such large forces have been deployed in the area. As it turns out, not everyone has read the leaflets that have circulated since the morning.

Around 3 p.m. a member of the Barbara staff puts a notice on the door which reads, "Closed due to a technical failure." By 3:30 the crowd on Świdnicka Street has grown tremendously. Many people are stopped by the police patrols to have their IDs checked. The policemen advise people to leave Świdnicka for their own safety. At the same time, the crew of the battleship "Potemkin" are gathering in the sports-equipment store Stadion. Four boys bring to the store cardboard boxes with holes in the bottoms. They will be the two sides of the battleship. A poster with a full-size portrait of Lenin has been attached to one of the boxes. It is somewhat too big, which is why it has been folded so that Lenin looks like a cephalopod. Simultaneously, on the other side of the street, the crew of the "Aurora" is gathering in a store called Merkury. Inside, there are many plain-clothesmen who closely watch everyone coming in. The crew manages to sneak unnoticed up to the second floor. A pregnant girl enters the store. The police do not stop her, and she easily reaches the fitting room. The "Aurora" crew follows her inside. They paint their faces red. The one standing on the ship's bow puts on his face a papier-mâché mask of Lenin. From under her sweater the girl produces the "fetus" — a wide tarpaulin band with holes in it. She covers the crew with the band.

In the meantime, an infantry unit has been gathering in the store called Feniks at the Old Market. Wearing red sweat suits, the boys roam the store and look at the sports equipment on display.

To the bus stop located a few blocks away come the Proletarians. They are members of the Solidarity units from the local factories — workers. The Proletarians, with red shirts folded in their pockets, are holding a rolled banner. They are standing, waiting for a bus.

The members of the Cavalry unit have been gathering in the courtyard of a church on Kazimierza Wielkiego Street. The church has a direct exit onto the street, and via side streets one can also get from there to Świdnicka. The Cavalrymen are a little nervous, and their commander tells them about the plan. A girl comes and brings some hats resembling those worn once by the [Soviet] soldiers of Budyonny. It turns out that there are too few of them. Other Cavalrymen come, too. They bring wooden hobbyhorses and wooden rifles. A moment of hesitation: Did cavalrymen use rifles? The young people are confused. Some of them say that wooden sabers would be better. Then two more people join them. They are carrying an original, used banner with the following inscription in

The Christmas Eve of the Great October Revolution, Wrocław, 1987. Documentary photo of Orange Alternative action. Courtesy Waldemar "Major" Fydrych

capital letters: "Anniversary of the Great Socialist October Revolution." Later it will be realized that the banner is as wide as the street.

After a while, the Angel of the Revolution enters the courtyard. The Cavalry-men help him into his costume: a white robe and huge red wings attached to his shoulders. On his head he has a wig made of long white hair, with a halo above it.

Not far away, near the Metropol hotel, is the gathering site of the Carolers. To the poles prepared in advance they attach a banner with the inscription, "Red Borscht." To the top of another long pole they fasten a big red star.

According to the schedule, at 4 p.m. the "Potemkin" with its crew consist-ing of four men comes out of the Stadion shop onto Świdnicka Street. The po-licemen standing nearby rush at them and tear the cardboard boxes into pieces. There is a lot of noise. The spectators who are close to the place run even closer to see what is going on. After a few minutes the police have everything under control and arrest the "Potemkin" crew.

At about the same time, five minutes after 4 p.m., the "Aurora" leaves the Merkury. The leading commissar, wearing a mask of Lenin, directs the crew to-ward the clock. A police van drives up to them. The members of the crew at the end of the group rub their shoulders against the side of the van. The driver steps on the brake. The spectators nearby begin to shout, "Revolution! Revolution!" The "Aurora" is approaching the clock. The police come and surround the crew. Other participants of the Happening take whistles out of their pockets and start whistling. The police are angry. The "Aurora" crew sits on the ground. The police drag them from under the tarpaulin one by one and arrest them. But the missing crew members are replaced by people from the crowd. The struggle continues. The police put more and more people under arrest. They take them to the vans parked on Ofiar Oświęcimskich Street.

Ten minutes after 4 p.m., the Infantrymen wearing red sweat suits run out, one after another, from the Feniks. They keep blowing their whistles. The police block access to Świdnicka Street and grab the Infantrymen. Only their commander manages to break through the police cordon. He reaches the struggling "Aurora." There, tripped up, he falls into a puddle. The police run up to him and drag him toward their vans.

Suddenly, everything on Świdnicka Street comes to a standstill. From an underground pedestrian passage emerges an African man with a red beret on his head. He walks by the still struggling crew of the "Aurora." No one reacts. The police, the happeners, and the passersby are all confused. The African paces slowly, with dignity. Everyone is watching the foreigner, who soon disappears into a side street. Then the police start doing their job again. They put under arrest not only the crew of the "Aurora" and the red-clad infantrymen, but they also stop those pedestrians who happen to wear red berets and scarves and take them to the police vans. They are protesting, since they do not know why they are being treated in such a way. The policemen do not answer any questions, just take those under arrest to their vehicles.

As the police are struggling with the "Aurora" crew and some pedestrians who happened by, a bus arrives at the stop just opposite the snack bar "Barbara." The Proletarians emerge from the bus wearing red shirts with an inscription, "I will work more!" They unfold some banners: "We want comrade Yeltsin back!" "We want an eight-hour work day for the employees of the WUSW!" [Regional Office of Internal Affairs, the official name of the central Wrocław police station], "We want Leon Trotsky's rehabilitation!" The spectators yell, "Yeltsin, Yeltsin! Trotsky, Trotsky! Revolution! Revolution! Red borscht!!!" The police put the representatives of the Proletariat under arrest. Only one of them surreptitiously dodges and starts running. He takes up a wooden rifle with a red flag attached to its barrel. The policemen follow him at high speed. They make an attempt to arrest him.

From the church courtyard out come the Cavalrymen, holding in their hands rifles and wooden hobbyhorses, the Budyonny-style hats on their heads. First they check if the way is clear. From the distance, they can hear shouts, "Revolution! Revolution!" Then they retreat to their former positions.

It is 4:20. Time for the Carolers. They are marching along Świdnicka Street with the "Red borscht" banner. Their leader is a figure in disguise holding a pole with the red star fastened to its top. The policemen who stand in front of the underground passage stop the Carolers with the banner. The figure in disguise crosses Świdnicka Street. He comes to the battlefield where just a moment before the Proletarians were arrested. The red star soars above the undulating crowd. Then it disappears. The police put the Carolers under arrest.

Budyonny's Cavalrymen attack once more. They rush out of the courtyard and run quickly to the underground passage, next to the plainclothesmen who are standing right there. The latter take out their walkie-talkies and say something into the microphones. The policemen blocking the passageway form a line. They grab the hobbyhorses, break the rifles. The commander of the Cavalrymen is struggling with a policeman. He lets the policeman attack, then pushes him back with the flagstaff. After a while, the flag is lost and the commander orders his men to retreat. They leave behind the hobbyhorses, take off their hats, no longer the cavalry proper they were before. Taking various side streets, they try to reach Świdnicka.

After a while, the Angel of the Revolution appears on the battlefield. He is unable to press through the crowd of spectators, so he turns back and approaches a hot-dog stand. A line forms behind him. The police interfere. The saleswoman, scared, puts up a notice, "Sorry, no buns." The Angel of the Revolution stops and asks her, "Do you still have ketchup?" "Yes," she answers. "Then two portions, please," says the Angel, stretching out both hands. The woman pours some ketchup on them. The Angel goes away, soon to be stopped by the police and arrested.

At the same time, the Cavalrymen, unrecognized by the police, reach the snack bar Barbara. What they see there is debris: everywhere on the street there are scattered cardboard boxes and pieces of red cloth. They come up to the bar. On the door there is still the notice saying, "Closed due to a technical failure."

At 5 p.m. a staff member opens the door and people can come in. The first to enter is a plainclothesman. He comes up to the counter and tries to place an order. "Can I have borscht, please?" "No borscht," is the staff member's answer. The plainclothesman, satisfied, leaves. The Cavalrymen take seats around one of the tables. The commander comes up to the bar and orders four bottles of strawberry juice. He puts them on the table. The Cavalrymen put on their Budyonny-style hats. They keep sipping the juice in peace and quiet. All of a sudden there is silence in the bar. A policeman standing on the sidewalk notices the Cavalrymen. He summons a higher-ranking officer. A police patrol enters the bar. They come up to the Cavalrymen still drinking their juice. "Can I see your IDs, please?" The Cavalrymen produce their IDs, asking no questions. The officer orders them to take off their hats. An elderly lady standing near the policeman fulminates, "Why are you bothering them? Don't you have anything else to do?" Hearing that, the other patrons start laughing. The police take the Cavalrymen outside. From the opposite side of the street comes a woman who says, "Boys, you've been wonderful!" The commander of the Cavalrymen snaps to attention. He salutes her and replies, "Thank you in the name of the Revolution!" The people in the bar applaud.

In the evening, after 5 p.m. About 150 people were arrested in consequence of the action. Among them were pedestrians who happened by: Everyone who by chance wore something red was suspected of taking part in the Happening. A hundred participants and witnesses of the action were detained in the social room of the police station on Łąkowa Street, the other fifty at the police station on Grunwaldzka Street.

The social room of the police station on Łąkowa is filled with the participants of the action and the pedestrians. The TV is on. They are showing the anniversary celebrations of the Great October Revolution in Moscow. The people in the room applaud, watching the dignitaries deliver their speeches. They stand up and start singing "The Internationale." The policemen try to silence them. In vain. One of the happeners starts writing something on a flag which is in the room—some letters, the beginning of a slogan. A policeman rushes into the room, pulls the flag down, and tramples on it. The "Revolutionaries" applaud. One by one, individual participants of the action are taken to be interviewed. After the interviews, they are brought to the exit where they are waiting for the others. The policemen try to make them go away, but to no avail.

At the police station on Grunwaldzka the atmosphere is gloomy. The crew of the "Aurora" is sitting by the wall, their faces painted red. They look as if they have been beaten to a pulp. The policemen treat them with great respect. After some interrogation, they let everyone go. Leaving the station, the happeners say goodbye to the policemen flanking the exit. The policemen wave back in a friendly manner.

Written in August 1989. Originally published in *Dialog,* 395. Translated by Marek Wilczynski.

•●

NEDKO SOLAKOV

Nedko Solakov (born 1957) is one of Bulgaria's best-known contemporary artists. He received traditional training in mural painting at the Art Academy in Sofia, and combines this classical background with Conceptual practices and a sense of the absurd to create installations, paintings, and performances that reference art history and play on the expectations of the viewer.

Top Secret, created between December 1989 and February 1990, consists of a file box filled with a series of cards detailing the artist's youthful collaboration with the Bulgarian secret police. The work caused great controversy when it was first exhibited in the spring of 1990, at the height of political changes to the long-standing Communist rule. Consequently, Solakov wrote the following text for a weekly newspaper as a public explanation of his artwork, as well as to counteract rumors that had begun to circulate after the exhibition about his involvement with the state security apparatus. The self-disclosing gesture in this artistic project (mentioned in the artist's résumé as Top Secret—Action with Colleagues*) is still unique in the context of post-Communist Europe, and since its appearance* Top Secret *has become an icon of its time.*

The Action is on (for the time being) . . .

Once upon a time there was a boy.
They say he was a smart and obedient one. He got the highest grades in school, he read books at home and he drew. He drew rabbits, hunters, houses with chimneys and aeroplanes with fivepointed stars on them destroying other airplanes with swastikas on them. He drew and read . . . He liked particularly the books with the adventure stories where the "good" guys won over the "bad" guys. He also liked spy stories. The brave Soviet "chekisti" and their Bulgarian colleagues Avakum Zakhov and Emil Boev were really attractive to him. They were making him confident that the enemies about whom it was spoken and written everywhere were not going to intrude upon his socialist fatherland.

The boy was growing up. He graduated with honors (a gold medal) from the prestigious high school for mathematics in his native town and was accepted right away as a student in the Academy of Fine Arts (he was not drafted into the army then because of an ailment which he had suffered in his early youth). His usual diligence and obedience went on here as well.

In the autumn of 1976 (when he was in his second year at the Academy) the boy went on a trip to Paris (his loving parents, whom he also loved, paid for the trip). Everything was wonderful — the Louvre, the Rodin [museum], the Dufy retrospective, a few porno movies. In the middle of the eight-day trip the tour leader of the group of Bulgarian tourists told him there were packages left by somebody for him and for B. (a kind older man, brother of a well-known professor) at the reception desk. To the boy's surprise his package contained "enemy" propaganda materials. The boy read this and that and handed the materials over to the tour leader with the words: "They are 'spitting' on Bulgaria!" The tour leader got worried and summoned right away a man from the Embassy to whom the boy gave the package, happy to have carried out his patriotic duty.

A few weeks later though (already back in Sofia) the boy was summoned by the head of the "personnel" department at the Academy, who told him with a secretive voice that there was this "comrade" here who wanted to talk to him. The "comrade" (a nice young man) asked for the "case" in Paris to be described in one or two pages. The boy did so. The "comrade" was satisfied and then asked an unexpected question: "Well, we are actually interested in . . ." and mentioned the name of a boy's colleague, one quiet and humble guy. "What's he like, is there something about him that strikes you as unusual, etc.?" The boy (diligent and obedient) answered that since it was necessary he would tell. Afterwards, filled with some peculiar pride, the boy shared that event with a friend and a girlfriend.

The nice young "comrade" had appeared again (only this time in secrecy — eye to eye). And thus little by little the boy had entered a meadow from where the flowers were gradually disappearing, the thorns were getting thicker, the grass and the bush grew up to his eyes. To tell you the truth the boy wasn't too active. But nevertheless when asked he answered (and always afterwards he wrote on a white sheet of paper leaving on purpose a blank white space at the top of the sheet) which exhibition was popular and which one was not, who had contacts with religious sects and who didn't, etc. Did the boy actually realize what he was doing? I would say yes and no. The boy had just trusted the institutions, had believed he was contributing to the realization of that great future society where everything would be great for everyone. Naturally he wasn't getting anything for all this (except maybe he was getting some strange feeling of security). While in the army he was transferred to another young man (with epaulets). Here, at the beginning, he also believed he was carrying out his soldier's duty. But this belief was getting shakier and shakier.

Thus came the summer of 1983. Once discharged from the army the boy had gathered all his courage together (is this the usual expression?) and had firmly refused to be used anymore. The "comrade" (with epaulets) had been trying hard to talk him into transferring to another "comrade" in charge of the intelligentsia. But the boy "stuck to his guns."

That was the beginning of a long and painful awakening. The boy's diligence and obedience were getting displaced little by little by other, a lot more manly, things. But the boy (the man) was still afraid. The fear must have shown itself in his paintings. That went on until his first child was born (the summer of 1986). And then the man realized that his path must be chosen categorically if he was to look straight in the eyes this child who had been carried around the blooming roses and daisies in its mother's womb during that sadly memorable May 1 of 1986.[1] And it seems the path he chose did not lead to the "bright future."

The audience trusted him. It trusted his drawings from the Enlightened by the Decisions and The Endurance of a Nation series from his one-man show in January 1988. It trusted as well his card index in the chest from the exhibition *The City,* his telescope with the title sign "View to the West" pointing from the roof of the 6 Shipka Street Gallery toward the red pentacle on top of the Bulgarian Communist Party headquarters (the telescope though had been mysteriously dismantled by the State security, which had long ago lost its confidence in the man). And his studio was filled with just such honest paintings and objects lying around in expectation of better times.

Could he have stopped with his frankness here?

He could have. It is very unlikely his contacts with the nice "comrades" from seven years ago would have come out in the open. It is not in the best interests of any political party or movement to bring out in public the full lists of just such names (you know why, don't you?).

But the man had made up his mind that this revelation should see the light of day as well. So he made a new card index in a chest. There he drew and described, using Pop art means, everything shameful and depressing which was still creeping around his ever more hurting heart. He described the case in question as well.

The man exhibited in public this card-index chest (called *Top Secret*) at the Club of Young Artists' exhibition entitled *End of Quotation* (April 20–May 26, 1990), and accepted internally once and for all that only he or she who can overcome his or her fears can be a true artist. It doesn't matter what kind of fear this

Nedko Solakov. *Top Secret.* 1989–90. Acrylic, drawing ink, oil, photographs, graphite, bronze, aluminum, wood, and shameful secret; 176 slips mounted in original index box, 5½ × 18⅛ × 15⅜" (14 × 46 × 39 cm). Collection the artist

may be — the fear of changing the direction of one's work in spite of the success it is gathering, or the fear of revealing oneself to the full at any cost and thus accomplishing an artistic act.

Many of his younger colleagues (and some older ones as well) understood and shook his hand. About a month after the opening of the exhibition, the Congress of the Union of Bulgarian Artists was held. The man thought somebody would bring up the "question" (his) in front of everybody but nobody did. Obviously (along the laws of safe existence) he should have kept quiet. But seeing that the conservatism in the Union was once again taking the upper hand he withdrew his initial decision not to run for Chairman of the Union and again put forward his candidacy. He felt morally obliged to help destroy this horrifying machine for oppression of artists called "Creative Union." He wanted his colleagues at last to feel free and confident in themselves (not in the Union), to start trusting the audience which had been waiting for them for a long, long time. He was elected Vice Chairman.

But the story doesn't end here. The rumor which was started after the *End of Quotation* exhibition that he was the man of the state security apparatuses in the Union was getting threateningly widespread. Many of his colleagues (obviously not into going to art exhibitions) had not even realized that the man himself had publicly disclosed his own past one month before the Congress. And that this "past" was very different indeed from the concept of the man of the State security in the Union. Thus a not altogether artistic campaign was under way. The man was forced to exhibit once again his *Top Secret* chest in the former office room of the Communist party at the Union. But since he knew not everyone would get to see it and the talk in the hallways and the cafés was going strong, he asked a newspaper, much respected by him, to publish the above words.

And at the end, stating that the boy, the man and myself are one and the same person, let me give you one more reason for my showing the *Top Secret* piece. I wanted it to be a warning to all young people who might be misled to fall into the meticulously woven webs of the Institution. Because if in two or three years time (or even sooner) some of these young people are asked by the future "appropriate services" whether some Communists, anarchists, etc. are having meetings together, these same young people may not hesitate to tell and this act would be perfectly normal and moral for them. I don't know if I, as an artist, should feel flattered that a work of mine has caused such a scandal. The whole of it turned into a sort of Happening (that is, an action where you don't really know what's going to happen next). But I am its author and it is up to me to put the tag with the right title and content of the work when its "finale" comes about.

I would like to believe that the artists in the Union of Artists and above all the audience, which I treasure the most, will understand.

Note
1. Date of Chernobyl nuclear accident. The Bulgarian government did not disclose the disaster to the public until several days later.

Written in 1990. Originally published in *Kultura* weekly newspaper (Sofia), June 22, 1990. Translated by Luchezar Boyadjiev.

CĂLIN DAN

In 1990 the Romanian art critic, curator, and media artist Călin Dan, along with sculptor Dan Mihălțianu and photographer Josef Király, formed subREAL, an artists group that takes as its subject the clichéd images and stereotypes associated with Romanian culture and politics, such as vampires and the dictatorship of Nicolae Ceausescu. The group, which currently consists of Dan and Király, often uses found images as material for its multimedia installations, as in the case of their "Art History Archive" project, for which they utilized the discarded photo archive of the official Romanian art magazine Arta.

The following text, written five years after the founding of subREAL, is a meditation on the group's projects and ideas, tracing the origins of their use of conceptual photography as a subversive purveyor of history, as well as giving a description of the media arts in Romania at that specific time.

Untitled Celebration

Dedicated to.

When subREAL took shape in the depressive Romanian summer of 1990, it was hard to predict that it would be more than another short-term survival operation. A lot of them have been launched in the darkness of the 1980s and killed immediately by the inexhaustible political censorship. But this time we were lucky: The oppressive system in Romania was too busy elsewhere after the big shake-up of December 1989. That is why next July we can celebrate the amazing fifth anniversary of the life and deeds of subREAL, because the [old/new] Power allowed us to exist. To this event are dedicated the following lines.

We're all stupid.

What is subREAL has still to be elucidated. First of all, [it is] a certain way to re-act toward an environment which just happened to be Romania. Then, it became a concept covering the ambiguous faces of that reality. Then again, the fact that Romania is just a piece in a huge subREAL context became obvious. But what is subREAL remains a question potentially addressed to everybody, since, modestly speaking, subREAL turns into being everybody and everything. For the moment, let's say that subREAL is all the information coming from the territory where stupidity and cynicism become one, since the world is stupidly cynical — or the other way around — cynically stupid.

A Group is a Conspiracy.

Such a radically confused concept needs a lot of energy to work with. This is why, technically speaking, subREAL was a group from the beginning. At the start, the structure was flexible, involving, around the founders, a number of people with potential subREAL sensitivity. It was the time of the installation *Alimentara (Food Store),* operating within the context of the "starvation decade" (the 1980s). This farewell reconstruction nevertheless required some material, like local canned food, smoked-and-salted pork bones (a delicacy during the times of Nicolae Ceausescu) and other products which turned into collectors' items under the pressure of the open market. For financial reasons also, *Alimentara* was an open subREAL event, a jam session where everybody brought his or her piece. In the end the guests didn't invest so much and then demanded to have their names labeled on things like old hams, broken eggs, salads, etc. It's hard to give up your identity, especially as an artist. Therefore, subREAL had to be limited for the time being to the initial group.

The mechanics of art.

The favorite medium of subREAL has been (is) the installation. Suffocated by material handicaps and exhausted by an abusive promotion in Western art, the installation was, in Romania, the key word for the freedom of expression during the dictatorship. During the 1970s and 1980s, to install was practically forbidden by the political censorship, with the help and approval of the old-media artists and their public, a silent majority rejecting on principle all "experiment." Those facts explain the inflation of (bad) installation—one of the characteristics of Romanian art in the 1990s. The difference cultivated by subREAL in that context belongs to specificity. Site-specific events have a very convenient hygiene—they appear briskly and they vanish in time. Nothing is left afterwards. Photography excepted, sometimes.

Memory erasure.

The main lesson of the underground period concerned the weakness of such media as installations and performances when their memorization is forbidden. To take pictures during the few alternative events held at that time was unusual. The technical culture of the artists was poor, and so were they. A camera was a luxury item. The few documents produced were usually confiscated after events by the ever-present secret police. Finally, a kind of exhaustion, a disgusted rejection of history went together with the local alternative scene. This mentality disappeared after 1989, partly.

Invent and Save.

In the case of subREAL, that experience was changed by the revelation that people can make history if they know how to fake it. What matters in the post-industrial era is not the fact but the information, not the object but its carrier. An aura of photographs, videos, texts is surrounding the subREAL "art pieces."

What is an installation? A very demanding sculpture, which needs more room, more technical assistance than a "normal" art piece, [which] is very difficult in terms of transportation and very fragile in the fight with natural enemies of art—dust and light. Installations, like humans, get old and ugly. Installations are time based; this is why they need photography.

Hit and Run.

Unsophisticated pieces (technically speaking) installed for a short period, documented in a sophisticated way and then dismantled. Sometimes remade in other locations. Just for the fun of making new pictures. The installation is a fluid medium; it takes the shape of the space that is hosting it. Looking at the pictures taken at the time, one can see the development of an autonomous aesthetics, more and more distant from the idea of documentation. Finally, the relation between photo and installations concerns the fiction of the image. subREAL is act-

subREAL. *Dataroom*. 1995. Photo installation, Künstlerhaus Bethanien, Berlin, 32'10" × 19'8" × 9'10" (10 × 6 × 3 m). Courtesy subREAL

ing like the production team of a science-fiction movie, building the setup for a five seconds shooting as carefully as if it would last forever. Since our favorite long-term project is called *Draculaland,* there must be a secret contamination between the Hollywood procedures and the subREAL obsessions.

Confession.
We love the mass production of the American movies and we would love to make one of them ourselves—a subREAL "Terminator," for instance.

Video break.
Since 1993 video has entered our [sub] lives, first under the cover of a small Hi8 camera, then by an addition in installation production. The first video installations of subREAL are, in a sense, an extension of photography, at least as far as the similarity with slides is concerned. The use of transparencies in some of our installations can be seen as a substitute for the video in a less-generous environment. Slide projections are the video of the poor (this is a good one!).

Photo-Hysteria.
Photography is an open manipulation, since it works with the basics of reality. No wonder the more insecure people are about themselves, the more they hate photography. Hatred of photographers is a common phenomenon in Romania, and it increased unexpectedly after the so-called changes to the internal politics. Taking pictures is a synonym of kidnapping a reality belonging to someone. And

the Romanians, brutalized by history, ended up becoming the accomplices of this oppressive reality around them. Therefore, their main concern is not to fight and change but to hide and protect. If subREAL is taking pictures of a shop window with political figures surrounded by *leberwursts,* of pathetic beggars or old cemeteries, the public opinion riots against a potential export of our Supreme State Secrets—Poverty and Ridicule. An interesting blend of guilt and pride makes the common people the most efficient fighters against the betrayal-by-image.

Trendy and Archived.

Both video and photography are prompt tools for exploring the chaos of the subREAL environment. An accumulation of images is the characteristic of the unofficial history of the group. The concept of archive entered our vocabulary relatively late (actually it was brought by the new fashion for archives, widespread in the last few years), but the archive reality was there from the beginning as the only method to absorb and systematize a random mass of information.

Practically all the coherent works labeled subREAL are issued from a process of accumulating data. From this tissue of information a structure is always extracted, because structures are there, in the massive mess of facts and images. Reality is, like installation, a fluid phenomenon, taking the shape of the space hosting it.

Manipulating.

Things are not that bad if you manage to use the situations, the institutions—and the people. The archive topic brought us back to the initial issue of the flexible subREAL structure. Using people's archives as a creative resource is a more realistic strategy than working directly with them; artists are easier to manipulate through their discourses than to stimulate through interaction.

META—the Romanian participation in the last (but not least, I'm afraid) São Paulo Bienal—was a subREAL-based event, using the private archives of six artists, as they developed under the pressure of the reality of the last fifteen years. The criteria for gathering 120 images were the amassing of themes and obsessions, the nonaesthetic side of life, which developed a nonresponse at the artistic level.

AHA

A step further is the Art History Archive project. Developed in Berlin, with the assistance of an environment traditionally more concerned with history than the Romanian one, the AHA is based on a ready-made archive, inherited from the official art magazine that covered the Romanian art scene between 1953 and 1993.

AHA is first of all an export-import operation. subREAL IMPEX. saved the photo material from the brutal indifference of the former publishers by placing it in a context where research and public access are potentially possible. Secondly, AHA is an interactive process involving people from various disciplines in order to debate the faith and destiny of Art, as proved by media users. What is left of art history after the discovery of photography, after the marriage of photography and printing, after the ideological collapse of modernism, Communism, etc.? What are photography and archives, at a time when digital compression develops another approach to the illusion of the deep frozen space?

Some interesting conclusions leap to the eyes when confronted with such material—going from the pre- to the post-history of the arts and from the national (Romanian) to the global areas. Some sad (?) evidence [exists] of the authority of figurative vs. aesthetic—on the unexhausted force of bad photography to compete with life on its very (sub)REAL ground.

Finally, AHA is the research field for a definition of subREAL-ity, as all accumulations are, potentially. Finally, photography, as life itself, is just a mass of unclassified information, waiting for the proper software and the proper operator. The (al)ready-made things are stronger than the inventions—at least at the end of the arts era.

Written in 1995. Originally published in *Imago: Another European Photography* (Bratislava: FOTOFO) (winter 95/96).

••

SLAVOJ ŽIŽEK

Slavoj Žižek was born in Ljubljana, Slovenia, in 1949 and received a doctorate in philosophy from the University of Ljubljana and a doctorate in psychoanalysis from the University of Paris. He is more widely known as a specialist in the psychoanalytic theory of Jacques Lacan than as a critic of the visual arts, although much of his work utilizes Lacanian thought to analyze popular culture. Žižek was politically active in the dissident movement in Slovenia throughout the 1980s and was a presidential candidate during the first multiparty elections held in 1990. Since 2000 he has directed a research group at the Kulturwissenschaftliches Institute in Essen, Germany.

In the following essay, Žižek writes about the difficulty of deciphering the intentions of the Neue Slowenische Kunst (NSK), an art collective that gained prominence in the early 1980s, and the fascistic imagery used by its musical branch, Laibach. According to Žižek, the typical NSK supporter assumes that the group treats the transgressive imagery of Nazism and fascism with ironical distance, despite the fact that the NSK offers no explicit admission of such. Žižek, however, contends that the opposite is true: the NSK plays the role of an utterly unironic supporter of what their imagery stands for, hoping to reveal publicly the difficult truth that transgression is acceptable when it is part of a private ritual or unspoken mandate.

Why are Laibach and NSK not Fascists?

Superego is the obscene "nightly" law that necessarily redoubles and accompanies, as its shadow, the "public" Law. This inherent and constitutive splitting in the Law is the subject of Rob Reiner's film *A Few Good Men*, the court-martial drama about two marines accused of murdering one of their fellow soldiers. The military prosecutor claims that the two marines' act was a deliberate murder, whereas the defense succeeds in proving that the defendants just followed the so-called "Code Red," which authorizes the clandestine night-time beating of a fellow soldier who, in the opinion of his peers or of the superior officer, has broken the ethical code of the marines. The function of this "Code

Red" is extremely interesting: it condones an act of transgression—illegal punishment of a fellow soldier—yet at the same time it reaffirms the cohesion of the group, i.e., it calls for an act of supreme identification with group values. Such a code must remain under the cover of night, unacknowledged, unutterable—in public everybody pretends to know nothing about it, or even actively denies its existence. It represents the "spirit of community" in its purest, exerting the strongest pressure on the individual to comply with its mandate of group identification. Yet, simultaneously, it violates the explicit rules of community life. (The plight of the two accused soldiers is that they are unable to grasp this exclusion of "Code Red" from the "Big Other," the domain of the public Law: They desperately ask themselves "What did we do wrong?" since they just followed the order of the superior officer.) Where does this splitting of the Law into the written public Law and its underside, the "unwritten," obscene secret code, come from? From the incomplete, "non-all" character of the public Law: explicit, public rules do not suffice, so they have to be supplemented by a clandestine, "unwritten" code aimed at those who, although they violate no public rules, maintain a kind of inner distance and do not truly identify with the "spirit of community."

The field of the law is thus split into Law *qua* "Ego-Ideal," i.e., a symbolic order which regulates social life and maintains social peace, and into its obscene, superegotistical inverse. As has been shown by numerous analyses from [Mikhail] Bakhtin onwards, periodic transgressions of the public law are inherent to the social order, they function as a condition of the latter's stability. (The mistake of Bakhtin—or, rather, of some of his followers—was to present an idealized image of these "transgressions," while passing in silence over lynching parties, etc., as the crucial form of the "carnevalesque suspense of social hierarchy.") What most deeply "holds together" a community is not so much identification with the Law that regulates the community's "normal" everyday circuit, but rather *identification with a specific form of transgression of the Law, of the Law's suspension* (in psychoanalytic terms, with a specific form of enjoyment). Let us return to those small town white communities in the American south of the twenties, where the reign of the official, public Law is accompanied by its shadowy double, the nightly terror of Ku Klux Klan, with its lynchings of powerless blacks: a (white) man is easily forgiven minor infractions of the Law, especially when they can be justified by a "code of honor"; the community still recognizes him as "one of us." Yet he will be effectively excommunicated, perceived as "not one of us," the moment he disowns the specific form of transgression that pertains to this community—say, the moment he refuses to partake in the ritual lynchings by the Klan, or even reports them to the Law (which, of course, does not want to hear about them since they exemplify its own hidden underside). The Nazi community relied on the same solidarity-in-guilt adduced by participation in a common transgression: it ostracized those who were not ready to assume the dark side of the idyllic *Volksgemeinschaft,* the night pogroms, the beatings of political opponents—in short, all that "everybody knew, yet did not want to speak about aloud."

It is against the background of this constitutive tension of the Law between public-written Law and superego that one should comprehend the extraordinary critical-ideological impact of the *Neue Slowenische Kunst,* especially of Laibach group. In the process of disintegration of socialism in Slovenia, they staged an aggressive inconsistent mixture of Stalinism, Nazism, and *Blut und Boden* ideology. The first reaction of the enlightened Leftist critics was to conceive of Laibach as the ironic imitation of totalitarian rituals; however, their support of Laibach was always accompanied by an uneasy feeling: "What if they really mean it? What if they truly identify with the totalitarian ritual?" — or, a more cunning version of it, transferring one's own doubt onto the other: "What if Laibach overestimates their public? What if the public takes seriously what Laibach mockingly imitates, so that Laibach actually strengthens what it purports to undermine?" This uneasy feeling is fed on the assumption that ironic distance is automatically a subversive attitude. What if, on the contrary, the dominant attitude of the contemporary "postideological" universe is precisely the cynical distance toward public values? What if this distance, far from posing any threat to the system, designates the supreme form of conformism, since the normal function of the system requires cynical distance? In this sense the strategy of Laibach appears in a new light: *it "frustrates" the system (the ruling ideology) precisely insofar as it is not its ironic imitation, but over-identification with it —* by bringing to light the obscene superego underside of the system, over-identification suspends its efficiency. (In order to clarify the way this baring, this public staging of the obscene fantasmatic kernel of an ideological edifice, suspends its normal functioning, let us recall a somehow homologous phenomenon in the sphere of individual experience: each of us has some private ritual, phrase [nicknames, etc.] or gesture, used only within the most intimate circle of closest friends or relatives; when these rituals are rendered public, their effect is necessarily one of extreme embarrassment and shame — one has a mind to sink into the earth.)

The ultimate expedient of Laibach is their deft manipulation of transference: their public (especially intellectuals) is obsessed with the "desire of the Other" — what is Laibach's actual position, are they truly totalitarians or not? — i.e., they address Laibach with a question and expect from them an answer, failing to notice that Laibach itself *does not function as an answer but a question.* By means of the elusive character of their desire, of the indecidability as to "where they actually stand," Laibach compels us to take up our position and decide upon *our* desire. Laibach here actually accomplishes the reversal that defines the end of psychoanalytical cure. At the outset of the cure is transference: the transferential relationship is put in force as soon as the analyst appears in the guise of the subject supposed to know — to know the truth about the analysand's desire. When, in the course of the psychoanalysis, the analysand complains that he doesn't know what he wants, all this moan and groan is addressed to the analyst, with the implicit supposition that the analyst *does* know it. In other words, i.e., insofar as the analyst stands for the Big Other, the analysand's illusion lies in reducing his ignorance about his desire to an "epistemological" *incapacity:* the truth about his desire already exists, it is registered somewhere in the Big Other, one has only to bring it to light and his desiring will run smoothly. The end of the psychoanalysis, the dissolution of transference, occurs when this "epistemological" incapacity shifts into "ontological" *impossibility:* the analysand has to experience how the Big Other also does not possess the truth about his desire, how his desire is without guarantee, groundless, authorized only in itself. In this precise sense, the dissolution of transference designates the moment when the arrow of the question that the analysand pointed at the analyst turns back toward the analysand himself: first, the analysand's (hysterical) question addressed to the analyst supposed to possess the answer; then, the analysand is forced to acknowledge that the analyst himself is nothing but a big question mark addressed to the analysand. Here one can specify Lacan's thesis that an analyst is authorized only by himself: an analysand becomes analyst upon assuming that his desire has no support in the Other, that the authorization of his desire can only come from himself. And insofar as this same reversal of the direction of the arrow defines drive, we could say (as Lacan does say) that what takes place at the end of the psychoanalysis is the shift from desire to drive.

Written in 1993. Originally published in *M'ARS* (Ljubljana: Moderna Galerija), vol. 3/4.

••

BORIS GROYS

Boris Groys (see biographical information on p. 162) wrote the following text about the IRWIN group, the visual-arts component of the Neue Slowenische Kunst, for an NSK publication. In it he argues that the predominant notion in the West that contemporary avant-garde art is, by nature, opposed to the establishment is complicated by some Eastern European artists, including IRWIN. He contends that the historical situation of Slovenian artists and all Eastern European artists offers no easy explanation of motives. Although the West prefers to regard them as "other," East Europeans were not, in fact, so isolated, nor were they eager to accept the total promise of utopia that the first historical avant-garde envisioned for themselves during the early decades of the twentieth century.

The IRWIN Group: More Total than Totalitarianism

When confronted with the works of the IRWIN group, most — and primarily Western — viewers and commentators immediately raise one characteristic question: with what aim and in what context do these artists make such extensive use of symbols of fascism or totalitarian Communism? On the one hand, they employ these symbols side by side with signs of contemporary modernist art usually associated with opposition to totalitarianism, thus making it impossible to suppose that the IRWIN group actually wants to engender an aesthetic of totalitarianism in its original form. On the other hand, their quotations from totalitarian propagandist art are not used according to the usual devices of modernist estrangement, distortion, or the visual "critique of representation" which would allow the position of the authors to be unambiguously identified as critical. Nor does reference to the programmatic statements of the group provide a way out of the initial bewilderment: in all of their programmatic documents the artists of the IRWIN group employ direct quotations from totalitarian rhetoric and combine them with references to modernist or postmodern criticism in exactly the same way they do in their artworks, so that the corresponding texts, if anything, double rather than disperse the initial bewilderment. Such parallelism of formal devices between purely artistic and interpreted practices is, incidentally, not at all characteristic of contemporary art. Inside this system it is usually assumed that the artist or critic will honestly decode, on the level of the text, that which is coded in the artistic work.

The uniqueness of the artistic practice of IRWIN lies, however, precisely in the fact that it questions the twentieth-century habit of assuming an opposition between the critical and the affirmative positions in art. The critical position is usually connected with the aesthetic of the artistic avant-garde: in this sense postmodern art can also be regarded as a continuation of avant-garde criticism, but only addressed to the avant-garde itself. The affirmative position is associated, by contrast, with the traditionalism and triviality of artistic means, and the apotheosis of such traditionalist affirmativism is often considered to be the totalitarian art of Nazi Germany or Stalinist Russia, which persecuted and suppressed the avant-garde. This (in the context of Western culture entirely natural) breakdown looks rather different, however, in Eastern Europe.

The crucial difference lies in the fact that the avant-garde in the East, unlike its Western counterpart, fulfilled not only a critical but also a thoroughly affirmative function. Everywhere the historical artistic avant-garde demanded emancipation from all criteria of quality, tradition, taste, or craftsmanship; or, to put it differently, from any kind of control by the consumer, the critic, or the viewer. It was the aim of this entire artistic strategy to deprive the consumer of art of his independent, external, and comfortable position: the viewer was to be involved in the production of the work of art through aesthetic shock or through the transformation of all his everyday surroundings. No longer would the taste and judgement of the viewer decide the fate of the work of art within the market system of supply and demand; instead the artist would completely transform the taste of the viewer. Corresponding projects for the complete transformation of the world according to the principles of the new and unified aesthetic were advanced by De Stijl in Holland or the Bauhaus in Germany; but they were proclaimed with the greatest radicalism by the Russian avant-garde—through the Suprematism of Malevich, but also the Constructivism of Tatlin and Rodchenko. In essence the demand was now being made for a kind of artistic dictatorship of the artist over the viewer, by means of which the viewer was supposed to be led beyond his accustomed cultural limits into the ecstatic space of his very life, taken as a continuous act of creation. In the West these utopian demands of the artistic avant-garde were never realized, and for this reason they remained merely a basis for criticism of the reigning consumerist society.

In Eastern Europe—at first in Russia, and then everywhere else, including Yugoslavia—developments were quite different. The Communists also declared their aim to be the rule of the producer—of the working class—over the consumer: the market and the usual system of consumption were liquidated. All of society was oriented toward a single process of the creation of a new life and a new human being; an external, purely consumerist position became impossible; and each individual became one element of a unified new world in which life was supposed to coincide with art. The Russian avant-garde, like its Eastern European counterparts, welcomed this realization of its artistic and social ideal. Certain Russian avant-garde artists made full use of the political power that was initially given them for the liquidation of the art market in the country, for the subordination of all art to control by a single party, and for the centralization and etatism of artistic life: a politically and economically totalitarian state was supposed to become a total work of art, insofar as this was what constituted the avant-garde project from the very beginning.

Of course the avant-garde was soon forced out of power, to the extent that its freedom from tradition was still defined in purely negative terms, as a rejection of traditional artistic forms. The victorious avant-garde demanded full artistic freedom, consisting of the expedient strategic manipulation means of traditional forms entirely subordinated to the artistic will to power. The art of Stalinist Soviet realism was just such a free manipulation. It was by no means mimetic or traditionalist and did not affirmatively reflect life as it is. In fact just the opposite was true: Socialist Realism used traditional artistic forms to create a phantasmagoric, utopian world of the paradisaical future.

The art of Nazi Germany was essentially the same. In both cases there was talk of creating an art without viewer or consumer—assuming one did not include in this definition Hitler and Stalin, who simultaneously appeared as its true creators: the populations of both empires appeared themselves within the art as its material. Here the traditional forms of art were utilized as tools for the most radical critique of the traditional conditions of life—all the way to their radical elimination. This is the source of the ecstatic and psychedelic character of Stalinist and Hitlerist art, which are more reminiscent of the contemporary phenomena of Surrealism or magic realism than the sober mimetic realism of the past.

IRWIN. *Geography of Time.* 1992. Mixed media. Installation view from the exhibition *Molteplici culture in Convento di S. Egidio,* Rome, 1992. Courtsy IRWIN

This brief excursus into the history of the interrelationship between the artistic avant-garde and traditionalism in Eastern Europe allows us to understand the artistic strategy of a whole series of contemporary Russian and Eastern artists, including those of the IRWIN group. When the IRWIN artists, in their works and in their texts, place quotations from European modernism and totalitarian art on the same level, they thus deconstruct the usual opposition between avant-garde criticism and totalitarian traditionalism in reference to the specific cultural experience of the countries. It is precisely this experience that shows the extreme diversity of strategies within whose framework it was possible to use various visual or verbal forms and, at the same time, the extreme closeness of these strategies to each other. Any criticism becomes affirmative as soon as it has attained victory—whether that be socialism in one country or avant-gardism within one work of art or text.

For far too long the political dichotomy of the cold war relieved intellectuals and artists of the luxury of trustworthy theoretical oppositions: the consumerist society of the West was criticized in the name of the total utopian project partly realized in the East, while the totalitarianism of the East was criticized with reference to the consumerist individualism of the West. For all of these years the artistic avant-garde of the West relied ideologically, in one way or another, on the ideals of Marxism, while the artistic avant-garde of the East, not much different from that of the West in terms of its external forms, was in one way or another oriented to Western ideals of individual freedom. And when the avant-gardists from the West accidentally met with avant-gardists from the East, both sides preferred to avoid overly close contacts—for the avant-gardists of the West considered the Eastern avant-gardists to be agents of imperialism and the CIA, while the Eastern avant-gardists considered the Western avant-gardists to be useful idiots of the Communist propaganda and the KGB. Today the cold war is over, and the entire world is confronted by the indistinguishability of East and West once hidden behind their obvious oppositions; Western society waited in vain for a glimpse of that long-expected "other" in the newly opened countries of the East. However, the picture which is only today being revealed to all was already presented by Eastern European art itself. Thus the works of the IRWIN group had already appeared, long before the end of the cold war in political life, as an artistic rendition of its end; they showed the total tautology of the world ideological constellation.

At a time when one sees frequent expectations of an influx to the West of new artistic forms from Eastern European art which were preserved untouched thanks to a national tradition which was not integrated into the international artistic process, the artists of the IRWIN group are showing the cultural history of Slovenia—as is characteristic for the other countries of Eastern Europe as well—constantly imported artistic models from the West as well as from the East, by no means considering itself to be some sort of isolated cultural space. The cultural situation in Eastern Europe is not determined by any specifically national or traditional artistic forms, but by the use of defined elements of internal artistic language in the framework of other strategies and contexts, in different combinations, with different intentions, and for the illustration of different ideologies from those that have their place in the West.

Precisely in order to demonstrate this circumstance, the IRWIN artists use quotations from Western modernist art as ideological signs within defined ideological configuration. This ideological, content-oriented motivation of artistic composition is a distinguishing trait of almost all Eastern art, which has never trusted those appeals, characteristic of Western art, to purely aesthetic formal criteria. For this reason the originality of the art of Eastern Europe consists not so much of a specific repertoire of particular artistic forms as of the idiosyncratic social and artistic-strategic application of already familiar forms and in the special attention directed toward the mechanisms of such usage. Of course, only a few artists of Eastern Europe are in a position to demonstrate these mechanisms in their own art consciously. But the artists of the IRWIN group are among them— and it is precisely for this reason that the works of its artists present a source of particular cultural interest.

Written in 1990. Originally published in IRWIN-Kapital, Co-Laborator (Edinburgh) and Institut-NSK (Ljubljana), 1991.

•●

A CASE STUDY: NEUE SLOWENISCHE KUNST

The art collective Neue Slowenische Kunst (NSK), based in Ljubljana, Slovenia, came to prominence in the early 1980s and has functioned ever since as one of the more complex, charismatic phenomena of the East European culture industry. Using a highly developed system of discursive instruments, aesthetic symbols, and performative techniques, NSK has employed music, video, exhibitions, writing, theater, graphic design, architecture, and public relations to investigate the relationship between art and ideology.

Institutional and transparent in its appearance but mutating and opaque in its behavior, the NSK organism bears traits of both a cult and a corporation. It defies classification by assimilating misunderstanding and incorporating contradiction and paradox into its self-reproductive apparatus. NSK's interventions—which range from establishing temporary NSK embassies on "foreign soil" to conducting Conceptual art experiments in the form of journeys—probe the memory and breakup of Yugoslavia for aesthetic possibilities and insinuate Slav content into the Western cultural sphere. Drawing inspiration from both avant-garde iconography and totalitarian ideology, NSK defines its artistic, methodological, and philosophic practice as "retro-avant-garde."

The movement began operating in 1984 as a union of three groups working in different mediums. While a number of subgroups have emerged and dissolved as specific needs arose (New Collectivism, Department for Pure and Applied Philosophy, Theater Red Pilot, Theater Noordung), the original groups which came together to form NSK are: the musical group Laibach; the visual-arts group IRWIN; and the Scipion Nasice Sisters Theater.

—Roger L. Conover

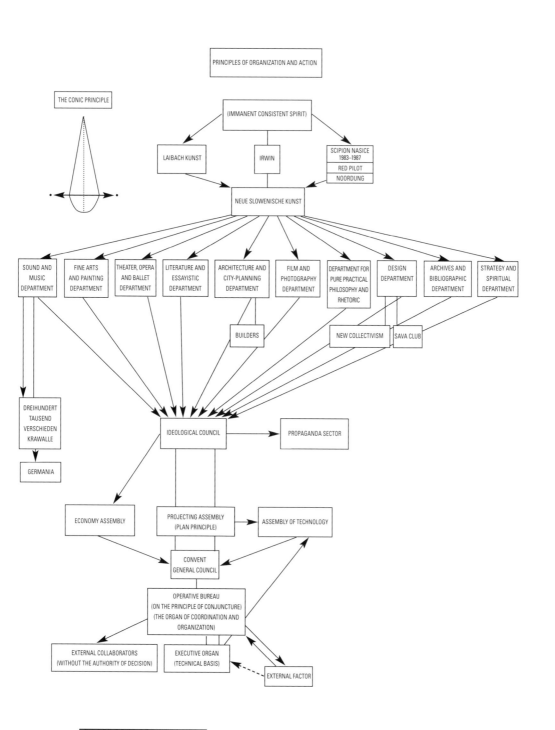

Chart of the NSK organization, 1984. Courtesy NSK

LAIBACH

The industrial band Laibach was established in 1980 in the mining town of Trbovlje, Slove-nia. Following its first concerts ("ideological offensives") in Yugoslavia, the group was banned from making public appearances and from using the name Laibach—the name of the Slovene capital (Ljubljana) under the Hapsburg Empire, which the Nazis revived dur-ing their occupation of the city. Laibach members lived "in uniform," personally renounced their individuality, and adhered to the strict collectivist aesthetic of the founding "Cove-nants." Laibach went on to release many bootleg records and CDs, transform their Euro-pean and American concert tours into political scandals, produce a strong inventory of visual symbols and icons (under the name Laibach Kunst), and become the subject of sev-eral documentary films. The alienating power and mystique surrounding Laibach remains without parallel in the Yugoslavian alternative culture scene of the 1980s and 1990s.

—R. L. C.

Laibach: 10 Items of the Covenant

1.

LAIBACH works as a team (the collective spirit), according to the principle of industrial production and totalitarianism, which means that the individual does not speak; the organization does. Our work is industrial, our language political.

2.

LAIBACH analyzes the relation between ideology and culture in a late phase, presented through art. LAIBACH sublimates the tension between them and the existing disharmonies (social unrest, individual frustrations, ideological opposi-tions) and thus eliminates every direct ideological and systemic discursiveness. The very name and the emblem are visible materializations of the idea on the level of a cognitive symbol. The name LAIBACH is a suggestion of the actual possibility of establishing a politicized (system) ideological art because of the influence of politics and ideology.

3.

All art is subject to political manipulation (indirectly—consciousness; directly), except for that which speaks the language of this same manipulation. To speak in political terms means to reveal and acknowledge the omnipresence of politics. The role of the most humane form of politics is the bridging of the gap between reality and the mobilizing spirit. Ideology takes the place of authentic forms of social consciousness. The subject in modern society assumes the role of the politi-cized subject by acknowledging these facts. LAIBACH reveals and expresses the link of politics and ideology with industrial production and the unbridgeable gaps between this link and the spirit.

4.

The triumph of anonymity and facelessness has been intensified to the absolute through a technological process. All individual differences of the authors are an-nulled, every trace of individuality erased. The technological process is a method of programming function. It represents development, i.e., purposeful change. To isolate a particle of this process and form it statically means to reveal man's negation of any kind of evolution which is foreign to and inadequate for his biological evolution.

LAIBACH adopts the organizational system of industrial production and the identification with the ideology as its work method. In accordance with this, each member personally rejects his individuality, thereby expressing the relationship between the particular form of production system and ideology and the individual. The form of social production appears in the manner of production of LAIBACH music itself and the relations within the group. The group functions operationally according to the principle of rational transformation, and its (hierarchical) structure is coherent.

5.

The internal structure functions on the directive principle and symbolizes the relation of ideology toward the individual. The idea is concentrated in one (and the same) person, who is prevented from any kind of deviation. The quadruple principle acts by the same key (EBER—SALIGER—KELLER—DACHAUER), which—predestined—conceals in itself an arbitrary number of sub-objects (depending on the needs).

The flexibility and anonymity of the members prevent possible individual deviations and allow a permanent revitalization of the internal juices of life. A subject who can identify himself with the extreme position of contemporary industrial production automatically becomes a LAIBACH member (and is simultaneously condemned for his objectivization).

6.

The basis of LAIBACH's activity lies in its concept of unity, which expresses itself in each medium according to appropriate laws (art, music, film . . .).

The material of LAIBACH manipulation: Taylorism, bruitism, Nazi Kunst, disco . . .

The principle of work is totally constructed and the compositional process is a dictated "ready-made": industrial production is rationally developmental, but if we extract from this process the element of the moment and emphasize it, we also designate to it the mystical dimension of alienation, which reveals the magical component of the industrial process. Repression of the industrial ritual is transformed into a compositional dictate and the politicization of sound can become absolute tonality.

7.

LAIBACH excludes any evolution of the original idea; the original concept is not evolutionary but entelechical, and the presentation is only a link between this static and the changing determinant unit. We take the same stand toward the direct influence of the development of music on the LAIBACH concept; of course, this influence is a material necessity but it is of secondary importance and appears only as a historical musical foundation of the moment which, in its choice, is unlimited. LAIBACH expresses its timelessness with the artifacts of the present and it is thus necessary that at the intersection of politics and industrial production (the culture of art, ideology, consciousness) it encounters the elements of both, although it wants to be both. This wide range allows LAIBACH to oscillate, creating the illusion of movement (development).

8.
LAIBACH practices provocation on the revolted state of the alienated consciousness (which must necessarily find itself an enemy) and unites warriors and opponents into an expression of a static totalitarian scream.

It acts as a creative illusion of strict institutionality, as a social theater of popular culture, and communicates only through non-communication.

9.
Besides LAIBACH, which concerns itself with the manner of industrial production in totalitarianism, there also exist two other groups in the concept of LAIBACH KUNST aesthetics: GERMANIA studies the emotional side, which is outlined in relation to the general ways of emotional, erotic, and family life, lauding the foundations of the state functioning of emotions on the old classicist form of new social ideologies.

DREIHUNDERT TAUSEND VERSCHIEDENE KRAWALLE is a retrospective futuristic negative utopia. (The era of peace has ended.)

10.
LAIBACH is the knowledge of the universality of the moment. It is the revelation of the absence of balance between sex and work, between servitude and activity. It uses all expressions of history to mark this imbalance. This work is without limit; God has one face, the devil infinitely many. *LAIBACH is the return of action on behalf of the idea.*

Written in 1982. Originally published in *Nova Revija* magazine (Ljubljana) 2, no. 13–14 (1983). Translated by members of Laibach.

•

Art and totalitarianism
are not mutually exclusive.
Totalitarian regimes abolish
the illusion of revolutionary
individual artistic
freedom.
LAIBACH KUNST is the principle
of conscious rejection
of personal tastes,
judgments, convictions (. . .);
free depersonalization,
voluntary acceptance
of the role of ideology,
demasking and
recapitulation of regime,
"ultramodernism" . . .

Published on the invitation for *Ausstellung Laibach Kunst* exhibition, April 28, 1982, at ŠKUC Gallery-Student Cultural Center, Ljubljana. Translated by members of Laibach.

He who has material power, has spiritual power, and all art is subject to political manipulation, except for that which speaks the language of this same manipulation.

Published in *VIKS* magazine (Ljubljana: ŠKUC & FORUM), no. 3 (February 1985). Translated by members of Laibach.

•

LAIBACH KUNST signifies the end of an era of movement, search, the end of stylistic and aesthetic inventions, and is:
—a more mature, critical evaluation of art,
—a choice which will rediscover history, return power to institutions and conventions,
—a remodeling of history as a successful method of violence/oppression of new artistic practices,
— the application of force to the point of complete control over values,
—a depersonification of authors,
—self-reproduction,
—the consequence of ideological dictate *(Gleichschaltung),*
—security for the aesthetic market *(Warenästhetik);*
LAIBACH KUNST conserves lasting values.

Published on the invitation for *Ausstellung Laibach Kunst—Monumental Retro-avant-garde* exhibition, April 21, 1983, at ŠKUC Gallery, Ljubljana. Translated by members of Laibach.

•●

SCIPION NASICE SISTERS THEATER

Scipion Nasice Sisters Theater was established as an underground theater in 1983 to inject retro-avant-garde principles into Yugoslav space. Unlike the other wings of NSK, the aim of this highly polemical theater was not self-reproduction, but obsolescence. Announcing its aim of self-abolishment in its founding act, it fulfilled its promise at a press conference following the performance of "Baptism below Triglav" in 1986. This performance remains a legendary event in the annals of Slovene theater, marking one of the high points of NSK cultural production and the fulfillment of the SNST's aims: the destruction of the classical stage by the theater that has no stage.
                                                                    —*R. L. C.*

Exorcism
The Second Sisters Letter

The dreadful image, in which art is dying as a reflection of ideologies and programs, is abandoned to the glory of the impossible schizo-reversal. The retro-art of the Scipion Nasice Sisters Theater shatters the mirror of the atmosphere of time and swears upon the desperate revolutionary spirit of the prophet.

NEUE
SLOWENISCHE
KUNST

THEATRE OF SCIPION NASICA

NSK symbol, used on the cover of
the program for the first international Scipion Nasice Sisters
Theater Tour, Edinburgh Festival,
1985. Courtesy NSK

The retro-hero rises in view of the victim's and executioner's destiny. With
the simultaneity of faith and doubt, in the feverish eroticism of emotion, shaped
in the mind, he begins the passionate schizo ritual of renewal. Blood runs from
old wounds. He sacralizes the duplicity into extra-temporal drama. The paradoxical non-dialecticity and extra-temporality are unmasked as a collective
method of *Ideologies, Religions,* and *Art.*

The Scipion Nasice Sisters Theater exorcises *Religion* and *Ideology* into a mirror image of *Art,* and as such abolishes it.

Originally published as programmatic text, 1984.

•

One-Minute Drama: Baptism below Triglav

(Bogomila, Cardinal)
BOGOMILA: I met him when he was roaming the city cafés. He came toward
me with a monstrous frozen laugh on his face, and so deformed, like a rigid, horrifying mask, he began to speak to me:
ČRTOMIR: The call must be made possible. The call must ring, must be heard. The
force which drives man's soul on the free path up and forward is purposeless.
CARDINAL: A black hand lies over him. The black hand of the spirit of Religion
and Ideology. Necessity has attracted him into its service and he performs it,
without being aware of it.
BOGOMILA: Can't he be stopped?
CARDINAL: His is a prisoner of Form. He is trapped in the spirit of Art.

Originally published in program for a theater performance, February 1986.

The Act of Self-Destruction
Artistic Event: Youth Day

In 1983 the SCIPION NASICE SISTERS THEATER composed a program founded solely on unknowns. The only item of this program which could be foreseen proceeded from certified political experience, that the unknown, which is simulated as the known, is always constructive, as it can be controlled and directed into the desired consequences. The SCIPION NASICE SISTERS THEATER was simultaneously developed as an idea about a THEATER and an idea about a STATE. IN 1987, the idea about the STATE in the SCIPION NASICE SISTERS THEATER achieved the level of state creativity. THE ARTISTIC EVENT OF YOUTH DAY, which was dedicated to the celebration of the YUGOSLAV youth, is the last theatrical project of the SCIPION NASICE SISTERS THEATER. With this project, the observation of the relation between the THEATER and the STATE and the THEATER as a STATE has achieved its climax. That is why the ARTISTIC EVENT OF YOUTH DAY is also an ACT OF SELF-DESTRUCTION OF THE SCIPION NASICE SISTERS THEATER as a STATE institution and STATE.

Originally published in *Neue Slowenische Kunst* (Zagreb: Grafički zavod Hrvatske; Los Angeles: AMOK Books, 1991).

IRWIN

IRWIN, the visual-arts constituent of NSK, is a group of five artists who established themselves as a collective within a collective in 1983. Using this organizational structure to forge a new cultural space, they have been systematically launching initiatives, which map, interrogate, and extend the boundaries of art as well as the possibilities of collaborative practice. In doing so, they often transform their exhibitions and performances into political actions that appropriate, annex, or neutralize other institutions and structures (curatorial, theatrical, editorial, political) to critical advantage. Together with Eda Čufer, IRWIN has authored many manifestos and texts and used documentary and archival research to give theoretical and historical traction to their visual work.　　　　　　—R. L. C.

Retro Principle: The Principle of Manipulation
with the Memory of the Visible Emphasized Eclecticism —
The Platform for National Authenticity

In the early twenties, Joseph Schillinger, an American cubist, wrote a book entitled *The Mathematical Basis for Art*, in which he classified the evolution of art into five different levels (which develop with accelerating speed):

1. the pre-aesthetic level; biological states of mimicry,
2. the traditional-aesthetic level; magic, rational-religious art,
3. the emotionally aesthetic level; an artistic expression of emotions, self-expression, art for art's sake,
4. the rationally aesthetic level; empiricism, experimental art, new art,

5. the scientific, post-aesthetic level; the fusion of artistic forms and material, the disintegration and end of art.

Added to these is the sixth level, which is partly incorporated in the last level and is unconscious, unformulated.

6. the emphatically eclectic level; all-aesthetic, an evocation of historical works, integration of individual homogeneous creations, nowadays called the retro principle, incorporating the five above-mentioned levels.

The retro principle is a sphere of historically present art, and means thinking about the past models of art in view of building a complete awareness of the dialectical evolution of Western art. The artistic interest abandons the sphere of the formal on account of the content, following the dictates of the motive. Nature ceases to be the model for creative design and is supplanted by culture as the second nature (being a mimesis of mimesis). The pivotal interest encompasses the rising awareness of the historical evolution of culture (dialectics), proceeding from the lower forms toward the higher ones (structure).

The sixth level is not a style or an art trend but a principle of thought, a way of behaving and acting. It builds on reinterpretations, re-creation of past models, keeping other trends at a distance. It is manifest throughout the history of art and is historically conditioned. It does not appear, however, in a mathematically linear fashion nor in terms of artistic supervision; on the contrary, it occurs in recurring intervals. Its subconscious basis is inherent in time. Operation within a field of thought—retro—requires that the retro principle be declaratively freed from the field of marginality.

The retro principle supports constant alteration of language and shifting from one pictorial expression to another. It eclectically refers to the history of art, choosing it, together with the entire cultural sphere, as the field of its operation. It makes use of various already existing language models, modifies itself through the past on the formal level, but remains intact on the conceptual one. Without giving up achievements of modernism and without seeking new formal patterns, it remains a principle of thought maintaining a process of assimilation. Its language reflects the concepts of *l'art de l'art* (art from art) and an elitist attitude toward art and society in which the applied typical equations do not determine the spiritual circle of a picture. Its own expressivity is eliminated, and a tendency toward the impersonal appears, exploiting the already existing personal expressions or typical (stylistic) equations.

The retro principle makes use of tradition in a direct and indirect way (quoted in its original purity). Due to the current interest in it, even a complete identification (a quotation) acquires a historically specific productive character. The unveiling of identity is carried out through a certain mode of reinterpretation which establishes space for a personal account, and the motive becomes the element which determines the method of execution (style). Historical facts are losing their special immanent character and their role in the context of time, being transformed into everyday conscious experience.

The artistic process is transformed into a demonstrative exploration of the previous language models by way of collective consciousness of individual visual forms.

Written in 1984. Originally published in *Problemi* (Ljubljana), no. 6 (1985).

NSK State in Time

Eda Čufer and IRWIN

Retro-avant-garde is the basic artistic procedure of Neue Slowenische Kunst, based on the premise that traumas from the past affecting the present and the future can be healed only by returning to the initial conflicts. Modern art has not yet overcome the conflict brought about by the rapid and efficient assimilation of historical avant-garde movements in the systems of totalitarian states. The common perception of the avant-garde as a fundamental phenomenon of twentieth-century art is loaded with fears and prejudices. On the one hand this period is naively glorified and mythicized, while on the other hand its abuses, compromises, and failures are counted with bureaucratic pedantry to remind us that this magnificent delusion should not be repeated.

Neue Slowenische Kunst—as Art in the image of the State—revives the trauma of avant-garde movements by identifying with it in the stage of their assimilation in the systems of totalitarian states. The most important and at the same time traumatic dimension of avant-garde movements is that they operate and create within a collective. Collectivism is the point where progressive philosophy, social theory, and the militarism of contemporary states clash. The question of collectivism, i.e., the question of how to organize communication and enable the coexistence of various autonomous individuals in a community, can be solved in two different ways. Modern states continue to be preoccupied with the question of how to collectivize and socialize the individual, whereas avant-garde movements tried to solve the question of how to individualize the collective. Avant-garde movements tried to develop autonomous social organisms in which the characteristics, needs, and values of individualism, which cannot be comprised in the systems of a formal state, could be freely developed and defined. The collectivism of avant-garde movements had an experimental value. With the collapse of the avant-garde movements, social constructive views in art fell into disgrace, which caused the social escapism of orthodox modernism and consequently led to a crisis in basic values in the period of postmodernism.

The group Neue Slowenische Kunst defines its collectivism within the framework of an autonomous state, as artistic actions in time to which all other spatial and material procedures of artistic creation are subordinated. This means that the procedure of the deconstruction and analysis of past forms and situations functions as the creator of new conditions for the development of the individual within the framework of a collective. One of the aims of Neue Slowenische Kunst is to prove that abstraction, which in its fundamental philosophic component—suprematism—explains and expels the political language of global cultures from the language and culture of art, contains a social program adequate to the needs of modern man and community. The NSK state in time is an abstract organism, a suprematist body, installed in a real social and political space as a sculpture comprising the concrete body warmth, spirit, and work of its members. NSK confers the status of a state not upon territory but upon the mind, whose borders are in a state of flux, in accordance with the movements and changes of its symbolic and physical collective body.

Written in 1992. Originally published in *NSK Embassy Moscow* (Koper: Gallery Loža, 1993). Translated by Jasna Hrastnik.

6 AN EMPTY PEDESTAL: BETWEEN FREEDOM AND NATIONALISM

After the fall of the socialist regimes in the region, the artificial barriers that separated Eastern European art from the rest of the world became more porous. But after more than a decade, the region has been unable to merge with the West, as many had envisioned, and there are residues from the old regimes that are common to all of the states of the former Soviet bloc. When the common enemy was lost, so too was a certain sense of a national self so long defined in opposition to a specific other.

The old totalitarian statues and monuments are gone, but the spaces on their pedestals remain empty, both metaphorically and in reality. To fill them, as the Latvian critic Helēna Demakova argues, has been more difficult than anyone could have imagined. The forms and ideology of the new era have not yet been established and simply do not fit into the frames left to us by history.

The search for new and freely established identities is a troubled process. One could turn to the roots of national tradition, as the Hungarian artist Imre Bukta does in his writings and installations. Others, like the Bulgarian critic and artist Luchezar Boyadjiev, who explores deconstructions of Balkan stereotypes in his tongue-in-cheek works, search for wider positions in the contemporary world. Bojana Pejić in her article on Serbian artist Marina Abramović demonstrates how generalizations in a complicated and multilayered region like the Balkans can seem straightforward but can ultimately be misleading.

In the mid-1990s, Russian artist and theoretician Anatoly Osmolovsky self-published a magazine called *Radek,* which he circulated in the Russian art community. He represents radical and left-oriented contemporary theory influenced by the Situationist International, by anarchism, and by the radical tenets of the Russian avant-garde. Another Russian art critic, Ekaterina Degot, tries to explain how contemporary art in Russia is suspended between local tradition, international expectations, and the challenges of Western art.

What some had envisioned as being an easy period of transition has, in fact, turned out to be a slow path full of misunderstandings and mistranslations on the part of both the West and the East. This chapter concludes with a case study of radical misinterpretation between East and West, sparked by a violent action perpetrated by the Russian artists Oleg Kulik and Alexander Brener at the international group exhibition Interpol, held in Stockholm in 1996.

—*Tomáš Pospiszyl*

LUCHEZAR BOYADJIEV

Born in 1957 in Sofia, Bulgaria, Luchezar Boyadjiev trained as an art historian and theorist before becoming an artist in the late 1980s. His work, which includes videos, installation, web design, and printmaking, deals with the communicative possibilities of art. He often uses his art as a tool to display social structures of Bulgarian society and to explore his own role as an artist both in his homeland and abroad. He was one of the founders of the Institute of Contemporary Art in Sofia.

The following text, written for the catalogue of the Third International Istanbul Biennial in 1992, addresses the fluctuating position that the Balkans occupy in the minds of their neighbors.

The Balkanization of *Alpa Europaea*

I.

Seen in their geographical location/relation, the Balkans appear to be both the Same and the Other of both Europe and Asia. This strange geosituation of a territory, "populated" by several incredibly same/different countries, could be explicated in the following manner:

II.
1. The Balkans as the Other of both Europe and Asia
Depending on the passive or aggressive "interpretative" ambitions/strategies of both out-of-the-Balkans reflecting subjects, the metaphorical status of the Balkans could be expressed figuratively through the metaphors of The Door or The Corner. Or if put in a diagrammatic form:

a. Door — passive strategies = regard for the Other:

Here the Balkans are the very epitome of transparency.

b. Corner — aggressive strategies = disregard for the Other:

EUROPE   THE BALKANS   ASIA

Here the Balkans become an especially heavily inflamed point of friction where all notions of transparency are annihilated.

Both of the above-described cases are defined geographically by the viewpoint of the out-of-the-Balkans reflecting subject. Without dependence on the character of his or her ambitions/strategies as cultural, political, economic, etc. ones, this ambiguous metaphorical status of the Balkans has received concrete realization throughout history in an alternating rhythm — the Balkans have been thought of as either a door or a corner at any given historical period. Only the passive or aggressive exercise of those ambitions/strategies determines the switches in the metaphorical orientation of the European and/or Asian viewpoints toward the Balkans. It should be clear that historically the metaphorical orientations of the European and/or the Asian viewpoints toward the Balkans have not necessarily coincided. That is, Europe and Asia have not always perceived of the Balkans as either a door or a corner at one and the same time. There have not only been switches in the orientation toward the Balkans from one of the two viewpoints, but there also have been times when one of the viewpoints thinks of the Balkans as a door while the other as a corner (and vice versa). All of the ethnic, religious, moral, aesthetic, military, financial, etc. specifics of these ambitions/strategies are irrelevant. The only relevant point is the character of the metaphorical orientation and the switches this character suffers from time to time.

As the Other of both Europe and Asia, the Balkans are a function of out-of-the-Balkans agents, their strategies and orientations. Because of that the most difficult times for the Balkans themselves come at times when there appears a switch in the metaphorical orientation of any one of the two of its Others — Europe and/or Asia. This is so because such a switch causes severe confusion over the sense of Balkan identity for the Balkan people themselves.

At the present time there is just such a switch taking place on the part of the European viewpoint. Up until recently Europe thought of the Balkans as a corner. In the European view the Balkans were at the same time a part, and not a part, of Europe — a corner. Now the Balkans are slowly being *turned into* a door. The only problem is that they are not awarded the right of choice to or not to turn *themselves* into a door *on their own terms.* This could only be done on European terms. For instance, as is well known in a corner, there appears an aftereffect, an *echo,* a reverberation of concepts belonging originally to the Center, but long ago disposed of by the same Center. The corner starts acting in accordance with these concepts, believing they are the right (central = good, etc.) concepts because they are the ones of *the Center* and thus the corner wants to fit in with *the Center*. But it turns out that the Center has long ago changed its concepts and the corner is way behind the times. Take the case of the "one nation — one state" concept and the present crisis in the (Balkan) former country — Yugoslavia. Serbia, being the legitimate child (= corner) of Europe, appears to be acting upon this old European concept now. And Serbia is being disowned by Europe, which refuses to acknowledge responsibility for its own child and its behavior — what was once thought of as a civilized action is now a monstrosity.

Strange, but by refusing *to be turned into* a door, a former corner is nevertheless becoming a center which terrorizes all the rest of the diagram. This former corner has taken a hostage — the very new concept of all-over Europeanness as it is being defined now.

2. The Balkans as the Same of both Europe and Asia

The Balkans are the coordinate system, a *screen* where Europe and Asia come together. The geographical reality of the geographical concept *Eurasia* is the Balkans. It could be claimed that at least one way to spell the cultural name of Eurasia is the B-A-L-K-A-N-S. It is the Balkan viewpoint itself that could metaphorically think of the Balkans as simultaneously a door and a corner. The emblem of the Balkans could be:

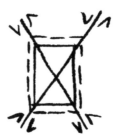

It is only the Balkan viewpoint itself that could think of the Balkans as the Same of both Europe and Asia. An integral part of the organic Balkan intuition for the world is this sense of belonging simultaneously to two very different in themselves cultural, political, etc. real worlds. This intuition is internalized in many different ways and on many different levels. The cultural anthropology of the Balkans, if it reaches a stage of classical scientific conceptualization, may read as a matrix for the Eurasian history.

The Balkan viewpoint is necessarily and naturally a schizoid one — in order to perceive of its own wholeness it has to think in at least two different cultural/historical coordinate systems.

Paradoxically the Balkans are the Same (as a thing in itself) only when they are the Other (as a thing for itself) and vice versa. Exactly who that concrete historical Other might be is simply a matter of circumstance. The relevant fact is the ever-present Same-Other dichotomy in the Balkan sense of identity.

More, the schizoid sense of Balkan identity is "fortified" further by the time-space dichotomy implicit in the door-corner metaphors. In the metaphor of *the door* there is only the concept of time and not of space. In the metaphor of *the corner* there is only the concept of space and not of time. The Balkan coordinate system suffers an *either space or time* dichotomy which, combined with the *either same or other* dichotomy, produces a monstrous "quadrochotomy" [*sic*] of split identity which is natural to the Balkans but could be calamitous for other geographical parts of the civilized Eurasian world. It is only when these other parts of the Eurasian world project disciplinary/civilizing measures/wishes, etc. toward the Balkans that the innate Balkan terror is being let loose. This is the terror of the nonidentity refusing acceptance of any (only) one given identity. In the state of health of the Balkans it is projected, as if on a screen, the state of health of Eurasia. If the Balkans are sick, that only means that either Europe or Asia (or both?) is sick. This author, for one, thinks that Europe now is deeply sick of not being able to come to terms with the perfidy of its own desire (actually, nondesire) to be one total whole. For Europe now claims intent to become united and at the same time is unable to cope with the consequences of its own claims for unification. Europe, it turns out, is unable to endure and tolerate the results of the realization of its concepts. And this is not happening for the first time in recent memory.

III.

Bulgaria might very well be the ultimate Balkan country, the ultimate door-corner of Eurasia. It is not only a matter of the many duplicities active in its present-day reality — religious, ethnic, political, economical, etc. ones. Some duplicities are just as active in some other micro door-corners of the Balkans. Take, for instance, Bosnia and Herzegovina. But take it for real — look at what happened there as a consequence of all this messing around with the identity problem in the Balkans. As opposed to the situation there, Bulgaria is exemplary on at least two more counts. First is the (so far) relatively tolerant interiorization and relatively peaceful coexistence in its present-day culture — reality of all identities. Tolerance, to the point of chaos, ripe with possibilities and potential (but for what?). And second, the past of this territory. Unlike Bosnia and Herzegovina (which, to the best of my knowledge, has never in the past been an independent state = political subject), Bulgaria, for all of the complicated centuries of its past, has alternately been *in* and *out* of history as if it was a supermarket. This was so depending on whether Bulgaria was an *autonomous political entity* (and thus, even though BG has its own history for any such particular periods, the whole of the fragmented independent BG — a "history" is of no importance for the general schemes of History and Historical development in Europe — so, when BG was independent it was *in* its own history but *out* of the European history; Bulgaria was at such times a corner of Europe), or *a part of some larger empire* or other type of political state organization (and thus, even though BG did not have at such periods its own history it was, paradoxically, part of the European history. So, when BG was dependent on some bigger political force it was *out* of its own history but *in* the European history; Bulgaria was at such times a door for Europe). Of course, the above argument could be reversed, especially if one believes in the general progress of humanity. The point is that Bulgaria has and is surviving now precisely because it takes very seriously, although intuitively, the whole issue of how to preserve its own nonidentity (in European and maybe Asian terms) as an identity (on Balkan terms). It is very possible that its present-day cultural "originality" follows exactly from this preserved, typically Balkan, confusing for others, quadrochotomous [sic] intuition for the ways the Eurasian world moves along the path of its own Historical progress. I don't want to sound too patriotic and/or overly optimistic but maybe it is not a simple coincidence after all that Christo (Javacheff), who so successfully rids the world of its utopian illusions, was born in this part of the Balkans. The point is that we have now as a fact the so-far-successful and peaceful (unlike in the former Yugoslav federation) Balkanization of this typically Balkan country in the situation of the present-day realities of Eurasia. And maybe that's quite an interesting thing to observe — the corner is turning itself (and is being turned by the Other) into a door, without forgetting that, in a way, it was a door (while still a corner), and imagining that even if it indeed becomes a door in the future, it will be, in a way, a corner (while being allegedly a door).

The emblem of Bulgaria could look like this:

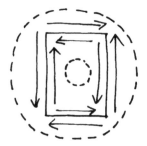

Repeated *ad infinitum* in all directions.

IV.

The space-time, door-corner quadrochotomy in the Balkans (read: Bulgaria) produces the "logic" of the heavily corporeal (body) metaphors. Because people (reflecting subjects) here are not very clear about the meaning of their abstracts and concepts, they tend to literalize these to extremes. The literalized intuitions for the world have at least the advantage of being tangible here and now, unlike the imported, and thus abstracted further, concepts. By being imported to the Balkans, the concepts from out-of-the-Balkans become an abstract square. So, the schizoid Balkan intellect suffers from the inflammation of the doubt which desires verification. The strange thing is that even if some imported concept (take, for instance, the newly fashionable one for the *utopia without illusions*) has a tangible reality here, it still needs to be verified further by special procedures. The paradigm of survival in the Balkans has always been the thought that utopia has to be stripped of its illusions. And yet, this is often forgotten by the Balkans themselves. So, top artists, thinkers, etc. every now and then tend to undertake projects in reconfirming the preciousness of the above paradigm. In a way this has become the visible side of the Balkan cultural originality. Take, for instance, the art of three young BG artists — Lyuben Kostov, Nedko Solakov, and Georgi Rouzhev.

1. During the several years just before and just after the political changes in Eastern Europe, Lyuben Kostov produced a group of works — wooden machines, which exemplify best the above statement. These machines, very operational indeed, acquire extremely anti-utopian meaning when seen in the context of real socialism as a perfect social technology for the realization of certain (European in origin) utopian visions.

It is a well-accepted fact now (at least in Bulgaria) that the original utopian values of socialism were substituted (first by Lenin, second by Stalin, third by other leaders) by the social technology of the construction of socialism. Among the most productive parts of this machinery should now be counted the Bolshevik party — a machine for overtaking political power, the Gulag — a machine for disciplining the mass collective bodies of socialism, all the way down to the machine-type formations such as the state security apparatus, the creative unions of the artists, writers, etc.

But what is interesting is the way in which values were substituted by the technologies and social machines. Generally speaking, this was the mechanism of literalization. The utopian socialist values were originally expressed in a metaphorical form. Later on they were taken at face value, as a plan for the construction of a utopian reality. The whole building up of the real socialism could be explained as a literalization of metaphors. At one point, for instance, the leading metaphors to be literalized as reality were the so-called *five-year plans*. At another (early on) it was Marx's metaphor that the true task of philosophy is not to explain the world, but to change it. This way of thinking/acting tended to naturalize everything. To see History, Society, etc., as mechanisms operating according to the same objective Laws that govern nature. And it is clear that the genetics of such literalization of nature go as far back as the Renaissance and the Enlightenment, the fifteenth and the eighteenth centuries. Take, for instance, Leonardo. He "pierced" the skin of nature with his eye, hand, and mind only to explicate the mathematical-mechanical laws of nature inherent in its construction. What he did afterwards was to apply these same laws to the science of technology, to draw up a "sketch," so to say, of the future technological progress of modern times. Marx, Lenin, etc., on their part, only applied the same procedure to history and society, thus marking the final state of the degradation of reason = the unquestioned faith in its power.

Of course, neither Leonardo nor anyone from the fifteenth to the eighteenth centuries is to be blamed in any way for this. But strangely all the parts, cog wheels, mechanics, all the way to the general plastic form of L. Kostov's machines, remind one of the models being made these days, reconstructing the original ideas — designs of Leonardo for the helicopter, the submarine, the clock, the gear, the airplane, etc. But this is a similarity of shape, not of function. For the only thing Kostov's machines are "producing" are the liberating, anti-utopian impulses for laughter, relief, satisfaction, impulses which tend to contribute to the dismantling of the reality of socialism.

The everyday life, the Street in real socialism, used to express its opposition to the ruling, literalized metaphors of power by producing its own anti-utopian metaphors. For instance, the convention of the BG Communist party (or any other public = official meeting that was taking place to simulate collective decision-making process, such as the Parliament, for instance) used to be called "a *machine* for voting," the leaders of the party, lined up on the Mausoleum, greeting the crowd, jubilating over the successful construction of socialism, were called "a *machine* for hand-waving," etc. L. Kostov's machines only *literalize* these subversive mass-metaphors, thus creating an alternative reality, a space for freedom of thought. His machines for applause, for congratulatory gesticulation, for painting, for bell ringing, for breaking down of idols and many other smart mechanisms are opponents of the power machine of socialism. Their own power rests in the effective way they deconstruct and "pierce" the *skin* of the simulative, symbolic reality of socialism. If Christo (Javacheff), by wrapping a building, simply stops its potential utopian emanations and changes the mass-perception of a natural and/or cultural object, L. Kostov goes as far as to *"unwrap"* piece by piece a whole system of symbolic reality.

2. The installation *New Noah's Ark* by Nedko Solakov, on the other hand, comes afterwards to fill in the symbolic space, thus "cleaned-up," by offering new mythologies of survival. But make no mistake, some years ago Solakov made his own contribution to the de-montage of socialism in numerous works — paintings and drawings, objects and installations, books and all other kinds of culturally subversive plastic gestures. His newest installation is meant to overcome the sorry past of socialism. It deals not only with the problem of survival but of deliverance as well. And this is done in a typically Balkanic, schizoid fashion. First Solakov dissimulates (in the sense Jean Baudrillard uses the term) his socialist past. He pretends not to have any values left and thus to be free for a new beginning. Then he takes on the ontologically powerful myth of Noah's Ark.

In its schizoid state of existence the Balkan creative intellect is "free" to manipulate everything in quasibombastic statements. Solakov is not satisfied only to dwell upon the now-fashionable quest for new "Messiahs" in the post-totalitarian value vacuum. He goes farther back. There is a need for ontological gestures, for a new world, for a new look beyond to transcend the current cultural Eurasian stalemate of identity intuitions. So it is Noah's Ark time once again. How could it happen? Who is to get into the Ark? *Whose* world, *what* world is to be saved? The deluge is here now. Noah is to be found somewhere in the concrete panel buildings (= catacombs?) of the Balkan city of Sofia (no less). So, crawl in, try to become one of the candylike strange creatures from the installation if you feel like you want to be saved. Maybe Solakov, in his endlessly self-confident Balkan ego thinks of himself as both Noah and a creature. Maybe you (the viewer) do so as well. Anyway, the viewer, wandering among the exhibits of the *New Noah's Ark,* is put into a corner which it is only up to him or her to see as a door. "O.K. Eurasia — where do you go from here?" That is the question Solakov's work puts forward now.

3. In a no less quasi-bombastic gesture (but in the far less bombastic media of photography) Georgi Rouzhev asks similar questions. In the *One-Dimensional Man Died* he sees himself as a Christlike figure (only shorter) symbolically striped of (ironed out of) any phallocentric potential. In a powerfully symbolic gesture of self-castration of identity Rouzhev disposes of the "privileged signifier," thus getting rid of the basic symbolic institution of European culture. The greatest narrative has come to an end — what's next? How is this next possible? Are we to come out of

the molehill for a new start or shall we still stick to the state of being (in Rouzhev's view) the Homo sapiens version of the *Alpa Europaea* (the Latin term for a mole)?

In another of his photographs, *Self-Portrait,* Rouzhev has wrapped (like Christo?) his head with his own long hair (just like Christ's hair, only longer) to produce an amazing statement of identity. With only eyes and mouth left visible, Rouzhev has turned himself into a strange sadomasochistic wild man (just like the one from the medieval illuminated manuscripts and tapestries). Is his hair becoming a mask, a *"natural"* mask to signify his own difference and identity nowadays? Is the image in the photograph an image of a Persona or just of a "face"? How could the production of identity be neutralized? Once again we have here a case of Balkanization of the entire humanistic problematic. And once again it is made painfully, tangibly, bodily apparent. This is a literalized metaphor of the Eurasian crisis of identity in a Balkanized version.

V.

So what's next? Hopefully the *Alpa Europaea* will pierce its own symbolic skin and find that its own mechanics have been transformed to fit the populace of the *New Noah's Ark.* It will still be the Same but maybe it will develop intuitions for the Other. The Balkan other?

Written in 1992. Originally published in the catalogue of the Third International Istanbul Biennial, 1992.

•●

IMRE BUKTA

The Hungarian artist Imre Bukta (born 1952) studied at the Dobó István Polytechnic College in Eger, Hungary. From his agricultural actions in the early 1970s to his grotesque objects and installations from the 1980s and 1990s, he has used materials associated with Hungarian agricultural life to create sculpture, photography, installations, and performances, endowed with his personal mythology. He quite literally designated himself an "agricultural artist."

In the following text he breaks down the distinction between human and animal nature by making both man and pig equal co-conspirators in an amusing fable. Although his art represents his own eclectic individuality, his approach elevates the elements of everyday existence to ritual symbols that are an important element of Hungary's collective identity.

A 1992 Guide for the Creation of Works of Art with Nature Themes

Go to a corner of Europe, or to another continent — on foot, if possible. Take four things with you.

Take a PANE OF GLASS through which to observe the environment. This will be your window on the four points of the compass.

Take a PIG to remind you that you are a human being. He will be your companion in solitude. You will be grateful if he allows you to scratch his ears.

But take GLUE with you, too, because after a few days the pig's curly hair will begin to irritate you very much. As a result, you will at first spend all your time straightening the curls and gluing them down. You will have to force yourself to resist the shameful temptation to make a paintbrush from his hair. If you do not, you will get used to it, even begin to like it, and when you get to the last hairs you will be sad that this simple, charming pastime has come to an end.

The fourth object you should take along is a PHOTOGRAPH of an ordinary cricket. The pig will be happy, because the cricket is his favorite creature, and his favorite pastime will be looking at it before he goes to sleep.

You will have to give up weighing the pig daily; if not, you should train it to weigh you, too. Do not try to establish boundaries around your environment. You cannot; your living area will be determined by where the pig goes.

A special relationship will develop between the two of you, something inexplicable, a deep respect that is apparent in everyday things — in the way each of you tries to be the first to say good morning, for example, and the way you both step back politely before answering the call of nature.

You will gaze into each other's eyes, your glances no longer modest, and you will feel as if you had already squeezed each other's hands or feet. Without even saying it, you will know that you are going to create a work of art together.

The day before you create the work of art, you will perform rituals together in joyous anticipation. This is something you have always done alone before. The two of you will tramp in the mud, look through the pane of glass, and husk corn together.

The next morning, you will get up earlier than usual, without a grunt, and wait for the sunrise, excited and wordless. You will take the still-warm hen eggs from your face, and the pig will drink his last herbal tea. You will ladle the daily portion of ground poppy seeds into one another's mouths. Then you will clean the pane of glass, put on your navy-blue suit, and stick a lily in your buttonhole. The pig will take a refreshing roll in the mud. Meanwhile, the sun's rays will illuminate the place where you have lived. You will be happy. Yet, after a short time, a profound sadness will overtake you, and you will suddenly feel that you must leave this place. Without looking back, you will start to run. You will take to the north, the pig to the east. Soon you will calm down. Both of you will know that your shared creation will hover above this place for a long time to come.

Written in 1991. Originally published in *Free Worlds: Metaphors and Realities in Contemporary Hungarian Art* (Toronto: Art Gallery of Ontario, 1991).

HELĒNA DEMAKOVA

Helēna Demakova (born 1959) is a leading critic, columnist, and curator in Latvia. She curated Latvia's submissions for the Venice Biennale in 1999 and 2001, served as cultural advisor to Latvia's prime minister, and is a member of the country's Parliament.

In the following text, presented as a speech at a Biennaal held on Saaremaa, an Estonian island, she discusses the premise and results of the "Monument" competition organized by the Latvian Center for Contemporary Art in 1995. When Latvia gained independence in 1991, it faced an issue familiar to all countries formerly under Soviet occupation—namely, the fate of its socialist monuments (as well as, in Latvia's case, the monuments left by previous occupying forces—Germans, Swedes, and Poles). The issue at hand, visual self-definition of the new republic, generated a lively discussion in the media and, ultimately, many Soviet-era monuments were removed, some replaced by works conveying a nationalistic ideology. The competition "Monument" was an open call for public art for spaces left empty in this process. All submitted proposals were exhibited at the Latvian Museum of Photography, and seventeen projects were chosen for realization in the cityscape. The exhibition functioned as an overview of Latvian contemporary art, but also prompted a review of the motives for creating monuments that express specific ideologies.

Monument Revisited

Over the last decades, it has been "modern" in certain academic circles to declare that history is an invention of nineteenth-century European positivism, which purported that the idea of history was somewhat different from the point of reference well known to many as having its beginnings in some stable in Bethlehem.

This European historicism reached its visual apotheosis in the monuments of the last century, the task of which, in the words of the German art historian Christoph Heinrich, was to ideologically fix a certain engaging view of history and then, as an expression of a collective desire, transcend it also to the future. As always, in every era, the purpose of monuments has been to act as an intentional memo, rising and recalling, but to this day the majority of monuments are thought of in terms of nineteenth-century bourgeois monuments.

The nineteenth century was precisely the time of the development of relatively stable bourgeois nation states. Monuments that elevated themes of national unity were especially popular. Their popularity also flowered in this century among those nations that made late entrances on the stage of history or among those nations for whom nationalism developed threatening parameters. Furthermore, apparently pan-national stale creations like the former Soviet Union, for example, exploited traditional monument forms, endowing them with naturalistic shapes and with some other unifying meaning, that is, a class or ideological content.

This also goes for Latvia, of which I am happy and proud to be a citizen, which belongs to the so-called latecomers, and has the experience of fifty years of Soviet occupation. Therefore, it is not surprising that after Latvia regained independence in 1991, the ideal of national unity and newly reinstated statehood aspired to create a diversity of forms of legitimization, visual ones among them.

The first waves of progressively increasing demands for independence at the end of the 1980s took place not in some neutral location but by the Freedom Monument built by the Latvian sculptor Karlis Zale in the 1930s. Riga Castle and "Brethren Cemetery" were also popular gathering places. National memory (which is hard to describe as a whole, but suffices conditionally and includes the greater portion of Latvians) at the time was directed toward a specific visual image of the past, of which monuments were also essential elements. The Latvian cultural landscape at the beginning of the 1990s is characterized by a tendency to renew many 1920s and 1930s monuments of the first republic which were destroyed during the Soviet era. In spite of meager resources, this was actually done in many places.

Gatis Blunavs. *Tram Tree*. Riga, 1995. Installation. Courtesy Latvian Centre for Contemporary Art

Present and seemingly future-directed aspirations to celebrate and remember manifest themselves as a desire to erect monuments to victims of Soviet repression, using, however, mainly the same prevailing stylistic approaches of the 1920s and 1930s that have been subjected to a certain Soviet Socialist Realism or naturalist transformation. In effect, [Auguste] Rodin plus Vera Mukhina was the prevailing visual vision under discussion. Clear thinking and a lack of funding thankfully won out, and this sort of monument has not yet been erected.

Nevertheless, the discussions continue and the group of, let's say, contemporarily oriented art critics and curators decided to contribute to this discussion. It was decided that visual concerns of our capital city of Riga were not only a matter for different kinds of politicians, interest groups, and growing corporate and commercial advertising, but also were part of the thinking of Latvian artists. The money which the Soros Centre for Contemporary Art has at its disposal for its annual exhibition will be spent this year [1995] on the project entitled *Monument*. It will be held in the city space of Riga. . . . The statements and information I will now give about the project are from a curatorial point of view. Deeper analysis of what has happened might come only when the whole event has left its traces. So instead of some philosophical and critical approach, I will try to inform you about what is going on and why.

As you may know, or might have experienced, many of the former Soviet monuments have been removed and demolished in recent years. Numerous sculptures of Stalin, some six in Riga, were removed in the 1950s. But, strangely enough, not only are there empty spaces where the former Soviet Socialist Realist or naturalistic monuments once stood. In the course of history, Riga has been ruled by Germans, Swedes, Poles, and Russians, and every new power did its best to remove the symbols of the previous order. Collective memory has been rewritten and reshaped according to existing canons. Even if we stress that individual testimonies are the more "truthful" messages of "true" history, they cannot but be influenced by the visual surroundings.

So the Russian *Victory Column* from the last century, [the monuments authorized by] German patrons, and so on were removed, and the sites which I would like to call strategic places in Riga are empty. They might have remained empty but, as you have already read, there is a new state with a new ideology which already claims to know what to do with the locations, as if ready for the new symbols. Riga is nearing its eight-hundredth anniversary in 2001, and there are already proposals for how to reoccupy the places which are architecturally appropriate for some new sculptures. These proposals, as you can imagine, are not even at the level of some stereotypical images of classical modernism.

Our idea was to use those spots, the places formerly occupied by Lenin, Kirov, and also by St. Christopher, Roland, or the *Victory Column* and several other locations, for contemporary art. The open competition for the exhibition *Monument* received over ninety entries. It is a contemporary scene in the sense that those proposals were made by contemporaries. We received projects starting with seventeen-year-old students from the College of Applied Arts to some eighty-year-old seniors who, until very recently, created Communist sculptures.

At this point the title of the exhibition legitimately became *Monument*. From the very beginning, it was clear that we were not going to select some kind of ideological sculptures, but art which adds something essential to the city. But *Monument* is the whole set of these ninety proposals, the cross section through different kinds of artistic thinking and through all generations, styles, and inclinations. Our *Monument* is intended to be a piece of history at the moment when the last entry is submitted, what was thought of about Riga at the end of the century. You might not call art ninety percent of what is seen among those sketches, drawings, and models, but nevertheless that is the status quo — the sum of what

Karlis Alainis. *Column.* Riga, 1995. Installation. Courtesy Latvian Centre for Contemporary Art

Aija Zarina. *Monument to Janis Rainis*. Riga, 1995. Installation. Courtesy Latvian Centre for Contemporary Art

we are together. But the subjective vision of the curator is how we might be, and that will be seen in the cityscape from among the thirteen selected Latvian artists who will build their works, and in the selection of four foreign artists from the countries that have shaped the fate of our capital. They are Raffael Rheinsberg from Germany, Robert Rumas from Poland, Dimitri Gutov from Russia, and Ulf Rollof from Sweden.

All ninety submitted proposals will be exhibited, . . . [and] the viewer will see how different and multilayered the so-called art scene in Latvia is. I think there is an answer to the question . . . How do the means of expression differ in Eastern Europe? The big difference is the art scene itself. It is not a creation of the art market or the strategies of most contemporary thinking, nor is it a baby spoiled by curators and critics. It is an amorphous mass consisting of academism from the last century, decorative expressionism of classical modernism, existing naturalistic realism, and contemporary art in the international (Western) sense. Everybody knows everybody, everything coexists in the same galleries and museums, most critics in newspapers praise all kinds of so-called art. I hate to use Hegel's expression "Das Ganze ist das Wahre" ("The truth is the whole") but that is how most progressive and democratic contemporaries feel. Luckily enough the curator is not obliged to be democratic in the final stage of his or her job, but our politicians don't need to know this. After a long and exhaustive fight with the cultural committee of the city, we got our green light. But again it was possible only in this society in a stage of transition in which those who at least granted permission barely realized what they agreed to. There have been a few (but not many) open-air projects in the cities of Europe: Skulpturenboulevard in Berlin and Sculpture Project in Münster in 1987; in Stockholm in the beginning of the 1990s; this year [1995] in the framework of ARS 95 in Helsinki; and so on. But hardly any capital would give the most visible places in its very center to seventeen artists to build huge and provocative works which will be fully noticed by the one million inhabitants of Riga. So one conclusion might be — to make history is to use confusion.

The very practical conclusions we reached in the course of the preparations are connected to the projects the artists submitted as their entries. Almost everybody took the word "monument" literally and conceived a project as a solid thing, many addressing the tension still possessed by the site of the former monument. We have given the place most pregnant with meaning of bygone times — the former location of the huge Lenin monument on the central axis of the city — to the Swedish artist, and here the Western attitude is apparent. Ulf Rollof will create a carousel with a red star in the middle of it made of red wax-dipped fir trees. The old statue is substituted, the city gets a reworked message — a carnivalesque star of the old symbol.

The bold exception in our context is the work of the young artist Andris Fribergs, which will be constructed in the park, by the city canal. Its title is *Joseph's Dogs Guard Paik's Ducks,* and it is a sound installation reacting to the passersby with the help of sensors.

As we have already noted, we mostly find tendencies connected to the essence of the same old bourgeois monument. Some of the artists with a completely serious approach created models dealing with the ideology of the new state in an affirmative way. These are statues of the brave Latvian women, symbols of boats, windmills of destiny, and other different clichéd symbols. One example you can see is the proposal of the senior lecturer of the Academy of Art. Here the symbol of Latvian ethnography — *Auseklitis,* which means the rising sun and has been overused as a symbol of the so-called singing revolution [sic] at the end of the 1980s — is presented in a completely serious way.

Another group created decorative images using poetic metaphors. Some correspond to the history of the place, like the idea of Kristaps Gulbis, where there was once a statue of St. Christopher. The surface resemblance with the former culture of knights again reworks something which has its own stereotypes in the collective memory of the popular description of history. The artists who are educated with a strong belief in the magic crafts of material, form, and storytelling also belong here.

The third group questioned the idea of the monument itself, its meaning and aims within society. The following five works from that group were chosen for construction: Aija Zarina's *Monument to Janis Rainis;* Eriks Brozhis's *For Local Calls;* Gatis Blunavs's *Tram Tree;* Karlis Alainis's *Column;* and Arturs Zemitis's and Edgars Mucenieks's *Rake.* These works question the mode of representation of the monument itself.

There are a few works which question the idea of the monument, some stereotype, event, or written history. These few works are still made by the well-known masters of the so-called Latvian avant-garde, and they add something extremely personal to the city, but at the same time relevant for contemporary society. I stress the relevance of these works as a modus of extraordinary thinking, as a disturbing situation which questions more than society itself. They question life and death, and also the natural and unnatural from the artist's point of view. They should remain a surprise to you when you come to the exhibition, but one work I will dare to mention here. Olegs Tillbergs will finally show his Russian fighter jet MIG 27, upside down, full of live bees.

In the above-mentioned context, it is evident how important the biennaal in Saaremaa [Estonia] also is for Latvian art, where different works, in a Latvian context, are shown. Both Latvian participants here, Anita Zabilevska and Juris Boiko, do not build monuments. They do not work with collective memory, reworking its symbols in any possible way. They work within themselves; they catch, of course, not the moment of revelation but the moments of cool self-observation in the middle of nonexisting or always changing coordinates. They show the constant movement from one point to another, a person as constantly evolving. Their photo and video works recall none of the stories about something. They may recall something which also by its visual appearance is called the contemporary art of the 1990s. So they belong to the big monumental body of that art, thus becoming the wide, outspread, ephemeral monument at the end of the century.

Speech presented at the conference "Fabrique d'histoire" at the Saaremaa Biennaal '95; transcribed and published in conference reader "Fabrique d'histoire" (Tallinn: Center for Contemporary Photography, 1995).

•●

ANATOLY OSMOLOVSKY

The Russian artist, writer, and theoretician Anatoly Osmolovsky (born 1969), together with Oleg Kulik and Alexander Brener, is recognized as one of the most radical and controversial contemporary Russian artists. Osmolovsky founded the group ETI (Expropriation of the Territory of Art) in 1989, staging spontaneous events in public spaces that were part-performance, part-political protest. In 1993 he joined the group Nesezudik, which, through its exhibitions, performances, and publications, emphasized the still-obvious chasm between East and West. His magazine Radek, *created in 1995, drew attention to developments in radical art that were suppressed by official politics in Moscow.*

The following selections from Radek *interpret the activities and motivations of other radical artists and serve to engender an atmosphere of artistic and intellectual dissidence among the greater Moscow art community. Initially the letter-format magazine was mailed to subscribers, but was eventually published electronically. In 1999 the art critic Oleg Kireev assumed production of the magazine, and its format changed to include writings by various authors. Osmolovsky continues to collaborate with fellow artists and cultural critics on political actions and installations, as well as on other publications.*

Selections from "Mail Radek"

Since the summer of 1995, I have been conducting my "mail-art" project. This involves sending to a group of twenty-five subscribers, leading art critics and journalists, letters ("epistles") in which I comment on the most extreme tendencies in Moscow radical art and provide an analysis of contemporary artistic methods. My approach is based on paying meticulous attention not so much to the "programmatic" representations of the radical artists as to the minutiae of their daily lives, as well as the internal processes by which they make or refuse to make choices. The main purpose of this project is to arrive at an understanding between the "art community" and contemporary radical artists by making clear the purposes and the inner motivations of the latter. This long-term project will be contained in the second issue of the journal *Radek,* which, due to a lack of funding, will appear in this untraditional manner.

Text no. 1

August 12, 1995
The mainstream of contemporary art will be determined by the poster for the next five years. The poster will become the matrix on which artistic, social, institutional, and political relations will be fixed. It will play the same role as children's illustrations played in the 1970s and 1980s. In this sense, contemporary action art, which has conducted a "shock reform," is designed to clear artistic space of relationships based on illustrations.

Anatoly Osmolovsky

Project: A. Osmolovsky
Proofs: A. Obukhova
Communication: A. Osmolovsky

Text no. 2

August 20, 1995
The fundamental vector in the development of the art scene in Moscow during the past year was the change in the modus operandi of radical art. Whereas previously it had actively sought out and gambled on scandal, now it was slowly shifting to acts of terror. There is a fundamental difference between the two. Scandal functions exclusively within the semiotic field—it is a violation of the symbolic structure of society. The dramatic action on Red Square ("Khuy" [Prick])[1] was played out exclusively within a semiotic field. With the exception of several "fight actions" conducted with the poets from the club Poezia and the actions at V. Podroga's seminar, my actions were oriented toward scandal, and terror was just a by-product. In Alexander Brener's actions (and all the more so in his intentions), on the other hand, the by-product is scandal, while the fundamental modality of his work is terror. Terror manifests itself in ways that affect the body: fighting, rape, bodily restraint, and, of course, murder (murder is Brener's idée fixe). Whereas I created the milieu embodied in the events of August 1991 (although not in the ideological sense), Brener is without a doubt a child of the events of October 1993.

The transition of radical art to terror completed one of its stages, as terror is not representative. (Real terrorists who oppose the laws of the state are always underground since, understandably, they are hiding their real identities.) The state defines terror as being at the outer fringes of what is socially tolerable and therefore flushes it out and suppresses it.

What does the future hold? Either there will be a development of terror, which will reach its limits and culmination, or there will be a transition to a postradical stage of more refined and active methods of resistance.

Anatoly Osmolovsky

Project: A. Osmolovsky
Proofs: A. Obukhova
Communication: N. Udaltsov

Note
1. An action organized by ETI in 1991 in which thirteen artists lay down in Moscow's Red Square to form the letters of the word "Khuy" [prick]. The artists were arrested and interrogated by the KGB.

Text no. 4
September 20, 1995
The new version of Moscow radical art will be made up of several aesthetic vectors:

1) Informational "scandal" — a mixing up and fusing of different information flows.
2) Creation of "social" visual props such as posters, leaflets, and stickers and
   their integration into various social spheres: political, economic, analytical, etc.
3) Disunification of artistic activity leading to a loss of specificity.

The following is a roster of artists and groups influencing the realization of the new version of Moscow radical art:

GENERAL IDEA
HANS HAACKE
TOSCANI [Oliviero Toscani] (advertising for United Colors of Benetton)
Art Club 2000
Guerrilla Girls
BARBARA KRUGER
Seymour Likely
Renée Green
INTERNATIONALE SITUATIONISTE
Robert Longo (early works)
CONSTRUCTIVISM (A. Rodchenko, G. Klutsis, E. Lissitzky, and others)
Raymond Pettibon
Alfredo Jaar (social works)
Damien Hirst
M. Kostabi
Pino Pascali
DADA
Cindy Sherman
POP ART (Andy Warhol, Robert Indiana, Robert Rauschenberg)
Martin Kippenberger
Komar and Melamid

Project: A. Osmolovsky
Proofs: A. Obukhova
Communication: N. Udaltsev

Text no. 8
October 9, 1995
How should one react to the actions of Dmitri Gutov, who, in response to an article by F. Romer [A. Panov], punched the latter in the face? This is a gesture of negative subjectivity wanting to be objective. Contemporary Marxism as developed by Gutov can reestablish its status of objectivity only by violent means; or, conversely, the desire to reestablish this status in contemporary conditions testifies to its inherent subjectivity. In Gutov's kind and seemingly domestic beard there lurks the grasping grin of "totalization" — the desire to restore the split unity of the world. Paradoxically, it is precisely his hidden grin that makes Gutov a contemporary artist.

"[There is] not the least reconciliation between the different 'linguistic games' which Kant referred to as abilities, knowing that they are separated by a gulf and that only transcendental illusion (Hegelian) can hope to totalize them in a real unity. However, he also knew that this illusion is paid for by terror . . . We paid dearly for our nostalgia for the whole and the unified, for the reconciliation of the conceptual with the perceptible, for transparent and communicable experience. Beyond the general desire to let down our guard and set our minds at rest, we hear the hoarse voice of the desire to recommence the terror and realize the phantasm, the dream of enveloping reality in our embrace."[1]

Project: A. Osmolovsky
Proofs: A. Obukhova
Communication: N. Udaltsov

Note
1. Jean François Lyotard, "Reply to the Question: What is Postmodernism?" *Ad Marginem* (Moscow, 1994), p. 323.

Text no. 9

October 9, 1995

All sorts of claims have been made vis-à-vis radical art, and it has been accused of many "sins." In ascending order these sins are: immorality, amorality, being third rate, lacking in talent, being decorative, inconsistency, and cowardice. I was even accused of betraying art ("Lock up the Party"). Why is it that that part of society, which traditionally served as its experimental laboratory, has turned into a conservative, culturally preservationist milieu? Whereas at the turn of the century the Bohemian milieu consisted of the lower middle classes, lumpen proletarians, and "easily aroused" young people, i.e., all those who yearned for free thought and were out to shock and take risks, today the makeup of the Bohemian milieu has changed dramatically. Nowadays it consists of the children of poor parents, invalids incapable of being socialized, frightened intelligentsia, and a very limited number of truly committed people who have actually pulled this "old-age home" into contemporary art. Most of these "Bohemians" are interested in peace, stability, a small amount of money to get by on, and having a good time. Of course, these "normal" people are motivated by fear and are seeking peace and tranquillity and are simply *defending themselves.* (It is naive to think that one can be sheltered and isolated in a situation in which political and criminal terrorism is paramount.) It seems likely that these people would use more radical means of defending themselves if they had even a small amount of *will and power.* Being at the same time spectators and consumers of modern art — of art whose place and qualities are ambiguous — they do not understand that in its essence this art is abnormal. It is just *not for them.* What a "tragedy!!!"

Anatoly Osmolovsky

Project: Osmolovsky
Proofs: A. Obukhova
Communication: N. Udaltsov

Text no. 20
Contemporary Art: Here and Now (rejection of museums)
November 10–December 9, 1996
"Artists, gallery owners, critics, and the public throng to wherever 'something is happening.' But the reality of this 'something happening' is the reality of money. In the absence of aesthetic criteria, it is possible and useful to determine the value of works of art on the basis of their profitability. This reality reconciles everything, even the most contradictory tendencies in art, provided that these tendencies have purchasing power."[2]

It is generally recognized that contemporary art is in a state of crisis that is becoming more profound every year. The infrastructure created in the 1980s is being destroyed, and there is a dearth of new ideas in the artistic community. Thousands of people employed in this field ("art system") are seeking employment in other areas. It appears that the visual arts that used to be the standard by which experimentation and innovation were measured in the past are yielding to other forms of expression. In reality the general cultural setting has changed so radically that the basic functions of contemporary art are no longer relevant. At the same time it must be recognized that the contemporary visual arts in many years of development have garnered considerable strategic experience in interacting with society. No other type of human activity can make this claim. The contemporary artist is acutely aware of the function and structure of contemporary society and is an expert in communication. With very limited means he is able to maximize the dissemination of information. Contemporary art is a platform for developing the most shocking, the most paradoxical, and the most fantastic forms of representation. Representation itself is never neutral and carries within itself a certain way of perceiving reality. The modern artist is primarily concerned with how the perception of the consumer is formed. This process has continued without interruption throughout the twentieth century, and there is no indication that any other area of the humanities has taken this function upon itself. In actual fact it is not modern art that is in a state of crisis, but the outdated model of its functioning created in the 1980s. This model contains at least several stereotypes:

> 1) a claim to innovation which created commodified art in the art market;
> 2) reliance on the market system of production and redistribution of art as the main determinant of its reliability and universality and, as a consequence, the tendency toward the creation of high-quality "art products";
> 3) obligatory achievement of museum status as a guarantee of historical worth.

What all of these points have in common is the conviction that art has an intrinsic value outside of the communicative event. Whereas the postmodernists accused classical modernism of being excessively ambitious without any basis in reality, criticized the position of the "genius" who made his works appear out of nothing, as well as classical modernism's claims to independence, etc., the newest art can also criticize the postmodern culture of contemporary art of being concerned with its preservation and monetary worth. In reality the only value that art possesses is within the confines of the process of its creation. Outside of this event any artifact (work of art) must be seen only as the documentation of this event outside of any relationship with a preceding artifact and works of art. Art that is valued in this way is truly "contemporary," as its main goal is to provide for maximum communication.

Contemporary art is not a commodity, nor is it an innovation or a universal value, which deserves to be conserved. How can it be defined?

In order to be contemporary, art must be specific to the utmost and functional, i.e., it must relate to the real world — politics, show business, music, analytical practice, medicine, etc. I do not mean that art should be subservient to the above-mentioned activities; what I am referring to is their mutual transgression. When art encroaches on politics, we save art from art and politics from politics. When art diffuses itself with some sort of analytical practice, a new type of activity is the result.

Among the many genres of contemporary art, the most current are those which are the most functional and communicable. The following is a list of the more important ones: performance, posters, strategic planning of representational activity, different types of design, club and institutional activity. The main task of the artist is to synthesize the different artistic genres into a unified system and to introduce this entity into another sphere of human activity. Under functionality I do not necessarily have in mind the positive "utility" of art as it was understood by the Russian Constructivists, but finding another mode for its existence. The introduction of art into real life could also be destructive, malignant, chaotic, and confusing. The Italian artist Oliviero Toscani provides one of the best examples of this approach. His ads for United Colors of Benetton are a synthesis of art and advertisement intended for a mass public. Toscani is not dependent on museums, galleries, or curators, nor does he define himself through the existing system of modern art but demonstrates a completely new approach to the functioning of art. His images are ubiquitous in all the Benetton stores and on Benetton products, where they fulfill a certain function (advertising, in this case), but bear a direct relation to art. Seen from a broader perspective, Benetton itself has become Toscani's artistic project. The most important aspects of his approach are the interaction of art with other types of activity and his attempts to build nontraditional relationships with society.

In this regard Jeff Koons is the culmination of one of the most important stages of modern art. He made use of the aesthetic of kitsch and camp, and brought to a dazzling conclusion the orientation toward the creation of high-quality long-lasting artifacts. It is at this point, one could say, that art bids farewell to the Museum as one of the forms of transcendence. Another key figure of the 1980s, in my opinion, was Cindy Sherman, who used photography to create classical paintings for museums. The ideology of the Museum was implicit in the works of these artists. The "current" (contemporary) artist breaks with this implication — the success of his works is tested by their inclusion into social processes and their ability to synthesize the creative milieu.

If we were to attempt to formalize the activity of the current artist by assigning it to a certain "genre," the most elementary form of this activity could be characterized as Situation. This term, which was introduced by the Situationist International, refers to the construction of some sort of social event. Situation is not performance and not a Happening; it is rather a hooligan prank, a provocation touching upon not so much the aesthetic sphere of functioning within the system of art as the sphere of political (in the broad sense) legitimacy. In the Moscow art community, the ETI movement [Expropriation of the Territory of Art; founded by Osmolovsky in 1989] and Alexander Brener worked in this genre. One of the latest situations created by Brener, which received some notoriety, was performed at the international *Manifesta* exhibition in Rotterdam. During a speech by the main sponsor of this event, Brener came up to the microphone and began commenting on the speech by using such words as "this is a lie, this is true," demonstrating on one hand the absurdity of such "accusations" and on the other hand their appropriateness precisely because of their absurdity. I believe that one of the most important elements of this gesture was its suddenness and spontaneity. It is precisely this factor that makes it possible to categorize this gesture as a situation rather than a performance. The gallery manager Marat Gelman works in a more complex and approximate version of this "genre." His project involving new Russian money was actually a situation rather than just an ordinary exhibition.

Another distinguishing characteristic of the contemporary artist is that he plans his works within the framework of complete projects. He does not think of his art as a succession of unrelated works but as a project, within the scope of which different works by him and other artists and documentation may be incorporated. Leading examples of this approach are Oleg Kulik's *Consignment of Animals* and Dimitri Gutov's *Lifshitz's Institute.* In my opinion an artist such as Oliviero Toscani also engages in this type of "project" approach, which is an attempt to conceive of art as a process rather than as an aggregate of works.

Finally, the most complex "genre" in current art is one in which a "milieu" is created, which encompasses the activities of several people united in a "disjunctive synthesis." The best-known current artist of this type is, of course, Quentin Tarantino. His main task is to create a milieu in which it does not matter to the participants of the process through which forms their flows of desire and creativity, whether literature, performance, objects, posters, exhibitions, film, theoretical articles, reviews, etc., are channeled.

The task of this type of current artist consists of initiating processes of positive disjunctive synthesis, intertwining different forms of activity, and taking part in events that completely differ in essence from each other: musical, political, theatrical, analytical, editorial, curatorial, etc. The topos of the current artist is the broadest possible, and it encompasses practically all areas of the humanities. This type of artist has turned from a creator of visual images into a creator of milieus and situations. This type of activity was well known in the past; one need only recall the activity of André Breton and David Burliuk, among others. This type of creative activity, however, was never formalized as "creative."

On the other hand, the process of creating situations and creative milieus is linked to political activity as it concerns the economic and political basis of society and the state. This process cannot help but enter into conflict with the laws and rules of late capitalist society, which essentially have not changed since the time of Marx's *Das Kapital.*

We may add the following points in addition to the above-mentioned ones relating to the 1980s:

1) *Communication instead of innovation;*
2) *Synthesis of social processes, milieus, and situations instead of creating products for the market;*
3) *A maximum of social functionality as a guarantee of historical and social viability.*

In rejecting the museum, current art stakes out a claim in favor of situation and communication in the present, and thus aspires to become a permanent event in art rather than a recollection of an event stored in a museum.

Projects: A. Osmolovsky
Proofs: G. Avanesova
Communication: *Chudozestvennyj Zhurnal* [art journal], no. 16

Note
2. Lyotard, op. cit.

Originally self-published by the author and *Chudozestvennyj Zhurnal* in 1995. Translated by Daniel Rishik.

•●

BOJANA PEJIĆ

Bojana Pejić (born 1948) graduated with a degree in art history from the University of Belgrade in 1974. As one of the most respected curators and art historians from Eastern Europe, she helped organize two important exhibitions in 1999: Aspects/Positions *at the Museum of Contemporary Art/Foundation Ludwig in Vienna; and* After the Wall: Art and Culture in Post-Communist Europe *at the Moderna Museet in Stockholm.*

In the following text, Pejić recounts the story of the artist Marina Abramović, who was initially invited to represent Yugoslavia in the 1997 Venice Biennale. Abramović's entry, entitled Balkan Baroque, *combined installation and performance and contained elements of both Eastern and Western culture. The Minister of Culture, disapproving of Abramović's piece, proceeded to fire the commissioners of the pavilion and appoint new ones who then rescinded the offer to Abramović and replaced her with landscape painter Vojo Stanić. One of the reasons for their decision was that Abramović had moved to Amsterdam in the 1970s and therefore was one of a diaspora of artists who were no longer considered Balkan enough. In the end, the curator of the Venice Biennale, Germano Celant, intervened and invited Abramović to exhibit at the Italian Pavilion. In her essay, Bojana Pejić illuminates the circumstances of this particular exhibition, and also the complexities and stereotypes associated with Balkan culture.*

Balkan for Beginners

> *L'universel, c'est le local moins les mûres.* — M. Torga, 1986

Among the Serbian and Montenegrin peoples, opera is not such a common genre of music, operetta even less so. Therefore, it should not be so strange that the operetta *Die Lustige Witwe* (1905), whose plot takes place somewhere in the "exotic" Balkans, was written by a foreigner, Franz Lehár, a Hungarian composer living in Vienna. This operetta, for which the musician found inspiration in South Slavic folk music, became the basis for another artistic production, namely, a silent film. The film, *The Merry Widow* (1925), an authentic European story, was directed in Hollywood by Erich von Stroheim, a "diasporic" Viennese who had moved to the United States in 1910. The film story is situated in a court where princes named Mirko and Danilo live; they wear fascinating garb that could easily be recognized, by those who come from the Balkan regions, as the folk costumes worn in the countryside of Crna Gora, the name the Italians literally translated as "Monte Ne(g)ro" ("Black Mountains"). Nevertheless, as indicated in the film's intertitles, the plot takes place in the country of "Monteblanco" ("White Mountains"), and it was shot in Griffith Park in Los Angeles. There the Montenegrin/Monteblancan courtyard is reconstructed, as well as suitable mountains which "act" as Balkan landscape. A female intruder, a body-conscious saloon singer, dashes into that male space and causes utter confusion among the local highland (handsome but macho) princes. In the Hollywood version, the widow is not European, but, as expected in patriotic Hollywood, American. The princes are rather confused by this type of femaleness, i.e., a *femme fatale,* since, in all the Balkan regions, a woman who is a singer, an actress, or a ballerina is given a quite different name ("a whore"). In those regions, in those times, femininity was defined by the institution of the Mother. The male-based milieu, occasionally though not frequently, produced a "third-gender," cross-dressing women, who fully took over men's roles due to the lack of sons in their families. Such biological females wore men's clothes and often bore men's weaponry.[1] As a foreigner, therefore, someone who comes from the outside, from the remote Center, from the "site" also known as *le grand Monde,"* this calamity widow first disturbs the existing patriarchal order, into which she then integrates. This "nationally pure" American woman, as she would nowadays be called, ends up happily in a multicultural marriage. In that union the "stronger sex" (the passionate and therefore bellicose local prince) is also ethnically pure. Marrying a Balkan man, the folk singer becomes a princess. From the American point of view, free of the geographical pedantry to which our Old Continent is highly sensitive, back home in the United States she was probably said "to have made IT in Europe."

Both the operetta and the film might heedlessly be assigned to Balkanism, and thus be interpreted as an image of the Balkans as a semiprimitive Margin, an image of the Other that simultaneously attracts and repels, which was, as usual, constructed by the Center(s), by turn-of-the-century Vienna, and by Hollywood in the roaring twenties. This assumption, nevertheless, must be dismissed if we know who commissioned the operetta in which the country of "Monteblanco" is charmingly caricatured. It was ordered, history claims, from Franz Lehár of Vienna by Petar I Karaðjorðjević himself, who became the king of Serbia in 1903. He was married to a Montenegrin duchess with whom he lived at the Montenegrin court from 1883 until 1890. Immediately after ascending the Serbian throne, he did not commission an operetta about his Serbia, but built a musical monument to Montenegro, the bordering "fraternal" country, represented — constructed — by that operetta as Margin.[2] In other words, the narrative about the widow does not match the story about antagonism between Center and Margin (and vice versa); it is rather a strictly Balkan affair conducted by the Margin itself.

Serenissima,[3] or How to Make IT

The choice of an artist to represent a country at the Venice Biennale is also a matter of internal affairs, and it is conducted by a national selector, a professional, a curator, or an art historian, with whose choice the international community does not interfere (which certainly does not mean that such a commissioner should utterly disregard the international art market). Thus, the story of Marina Abramović, Yugoslavia, Montenegro, and this year's Biennale [1997] is the one in which no foreign or "enemy" forces interfered. Also, this story is not about some imaginary country called "Monteblanco," but about a concrete political landscape. Montenegro (Crna Gora) is the republic which, after Communist Yugoslavia disintegrated, remained in a more or less happy marriage with the republic of Serbia (Srbija), which still contains the autonomous regions of Kosovo and Vojvodina. Together they make up the actual Federal Republic of Yugoslavia. According to an agreement between the federal and Montenegrin ministries of culture, Petar Čuković was appointed Yugoslav commissar [of the Venice Biennale pavilion] this time; he is an art historian from Montenegro, and also director of the National Museum of Montenegro in Cetinje. Information about the meeting of the two ministers of culture, in which the choice of the commissar was confirmed, was submitted to the public in the Podgorica daily *Pobjeda* on January 23, 1997. As commissar, Čuković invited Marina to represent Yugoslavia in the Biennale and exhibit her work in the Yugoslav pavilion in the Giardini. It is not unimportant to mention that since 1938, when Yugoslav artists started exhibiting their work in the national pavilion,[4] the name "Yugoslavia" has remained on it, no matter *which* Yugoslavia it was: the *first,* semi-capitalist country which lasted between World Wars I and II; the *second,* socialist (Titoist) Yugoslavia which lasted between World War II and the first Yugoslav war in Bosnia and Herzegovina; or else the *third,* Montenegro-cum-Serbia community that is also called Yugoslavia. In this pavilion, by the way, none of the Yugoslavias have presented a woman artist in a monographic way.

Marina Abramović has been living in Amsterdam since 1976; still, she has staged performances or participated in international exhibitions held "back home." After a certain time needed to think the invitation over, she accepted. Abramović's decision to accept was certainly triggered by the long students' anti-regime demonstrations that started on November 17, 1996, in Belgrade, which inaugurated peaceful and humorous forms of civil and urban conduct, new to the Balkans—the protest started with an intention of changing the immediate present in order to achieve a (democratic) future.

Deciding to represent Yugoslavia as an artist, she bore in mind that that was the very country whose national(istic) politics had been primarily responsible for the recent war in the Balkans. During that war and because of it, the past of all cultures existing in that area was erased, their present imperiled by mutual hatred, and thus their future postponed. No less importantly, the major victims of that war were women, primarily Muslim, but Serb and Croat as well. During the war, feminist groups from all of the regions of ex-Yugoslavia, as well as from abroad, reacted to this terrible situation for women. A telegram from London, from an Australian radio journalist (a woman) working for the Women's Environment Network, was sent to Zagreb in 1993, requesting an interview about the rape of women in "rape camps in Bosnia/Croatia," with "preferably a survivor + someone who speaks English."[5]

All these elements are intertwined in *Balkan Baroque,* the work conceived by Marina Abramović for the Yugoslav pavilion. This work stemmed from her theater performance *Delusional* (1994), in which she used, among other things, as a metaphor for the recent combat in the territory she had been born in, a stage consisting of glass cages in which there were approximately four hundred live rats. Apart from an installation inside the Yugoslav pavilion, she planned to carry out performances in front of it for three consecutive days, during the press opening of the Biennale. After the exhibition was closed, the installation, the cost of which has been estimated at 150.000 DEM, would become the property of the National Museum of Montenegro, as the artist herself suggested. The sum, a third higher than the cost of the work itself, was necessary for its realization, as well as to cover expenses usual for a national pavilion (catalogue, sojourn in Venice during preparations, and purchase of video equipment). No reception was planned for presentation in the Biennale (not even a modest one, just with šljivovica [plum brandy]), nor the personal appearance of Claudia Schiffer, who would this time (once again) stroll around in Montenegrin folk costume, advertising the Mediterranean tourism of Montenegro.

Marina Abramović: A (Nationally Correct) Portrait

Marina Abramović was born in 1946 in Belgrade, where she studied painting at the Academy of Fine Arts; her professor was an abstract painter who struggled, even in the early 1950s, for the victory of modernism in Communist Yugoslavia. Following a short period of Socialist Realism, which was the official aesthetic before 1948 (when Tito's Yugoslavia stepped out of the Soviet fraternity and deceived "papa" Stalin), modernism was accepted in Titoist Yugoslavia as "official" art. Abandoning modernist canons, Abramović, like many other Yugoslav artists after 1968, focused on Conceptual art, post-object art, and performance art. In 1973 she started staging performances, both "at home" and abroad.

According to the post-Communist *doxa* [the Greek work for belief, opinion], Yugoslav Communism forbade and/or suppressed national content in works of art, due to its "supranational" orientation (characteristic of Marxist theory in general). Nonetheless, such meanings in a work of art were utterly irrelevant for all modernists, no matter in which part of the world they lived. Modernism and its theory, as defined after World War II, viewed abstraction as "universal" language. For the generation of artists formed by and during 1968, who lived (even in the socialist Yugoslavia) in the transnational idealism of the early 1970s, a national work of art (e.g., "Slovenian" performance, "Croatian" video art, or "Serbian" minimalist music) could, in the seventies, only be a laughing issue. In the late 1980s, when the theses of *Heimat* and *Heimatkunst* were actualized among Balkan peoples, the Croatian philosopher Milan Kangrga made a statement in an interview which, I trust, Marina Abramović could also underwrite. He said: "Homeland is not only the place we were born in; Homeland is also a spiritual landscape that we acquire over the entire course of our lives."

Today, however, in the age of "post-Communism," the category of national identity was promoted to the favorite, if not the criterion, *sine qua non* for appraisal of works of art. Following this twisted logic, I must admit, although involuntarily, that the invitation to Marina Abramović to represent Yugoslavia in Venice was an invitation which could have gone to "right" hands (but did not).

I am going to disregard, if possible, the twenty-year-long praxis of Abramović, which has, after all, been denied by no professional in the previous or present Yugoslavia (whether he or she was in favor of her art or not). So, if we disregard art, and if we view the artist's family origins from the standpoint of the Serbian and/or Montenegrin intelligentsia in power, Marina Abramović turns out to be the "ideal" (political) choice. She and her brother, Velimir, were born in a doubly mixed marriage. Their father, Vojo Abramović, is a man, and their mother, Danica Abramović (born Rosić), is a woman. Except for this mixture, characteristic of marriages in the Balkans (before, during, and after Communism), I should add that Marina's parents speak the same language, and that they grew up in families which both observed the Christian Orthodox religion. The population of the Balkans can, beside this, also be affiliated with the Roman Catholic or Muslim religions.

The history of Marina Abramović's family, both on her mother's and her father's sides, is a story of the Balkans in which landscapes, influenced by (un)fortunate political circumstances, undergo permanent renaming. The only continuity that could hold here was *discontinuity*. Marina's father was born in Montenegro in 1912, at a time when it was still an independent country, which dethroned its own king by parliamentary decision so as to join the union of South Slavic countries, the Kingdom of Serbs, Croats, and Slovenes (SCS), established in 1918. The rulers, members of the Serbian Karaðjorðjević dynasty, were too busy solving the national issues in the country to commission operettas from abroad, as their grandfather had. Another reason was that they were more interested in "pure" fine arts, and so they invested a lot in the improvement of the local landscapes, and built magnificent monuments. (These were destroyed by the Communists, who, having come to power, tore down everything that was connected to a national hero they suspected as "politically incorrect.") Apart from the nations already mentioned, there also existed Montenegro, Macedonia, and Bosnia. The country consisting of these parts was constituted after World War I, during the process called "Balkanization" in political history, the process that designates the creation of new countries or "small fatherlands." (In passing, the Balkan peninsula was only named such in 1806, and its godfather was a German, not a local, geographer.) These countries were built on the ruins of the Ottoman Empire on the one hand, and of the Hapsburg monarchy on the other. Following the Great War, when the institution of the Unknown Soldier was inaugurated, the Kingdom of SCS embraced it and built the first Tomb to the Unknown Soldier in 1922. It was later torn down, so that Ivan Meštrović (a Croatian sculptor who was the favorite artist of the Serbian regime, as well as the *artist royal* of the kingdom) could, between 1934 and 1938, build a new, magnificent, multinational monument with eight female caryatids. Each of these Mothers represented one of the different peoples which comprised the new state. This artist was also well-liked in Communist Yugoslavia, and the chapel in which Njegoš (1747–1830), a Montenegrin patriarch, ruler, and philosopher, had wished to be buried, was torn down to make room for another pretentious monument designed by him, this time in Njegoš's honor. Moreover, the top of the mountain had to be removed, since the memorial was so enormous. Apart from Mothers, Meštrović's most frequent artistic motif was the Widow, as a rule unmerry in the Balkans. According to an anecdote that dates back to those times, a mother, clad in mourning clothes, came to the ministry of defense, requiring a lifetime pension. She claimed to be the widow of the Unknown Soldier!

Marina's maternal grandfather, who was also born in Montenegro, was a priest, and in 1930 he became the patriarch of the Serbian Orthodox Church. In 1921 Marina's mother, Danica, was born in the Kingdom of SCS, in Serbia. That year the first constitution of the kingdom was adopted; according to the official census, it was determined that three-quarters of the country's population lived on agriculture and fishing. According to the same source, three-quarters of the people listed in the census were illiterate. That was the year when avant-garde art appeared along with the (not-quite-happily) united South Slavs. In resistance to "universalistic" academicism, the international periodical *Zenit (Zenith)* was founded, with Ljubomir Micić as its editor. It was published, first in Zagreb and then in Belgrade, from 1921 to 1926. *Zenith,* "a journal published to the astonishment of all Serbs, Croats, and Slovenes," was a "small review" just like the ones that had flooded Europe in the 1920s. It supported the negation of everything that existed, but it also supported "Balkanization of the Merry Widow of Europe." In 1922 Dragan Aleksić from Zagreb also introduced Dadaism as "a child of Communism," and described the circumstances in the Balkans with the slogan: *Paradox is the condition of existence!!!*

When a monarchist dictatorship was introduced in 1929, the Kingdom of SCS was renamed the Kingdom of Yugoslavia. Many liberal, "paradoxical" periodicals were forbidden in a completely nonparadoxical way. (The State's excuse was a lack of paper!) From today's "post-Communist" perspective, to forbid the work of the Communist party of Yugoslavia of that time was an absolutely correct decision. According to such a standpoint, to organize Partisan resistance against the fascist occupation in 1941 was a mistake as well. The Yugoslav ruler, the king of Serbia, took shelter in London, from which he sends a telegram to his nation(s): "We arrived well." In 1943 Tito sent a dispatch through a messenger to his partisans: "I am nearby." Since postwar Belgrade lacked housing, due to the bombing carried out by the *Wehrmacht* on April 6, 1941, without a declaration of war, Tito moved into the king's court/residence in 1945. Later, when the country got back on its feet by means of "everybody-pull-now socialism," new villas were built for him in all the republics of Yugoslavia, or old ones from the ex-kingdom were adapted in his honor.

Marina's parents got to know each other while in the Partisans. They believed in anti-fascism, the revolution, and the future, which was then imagined as Communism; unlike their parents, they did not believe any more in their King, Nation, or God. By the way, at that time, God somehow vanished from the Yugoslav territory. (In spite of serious historical research, Communist historiographers could not determine the exact date of His death, but there have been some serious claims that it happened somewhere after 1941, but before 1945.) "Tito's" Yugoslavia was proclaimed and internationally recognized in 1945. The Abramović children were born and grew up in the second, Socialist Federal Republic of Yugoslavia, which was, as many post-Communist and post-Yugoslav historians claim, founded by Josip Broz Tito (1892–1980), himself alone, and no one else. Tito was the first, the only, and the last president of Yugoslavia, general secretary of the Communist party, Ph.D. in military science, etcetera, etcetera. Since he was one of the initiators of the Nonaligned Movement, which a great number of postcolonial countries joined after 1961, Yugoslavia was given the Art Museum of Nonaligned Countries, whose collection contains gifts received by "our comrade Tito" in his travels around the Third World. That was the time when we welcomed him in peaceful (i.e., well-organized) street demonstrations. The museum was not founded in Belgrade, but was situated, during the Sturm und Drang of decentralization, in Titograd, Montenegro (the city called Podgorica before and after Communism) from which the Yugoslav participation in the Venice Biennale in 1997 was organized. When Tito died, one Third Worldist, a president of a postcolonial country, optimistically stated: "He was a rare leader who departed without fear of what would happen after he was gone."[6] Tito never left the making of historical films, which glorified the Yugoslav National Liberation War, to gentlemen from Hollywood, but entrusted it to comrades from his ranks. They filmed stories about Partisan victories in original locations, in Bosnia-Herzegovina, where crucial battles had taken place in 1943. In the 1960s, those were the locations in which grandiose, modernist (abstract) monuments were built to honor the Yugoslav socialist revolution realized through the war. Of all the actors who impersonated Tito, he was said to have liked his "imported self" the best — that was Richard Burton as "Tito."

The Abramović children, just like all other children, played cowboys and Indians, or Partisans and Germans in the street. As schoolchildren they wore, in performances for State holidays, the red scarves of Tito's pioneers around their necks. A Slovenian girl, a pioneer whose parents were traveling for the first time to a capitalist country, at the beginning of the 1960s, asked them to bring her a gift from Paris — a color photo of Tito. That was the country in which red icons of Marx, Engels, Lenin, and Tito (Stalin as well, but only until mid-1948) were carried in parades honoring the First of May, the same way as icons of venerated saints (naturally, not favored in Yugoslav Communism) are carried in religious processions.

Although Tito passed away in "his" Yugoslavia in 1980, he had only started to fade away in these Balkan regions simultaneously with Vladimir Ilyich, whose absence from the squares of "his" Marxist-Leninist world had already begun by the end of the 1980s. The exact date of Ilyich's second (and final) death cannot be determined quite precisely; however, it is certain that he met his death after November 1989. The East without the Wall, without Lenin, with "democracy" looming on the horizon, rendered jobless Ernst Lubitsch's woman commissar Ninotchka (played by Greta Garbo and filmed back in 1937). This film was a means of anti-Communist propaganda in America until 1941, and in Europe from 1948 to 1952, in the coolest years of the cold war. Nevertheless, it was never shown to us in Yugoslavia because it caricatured Soviet Communism, although the Yugoslav film library, whose film archive was the third largest in Europe, owned a copy of it. James Bond, who now also became jobless, was very popular in Yugoslavia, and even we, citizens of Tito's Yugoslavia, could witness his anti-Communist adventures. The return to the new/old "Mother" Russia inspired Boris Yeltsin to make his nation (as well as Africa) face the truth about civilization: "Our country has not been lucky. Indeed, it was decided to carry out this Marxist experiment on us — fate pushed us in precisely this direction. Instead of some country in Africa, they began to experiment on us. It has simply pushed us off the path that the world's civilized countries have taken."[7] In 1987, prior to this statement, Nation, Tradition, Church, and Patriarchy *y compris* had already started to "happen" to those of us living in Serbia. That was the moment when a satirist from Belgrade declared: "Milošević was the first man in Yugoslavia who grasped that Tito was dead." Then the other Yugoslav republics started "experiencing" their own Nations.

Marina Abramović was invited to take part in the Venice Biennale by the third Yugoslavia, which is still not acknowledged by the international community, whose culture and sport were, nonetheless, exempt from the international embargo. Hence, the new Yugoslavia could, for the first time, take part in the Biennale held in 1995. At that time, the exhibition in the Yugoslav pavilion contained works of an artist born in Yugoslavia, and also living, for two decades now, somewhere in the Center (i.e., in Paris); still, his address was not a problem then. In the case of Marina Abramović, it seems to be so.

Opera called Heimat, Oh, Heimat

Post-Communist discourses that have, in the last few years, been taking place in the territory once simply called "the East" are engaged in "remaking history," namely, in rewriting national histories of peoples/countries/states from the time before Communism. They are also engaged in putting entries about artistic tendencies which were proscribed, or at least unwelcome, under the Communist regime onto the map of art history. Similar discourses also exist in the states built on the ideological and factual ruins of the former Yugoslavia—those that have slipped from state Communism into (more or less manifest) state nationalism. Redefinition of national identity and of the nation, defined by Benedict Anderson as "imagined community," points out that "the nation is always conceived as a deep, horizontal comradeship."[8] This redefinition denotes constructing or inventing tradition, articulating the archaic, searching for "roots'" as well as looking for a foundation in religion. While a number of newborn Balkan states find it highly important that they prove their culture to belong exclusively to Europe (and not to the Balkans as well), some other countries insist on their own cultural self-sufficiency, the consequence of that being the making of enemies. Existence or invention of enemies creates a need for protection of what is "inside" from what is "outside." "Nationalism is an urban movement which identifies with rural areas as a source of authenticity, finding in the 'folk' the attitudes, beliefs, customs, and language to create a sense of national unity among people who have other loyalties. Nationalism aims at . . . rejection of cosmopolitan upper classes, intellectuals, and others likely to be influenced by foreign ideas."[9]

Implicitly, all these discourses are dealing with placing one's own culture in a European context, in which all these countries would still have a status similar to that of other small European cultures, cultures of small languages that must be translated, even if they had not experienced Communism or survived it (with or without wars). In the text "Mediterranean Monads" (1996), in which Petar Čuković considers six "stations" in Montenegrin modern art, he, who was to have been Marina Abramović's host in the Yugoslav pavilion in Venice, says: "An important trait . . . connects the greatest number of these artists, and it naturally also reveals something about the fate of small cultural milieus to which Montenegro belongs as well. Those are the artists who spend the greatest parts of their lives in *diaspora,* the greatest part of their works being created in *diaspora,* in spite of the fact that at the deepest levels of their beings . . . the being of their homeland murmurs. But the diaspora has actually been, until the most recent times, the fate of the arts of all the South Slavic milieus." He goes on to say: "Still, the modernity of our artists is not an 'easy' kind of modernity at all costs, and it is not free of difficult drama: it is, in fact, some kind of 'slow modernity.'"[10]

However, the minister of culture in the Montenegrin government, Goran Rakočević, holds a completely different opinion on the diaspora of national artists. The fact that Roman Opalka, an artist of Polish origins, had been living for decades in the United States, did not, for example, prevent the Polish minister of culture, as well as the ever-so-persistent Anda Rottenberg, the Polish commissar at the Biennale in 1995, from presenting this artist in the national pavilion.

After many commentaries appearing daily in the regional (Serbian and Montenegrin) press over several months (some of them benevolent and some not so) mainly dealing with the costs required for realization of Marina Abramović's project *Balkan Baroque,* all the pros and cons were terminated at the end of March 1997 by Minister Rakočević. Rakočević (appointed to that post in December of last year) expressed his "personal attitude," claiming, naturally, that he was not calling Marina Abramović's artistic personality into question. He said: "Nonetheless, it is my obligation, being primus inter pares of Montenegrin cultural politics, to defend and support what is its integral and original interest, what results in recognizable and convincing artistic effects that are received well by the Montenegrin cultural and general public." He went on to add that the financial plan for the presentation was a controversial issue.

The ministry of culture of the former Yugoslavia did not interfere so much with the aesthetic their country exported to the Biennale, but they were rather reluctant to finance a presentation if it did not mirror "national pluralism," and did not include artists belonging to "all the nations and nationalities." In fact, they still cared the most for artists-delegates from Croatia, Slovenia, and Serbia, whence the selectors also came. In the interwar period (i.e., 1945–91), the Yugoslav commissioner for the Biennale came from Macedonia only once, and from Bosnia and Herzegovina and Montenegro — never. Only in 1968 was our commissioner a woman who, however, selected three male artists. But neither did Communist comrades understand, nor has the post-Communist gentry yet learned to grasp, that an exhibition of contemporary art in general, and an international manifestation in particular, must cost. Fritz Lang in Jean-Luc Godard's film *Le mépris* (1963) recites ironically a sentence suitable for the anti-commercial attitudes which marked the 1960s; still, it is a statement that holds, willy-nilly, even today. Lang/Godard says: "When I hear the word culture, I reach for my checkbook!" This quotation may sound utterly ironic, because the FR of Yugoslavia has, in the last couple of years, been undergoing an economic crisis, for which, internally, the international sanctions have been exclusively blamed. In 1993, at a time of total lack of food, when the average pension in Belgrade was 20 DEM, I watched, nevertheless, on private TV channels in Belgrade, commercials for slimming products. The same channels constantly showed commercials for private gun shops. (This could have inspired some male citizen, no matter whether he knew the history of Nazism or not, to connect the word "culture" with the mentioned commercial product.) State television, known as TV Bastille, broadcasted, in its prime-time news, long reports about the war. After the end of the news, calls by battered women to the SOS help line in Belgrade, which is at the service of all the women who suffer family (and other) violence, rose by forty percent.

In addition to his extensive statement, Minister Rakočević continued (quite privately) to disagree with the already made choice of Marina Abramović, whose international fame he was forced to grant. His disagreement was "primarily due to my personal point of view that this outstanding opportunity ought to be used to represent authentic art from Montenegro, free of any complex of inferiority for which there is no reason in our exquisite tradition and spirituality . . . Montenegro is not a cultural margin and it should not be just a homeland colony for megalomaniac performances. In my opinion, we should be represented in the world by painters marked by Montenegro and its poetics, since we have the luck and honor to have brilliant artists of universal dimensions living among us." His statement ended with a quotation, *"Dixi et salvi animam meam,"* and its title — apparently given by the editorial staff — was as follows: "Montenegro is not a Cultural Colony."[11]

The "Essence" of Margin

Terms such as margin, or province — "sites" also known in the Euro-American West as *nice places to come from* — unavoidably imply that there is such a place in which margin or province is imagined, i.e., constructed as the Other. Ever since the inception of liberal capitalism, the Other is usually a "place" geographically removed from Europe; it is a screen in which the West inscribes the Other as exotic, original, primitive, or "natural." But the Other can also be in the "old" continent, in the Balkans, for example. The myth of the Balkans, necessarily reactualized during the war in Bosnia-Herzegovina, is an image of the Other in which the Balkan peninsula is a perpetual source of bellicose confrontations, as suggested in the verb "to balkanize," which means "to break up into small, mutually hostile political units, such as the Balkan states after World War I" (*Webster's Dictionary of the English Language,* Toronto, 1976). This construction of the Balkans as the Other is an image created from the outside, and is summed up by Slavoj Žižek: "For a long time, the 'Balkans' have been one of the privileged sites of phantasmic investments in politics. . . . The fantasy which organized the perception of ex-Yugoslavia is that of 'Balkan' as the Other of the West: the place of savage ethnic conflicts long since overcome by civilized Europe; a place where nothing is forgotten and nothing learned, where old traumas are replayed again and again; where the symbolic link is simultaneously devalued (dozens of cease-fires are broken) and overvalued (primitive warrior notions of honor and pride).

"Against this background, a multitude of myths have flourished. For the 'democratic Left,' Tito's Yugoslavia was the mirage of the 'third way' of self-management beyond capitalism and state socialism; for the delicate men of culture it was the exotic land of refreshing folkloric diversity (the films of Makavejev and Kusturica); for Milan Kundera, the place where the idyll of *Mitteleuropa* meets oriental barbarism; for the Western Realpolitik of the late 1980s, the disintegration of Yugoslavia functioned as a metaphor for what might happen in the Soviet Union; for France and Great Britain, it resuscitated the phantom of the German Fourth Reich disturbing the delicate balance of European politics; behind all this lurked the primordial trauma of Sarajevo, of the Balkans as the gunpowder threatening to set the whole of Europe alight. . . . Far from being the Other of Europe, ex-Yugoslavia was rather Europe itself in its Otherness, the screen on to which Europe projected its own repressed reverse."[12]

The post-Communist age, and its theoreticians and practitioners in charge, would certainly benefit from some observations made by postcolonial discourse. Eurocentric and Euro-American approaches to countries and peoples which do not belong to Europe, and which are defined as the Other, have been seriously undone in the past two decades within postcolonial discourse. In such discussions, naturally, the first thing to be analyzed is Western literature, visual arts, or film, in all of which what Edward Said calls "Orientalism" is being constructed. Besides this image projected by the Center to the distant Other, the image that comes from without, another form of construction, seems as important: a "diasporic Second Worldist," as she defines herself. Gayatri Spivak focuses on this phenomenon. She critically evaluates the method applied by postcolonial intellectuals in her native India, when writing "Third Worldist Alternative Histories." When he (and it is, as a rule, a man) becomes involved in "remaking history," and when he speaks "from within," therefore, with no pressure from colonizers (and their language), he as a rule takes a stand of "nativist ethnicist culturalism." Spivak contends: "The new culturalist alibi, working within a basically elitist culture industry, insisting on the continuity of a native tradition untouched by Westernization whose failures it can help to cover, legitimizes the very thing it claims to combat." She continues: "The discipline of history in India—conservative in its choice of canonical method even when radical in its sentiments—resists efforts, especially from the inside of the discipline to remake the disciplinary method. . . . This is again a reminder that there are other battles to fight than just metropolitan centrism. This too is a difference between internal colonization and decolonization."[13]

In the countries that are on their way to "future" democracy and future capitalism as well, the "personal attitude" of a post-Communist minister (of culture) acquires almost the same weight as an attitude of some minister in the Communist ancien régime had. Polish author Leszek Kolakowski, *enfant terrible* of Marxism, completed an essay about that regime, rewriting, i.e., undoing legends from the Old Testament, to which he added "historically materialist" morals. In his *Key to Heaven* (1964), after remaking the narrative about the ass, Balaam, and the angel, he concludes: "It goes against reason that one can use it to argue against absolute reason."[14] When a politician from a state that considers itself post-Communist expresses his "personal" attitude, that attitude becomes the attitude of "absolute reason," and it has a different weight from a personal attitude stated by a politician in Western democracies. The personal attitude of dissatisfaction stated by Chancellor Kohl on the occasion of the project by Christo and Jeanne-Claude entitled *Wrapping of the Reichstag* did not prevent the Berlin Senate from making the opposite decision; thus, the installation could take place.

One day after the above-mentioned "private statement," Marina sent her official statement to the press, in which she terminated all communication with all *Heimat* institutions responsible for the Biennale. In a new *communiqué de presse,* the minister announced on March 24, 1997, that the Association of Artists of Montenegro (meeting in expanded formation) had decided, at a session held that very day, which painter to send to the Biennale. On that occasion, a new commissioner, who was supposed to bring the Yugoslav presentation to happy fruition, was also chosen. Marina Abramović received an official letter in which the minister himself informed her about the final decision, hoping for "further cooperation." *Ciao* Marina, *Auf Wiedersehen Balkanski Barok, Au revoir* exotic Communism. Tradition, *Mater omnium bonarum artium*, is back in the ever-so-exotic post-Communist Balkans. Paradox is — still — the condition of existence!

How does the Margin, or how do we-as-margin, see itself/ourselves from within? A TV show produced by TV Sarajevo back in 1988, when the "fraternal" Yugoslav republics of those times watched common programs, was devoted precisely to a topic that used to be touchy among the Balkan-Yugoslav peoples (and has still remained so), i.e., provincialism. Laszlo Vege, a Hungarian theater critic from Vojvodina, gave the following definition of (our) provincial *Weltanschauung* at that time, which still seems to hold: "When you live in the provinces, people are constantly trying to persuade you that you live in an opera, while you are, actually, living in an operetta all the time!" When it views itself in the operetta manner, Margin does it with self-irony and humor, and it views "le Grand Monde" in the same critical way as well. When it defines itself in terms of opera, Margin manifests its own divided *ratio*. It imagines itself either as the Center of the World, seen by nobody as such, or as the End of the World; both attitudes imply (local) patriotism colored with bitterness.

The Balkans, Baroque, and Wolf-Rat

Balkan Baroque is a piece with dancing (video) and singing (performance) in which Marina Abramović, in using installation and performance, intertwines elements from both Eastern and Western traditions. Those traditions have intersected, confronted, met, and parted in the course of centuries in the Balkan Peninsula. On the one hand, it is Byzantine tradition to which Christian Orthodox countries of the Balkans owe "the theory of the icon," which they adopted in the early Middle Ages, and continued to develop throughout the centuries, in spite of the Turkish rule that steadfastly maintained their positions in these areas until the Balkan wars of 1912–13. The Orthodox religious image, icon or fresco, is based on "inverse perspective" and not on Albertian central perspective that presents an illusion of space, constructed in Renaissance pictures as space-with-depth. Respecting the neo-Platonist aversion toward the third dimension,[15] which is considered the "earth dimension" — dimension of Matter, of the body — Byzantine art, as well as the types of art deriving from the same spiritual background, never accepted freestanding sculpture. It is so even in the Baroque, which came to Balkan regions only in the seventeenth century, and which is, in Western culture, unimaginable without sculpture. Serbian and Montenegrin Baroque can, hence, only be felt in iconostases, wooden screens laid with icons with rich engravings. In Croatia and Slovenia, for example, countries in which the Roman Catholic religion is practiced, Baroque sculpture is highly developed in the variant in which style, when dislocated from the Center and brought to Margins, becomes "unclean," interesting, and "rustic." Only when it is dislocated from the Center and accepted (always late) in the Province, in which every "universalistic" style becomes "lunatic," the dogma is here transformed into freedom (sometimes also known as chaos).

Marina Abramović. *Balkan Baroque.* 1997. Performance and video installation. Courtesy Sean Kelly Gallery, New York

The Christian Orthodox religion accepts only two-dimensional represen-tation, a flattened image, a picture without depth. Clement Greenberg also points to this flatness of Byzantine art when elaborating his modernist the-ory of painting.[16] For an icon or fresco painter in this spiritual context, the icon is a conveyor of the second dimension; that is precisely what enables the human eye to reach the "fourth dimension," the dimension of the Soul. Icons used to be painted by monks, collectively and anonymously; this art met "artistic subjectivity" only in the sixteenth century, when one icon was made by one artistic hand. The greatest respect was shown for icons called archeiropoietic (untouched by the human hand), images not painted, but al-legedly created by contact with and emanation from a sacred personage. On such an image, the Shroud of Turin, André Bazin builds his cinematographic theory. From this film theory, video theory also easily follows. It is inscribed in videotape, and a picture in videotape is neither touched by human hands nor can be seen by the human eye, as opposed to film stock, which is touched by human hands during film editing.[17]

Video images in the *Balkan Baroque* installation are spatially organized as a triptych, in the middle of which there is a life-size self-portrait in which Abramović presents herself as her dual or divided self. In the first part, she is dressed in a white topcoat, and acts as a scientist-zoologist who tells the story of the creation of wolf-rats in the Balkans, animals that, when placed in un-bearable conditions (like humans in war), begin to destroy each other. In the second part, she is transformed into a woman — a "typical" Balkan tavern singer who amuses the (male) audience — dancing, as if possessed, to the sounds of a folk melody, originating from eastern Serbia and Romania. On her left and right, there are video portraits of her mother and father. This structure consisting of three parts opens up the possibility of being read as an iconostasis, or rather as a "kinetic iconostasis," as suggested by Annette Michelson's analysis of Dziga Vertov's film *Three Songs of Lenin* (1934).[18] On the iconostasis, the sanctuary screen dividing the Earth (narthex) and Heaven (altar) zones in the church, exactly above the Royal Door, there is an icon of the Savior flanked by the Mother of God on his right, and St. John the Baptist on his left. This composition is called Deesis. The Savior and the Mother of God are seen here as mediators between heaven and earth, while the iconostasis itself is located on the boundary line and connects/divides the human and the divine. In frescoes, which allow wider narration, Deesis is always painted in the images of Judgment Day, prior to which the Mother of God begs her son not to be too strict a judge.

How is it at all possible to recognize in this work of art, which I have so far read as one that can be recognized as belonging to one spiritual tradition, something belonging to the Baroque, the other tradition that is considered "imported" to the Balkans? Baroque, as the art of the Counter-Reformation, could not find much fertile ground in Christian Orthodox countries, paranoically allergic to Catholicism and all that originates from it. The Baroque layer in this work by Marina Abramović may be viewed through Walter Benjamin's optics: "The Baroque apotheosis is a dialectical one. It is accomplished in the movement between extremes."[19] In respect to Benjamin, I tend to read *Balkan Baroque* as *Trauerspiel,* a theater play originating in German Baroque, in which Benjamin situates his concept of the "allegorical mind." In Baroque, as it is well known, an absolutist maxim was in force: "Do everything for the people, nothing with the help of people." These theater plays, created during the Thirty Years' War, were often said "to have been written by animals for animals." However, Benjamin says that to contemporaries, people living in the seventeenth century, these theater plays looked "completely natural, because they reflected the image of their own lives." Benjamin claims that the favorite source of material for these plays was the history of the East, where they could find—especially in the Byzantine empire founded on theocracy—"the absolute power of the emperor, developed to a degree unknown to the West." Hence, we should not be suprised that in Louis XIV's France, Byzantine historians were discovered and translated. The German tragic drama *Trauerspiel,* as its name suggests (*Spiel:* play; *Trauer:* mourning or grief), does not originate from Classical Greek tragedy, but stems from medieval mystery plays and from Christian themes of mortification of the flesh. Such theater plays reflect "on the tragedy of the human embodiment, and hence on the dual life of humans (both animal and divine, fleshly and spiritual)."[20]

The self-portrait with parents contains three video images that are reflected in the surface of the water that fills Abramović's three copper sculptures, vessels which suggest some form of spiritual purification. The act of purification is also present in a more dramatic way in the performance in which the artist cleans animal bones for hours, scraping the last bits of meat from them. This purification "to the bone," as suggested by the expression itself, this clearing away of ballast (beautiful or ugly, pleasant or unpleasant, personal and collective), becomes an individualized work of mourning, without which no rite of passage can occur. Without this it is not possible to create, imagine, or hope for the future, without a feeling of hatred.

Notes

1. Cf. René Grémaux, "Woman Becomes Man in the Balkans," in Gilbert Herdt, ed., *Third Sex, Third Gender* (New York: Zone Books, 1994), pp. 241–81.

2. I found the following information after my text was published in 1997: As soon as *The Merry Widow* was released in France, the prince of Montenegro, Danilo Petrović, brought charges against the American producer because of the insult, and won in the court proceeding. See Dejan Kosanović and Dinko Tucaković, *Stranci u raju (Strangers in Paradise: Foreigners in Yugoslav Films, Yugoslavs in Foreign Films)* (Belgrade: Stubovi kulture, 1998), p. 85.

3. The old Venetian Republic used to be called La Serenissima.

4. Cf. Želimir Košćević, *Venice Biennale and Yugoslav Modern Art 1895–1988* (Zagreb: Galerije Grada Zagreba, 1988).

5. See *Kruh i ruže,* Fall 1993. Zagreb: Ženska infoteka, back cover.

6. Cf. Goranka Matić, *Days of Grief and Pride,* a photographic album (Belgrade: Vreme Knjige, 1995), no pagination.

7. Boris Yeltsin, speech at a meeting of "Democratic Russia," Moscow, June 1, 1991, quoted in Krishan Kumar, "The End of Socialism? The End of Utopia? The End of History?" in Krishan Kumar and Stephen Bann, eds., *Utopias and the Millennium* (London: Reaction Books, 1993), p. 63.

8. Benedict Anderson, *Imagined Communities* (London and New York: Verso, 1983); quote is from the second edition, published in 1991, p. 7.

9. Bruce King, quoted by Timothy Brennan, "The National Longing for Form," in Homi K. Bhabha, ed., *Nation and Narration* (London and New York: Routledge, 1994), p. 53.

10. Petar Čuković, "Monadi Mediterranée," in *I punti dell'arte moderna montenegrina* (Rome: Palazzo degli Esposizioni, 1996), pp. 3 and 4.

11. See *Pobjeda,* Podgorica, March 19, 1997.

12. Slavoj Žižek, "Taking Sides — A Self-Interview," in S. Žižek, *The Metastasis of Enjoyment* (London and New York: Verso, 1994), p. 212.

13. Gayatri Chakravorty Spivak, "Who Claims Alterity?" in Barbara Kruger and Phil Mariani, eds., Remaking History (Seattle: Bay Press, 1989), pp. 281 and 291.

14. Leszek Kolakowski, *Der Himmelsschlüssel* (Munich: R. Piper Verlag, 1965), p. 40. Polish original: *Klucz niebieski* (Warsaw: PIW, 1964).

15. Cf. Eric Alliez and Michel Feher, "Reflections of a Soul," in Michel Feher et al., eds., *Fragments for a History of the Human Body,* Pt. 2 (New York: Zone, 1989), pp. 47–84.

16. See Clement Greenberg, "Byzantine Parallels" (1957) in C. Greenberg, *Art and Culture* (Boston: Beacon Press, 1961), pp. 167–70.

17. See Bojana Pejić, "Living On: Video Lines," in Davor Matičević, ed., *Dalibor Martinis* (Zagreb: Museum of Contemporary Art, 1990), pp. 42–53.

18. See Annette Michelson, "The Kinetic Icon in the Work of Mourning: Prologomena to the Analysis of a Textual System" (Intertitles to *Three Songs of Lenin,* 1934), *October,* no. 52 (1990), pp. 16–39.

19. Walter Benjamin, *The Origin of German Tragic Drama* (London: New Left Books, 1977), p. 160. German original: *Der Ursprung des deutschen Trauerspiels* (Frankfurt am Main: Suhrkamp, 1978).

20. Bryan S. Turner, "Introduction," in Christina Buci-Glucksaman, *Baroque Reason* (London: Sage Publications, 1984), p. 8.

Written in 1997. Originally published in *New Moment* magazine (Belgrade), no. 7 (spring 1997). Translated by Vanja Smoje.

EKATERINA DEGOT

The Russian art historian, critic, and curator Ekaterina Degot was born in 1958 in Moscow. She held the position of cultural critic at the prominent Russian newspaper Kommersant *from 1993 to 2000. Currently she teaches at the Russian State University for the Humanities in Moscow and at the Pro Arte Institute in St. Petersburg. Her publications include a study of Russian Conceptual art and a book on contemporary Russian art, published in 2001, which brings together examples of Socialist Realist art and postwar neo-avant-garde art for the first time.*

In this essay, Degot assesses the intricate identities of Russian contemporary artists during the 1990s. Her particular focus is on the violent hostility of the artists Oleg Kulik and Alexander Brener as they confront the oppressive social system, the problem of cultural identity, and the rigid approach to artistic expression.

The Revenge of the Background[1]

As everywhere in the world, in Moscow's trendy magazines — mostly rave magazines, but also new art magazines, which don't differ so much from the former ones — texts are usually unreadable, nor are they intended to be read at all. The page can be printed all over with big psychedelic flowers, and the background seems integral and continuous under the tiny importunate letters which, apparently, only disturb the vital flow. The background thus takes its revenge on the text, or, to put it differently, on the art of the twentieth century which has become text. The Black Square or the modernist grid are literally put up against the background, censoring it while displaying it.

The 1990s were, at first glance, about body and performance, but this was — and still is — only part of the game. Having assumed the responsibility for the whole of the century, the nineties try to rehabilitate the Real, the Body, the Author, the Female, the Accidental — even the Failure and the Inarticulate — everything discriminated against in modernism, everything violated in its rights by the structure of representation. The art of the nineties proclaims "Ars brevis, vita longa" — re-reading Guy Debord's critique of "mere representation" as politically oppressive, commercializing, and aesthetically defective, nothing but an *ersatz* of what has been directly lived. The profound distrust of "cultural identities" as rigid, flat, and simulating leads to the discovery of something that lies behind them, something real and physical, more authentic: the background.

This aesthetic and political ecology — the representation of underrepresented — goes to extremes in the work of the Moscow artist Oleg Kulik who, for some years now, has been coming out against anthropocentrism with his maniacal "Zoophreny" project, in which he proposes to interbreed human beings with animals and to grant equal rights to the latter, including the right to vote. Founding the "Party of Animals," Kulik proclaims himself an animals' candidate for Russia's presidency. He mostly exposes himself as a dog, naked, chained up or gives speeches mooing like a cow, or imitates sex scenes with animals on video or in photographs.

Kulik's voiceless Other, of course, is Russia, which becomes obvious in his more explicitly political performances such as "I like Europe, Europe does not like me," presented in Berlin (1996), a performance in which his "alter ego," a dog, was surrounded by real German police dogs under the colors of United Europe. Contemporary Russian art belongs simultaneously to two equally powerful contexts — sharing all the problems of self-examination typical of the international art scene, it bears at the same time the whole burden of old Russian identity issues. In Russia, speaking about representation, about the "inward" and the "external," is inevitably speaking about Russia as opposed to the West, the West being the only reference and place to be represented when mentioning the unrepresented. When [it is] the unrepresentable, the reference is unavoidably to Russia.

In a brutal and naturalistic way, Kulik stages the classical Russian identity of that which is excluded, as formulated in the early nineteenth century: Russia is absent from the "Weltbild," since it entered the world scene too late to be embraced in the Hegelian panorama of history. Simplifying to an almost inadmissible degree, it could be said that the bitter discovery of this fact resulted in a reconsideration of values in which Russia was positively defined as something "logically different" — mysterious and incomparable. Confronted with that same problem of not-fitting-into-the-picture for the nth time in Russian history, Russian artists take the opportunity to explore the nationalist anti-Western issues which were rather alien and no challenge to most of the artists of the Conceptual generation. Seeing herself as a victim of representation, Russia does not feel so much underrepresented as overrepresented, or, to be more precise, violated by compulsory representation. "A lack of identity is better than an imposed identity," says Moscow artist Georgi Litichevski; another artist, Yuri Leiderman, points out that the West is always forcing Russia to have some "soil," some "ground," "which we must constantly tell them about." The Russian artist perpetually finds himself or herself between the Scylla and Charybdis of two representational mechanisms which are switched on automatically and ruthlessly. In Russia, where twentieth-century art with its ideology of individualism and unrestrained freedom is still a foreign phenomenon of invested dreams, being a "contemporary artist" means to represent Western culture (with all its connotations), as shown by mass-media shows in order to appear "up to date," more Western-like. In the West, on the other hand, a Russian artist must inevitably represent Russia. Western curators are almost never interested in him or her personally, but in having "an artist from Russia," best of all a typical one, i.e., a representative one, particularly one representing the political reality, chaos, and disruption.

A Russian artist can neither identify with the Western art scene (which is mostly reluctant to admit him or her) nor with Russia (being a Western-oriented intellectual and/or a Jew, which in Russia has always been almost the same). Moreover, in both cases he or she is a mere symptom, sharing the nineties general distrust of representation, signs, and symptoms. That is why he or she feels like a kamikaze of representation, crashed by the machine of symbol production. And to preserve himself or herself as a subject, he or she can find a way out only by becoming a virus, destroying the whole system.

This can explain the aggressive gestures of another leader of Moscow Actionism (besides Kulik), Alexander Brener, whose performances sometimes result in the destruction of another artist's works. What Brener is desperately destroying is, in fact, a whole system of cultural identities, a structure of conventions and expectations.

Brener repeats the crucial ideas of the Russian avant-garde of the 1910s when he writes with pathos: "The great Western system is coming to its end. The mighty architecture of hypocrisy . . . is perishing under the pressure of the hopelessly lying, corrupted newcomers from the East. Neither the Muslim world nor Russia can fit into the giant computer. They are incapable of either withdrawing quietly and with dignity or joining it with a cry of despair. So they have no choice but to destroy it." Now, in their quest for identity as otherness, Russian artists even try a controversial identification with the Islamic world, producing geopolitical phantasms such as the posters made by the AES group, representing European and American capitals in the twenty-first century conquered by hordes of Bedouins and covered by a multitude of mosques. Thus in Russian art the "ecological" project of liberating the repressed is less present than the "critical" one (the critique of the privileged image, of systems of oppression) or even the "terrorist" one in which the artist, as a new Luddite, violently destroys the representational machine, not necessarily physically, but verbally, by mooing like Kulik or by howling (the installation "After Postmodernism You Can Only Howl" by Anatoly Osmolovsky deafened the visitor with the loud recorded howling of artists whose photographic identities were shown in the same room).

This explains how the operative and socially interactive character of the art of the nineties is interpreted in Russia. While the international trend is for an artist to make a gesture of solidarity and intersubjectivity in a genuine, pure, almost simple-hearted way, an artist can offer candies to the visitors, invite them to his or her own flat reconstructed in the gallery, treat them to a foot massage, give a grant to another artist or a prize to a critic—Russian artists of the nineties, surprisingly, take this "aesthetics of conviviality" (according to French critic Nicolas Bourriaud) with a grain of bitter sarcasm. Sometimes they even turn it into the aesthetic of hostility and envy: Kulik bites; Brener throws a basin with water into the crowd and raw eggs into the audience who came to listen to his "sermon"; Gia Rigvava organizes a live TV show in which artists and critics are rudely interrupted by the interviewers; Alyona Martynova displays her self-portrait as a prostitute with a price list for her services, which help her to survive as an artist. Even newborn babies are shown pictures of aggression (a project by Ludmila Gorlova).

All these gestures have political connotations. It is obvious that the artists of the nineties criticize art as a commodity. Yet Western artists, in their communicating gestures, refer to commerce and economics, organizing fake (and real) institutions, enterprises, and dialogues, while the art of their Russian colleagues is exclusively about power and language as power, which is anti-economical. Never in her history has Russia had an economic identity; she is connected to the rest of the world in a purely political way—with politics understood as terror and domination, not as a parliamentary system of representation. "True democracy is the law of the jungle," proclaims Kulik. In a project by Dmitri Gutov for the Interpol show, artists and curators were to unveil their mutual resentment and to abuse each other at a pre-opening dinner; the episode was to be recorded on video and displayed together with the leftovers of the food. The transparent exchange of images and ideas is over; what reigns here is decay, Bataille's "crachat," where analysis is no longer of any use.

New Russian art transcends aesthetic ecology; it is inwardly, almost suicidally, critical. Being extremely critical to logocentricism, it is still irreducibly logocentric even when it works with the body, since exhibitionist gestures are nothing but a desperate attempt to overcome the development of discourse. We have arrived at an inflation of words (so obvious on the pages of the art magazines conquered by the background, which makes the text unnecessary) and an inflation of artistic means. If Moscow Conceptualism, with its minimalist origins, was the art of the time of "deficit," the new Moscow scene can be called the art of "inflation," of opaque economy, of the decay of illusions. What remains, however, is the question of which way this art is influenced by the fact that in a poor and backward country like present-day Russia, there are no structures and no institutions for contemporary art, and of what general importance this art can be. But Russia has always seen herself as a living prophecy of the world's destiny, and so do the artists. In some respects, they are right: in a sense, the scene of the nineties all over the world prefers to produce the discourse of resentment and of pariahs, no matter what the real economic situation is like. And when everybody is "the Other," there is no place even for the comforting thought of structure. As Bataille once more says, "Intellectual despair culminates neither in cowardice nor in dreaming, but in violence."

Note

1. The grid (that Rosalind Krauss has written about in her famous essay) or the Black Square, these emblems of modernism, seem to liberate art from its representational function, but at the same time are nothing but representations of the surface of the picture or of the square frame of its background, which thus plays the role of "nature." This rupture between signifier and signified within the same work, which never occurred in art history before, is inherent to the aesthetics of modernism, which sees every work of art as a text, and to its ideology, which consists in an "elitist" approach. This structure, the structure of a sign, or, to put it differently, the structure of alienation, is precisely what the artist of the 1990s is reluctant about, finding it far too mechanical and discriminating. Any language, from this point of view, is repressive.

Written in 1997. Originally published in Silvia Eiblmayr, ed., *Zones of Disturbance* (Graz: Steirischer Herbst, 1997).

CASE STUDY: EAST AGAINST WEST

The following texts were written in the aftermath of the *Interpol* exhibition held at the Färgfabriken Centre for Contemporary Art and Architecture in Stockholm in 1996. The exhibition was conceived by Jan Åman, Director of Färgfabriken, and by Russian critic and curator Viktor Misiano. The show, planned over a two-year period, was intended to encourage a dialogue between artists from both the East and the West. It was felt that since the fall of the Berlin Wall in 1989 the cultures on either side of it had failed to reconcile the disparities between them and that this exhibition would help to deal with the issue. However, the show became notorious for the surprising and—to some—offensive actions carried out by two artists during the opening festivities.

One of the artists, Oleg Kulik, performed as a dog chained to a doghouse. He claimed that spectators kicked him, and he reacted to the aggression by attacking them. Kulik was eventually arrested at the scene for biting several people during the opening. The other artist, Alexander Brener, stopped his performance piece suddenly and destroyed the installation of the artist Wenda Gu, which was installed nearby. These actions, unbeknownst to the curators, artists, and guests present, were all the while encouraged by the Russian curator of the show, Viktor Misiano.

The destruction of Gu's artwork and the violent behavior by Kulik obviously caused a flurry of reactions, many of them documented here. The first example is a letter of protest signed by many of the artists in the exhibition and some members of the press. They condemn the actions of both artists as a desecration of the purpose of the show—to open a dialogue on equal terms between East and West. The second letter, a rebuttal by Viktor Misiano, alleges that the authors of *An Open Letter to the Art World* cannot accept the catastrophic actions by Kulik and Brener because, blinded by their own ideology, they misconstrued the artists' actions as totalitarian and fascistic.

That same year, Kulik was slated to participate in the *Manifesta I* exhibition in Rotterdam with his performance as a dog. Due to the scandal surrounding the *Interpol* calamity, the curators in Rotterdam asked Kulik to offer a public explanation of his work to help substantiate his intent. The text, entitled "Why Have I Bitten a Man?" suggests that his aggression was merely a reaction and a symbol of the futility and irrelevance of East-West communications.

Wenda Gu, in his essay "The Cultural War," takes a more measured approach to the situation. Although his work was destroyed by Brener, Gu disavows those who oppose Brener because he violated the work of a fellow artist. Gu understands Brener's artistic statement on a higher level, but posits that his act was not successful in subverting the system as he had hoped.

The final essay in this case study is by Igor Zabel, who is Curator of the Moderna Galerija in Ljubljana. It was written one year after the *Interpol* exhibition and reflects on the problematic rhetoric between East and West, in the art world and in other areas of society. Zabel indicates that the shifting identities of East and West during the cold war and afterward reveal a power struggle on both sides, and concludes that there is no parity between East and West, but rather another period in which the "other" is repositioned.

—Clay Tarica

An Open Letter to the Art World

We would like to inform you about what happened at the opening night of the exhibition *Interpol*—a global network from Stockholm and Moscow on February 2, 1996, at the Färgfabriken Centre for Contemporary Art and Architecture in Stockholm.

I. Fact: The Interpol Scandal

Alexander Brener, Oleg Kulik, and the Russian curator Viktor Misiano were part of the *Interpol* project, a collaborative exhibition based on the idea of network and exchange, which opened at the Färgfabriken in Stockholm on February 2. Their intervention in the show, after two years of preparation, took the form of deliberate acts of destruction—physical, mental, and ideological aggression—directed against the show, the other artists in the show, the visitors, and against art and democracy.

For Oleg Kulik's performance, he played the role of a chained, dangerous dog, and physically attacked visitors (who were seriously shocked and hurt). He also blocked circulation around the show, and began to destroy artworks by other artists, mainly those by Wenda Gu (China/USA) and Ernst Billgren (Sweden).

Alexander Brener stopped in the middle of his opening drum performance, and totally destroyed the main, central installation of the exhibition, a twenty-meter-long tunnel of human hair, made by the Chinese/American artist Wenda Gu.

The opening was turned into total chaos, with large numbers of visitors being mentally shocked, and some physically hurt.

Brener's and Kulik's brutality was unexpected, and contradicted the intentions they had declared to the Swedish curator before the opening. Kulik was to perform as a dog, but the emphasis was on endurance. He would react only when and if provoked. Brener had declared that he had left art to become a "rock star" and wanted to do a drum performance.

On the day after the opening, during a press conference organized by Färgfabriken, the Russian curator of the show, Viktor Misiano, described and legitimized this destruction as dynamic artistic action, which he also called "a new experience" in the catalogue. Alexander Brener, for his part, said that the exhibition had no reason to exist, since it was the "art of slaves," and that he was satisfied with his action.

2. Warning

Through this open letter we want to inform the art world (artists, critics, curators, institutions) of the consequences of collaboration with these people, and to help them see that:

1. What happened at this show reveals the true nature of what Misiano calls "a completely new experience."

2. Misiano is using theory to legitimize a new form of totalitarian ideology. His discourse plays with and uses the discourse of art, but in fact has nothing to do with art theory. It is what we would call hooliganism and skinhead ideology. His ultimate ambition is destruction and chaos, in the name of "the new experience." He wants to destroy the art world, since "the only reason for art to exist today is the debate about the destruction of the art world."

3. We want to inform Hans Ulrich Obrist, Andrew Renton, Rosa Martinez, and Katalin Neray of the *Manifesta* team of curators (Misiano declares in the *Interpol* catalogue that the other curators of the *Manifesta* "have positively accepted" Misiano's own idea that a curator must "create the new experience")—and we want to inform everyone else in contact with these three people that they are involved in a direct attack against art, democracy, and freedom of expression.

This attitude denies every possibility of dialogue between the (former) East and the West. It is a speculative and populistic attitude that cannot be accepted as a basis for dialogue. Brener and Kulik do not accept or respect the opinions or expressions of others: They do not even accept the work of fellow artists.

Using this alibi of the discourse about the final step in art, Brener is willing to occupy a position as a curator's artist who denies the possibility of art today. Brener, Kulik, and Misiano also represent an attitude that excludes female artists.

To carry out these attacks on the art world at an alternative, independent new art space in Stockholm—peripheral to the main art world—cannot be interpreted as anything other than following the classical model of imperialist behavior. Why didn't this happen in the Russian Pavilion at the Venice Biennale this summer (curated by Viktor Misiano)?

3. Excerpts from the Catalogue

Brener writes: "I intended to become a dissident and deal out my blows in the dark, and not participate in a game which has already been lost. Maybe the football hooligans will prove to be my supporters, and not artists and intellectuals. I am prepared for this."

Misiano writes: "Artists should produce accidents. Otherwise nobody would pay any attention. How can you find the resources to pay any attention, any interest, to art after having read five pages of kidnapping, killing, corruption, murder? Of course this is imposing a specific condition on society and culture.

"So the critics are becoming artists themselves, working in the same way as the artists—like the artists that work in the streets as hooligans. They have to produce scandals!

"You have to accept this model of 'accidents.' And what must be communicated is a killer attitude.

"You should shock people, and you should give with your physical gestures and your physical presence some obvious visual synopsis of what they are experiencing. And they are experiencing terrible things. So you must be terrible."

Olivier Zahm, art critic living in Paris, chief editor of *Purple Prose*, France; Elein Fleiss, chief editor of *Purple Prose*, France; Jan Åman, curator (along with Misiano) of *Interpol*, director of Färgfabriken, Sweden; Catharina Ahlberg, Catti Lindahl, Thomas Lundh, Magnus af Petersens, Färgfabriken; Matthias Wagner K, artist participating in *Interpol*, Germany; Birgitta Muhr, artist participating in *Interpol*, Sweden/Germany; Wenda Gu, artist participating in *Interpol*, China/USA; Ionna Theocaropoullou, artist/architect participating in *Interpol*, Greece/USA; Ulrika Karlsson, artist/architect participating in *Interpol*, Sweden/USA; Dan Wolgers, artist participating in *Interpol*, Sweden; Ernst Billgren, artist participating in *Interpol*, Sweden; Bigert & Bergstrom, artist participating in *Interpol*, Sweden; Johannes Albers, artist participating in *Interpol*, Germany; Fredrik Wretman, artist, Sweden.

All the signatories to this open letter were physically present during the events in Stockholm.

Published in *SIKSI (SIKSI: The Nordic Art Review)* 11, no. 1 (spring 1996).

Response to an Open Letter to the Art World

Viktor Misiano

Interpol was considered an experiment. It was based on a dialogue between artists, on their collaboration and readiness to share the process of forming the exhibition. *Interpol* was to become a metaphor of the new Europe, where there is no more East and West but only independent subjects whose mutual attempts are aimed at the development of a new postideological order. *Interpol* was a project on democracy.

The project, identifying life and art, has resulted in a direct confrontation, both in art and life. *Interpol* participants have fiercely divided into two opposing groups: East and West have been constituted again. The action of Alexander Brener, who physically damaged the exhibition, became the symbolic core for one group. The action of Maurizio Cattelan, who transmitted quite a large amount of money as a prize to the magazine *Purple Prose,* became another group's core. In other words, in this project, devoted to the problem of communication, the East formed around the understanding of communication as a circulation of destruction and protest, and the West around its understanding as a circulation of money.

Then the letter appeared—a manifesto and a program of confrontation. This document is significant as it is a pure ideological fact: it was born out of ideological phobia.

Only ideology allows itself to manipulate terminology. Russian artists and the curator are accused of antidemocracy and totalitarism and also (several times and in public) of fascism. Obviously, though, the terms "extremism" and "anarchism" would have been much more appropriate here, as reflecting an individual protest and not mobilization of the masses. But "Russian anarchist" is probably too romantic a term, and ideology has to present a disgusting image of an enemy.

Ideology allows itself to use texts at will, to use their content and senses. Thus, quotations from my material in the catalogue, describing the Moscow scene's collisions with an analytic distance and even with some bitterness, were presented as a program of propaganda for the described subject.

Ideology misses contradictions. Could it be possible that the organizers of the exhibition had to wait for the opening, after more than two years of acquaintance, in order to understand that they had invited "Russian fascists"? In the letter they use extracts from the catalogue they had published themselves, i.e., they share the responsibility for the fascist propaganda. According to all rules of ideology, the more aggressive those contradictions are, the more aggressive is the tone of accusations.

Ideology sanctions confrontations: it doesn't take into account any individual dimension but only constitutes groups, mobilizes masses. Thus, nobody suggested to the Russian participants of *Interpol* that they sign this letter, though most of them do not identify themselves with the destructive gestures of Kulik and Brener. What's more, the Slovenian artists IRWIN were also excluded. This is ridiculous, Ljubljana is the West for Russians, but the logic of confrontation has dictated the Western sanction: Ljubljana is the East.

Ideology deprives any phenomenon of its heterogeneity. It presumes only something very schematic: its disclosure and disapproval. Thus, the letter was signed both by those who know neither the context of the project nor the contexts of the Moscow art scene, nor the works of the three "enemies of mankind," and by those who know, or ought to know, and who can say something more than to give it the label "fascist." Analysis is substituted here by rhetoric. Ideology also contradicts any fruitful polemics: the logic of writing places you either on this or that side of the barricades. You have to be either with Brener and Kulik (even if it contradicts your ideas) or escape to another side, having made an expiatory gesture *mea culpa* (even if it also contradicts your ideas). There could be no third way.

That's why the letter, distributed by the Western participants, evokes only one association in Eastern minds—well known from their childhood: the pogrom ideological texts of Stalin's era.

When do the ghosts of the past start to haunt us? When something is wrong in our present. When does the West have to invent the East? When the West doesn't feel very secure. In fact, nothing that happened in Stockholm can be understood without taking into consideration one obvious fact: *Interpol* had ended in catastrophe, besides or even before Brener and Kulik acted. No Russian (and not even Russian) work was realized, for organizational reasons. The exhibition didn't exist: it hadn't been made, it was destroyed. The programmed destruction of Brener and Kulik was a result and not the cause of the catastrophe (that doesn't justify their actions but only clarifies the context). Thus, the ideology of confrontation, as any ideology does, finalizes the events, disguising the reality.

Interpol was to become an experimental investigation of democracy. In this sense its catastrophic result is highly symptomatic and didactic. It unveiled the contradictions of new Eastern democracies, still very immature and uprooted, where there appears a single temptation: to try its fragility, test its borders. Brener's gesture is a conscious opposition to a classical liberal thesis that your own freedom shouldn't contradict another's freedom. *Interpol* has also shown the emptiness of the old Western democracy. It has demonstrated its total inability to resist something that is not regarded as democracy in a democratic way. *Interpol* showed the potential character of all prejudices that hide behind democratic rhetoric. That was the basis of Oleg Kulik's provocative action: performing as an aggressive chained dog. He, in fact, represented that image of Russia which is rooted in the Western collective subconscious.

Slavoj Žižek's words, spoken some time ago, could be regarded as a prophecy: "Sarajevo of today is Europe tomorrow." In fact, in the vacuum of democracy, conflict has become the most effective method of acquiring an identity. It becomes seductive for those who proclaim their otherness through aggressive manifestation. It becomes seductive also for those who resurrect the tradition of unmasking the *"mauvaise conscience"* and use the slogan *"continuer le combat"* in confrontation with this otherness. Identity, replacing frustration, returns will and integrity to an individual. So slow was the preparation for the project that the dream of its realization was shaken, the dates shifted, artists' projects were not presented, etc., so effectively and energetically did the vehicle of hatred work—thousands and thousands of copies of the denunciatory letter were sent daily all over the world. And the last thing, this confrontation exists in the context of an unspoken partnership: the confrontational scandal serves to promote both new names from Russia and new institutions from Stockholm.

The confrontational pathos of the authors' letter marks a new period of artistic dialogue between Russia and the West. I've witnessed the solidarity of the West with the underground of the Soviet age, then with the quick rise of Gorbachev's *perestroika*, and then with the infrastructure crisis of the transitional post-Soviet time. Each time the dialogue was unequal: it was built upon helping, sympathy, and correctness. Nowadays, all attempts to isolate and push Russian artists from the European scene mean only one thing: we are here already, in Europe, we are equal. Thus, confrontation is a European problem, and Europe needs to take responsibility. Here we can see a positive aspect of the negative experience of *Interpol*.

And the last thing. One should keep in mind that isolation and discreditation of a small group of Russian intellectuals who are ready for European dialogue is very dangerous and politically irresponsible. There are real fascists in Russia and, unfortunately, there are a lot of them. And if they come to power, we will be far from exchanging open letters.

Moscow, March 1996

Published in abbreviated form in *Flash Art International* 29, no. 188 (May–June 1996); complete version subsequently published in *SIKSI (SIKSI: The Nordic Art Review)* 11, no. 2 (summer 1996).

Why Have I Bitten a Man?

An open letter from Oleg Kulik

I am distressed that an absolute clearness of my performance "Dog House" (within the borders of *Interpol*) hasn't saved it from a wrong interpretation.

Why have I stood on all fours? Why have I become a dog?

My standing on hands and knees is a conscious falling-out of a human horizon, connected with a feeling of the end of anthropocentrism, with a crisis of not just contemporary art but contemporary culture on the whole. I feel its oversaturation of semiosis as my own tragedy, its too-refined cultural language that results in misunderstanding, estrangement, and people's mutual irritation.

I thought that in Russia one could feel these processes as nowhere else. I thought that we were Different, and the cause was inside us, in eternal ambitions of cultural superpower in the situation of insolvent actual cultural events. In Moscow I became a dog, I growled there and demonstrated a dog's devotion to an artist's ambitions. I was not going to export an artist's experience without a language outside the Muscovite context. But while getting to know the Western context, I found out that my program is applicable there as well. Art as an addition to a supermarket seems an impasse to me.

For me, human stopped being associated with the notions "alive," "feeling," and "understanding" and started to be associated with the notions "artificial" and "dangerous." I began to look for some basis outside human. But overhuman

Oleg Kulik. *Dog House.* 1996. Performance at Interpol, Färgfabriken Centre for Contemporary Art and Architecture, Stockholm. Courtesy the artist

for me is our bestial nature, which doesn't need any explanation from the outside.

I was invited to Stockholm by the curator of the exhibition, Jan Åman, and the artist Ernst Billgren, who proclaimed that within that project built upon communication, he preferred a dialogue with animals to a dialogue with people. I was invited as a dog, as a *readymade.* I was surprised how quickly they'd reacted to my "zoofrenic" image.

I came to Stockholm and was open to any variant and form of collaboration. To my surprise Ernst Billgren's ready work was waiting for me: he was not prepared for any kind of collaboration. So I was made to become something different from what I could have become in a dialogue. I became a "reservoir dog." Indifference, frenzy, and falsification were in the atmosphere of Färgfabriken—the initiator of the project on communication between East and West. This is what I have experienced together with my Muscovite friends, participants of *Interpol.* A work of art stopped becoming an act of communication, and only enforced alienation and misunderstanding between people. This is an endless loop.

In the exposition, nothing was left of the primary idea—neither of its sense (the idea of communication ended in rhetoric, to the practical desire of using different foundations of the support of contacts with Eastern Europe) nor of its practical idea (we witnessed how the organizers had miscarried the Moscow projects). Being in the first place an artist and only then a person on all fours, "a dog," it was unbearable to take part in a farce.

But that is not the case. For me art remains a zone of not-falsified, real values and notions. I can't reject this position. To keep my own authenticity I am ready to become a dog or a bird, an insect or a microbe.

In Stockholm I didn't bite just a person but the person who had ignored the sign "dangerous" beside my dog house. By my action I proclaimed one idea: keep away from communication, think about your own and the world's future. This turned out to be impossible.

Obviously I am ready to apologize to those who became victims of my action: I've done it personally in Stockholm and now I am ready to confirm it in writing.

I hope I wasn't too pathetic for a dog.

Originally published in Eda Čufer and Viktor Misiano, eds., *Interpol: The Art Show Which Divided East and West* (Ljubljana: Irwin; Moscow: Moscow Art Magazine, 2000). Translated by Neil Davenport.

The Cultural War

Wenda Gu

Interpol was the joint production of Viktor Misiano, the director of the Contemporary Art Center in Moscow, and Jan Åman, the director of the Centre for Contemporary Art and Architecture in Stockholm. Two years ago they began a dialogue about the physical and psychological separation of the Berlin Wall, whose demise has not eliminated the differences between the larger political, social, and ideological structures of the East and the West. Instead, it intensifies the direct confrontation and reveals the psychological wall which is more difficult to surpass. *Interpol* was an international exhibition meant to address this phenomenon in art.

Initially the curators chose artists from Sweden and Russia. The international participants were invited later. As a Chinese who has been living in New York for eight years, my role was as a third party working in between the two groups. I have a special sensitivity toward these kinds of conflicts because of my past and present experiences with both socialism and capitalism. The Russian artists, under the direction of their curator, Misiano, frequently attempted to conceptually control the planning of the whole exhibition, and even the show's catalogue. Evidently, it reflected the ambition of these Russian artists, who, from a collapsed superpower nation, the former Soviet Union, still have a somewhat twisted notion of their former strength. Comparatively, the Swedish artists, who live in a privileged social democracy, have never really experienced hardship and tragedy, not even during World War II. Because of these disparate experiences, the two groups approach theoretical dialogues from completely different perspectives. At the time of the show's planning, I was wondering how to represent these conflicts behind the two groups. The Moscow meeting let the romantic Swedish artists understand how they were in the shadow of Russian aggression. They felt that the artistic dialogue and the theoretical collaboration were just a pretense and a reflection of the political, cultural, and economic power game.

I decided to construct a pure hair tunnel made of Russian and Swedish hair which had been collected from barbershops since July 1995. In the middle of the tunnel, I suspended a genuine rocket, loaned to me by the Royal Swedish Army. The visual impression was that of running through the long, narrow hair tunnel as a hint of using military action to control the cultural battle. I wanted this work to stand as a referee of cultural confrontation. As Alexander Brener began playing his drums and screaming at the opening, I paid special attention to him, as I was videotaping the performance. I realized that he was not emotionally engaged with his playing. Rather, he was watching the crowd's behavior and was paying close attention to my every move. I then left the exhibition space momentarily to meet friends in an adjacent part of the building. One minute later, a German artist ran up to me shouting that my work had been destroyed by Brener. I followed him back to the show to find the audience of about one thousand shocked into absolute silence, staring at my piece. At that moment, I was very emotional; I had never experienced this kind of situation before. The work looked like a place after a terrorist bombing. In a few minutes the audience regained its composure; people called news reporters and local radio and TV stations, while the Center notified the police. The French art critic Olivier Zahm screamed, "This is absolutely a neofascist action!" The other French writer, Elein Fleiss, came to me and stated that if I would like to file a lawsuit, she would be a witness. When the police arrived, they arrested the other Russian artist who had been playing a chained, naked dog, attempting to attack and bite a two-year-old baby. Some audience members actually kicked him in the face. Meanwhile, Brener had fled the scene.

Some people have predicted that the essence of the twenty-first century will be the conflicts among nations, races, and cultures. But cultural conflicts have always been a part of human civilization; bloody religious wars are obvious examples. Historically, cultural "battles" were hidden behind gentlemanly intellectual discussions and controlled by geographical separation. To paraphrase a Chinese idiom, we can now "fight at close quarters; engage in hand-to-hand combat. We can speak frankly, not mincing our words." This is our migratory cultural reality. At a press conference the following day, I pointed out that the incident was not personal—I saw this "performance" as a mirror reflecting a political and economical power game. I did not want to label the actions as neofascist or neonationalistic, as in art we need to analyze events on different levels. The actual action was a "crime." On an artistic level, it was a repetition of old Dada ideology. On a purely ideological level, it relates to deep historical, cultural, social, and political backgrounds. The artists and Misiano are not neofascists; they are Russian Jews who are not embraced by Russian nationalists in their own country. In the Western artistic circuit, Misiano is well respected as a scholar and organizer. Yet within his own country, he encourages artists to act with aggression. Their ideology and actions abroad have many links to nationalism and Communism—the latter of which has many tendencies similar to Nazism, with an inherent dictatorial format.

The mind-set of Brener reflects the reality of Russia today—politically, economically, and socially degenerated, a chaotic, frustrated society. In the past,

Wenda Gu. *United Nations Sweden & Russia.* 1996. Site-specific installation for Interpol, Färgfabriken Centre for Contemporary Art and Architecture, Stockholm. Hair, Swedish Royal Airforce rocket, and European Community flag, 6'12 × 7 × 10' (25.6 × 2.1 × 3 m). Photograph after its destruction by Alexander Brener. Courtesy the artist

Russia has played as a superpower; now, due to its current environment, its great confidence has dissipated. The Swedes find their actions inconceivable, but having come from Communist China to the United States, I can understand it from both perspectives. These well-known Russian artists went against Communism with pride. With the downfall of Communism, these heroes lost their target of attack.

They shifted their attentions to the power structure of Western materialism. On the other hand, they hate being subservient. This kind of irresolvable predicament is their ideological base. The Russian artist Dimitri Gutov repeatedly said to me, "I hate Russia today and I hate contemporary art." But he is a representative of Russian contemporary art, so this is a paradox. Interestingly, the criticism of this incident from the European community was more theoretical. But an American point of view offers simply one answer: process a lawsuit and put him in jail.

On an artistic level, Brener's action has no significance. The old Dadaists threatened to destroy all art museums, but ironically, after fifty years, the museum system not only has not disappeared, it is also the goal for most artists. Brener had not come to terms with this separation of ideology versus fruition as he blindly acted out old Dadaist concepts. Was his intent to mimic acts of such predecessors as Marcel Duchamp, Piero Manzoni, or the more contemporary Jeff Koons? If so, where is the sophisticated subversion and "silent violence" of the toilet, cans of shit, and pornographic photos? Destructive happenings have occurred in the past which now appear as insignificant and only for the sake of publicity. Brener has not considered the sophistication of today's media: his old-fashioned shock tactics will be dismissed. Instead of addressing his actions, he immediately fled the scene. He doesn't have the guts of the terrorists who sacrifice themselves for their beliefs. In our reality, art stands for freedom and is regulated by democracy. These counterparts direct human development.

Misiano said that this incident creates an essential stage for the dialogue between Eastern and Western Europe. I believe his words make some sense. But we still have the responsibility of knowledge, basic humanity, and common destiny. From his words, as a human, Misiano loses his basic position; as an intellectual, he loses his responsibility. There were many people from the audience who came to me expressing their sorrow. I repeatedly replied to them that I interpreted Brener's "destruction" as a "special participation" in my global art project. One Russian artist came to me inquiring if the art center had any insurance. A Slovenian artist said, "If you can get money from the insurance company, you can use it to sponsor Misiano's wife's art magazine and these Russian artists." While still deliberating over the incident itself and recognizing their blind lust for gain, I could only respond with a laugh. For the sake of my global project, I said to Brener, "Thank you for your 'collaboration' and have a good trip back to Moscow." Misiano came to me and said, "I remember there was a postage stamp with a picture: Stalin and Mao are shaking hands—Russian and Chinese are great friend." The *Interpol* incident has left ice-cold relations between the Swedish, international, and Russian artists. My installation bears witness to this cultural war.

Originally published in *Flash Art International* 29, no. 189 (summer 1996).

Dialogue

Igor Zabel

In September 1994, the Russian artist Ilya Kabakov spoke at the AICA Congress in Stockholm. He was describing his experience of a "culturally relocated person." One of the aspects of Western culture he was interested in was the permanent tendency to criticize, provoke, and even destroy within this culture. He compared his experience of this tendency to the experience of an orphan living in a children's home who is visiting the family of his friend. This friend is sick of his home, and his behavior is aggressive and insulting, while the visitor himself sees a totally different picture: a nice home and kind and intelligent parents. But there is another thing that is essential: the friend's family is strong enough that it is not in danger because of the boy's outbursts. The same is true of Western culture, says Kabakov, and continues: "Western culture is so vital, so stable, its roots are so deep and so alive, it is so productive that it, speaking in the language of the parable above, absorbs, recasts, and dissolves in itself all destructive actions by its own 'children,' and as many believe, it sees in these actions its very own development—what is elegantly referred to here as 'permanent criticism.' But I would like to add a footnote here: this criticism, like the destruction itself, is permitted, if it can be so expressed, only from its own children. That same mom described above would have behaved quite differently if I had started to act up at the table the same way as her son. Most likely she would have called the police."[1]

It did not take too long, less than a year and a half, for the event Kabakov was somehow predicting really happened. It took place during the opening of an exhibition called *Interpol* in the Färgfabriken Centre for Contemporary Art in Stockholm; an exhibition trying to establish "a global network" between Stockholm and Moscow. One of the participants, the Russian performance artist Alexander Brener, destroyed a work of another participant, the Chinese-American artist Wenda Gu; and another Russian artist, Oleg Kulik, who appeared in the show as a dangerous dog on a chain, who actually bit some people, was attacked by the audience and was later taken away by the police.

There have been a lot of discussions (and even more rumors and gossip) about the *Interpol* scandal. I believe that the affair is so attractive because it is not just another scandal in the art world. It implies an extremely serious question: the relationship between East and West, and it indicates that the relationship is far from idyllic. I believe that it was not the intervention of the police which had made this tension explicit (after all, one should expect such intervention) but "An Open Letter to the Art World,"[2] (see pp. 345–47) signed by a group of artists and other participants of the show (all from the West) and broadly distributed. What is surprising is the fact that the letter was written and signed by artists and critics whose position is essentially based on the tradition of "permanent criticism," referred to by Kabakov. Of course, they were not necessarily expected to agree with Kulik's and Brener's actions, but one would at least think they would be more careful in the way they criticize them, since the tradition of twentieth-century art offers a number of examples of aggressive, destructive, and subversive actions which have, by now, attained a status of historical or even canonical fact.

Some examples of destroying other artists' works are now considered to be major points in the development of modern art. (Immediately I can think of at least two examples: the best known is, perhaps, [Robert] Rauschenberg's *Erased de Kooning;* another is the so-called Wolfsburg Affair from October 1961: "At the opening of the exhibition *Junge Stadt sieht junge Kunst,* Arnulf Rainer paints over the etching *Mond und Figuren II* by Helga Pape, which had won second prize, with black paint and attaches a label with the inscription: 'Painted over by Arnulf Rainer.' Rainer is arrested and sentenced to a fine for willfully damaging a work of art.")[3] The "Open Letter," however, is not simply a protest against the two Russian artists and their actions; it attacks them, as well as the Russian curator Viktor Misiano, with direct but, at the same time, very general and imprecise *political* accusations: "a new form of totalitarian ideology," "hooliganism and skinhead ideology," "a direct attack against art, democracy, and the freedom of expression," "speculative and populistic attitude," "classical model of imperialistic behavior," "attitude that excludes female artists." In short, the "Open Letter" treats the destructive actions of both Russian artists as being eminently political rather than artistic statements.

One could easily dismiss the "Open Letter" as ridiculous and reactionary since it lacks any precise analysis and reflection and because its criticism (as well as the position and the values this criticism implies) is just a set of phrases. I believe, however, that we have to understand this letter as a kind of "slip," i.e., that we have to recognize its symptomatic value; and it is this value that makes it so very interesting. One has to ask oneself: what made a group of artists and critics who (at least some of them) ascribe to a line of critical and subversive art, write a letter (and distribute it all over the world) in such a style which could easily be used by a representative of any conservative or totalitarian system? What made them blind to the style and form of their own writing? What made them directly and roughly denounce the artists (as well as the curator who was trying to understand the destructive actions as artistic statements) as being politically incorrect and against art, democracy, freedom of expression, and women— only because they did something which is well established in the tradition of twentieth-century art as a legitimate means of artistic expression, however radical and problematic?[4]

I do not believe that those who have signed the letter consider Rauschenberg and Rainer to be "hooligans," "skinheads," and "enemies of art, democracy, and freedom of expression." We must, therefore, conclude that Brener's action must be seen in an important aspect different from, say, Rainer's. And since they have done exactly the same thing: destroying the work of a fellow artist at the opening of a group show, the difference has to lie elsewhere. I believe that Kabakov is, with his "footnote," indicating the correct answer to this question: the Russians do not belong to the "family." Rainer's action is included in a certain code where it has a precisely determined meaning and value; on the other hand, the position of Brener's action seems to be at the point where two codes clash. Thus, his action could not be legitimized by the code that it was actually questioning and attacking.

There are two sentences in the "Open Letter" that I find essential: "This attitude denies every possibility of dialogue between the (former) East and the West. It is a speculative and populistic attitude that cannot be accepted as a basis for dialogue." Something has been made very clear here. Brener and Kulik are not two individual artists. They are not even Russians; they represent "the East"— politically correctly called "the (former) East." The "Open Letter" makes clear that the problematic point of the *Interpol* scandal is not the behavior of individual artists. Brener, Kulik, and Misiano only represent an "attitude," which actually is the "attitude" of the East. This coincides with the fact reported by Misiano, that only Western artists were invited to sign the letter: "Nobody suggested to the Russian participants of *Interpol* that they sign this letter, though most of them do not identify themselves with the destructive gestures of Kulik and Brener. What's more, the Slovenian artists IRWIN were also excluded. This is ridiculous. Ljubljana is the West for Russians, but the logic of confrontation has dictated the Western sanction: Ljubljana is the East."[5]

Interpol was obviously more than just a group show. Its main problem was not a network between different artists and different artistic attitudes and practices. The show was about the West-East dialogue. And actually, the result of the "scandal" at the opening was a sharp division and confrontation between Eastern and Western artists. The show, says Misiano in the same text, "was to become a metaphor of the new Europe [and] a new postideological order (where there is no more East and West)." Nevertheless, the confrontation remains. The East is still the East, although it is now called "the former East." (Does anybody speak about "the former West"?) The idea of a global network in the postideological new Europe, a model (presumably) replacing the topography of the East-West division, proved to be a veil covering the actual conflicts and confrontations. Even more, such rhetoric can actually serve as a means in such a conflict. A conflict, that is, which is essentially based on the will to establish a dominant position in the discourse and thus in the practice itself.

A dialogue is only possible on a certain common basis which both parties in the dialogue accept. For example, if I want to discuss something with somebody, the meanings of the words we use have to be established and clear to both of us. The quoted sentences from the "Open Letter" make clear that it was exactly on this level, the level of accepting a common basis, that the West-East dialogue had failed. The Easterners did not accept the terms of the dialogue, which were supposed to be "natural" for the Westerners. By not accepting these terms, Brener, Kulik, and Misiano (representing the East) deny "every possibility of dialogue between the (former) East and the West," since their own attitude "cannot be accepted as a basis for dialogue." I believe that one of the best descriptions of these problems was given by Lewis Carroll in *Through the Looking Glass:*

> "When I use a word," Humpty Dumpty said, in rather a scornful tone, "it means just what I choose it to mean — neither more nor less."
> "The question is," said Alice, "whether you can make words mean so many different things."
> "The question is," said Humpty Dumpty, "which is to be master — that's all."[6]

Thus, one could perhaps say that the struggle for a dialogue, or better, the struggle for the terms of a dialogue, represents the struggle for the position of the master.

The *Interpol* scandal demonstrated that the West-East division persists and that it was not surpassed with the fall of the Communist regimes. Furthermore, this division is clearly not confined to the area of art. As the ideological oppositions between the capitalist and the socialist systems are no longer functional, it has been replaced, for example, with the idea of the "clash of civilizations." Again, I believe that at the basis of this "clash" lies the struggle over the most basic, "human," and "natural" issues which themselves correspond to a certain power structure. For example, Samuel P. Huntington,[7] who has introduced the idea of the "clash of civilizations," also describes how the West ensures its domination by presenting its interests as the interests of the "world community" and how it presents its own fundamental values as universal, while in fact they are not valid within most other civilizations. Of course, one may assume that the concept of a world consisting of basically different (and often hostile) civilizations also corresponds to a certain strategy of power and control. The idea of the "clash of civilizations" is actually more than just an attempt at a neutral description of the contemporary world. It introduces a certain system of interpretation and representation, which is directly applicable in the international policy. One could, for example, notice how important American specialists in foreign affairs started to use Huntington's terms in describing conflict areas such as Bosnia.

The East-West "conflict," as far as art is concerned, develops in an essential aspect on the level of the fight for codification of the field and thus for its domination. It is this codification which determines the terms of the dialogue or, as Humpty Dumpty has said, which chooses their meaning.

The sharp political division between the East and the West during the cold war period also implied a confrontation of two artistic models: the modernist art in the West and the Socialist Realism in the East. Western art has presented itself as the "natural" development of genuine art as opposed to the politically suppressed art of Socialist Realism and its derived forms, which was not supposed to be genuine art but simply political propaganda. In light of this understanding, Eastern artists have been understood as a kind of underdeveloped and suppressed Western artists, and it was thought that they would immediately join the general developments in the West if they would be free to do so.

The identification of Western art of this century with modern art as such (this identification was actually a part of the "Western universalism," as it is described by Huntington) introduced a subtle dialectic of domination. The essential success of this dialectic lies in the fact that it was, to a great extent, accepted by Eastern artists themselves. Modern art was thus located in the West. But, as Western art is universal, Eastern artists also belong to the same idiom; however, they form only its periphery. All the constitutive structures, institutional, conceptual, and commercial, are located in the West. Thus they are controlled by it. The East more or less accepts (with some delay) and repeats the main currents of Western art. (I remember a participant at the CIMAM Congress in Dubrovnik in 1987, who directly said that *all* the important modern art was produced in the West and none in the East.) The function of Eastern modernism, inside this constellation, thus was often not to represent an autonomous statement and position but to serve as a confirmation of the original Western artist or particular movement. In her article "Abstract Expressionism, Weapon of the Cold War," Eva Cockcroft describes an example of using innovative Eastern art for strengthening the position of the West, regardless of the actual role and meaning of this art inside its original context: "During the post-Stalin era in 1956, when the Polish government under Gomułka became more liberal, Tadeusz Kantor, an artist from Kraków, impressed by the work of Pollock and other abstractionists which he had seen during an earlier trip to Paris, began to lead the movement away from Socialist Realism in Poland. Irrespective of the role of this art movement within the internal artistic evolution of Polish art, this kind of development was seen as a triumph for 'our side.' In 1961 Kantor and fourteen other nonobjective Polish painters were given an exhibition at the MoMA [Museum of Modern Art]. Examples like this one reflect the success of the political aims of the international programs of MoMA."[8]

Such a constellation permits a very limited acceptance of Eastern artists into the central "area" of art. An average Eastern artist has, in his effort to produce modern art, remained a kind of "incompletely realized Western artist," and thus a second-class artist. (It was, of course, only natural that the "Second World" produces second-rate art.) Most often, the Eastern artists who have succeeded in the West are those who have actually moved there and became its integral part. Still, some Eastern artists have reached a certain international response, partly due to their quality and the genuine interest of some Western critics and curators, but also because they could serve as evidence of the universal value of modern art and, as mentioned above, as an affirmation of the Western artists and artistic developments. Nevertheless, the codification of the field and the construction of its history and tradition resulted in a marginalization or total ignorance of important Eastern phenomena. For example, Eastern avant-garde artists of the sixties and early seventies simply do not exist in historical surveys of art of this time, except those who have moved to the West.

Establishing itself as the center, West has also established itself as a general reference point. East-East communication, inasmuch as it has existed at all, has been running via the West. This was even present in the recent project, the *Europa-Europa* exhibition, at the Bundeskunsthalle in Bonn. I found this show very important for presenting a number of lesser-known or unknown artists and works. (Among others, it made us aware of the fact that certain important achievements of, say, Carl Andre, Barnett Newman, and others were preceded for more than half a century by the works of artists like Alexander Rodchenko, Olga Rozanova, and others.) Still, the criteria for selecting the contemporary section seemed to depend, to a great extent, on the artists' international reputation (which actually means their reputation in the West).

I believe that we are witnessing a somehow different situation now, i.e., a change from the Eastern artist as an "incompletely developed Westerner" to the Eastern artist as a representative of a different and exotic culture. In the above-mentioned speech about the "relocated person," Ilya Kabakov also mentions how an artist who is coming from the East or from the Third World is, in advance, committed to represent his origins:

"Belonging to some 'school' now—be it Russian or Mexican, French or Czech— is perceived as a negative ethnographic factor hindering the artist to a certain degree from entering into the Western artistic community on an equal footing. However, the artist who has arrived from these places often himself doesn't know about this circumstance; this 'hump' on his back appears only in the new place upon crossing the border, and as Boris Groys wrote, like a growth on his back, it is visible to everyone except the owner of that back. This is precisely the same thing as when a critic in an offhanded manner writes: 'the young artist from India,' or 'the famous Mexican painter'—everyone silently understands what this epithet means."[9]

I believe that this change demonstrates an important modification in the field of East-West relationship, a shift that is connected to the *détente* process and the eventual collapse of the socialist regimes. During the time of the cold war, in a situation where the political and ideological confrontations ensured a firm, bipolar structure and therefore balance and control, Western modern art easily claimed to be universal. The post–cold-war era does not supply such controlling mechanisms any more. The necessary result is that the situation of art (as well as other related fields) has to be redefined. The freedom of traveling, for example, could be a universal value and a proclaimed right only as long as the bipolar system made it impossible for a large majority of (Eastern) people to travel freely. As soon as these limitations disappeared, the right of free travel had to be reduced.

As opposed to the proclamation of the universal value of Western modern art during the cold war period, post–cold-war ideology stresses the differences. (On a more global level, a similar development can be observed in the discourse of so-called multiculturalism.) As the ideological and political differences disappeared, the East is now established through "cultural" and "civilizational" differences, which are by themselves a starting point of conflicts, of the "clash of civilizations." (In his description of the *Interpol* incident, Wenda Gu, the artist whose work was destroyed by Brener, spoke very openly about the "cultural war.")[10]

The idea of modern art originally did not need the idea of a "dialogue"; the "substance," so to speak, was common, the only question was to what extent and how it was realized. Through the idea of "civilizational differences," however, the Easterner is established as the "other," thus an intercultural and inter-civilization dialogue is necessary. An Eastern artist now becomes attractive for the West not as somebody producing universal art, but exactly as somebody who reflects his particular condition. He is not only an artist, but particularly a Russian, Polish, or Slovene artist, or simply an Eastern artist.[11] This was clearly present in the *Interpol* incident. Renata Salecl, in her analysis of Kulik's actions, wrote about this question: "The paradox . . . is that Kulik was invited as a particularity—as a Russian dog. I am certain that if an American artist were to play a dog, he would be of much less interest for the international art scene than the Russian artist is. We all know that the majority of people in today's Russia live a doglike life. And the first association a Westerner makes in regard to Kulik's performance is that he is representing this reality of contemporary Russia. Kulik-dog is therefore of interest for the Western art world because of the fact that he is the Russian 'dog.' . . . And, in regard to Kulik's performance it can be said that the West finds an aesthetic pleasure in observing the Russian 'dog,' but only on condition that he does not behave in a truly doglike manner. When Kulik ceased to be the decorative art object—the Eastern neighbor who represents the misery of the Russian doglike life—and started to act in a way that surprised his admirers, he quickly became designated as the enemy."[12]

In short, the idea of the West-East dialogue could be understood as a way of reorganizing these relationships after the end of the cold war era, i.e., as a way to deal with the "other." If earlier the dominant position was achieved through the universal value of Western modern art, it is now achieved through the definition of the "other" and, at the same time, through the definition of the basis of communication.[13] As Wenda Gu reports, Misiano said that "this incident creates an essential stage for a dialogue between Eastern and Western Europe."[14] But it seems clear that this "stage" includes a reorganization of the very field of a dialogue and thus opens the question, "Who is to be master?" Unavoidably, the Western pole of the "global network" could only see mere aggression, imperialism, and destruction in this attempt.

Notes:

1. Ilya Kabakov, "A Story about a Culturally Relocated Person," speech at the XXVIII AICA Congress, Stockholm, September 22, 1994; reprinted in *M'ARS* (Ljubljana), no. 3–4 (1996).

2. The letter was signed by Olivier Zahm, Elein Fleiss, Jan Åman, Catharina Ahlberg, Catti Lindahl, Thomas Lundh, Magnus af Petersens, Matthias Wagner K, Birgitta Muhr, Wenda Gu, Ionna Theocaropoullou, Ulrika Karlsson, Dan Wolgers, Ernst Billgren, Birgert & Bergstrom, Johannes Albers, and Fredrik Wretman.

3. Dieter Schartz, "Chronology" in *Wiener Aktionismus/Viennese Actionism* (Klagenfurt: Ritter Verlag, 1998), vol. 1, p. 168.

4. Recently, Brener has caused another big scandal by attacking a painting by Malevich in the Stedelijk Museum in Amsterdam. This action again, and even more radically, opens up the question of artists' attacking and destroying works of other artists. Personally, I think that such actions are highly problematic and not something one could easily agree with. Also, I believe that an artist who has destroyed such a work has to take full responsibility for his action. Attacking a work of art does not necessarily imply a relevant artistic position and statement, but sometimes it does. In such cases, the destructive and unlawful behavior has a function and meaning, and we have to regard it as a relevant statement — like, I believe, in Brener's case. Personally, I do not agree with Brener's attacks on Wenda Gu's and Malevich's works (no more than I agree with the destruction of the works by de Kooning or Helga Pape), but, of course, these attacks were not meant to be agreed with. They are deliberate hooliganism which, however, has a deep meaning in the context of Brener's artistic position. If those who have written the *Open Letter* would actually read Brener's text in the *Interpol* catalogue instead of just searching for politically incorrect and compromising quotations in it, they could perhaps understand it.

5. Viktor Misiano, "Response to an Open Letter to the Art World," *Flash Art International* 29, no. 188 (May–June 1996), p. 46. (The quotation discloses one of the reasons why I am so interested in this affair. As I am based in Ljubljana, my position is in advance determined by the discourse of the West-East dialogue.)

6. Lewis Carroll, *Alice's Adventures in Wonderland & Through the Looking Glass* (Toronto and New York: Bantam Books, 1981), p. 169.

7. Samuel P. Huntington, "The Clash of Civilizations?" *Foreign Affairs*, no. 3 (summer 1993), pp. 22–49. Professor Huntington has expanded and elaborated the questions dealt with in the article in his recent book, *The Clash of Civilizations and the Remaking of World Order* (New York: Simon & Schuster, 1996).

8. Eva Cockcroft, "Abstract Expressionism, Weapon of the Cold War" in Francis Frascina, ed., *Pollock and After: The Critical Debate* (London: Harper & Row, 1985), p. 132.

9. Kabakov, op. cit.

10. Wenda Gu, "The Cultural War," *Flash Art International*, 29, no. 189 (summer 1996), pp. 102–03.

11. In recent Western discussions about contemporary Russian art, especially about artists like Brener and Kulik, such an attitude was often present. One can easily notice how these artists came to represent the wild, aggressive, irrational, non-understandable, dangerous, animal-like essence of "Russia" (or, perhaps, the "East" in general), and how their actions are received with a mixture of fascination, admiration, fear, hatred, and, of course, pleasure.

12. Renata Salecl, "Love Me, Love My Dog," *Index, Contemporary Scandinavian Art and Culture*, no. 3–4 (1996), p. 117.

13. Perhaps it would be more accurate to say that this new strategy is still often combined with the idea of "universalism."

14. Gu, op. cit., p. 103.

First presented at the international conference "On the Edge," organized by the Croatian section of AICA Zagreb, 1997; published in *Art Press*, no. 226 (July–August 1997), under the title "Dialogue East–West: East is East?"

Acknowledgments

Anthologies by their nature reflect the efforts of many contributors, but producing this volume required the assistance of an unusual number of colleagues, whom we would like to thank here.

Laura Hoptman first proposed the idea for this book. Noting that the many languages spoken in Central and Eastern Europe make written sources for the visual arts virtually inaccessible to readers outside the particular country in which an article was written, she pointed out that an anthology in English would be of great use not only to an interested public in this country but also to readers in the region itself. At her suggestion we asked Tomáš Pospiszyl to participate as co-editor of the publication. He had recently produced an anthology of American art criticism translated into Czech, making him a particularly apt collaborator. We are deeply indebted to both for conceiving such an ambitious volume and producing and organizing it so expertly. We also thank Ilya Kabakov for providing us with an insightful and eloquent Foreword. Majlena Braun and Clay Tarica of the International Program undertook extensive research and worked tirelessly to ensure the book's accuracy and to keep the project on schedule.

We would also like to thank the many artists, critics, historians, and writers who generously allowed us to include their texts and reproduce their artworks in this anthology. They, as well as the publishers of the books, catalogues, and journals in which these texts and images first appeared, offered extensive help in reviewing translations and clarifying the dates and circumstances of the initial publications, for which we are most grateful.

The International Council of The Museum of Modern Art has generously sponsored the publication of this book as the first in a series of volumes of primary documents on art in translation. We would especially like to thank the Council's President, Jo Carole Lauder, and its Executive Director, Carol Coffin. We are also indebted to The Trust for Mutual Understanding—and to its director, Richard Lanier—for supporting Mr. Pospiszyl's residency in New York.

At the Museum we are indebted to Joanne Greenspun, our compassionate but resolute editor, and her colleagues in the Department of Publications: Michael Maegraith, Publisher; Harriet Bee, Editorial Director; Lawrence Allen, Publications Manager; Marc Sapir, Director of Production; and Christopher Zichello, Production Manager. Gina Rossi, Senior Book Designer, devised a clear design for a complex book, and Jennifer Tobias, Librarian, graciously navigated our constant search for books. In addition, we wish to thank Glenn D. Lowry, Director, and Robert B. Storr, Senior Curator of Contemporary Art, for their advice and encouragement. We also received invaluable assistance from several young scholars holding fellowships and internships at the Museum: Maria Vassileva (whose research position was funded by CEC International Partners, for which we are especially grateful to Fritzie Brown of its ArtsLink program); Tetyana Kasyanenko; Joanna Raczkiewicz; and Georgia Scherman.

As the organization of the book developed, we relied extensively on a select group of consultants (pp. 364–65) in ensuring that we had chosen the most important writings in each category. Roger Conover, Executive Editor at MIT Press, our distributor, encouraged us throughout the long project with his enthusiasm and knowledge of the subject. We are also grateful to Timothy Benson and Stephanie Emerson of the Los Angeles County Museum of Art for enabling us to coordinate our publication with their related volume, *Between Worlds: A Sourcebook of Central European Avant-Gardes,* and to David Elliott, Director of the Mori Art Museum, Tokyo, for sharing with us his extensive experience with artists and institutions in Central and Eastern Europe.

We would like to thank the able translators with whom we worked: John Batki, Eric Dluhosch, Cynthia Martin, Daniel Rishik, Julian Semilian, Maja Soljan, Branka Stipančić, Marek Wilczynski, and Alex Zucker. We are also very grateful to the scholars and artists who offered information for the introductions to the individual essays: Nada Beroš, András Böröcz, Roger Conover, József Mélyí, Viktor Misiano, Andrei Monastyrski, Miklós Peternák, Nedko Solakov, Branka Stipančić, and Igor Zabel.

Among the numerous other scholars, artists, and curators who gave so freely of their time were: Jaroslav Anděl; Judit Angel; Sonia Avadzijeva; Josef Backstein; Kamen Balkanski; Tamas Banovitch; Marek Bartelik; Norton Batkin; László Beke; Dunja Blažević; Iveta Boiko; Barbara Borčić; Wiesław Borowski; Jeffrey Buehler; Paulina Celinska; Irina Cios; Codruta Cruceanu; Edina Csoka; Jasmina Cubrilo; Leida Curri; Aleksander Davić; Branka Davić; Ana Devic; Svetlana Djukić; Octavian Esanu; Jana Ferjan; Natalia Filonenko; Alfred Friendly, Jr.; Katherine Gates; Jana Geržová; Saša Glavan; Aleksander Glezer; Arthur Goldberg; Elizbeta Grygiel; Marek Grygiel; Marina Gržinić; Dulce Guerrero; Vít Havránek; Dóra Hegyi; Lóránd Hegyi; Sirje Helme; Ludvík Hlaváček; Mária Hlavajová; Lejla Hodzić; Ludmila Ivashina; Małgorzata Jurkiewicz; Magdalena Kardasz; Oleg Kireev; Julia Kolerova; Yuri Konovalov; Marko Košan; Želimir Koščević; Aleksandr Kosolapov; Charlotte Kotik; Elisabeta Koto; Miroslav Kulchitsky; Elena Kurliandtseva; Marta Kuzma; Lech Lechowicz; Peret Lindpere; Eve Linnap; Małgorzata Lisiewicz; Roxana Marcoci; Diana Maria; Julia Mayover; Viktor Mazin; Lidija Merenik; Miran Mohar; Stefan Morawski; Ludmila Motsiuk; David Nalle; Katalin Néray; Pavla Niklová; Beata Nowacka; Jana Oravcová; Natalia Orlova-Gentes; Anca Oroveanu; Melentie Pandilovski; Birute Pankunaite; Aleksandr Perepelytsya; Dan Perjovschi; Lia Perjovschi; Gabriela Petrea; Victor Platchikhin; Gregor Podnar; Paweł Polit; Marjetica Potrč; Andrzej Przywara; Mikhail Rashkovetsky; Neil Rector; Alla Rosenfeld; Anda Rottenberg; Helmutas Sabasevicius; Magda Savon; Beti Serovč; Jiří Ševčík; Jana Ševčíková; Darko Šimičić; Vladan Šír; Agnieszka Skalska; Milada Ślizińska; Alexander Soloviov; Igor Španjol; Sven Spieker; Dejan Sretenović; Ekaterina Stukalova; Janos Sugár; Eva Szabó; Annamaria Szoke, Katalin Szoke; Aneta Szyłak; Adam Szymczyk; Goran Tomčić; Margarita Tupitsyn; Viktor Tupitsyn; Olesya Turkina; Nebosja Vilić; Yuri Volkogonov; Janka Vukmir; Hanna Wróblewska; Olga Zahorbenska; Nina Zaretskaya; Anna Zdobiak; and Philip Zidarov.

Jay A. Levenson
Director, International Program
The Museum of Modern Art

Editors and Consultants

Editors

Laura Hoptman is Curator of Contemporary Art at the Carnegie Museum of Art, a post that includes the organization of the 2004 Carnegie International exhibition. Previously, she served as Assistant Curator in the Department of Drawings at The Museum of Modern Art, where she organized exhibitions that include *Drawing Now: Eight Propositions; Love Forever: Yayoi Kusama, 1958–1968;* and numerous one-artist projects by contemporary artists such as Ricci Albenda, John Bock, Maurizio Cattelan, John Currin, Elizabeth Peyton, Rirkrit Tiravanija, and Luc Tuymans. As guest curator at the Museum of Contemporary Art in Chicago in 1994–95, she organized *Beyond Belief: Contemporary Art in East Central Europe,* the first exhibition of contemporary art from the region in the United States since the revolutions of 1989–90. She is the author of a monographic study of the artist Yayoi Kusama, published by Phaidon in 2000, as well as numerous catalogues and articles published in *Frieze, Parkett,* and *Harper's Bazaar,* among others.

Tomáš Pospiszyl worked as an exhibition manager for the Office of the President of the Czech Republic in the early 1990s. Between 1997 and 2002, as Curator of Contemporary Art at the National Gallery in Prague, he organized numerous exhibitions, including one on the artist Jindřich Prucha. His published essays in exhibition catalogues include ones on Kim Adams for Power Plant in Toronto (1991) and on Marketa Othova for the Carnegie International (1999–2000). He edited the Czech anthology *In Front of a Picture: An Anthology of American Art Theory and Criticism from Clement Greenberg to Dave Hickey* (1998). Currently he is an editor of the international art magazine *Umělec/Artist,* published in Prague.

Consultants

Ruxandra Balaci, art critic and curator; Deputy Director of the newly founded Museum of Contemporary Art in Bucharest; Co-Director of the art magazine *Atelier;* contributor to *artpress* and to the catalogues for *Manifesta 2, After the Wall,* and *Boundless Borders;* Commissioner of the Romanian Pavilion at the 49th Venice Biennale.

Nada Beroš, art critic, curator, editor, and lecturer based in Zagreb, Croatia; Curator at the Museum of Contemporary Art in Zagreb since 1994; founder of *Jezevo Motel,* an ongoing independent multidisciplinary project on illegal migration; co-founder and editor-in-chief of the online magazine *art-e-fact.*

Iaroslava Boubnova, art critic and curator, lives and works in Sofia, Bulgaria; Founding Director of the Institute of Contemporary Art, Sofia; lecturer, since 1997, in the Visual Arts Department, The New Bulgarian University; Curator of *Manifesta 4* in Frankfurt, Germany.

Roger L. Conover, Executive Editor at The MIT Press; Co-Curator of *In Search of Balkania* (Neue Galerie, Graz, 2002); author/editor of many articles and books on avant-garde figures and subjects, such as Arthur Cravan and Mina Loy.

Milena Kalinovska, independent curator, formerly Director of the Institute of Contemporary Art, Boston, and associate curator of the New Museum, New York; organized exhibitions such as *Boston School* (1996), *The New Histories* (1997), and *Beyond Preconceptions: The Sixties Experiment* (2000–2001); contributor to *Trans* magazine, *Words of Wisdom, ICI,* and *New York,* among others.

Edi Muka, curator, lives and works in Tirana, Albania; Director of the *Tirana Biennale 2*; Curator of the International Program at the National Gallery of Arts in Tirana; Guest Professor at the Academy of Fine Arts, Tirana.

Miklós Peternák, art historian, Professor at the Hungarian Academy of Fine Arts, Budapest; Director of C3: Center for Culture and Communication, Budapest; Co-Curator of the exhibitions *The Butterfly Effect* (1996), *Perspective* (1999), and *Vision* (2002) all at the Mücsarnok, Budapest.

Piotr Piotrowski, Professor and Chair of the Art History department, Adam Mickiewicz University, Poznań, Poland; Former Senior Curator for Contemporary Art, National Museum, Poznań; author of: *Meaning of Modernism: On Polish Art after 1945* and *In the Shadow of Yalta: Art and Politics in Central Europe, 1945–1989* (forthcoming); contributor to *Central European Avant-Gardes: Exchange and Transformation, 1910–1930.*

Igor Zabel, critic and curator; Senior Curator at the Moderna Galerija, Ljubljana, Slovenia; Coordinator of *Manifesta 3*, Ljubljana (2000); author of articles in *Art Journal, artpress, Index,* and *Moscow Art Magazine*; contributed essays to catalogues for *After the Wall* (1999), *L'autre motif de l'Europe* (2000), and *Words of Wisdom* (2001), among others.

Selected Bibliography

General

Aulich, James, and Tim Wilcox, eds. *Europe without Walls: Art, Posters, and Revolution 1989–1993.* Manchester: Manchester City Art Galleries, 1993.

Badovinac, Zdenka, and Mika Briški, eds. *Body and the East from the 1960s to the Present.* Cambridge: MIT Press, 1999.

Berswordt-Wallrabe, Kornelia; Kornelia Röder; and Guy Shchraenen. *Mail Art: Osteuropa im internationalen Netzwerk.* Schwerin: Staatliches Museum Schwerin, 1996.

Bonami, Francesco, et al. *Manifesta 3: Borderline Syndrome: Energies of Defence.* Ljubljana: Cankarjev Dom, Cultural and Congress Center, 2000.

Boubnova, Iaroslava. *Crossroads in Central Europe: Ideas, Themes, Methods, and Problems of Contemporary Art and Art Criticism.* Edited by Katalin Kescrü. Budapest: Association of Hungarian Creative Artists, 1996.

Crowley, David, and Susan E. Reid, eds. *Style and Socialism: Modernity and Material Culture in Post-War Eastern Europe.* Oxford and New York: Berg Publishers, 2000.

Dan, Călin; Nina Gzegledy; and YYZ Gallery. *In Sight: Media Art from the Middle of Europe.* Toronto: YYZ Artists' Outlet, 1995.

Elliott, David, and Bojana Pejić, eds. *After the Wall: Art and Culture in Post-Communist Europe.* Stockholm: Moderna Museet, 1999.

Farver, Jane, ed. *Global Conceptualism: Points of Origin, 1950s–1980s.* New York: Queens Museum of Art, 1999.

Hegyi, Lóránd. ed. *Aspects / Positions: 50 Years of Art in Central Europe 1949–1999.* Vienna: Museum Moderner Kunst Stiftung Ludwig, 1999.

Hoptman, Laura J., ed. *Beyond Belief: Contemporary Art from East Central Europe.* Chicago: Museum of Contemporary Art, 1995.

Bosnia–Herzegovina

Blažević, Dunja, ed. *Meeting Point: First Annual Exhibition of the Soros Center for Contemporary Arts.* Sarajevo: Soros Center for Contemporary Art, 1997.

Oprez! Radovi!/Under Construction: Third Annual Exhibition, Soros Center for Contemporary Art—Sarajevo. Sarajevo: Soros Center for Contemporary Art, 1999.

Bulgaria

Ars ex Natio. Sofia: Soros Center for Contemporary Art, 1998.

Boubnova, Iaroslava. *Bulgariaavangarde: Contending Forces 2.* Munich: Künstlerwerkstatt, 1999.

———, and Haralampi G. Oroschakoff, eds. *Bulgaria Avant-Garde.* Cologne: Salon Verlag, 1998.

Boyadjiev, Luchezar. *Revolution for All.* Manchester, England: Holden Gallery, 1998.

Kiossev, Alexander, ed. *Post-Theory, Games, and Discursive Resistance: The Bulgarian Case.* New York: State University of New York Press, 1995.

Luchezar Boyadjiev. Berlin: Institut für Auslandsbeziehungen, 1992.

Solakov, Nedko. *Multimedia Installation: The Superstitious Man.* Skopje: Museum of Contemporary Art, 1994.

Croatia

Cameron, Dan; Catherine Millet; and Lóránd Hegyi. *Braco Dimitrijević: Slow as Light, Fast as Thought.* Vienna: Museum Moderner Kunst Stiftung Ludwig, 1994.

Cramer, Sue, and Branka Stipančić, eds. *The Horse Who Sings: Radical Art from Croatia.* Sydney, Australia: Museum of Contemporary Art, 1993.

Croatian Photography from 1950 to the Present. Zagreb: Museum of Contemporary Art, 1993.

Dimitrijević, Nena, and Klaus Pohl. *Braco Dimitrijević: Against an Historic Sense of Gravity.* Darmstadt: Das Museum, 1995.

Gattin, Marija. *Gorgona, Gorgonesco, Gorgonico.* Zagreb: Museum of Contemporary Art, 1997.

———; Leonida Kovač; and Jadranka Vinterhalter. *To Tell a Story.* Zagreb: Museum of Contemporary Art, 2001.

Gorgona. Self-published magazines, 1961–66. Copies in the Special Collections Library at The Museum of Modern Art, New York.

Iveković, Sanja. *Is This My True Face?* Edited by Tihomir Milovać. Zagreb: Museum of Contemporary Art, 1998.

———. *Tragedy of a Venus.* Zagreb: Museum of Contemporary Art, 1976.

Otok – Island / Simpozij–Symposium. Zagreb: Soros Center for Contemporary Art, 1997.

Stipančić, Branka. *Dimitrije Bašičević Mangelos.* Zagreb: Galerije grada Zagreba, 1990.

———, ed. *Words and Images.* Zagreb: Soros Center for Contemporary Art, 1995.

Susovski, Marijan. *Exat 51: New Tendencies, 1961–1973.* Lisbon: Centro Cultural de Cascais, 2001.

———, ed. *The New Art Practice in Yugoslavia 1966–1978.* Zagreb: Museum of Contemporary Art, 1978.

Czech Republic

Brunclík, Pavel, ed. *Adriena Šimotová: Retrospektiva.* Prague: The National Gallery in Prague and Gallery Pecka, 2001.

Bydžovská, Lenka; Vojtěch Lahoda; and Karel Srp. *Czech Modern Art 1900–1960: The Modern Art Collection, the Trade Fair Palace.* Prague: The National Gallery in Prague, 1995.

Havránek, Vít. *Action Word Movement Space.* Prague: City Gallery of Prague, 2000.

Judlová, Marie, ed. *Focal Points of Revival: Czech Art 1956–1963.* Prague: City Gallery of Prague and Institute for Art History, 1994.

Knížák, Milan. *New Paradise.* Prague: Gallery Mánes and the Museum of Applied Arts, 1996.

Kolíbal, Stanislav, and Jan Rous, eds. *Stanislav Kolíbal: Retrospektiva.* Prague: The National Gallery in Prague, 1997.

Pospiszyl, Tomáš. *David Černý: The Fucking Years. The Life and Work of an Artist.* Prague: Divus, 2000.

Rostislav, Švácha, and Eric Dluhosch, eds. *Karel Teige: L'enfant terrible of the Czech Modernist Avant-garde.* Cambridge: MIT Press, 1999.

Smolíková, Marta, ed. *Orbis Fictus: New Media in Contemporary Arts.* Prague: Soros Center for Contemporary Art, 1996.

Srp, Karel. *Karel Miler, Petr Štembera, and Jan Mlčoch, 1970–1980.* Prague: City Gallery of Prague, 1997.

———. *Lukáš Jasanský, Martin Polák, Pragensie.* Prague: City Gallery of Prague and Jaroslav Jonáš Něnička, 1998.

Zemánek, Jiří. *Milan Grygar.* Prague: The National Gallery in Prague, 1999.

Estonia

Artists of Estonia. Tallinn: Soros Center for Contemporary Art, 1998.

Breze, Andris. *Beyond Control: Critical Transition in the Baltic Republics.* Vancouver: Presentation House Cultural Society, 1991.

Dodge, Norton T., and Alla Rosenfeld. *Art of the Baltics: The Struggle for Freedom of Artistic Expression under the Soviets, 1945–1991.* New Brunswick, NJ: Rutgers University Press, 2001.

Liivak, Anu, ed. *Tallinn-Moskva, 1956–1985.* Tallinn, Estonia: Tallinn Art Hall, 1996.

Linnap, Peter, ed. *Fabrique d'histoire: Saaremaa Bienala 1995.* Tallinn, Estonia: Center for Contemporary Photography, 1995.

Myth and Abstraction: Actual Art from Estonia. Karlsruhe: Badischer Kunstverein Karlsruhe, 1992.

Rottenberg, Anda, ed. *Personal Time: Art of Estonia, Latvia, and Lithuania, 1945–1996.* 3 vols. Warsaw: The Zachęta Gallery of Contemporary Art, 1996.

Federal Republic of Yugoslavia

Andjelković, Branislava, and Branislav Dimitrijević. *Map Room.* Belgrade: Center for Contemporary Art, 1997.

Drathen, Doris von; Friedrich Meschede; and Bojana Pejić. *Marina Abramović.* Stuttgart: Edition Cantz, 1993.

The Gaze Scenes. Belgrade: Soros Center for Contemporary Art, 1995.

Konverzacija: A Short Notice Show. Belgrade: Museum of Contemporary Art, 2001.

Merenik, Lidija, and Dejan Sretenović, eds. *Art in Yugoslavia 1992–1995.* Belgrade: Fund for an Open Society and Radio B92, 1996.

Hungary

Barnabás, Bencsik, and Suzanne Mészöly, eds. *Polyphony: Social Commentary in Contemporary Hungarian Art.* Budapest: Soros Center for Contemporary Art, 1993.

Be, Käthe, and László Beke. *Gedächtnis-Räume: Hommage für Miklós Erdély*. Berlin: Künstlerhaus Bethanien, 1992.

Fráter, Zoltán, and András Petöcz, eds. *Medium-Art: Selection of Hungarian Experimental Poetry*. Budapest: Magvetö, 1990.

Mészöly, Suzanne, ed. *Modern and Contemporary Hungarian Art, Bulletin 1985–1990*. Budapest: Soros Foundation for Fine Art Documentation, 1991.

_____. *SVB Voce: Contemporary Hungarian Video Installation*. Budapest: Soros Foundation for Fine Art Documentation, 1991.

Miklós Erdély. Rome: Galleria Spicchi dell'Est, 1992.

Miklós Erdély, 1928–1986. Székesfehérvár: István Király Múzeum, 1991.

Nasgaard, Roald. *Beyond Borders: Hungarian Video Art from the Late 1980s*. Toronto: Art Gallery of Ontario, 1991.

_____. *Free Worlds: Metaphors and Realities in Contemporary Hungarian Art*. Toronto: Art Gallery of Ontario, 1991.

Naturally: Nature and Art in Central Europe. Budapest: Ernst Museum, 1994.

Latvia

Breze, Andris. *Beyond Control: Critical Transition in the Baltic Republics*. Vancouver: Presentation House Cultural Society, 1991.

Demakova, Hēlena. *Different Conversations: Writings on Art and Culture*. Riga: Visual Communication Department, 2002.

Dodge, Norton T., and Alla Rosenfeld. *Art of the Baltics: The Struggle for Freedom of Artistic Expression under the Soviets, 1945–1991*. New Brunswick, NJ: Rutgers University Press, 2001.

Rottenberg, Anda, ed. *Personal Time: Art of Estonia, Latvia, and Lithuania, 1945–1996*. 3 vols. Warsaw: The Zachęta Gallery of Contemporary Art, 1996.

Macedonia

Abadzieva Dimitrova, Sonja. *Radiations: Recent Macedonia Art*. Skopje: Museum of Contemporary Art, 1998.

Petrovski, Sonia. *Anthology of Macedonian Art 1894–1994*. Skopje: Museum of Contemporary Art, 1994.

Petrovski, Zoran. *9 1/2: New Macedonian Art*. Skopje: Museum of Contemporary Art, 1995.

Vilic, Nebojša, ed. *Few Candies for Venice: Art in Macedonia at the End of the Millennium* (published on the occasion of the XLVIII Venice Biennale). Skopje: Laurens Coster, 1999.

_____. *N.O.A.: Reflections on New-Object Art*. Skopje: Horizons Unlimited, 1996.

Poland

Borowski, Wiesław. *Galeria Foksal 1966–1988*. Warsaw: Galeria Foksal SBWA, 1994.

Chrzanowska-Pieńkos, Jolanta, and Anda Rottenberg, eds. *Alina Szapocznikow 1926–1973*. Warsaw: Institute for the Promotion of Art Foundation, Zachęta Gallery, 1998.

Kantor, Tadeusz. *A Journey Through Other Spaces: Essays and Manifestos, 1944–90*. Berkeley: University of California Press, 1993.

Lauf, Cornelia. *The Wealth of Nations: Centre for Contemporary Art, Ujazdowski Castle, Warsaw*. Ghent, Belgium: Imschoot, 1993.

Pakesch, Peter; Andrzej Przywara; and Madeleine Schuppli. *Pavel Althamer at Kunsthalle Basel*. Basel: Schwabe & Co., 1997.

Piotrowski, Piotr. *Meanings of Modernism: Towards a History of Polish Art after 1945*. Poznań: Rebis Publishing, 1999.

_____, ed. *Zofia Kulik: From Siberia to Cyberia*. Poznań: Museum of Art, 1999.

Pirie, Donald; Jekaterina Young; and Christopher Carrel, eds. *Polish Realities: The Arts in Poland 1980–1989*. Glasgow: Third Eye Centre, 1990.

Polit, Paweł, and Piotr Woznakiewicz, eds. *Conceptual Reflection in Polish Art: Experiences of Discourse: 1965–1975*. Warsaw: Centre for Contemporary Art, Ujazdowski Castle, 2000.

Rottenberg, Anda. *Art from Poland, 1945–1996*. Warsaw: Zachęta Gallery, 1997.

Wodiczko, Krzysztof. *Critical Vehicles: Writings, Projects, Interviews*. Cambridge: MIT Press, 1999.

Wróblewska, Hanna. *Katarzyna Kozyra: The Men's Bathhouse* (published on the occasion of the XLVIII Venice Biennale). Warsaw: Zachęta Gallery, 1999.

Romania

Babeti, Coriolan. *Horia Bernea*. Bucharest: National Museum of Art, 1997.

Cârneci, Magda. *Art of the 1980s in Eastern Europe: Texts on Postmodernism*. Bucharest: Mediana Collection, 1999.

Experiment in Romanian Art since 1960. Bucharest: Soros Center for Contemporary Art, 1997.

Balaci, Ruxandra. *Geta Bratescu*. Bucharest: The National Museum of Art, Romania, 1999.

Grigorescu, Dan. *From Poison to Coca-Cola: Notes on the Twilight of Postmodernism*. Bucharest: Editura Minerva, 1994.

_____. *Idea and Sensitivity: Trends and Tendencies of Romanian Contemporary Art*. Bucharest: Meridiane Publishing House, 1998.

Grigorescu Ion: Documente 1967–1997. Bucharest: The National Museum of Art, Romania, 1998.

Steriadi, Jean. *Călin Dan*. Bucharest: Meridiane Publishing House, 1988.

subREAL: Akten=Files. Berlin: Neuer Berliner Kunstverein and Künstlerhaus Bethanien, 1996.

subREAL: Art History Archive. Bucharest: The Romanian Ministry of Culture, 1999.

Slovakia

Hlavajová, Mária, ed. *Interior vs. Exterior, or On the Border of (Possible) Worlds*. Bratislava: Soros Center for Contemporary Art, 1996.

Kuchárová, Irena, and Marta Ciranová, eds. *Sixties*. Bratislava: Slovak National Gallery, 1995.

Restany, Pierre, and Mlynárčik, Alex. *Ailleurs*. Paris: Galerie Lara Vincy, and Bratislava: Slovak National Gallery, 1994.

Rusínová, Zora, ed. *Action Art, 1969–1989*. Bratislava: Slovak National Gallery, 2001.

Slovenia

Badovinac, Zdenka; Renato Brilli; and Igor Zabel. *V.S.S.D.* (published on the occasion of the XLVI Venice Biennale). Ljubljana: Moderna Galerija, 1995.

_____, and Igor Zabel. *P.A.R.A.S.I.T.E.: Slovene Art of the Nineties*. Ljubljana: Moderna Galerija, 1995.

Borčić, Barbara, ed. *Videodokument: Video Art in Slovenia, 1969–1998*. 3 vols. Ljubljana: Open Society Institute and Soros Center for Contemporary Art, 1999.

_____; Vanesa Cvahte; Lilijana Stepančić. *Media in Media*. Ljubljana: Open Society Institute and Soros Center for Contemporary Art, 1997.

Čufer, Eda, ed. *NSK Embassy Moscow: How the East Sees the East*. Koper, Slovenia: Loza Gallery, 1992.

New Collectivism: Neue Slowenische Kunst. Zagreb: Graficki Zavod Hrvatske, and Los Angeles: AMOK Books, 1991.

Neue Slowenische Kunst. Zagreb: Graficki Zavod Hrvatske, 1991.

Podnar, Gregor. *Somewhere Else*. Ljubljana: Galerija Škuc, and Weimar: ACC Galerie, 1999.

Zabel, Igor. *OHO: A Retrospective*. Ljubljana: Moderna Galerija, 1994.

_____. *Aspects of the Minimal: Minimalism in Slovene Art, 1968–1980*. Ljubljana: Moderna Galerija, 1990.

_____. *Disclosed Images: The Young Slovene Art of the Seventies and the Eighties*. Ljubljana: Moderna Galerija, 1989.

Socialist Federal Republic of Yugoslavia

Abramović, Marina. *Marina Abramović*. Paris: Musée National d'Art Moderne, Centre Georges Pompidou, 1990.

Metaphysical Visions – Middle Europe: Deconstruction, Quotation, and Subversion. Video from Yugoslavia. New York: Artists Space, 1989.

Todosijević, Raša. *Texts*. Tübingen: Edition Dačić, 1977.

Soviet Union / Russia

Atkinson, Conrad, and Andrei Monastyrski. *Conrad Atkinson, Andrei Monastyrski: Particular Histories*. Moscow: Club of Avantguardists, 1990.

Baigell, Matthew, and Renée Baigell. *Peeling Potatoes, Painting Pictures*. New Brunswick, NJ: Rutgers University Press, 2001.

_____. *Soviet Dissident Artists: Interviews after Perestroika*. New Brunswick, NJ: Rutgers University Press, 1995.

Bowlt, John E. *Russian Samizdat Art: Essays*. New York: Willis, Locker, and Owens, 1986.

Bown, Matthew Cullerne. *Contemporary Russian Art*. London: Phaidon, 1989.

Čufer, Eda, and Viktor Misiano. *Interpol: The Art Exhibition which Divided East and West.* Ljubljana: IRWIN and Moscow: *Moscow Art* magazine, 2000.

Degot, Ekaterina. *Contemporary Painting in Russia.* Roseville East, NSW: Craftsman House, 1995.

Dodge, Norton T., and Alla Rosenfeld. *Nonconformist Art: The Soviet Experience, 1956–1986.* New York: Thames and Hudson, and New Brunswick, NJ: Jane Voorhees Zimmerli Art Museum, Rutgers University Press, 1995.

Efimova, Alla, and Lev Manovich, eds. *Tekstura: Russian Essays on Visual Culture.* Chicago: University of Chicago Press, 1993.

Fuchs, Rudolf Herman; Viktor Mazin; et al. *Kabinet: An Anthology.* St. Petersburg: Inapress and Amsterdam: Stedelijk Museum, 1997.

Gerlovina, Rimma, and Valeriy Gerlovin. *Russian Samizdat Art: 1960–1982.* Chappaqua: Chappaqua Library Gallery, and New York: Franklin Furnace, 1982.

Gleser, Alexander. *Contemporary Russian Art.* Paris: Third Wave Publishers, 1993.

———. *Kunst gegen Bulldozer: Memoiren eines russischen Sammlers.* Frankfurt: Ullstein Verlag, 1982.

Groys, Boris. *The Total Art of Stalinism: Avant-Garde, Aesthetic Dictatorship, and Beyond.* Princeton: Princeton University Press, 1992.

Interpol. Stockholm: Färgfabriken Editions, 1996.

Johnson, Kent, and Stephen M. Ashby, eds. *Third Wave: The New Russian Poetry.* Ann Arbor: University of Michigan Press, 1992.

Lingwood, James, ed. *Eric Bulatov.* London: Institute of Contemporary Art, and Zürich: Parkett Publishers, 1989.

McMillan, Priscilla Johnson. *Krushchev and the Arts: The Politics of Soviet Culture, 1962–1964.* Cambridge: MIT Press, 1965.

Prigov, Dmitry. *Texts of Our Life: Essays in Poetics.* Keele, England: Keele University Press, 1995.

Rabin, Oskar. *L'Artiste et les bulldozers: être peintre en URSS.* Paris: R. Laffont, 1981.

Ratcliff, Carter. *Komar and Melamid.* New York: Abbeville Press, 1989.

Ross, David, ed. *Between Spring and Summer: Soviet Conceptual Art in the Era of Late Communism.* Cambridge: MIT Press, 1990.

Tamruchi, Natalia. *Moscow Conceptualism, 1970–1990.* Roseville East, NSW: Craftsman House, 1995.

Tupitsyn, Margarita. *After Perestroika: Kitchenmaids or Stateswomen.* New York: Independent Curators, 1993.

———. *Margins of Soviet Art: Socialist Realism to the Present.* Milan: Giancarlo Politi Editore, 1989.

———. *Sots Art.* New York: The New Museum of Contemporary Art, 1986.

Wallach, Amei. *Ilya Kabakov: The Man Who Never Threw Anything Away.* New York: Harry N. Abrams, 1996.

Credits

Photographs of works of art reproduced in this volume have been provided in most cases by the owners or custodians of the works, identified in the captions. Individual works of art appearing herein may be protected by copyrights in the United States of America or elsewhere, and may thus not be reproduced in any form without the permission of the copyright owners. The following copyrights and credits appear at the request of the artists, their heirs or representatives, and/or owners of the works.

Numbers refer to page numbers.

Photographs

Jack Abraham: 18, 49, 168, 172, 260, 267; © 2002 Artists Right Society (ARS), New York / ADAGP, Paris: 260; © 2002 Artists Right Society (ARS), New York: 49; © Stefan Bertalan: 54; © Luchezar Boyadjiev: 304–306, 308; Mila Bredikhina: 350; Boris Cvjetanović: 84; Courtesy Braco Dimitrijević: 123, 148–53; eeva-inkeri, New York: frontispiece; © Peter Freeman, Inc, New York: cover; © Rimma Gerlovina: 267; Courtesy Aleksandr Glezer: 13, 69; Ion Grigorescu: 201; Miljenko Horvat: 133, 135; © Aleksandar Battista Ilić (in collaboration with Ivana Keser and Tomislav Gotovac): 193–95; © IRWIN: 290; © Sanja Iveković: 204–19; Robert Jankulovski: 186; Courtesy Ilya Kabakov: 39; © Eustachy Kossakowski: 79, 103; © Katarzyna Kozyra, Courtesy Zachęta Gallery, Warsaw: 243; © Vladislav Mamyshev-Monroe: 197, 238; Michailov and Shestakov: 279; Mieczyslaw Michalak: 257, 274; © Andrei Monastyrski: 176, 179, 180; The Museum of Modern Art, New York, Thomas Griesel: 66, 69; © NSK: 293, 298; © Marko Pogačnik, I. G. Plamen (Iztok Geister): 93; Tadeusz Rolke: 90; © Jan Sagl/Anzenberger, Vienna: 58; Courtesy Nedko Solakov: 279; © subREAL: 283; Branko Tasev, © Zaneta Vangeli: 189; Piotr Tomczyk, © Piotr Stanislawski, Paris: 198; © Krzysztof Wodiczko, Galerie Lelong, New York: 155; Courtesy XL Gallery, Moscow: 168.

Text Copyrights

© 1980 *Artforum* magazine and Komar and Melamid: 258–71; © 1978 Zdravka Bašičević: 80–85;© Wiesław Borowski, Hanna Ptaszkowska, and Mariusz Tchorek; courtesy of the Archive of the Foksal Gallery Foundation: 88–91; © 1992 Luchezar Boyadjiev: 304–11; © 1977 Geta Bratescu: 200–203; © 2001 Imre Bukta, courtesy of the Art Gallery of Ontario, Toronto, Canada: 311–12; © 1995 Călin Dan: 281–85; © 1997 Ekaterina Degot and Steirischer Herbst, Graz: 340–43;© 1995 Helena Demakova and Center for Contemporary Photography, Tallinn: 313–18;© 1976 Braco Dimitrijević: 141–46; © 1977 Nena Dimitrijević and Muzej Suvremene Umjetnosti, Zagreb: 124–40; © 1980 Dániel Erdély and György Erdély: 96–101; © 1995 Andrei Erofeev: 37–53; © 1993 *Gazeta Gdańska*: 254; © 1993 *Gazeta Wyborcza*: 250–51; © 1979 Boris Groys: 162–74; © 1991 Boris Groys: 288–92; © 1996 Wenda Gu: 351–54; © 1997 Jiřina Hauková: 29–37; © 1985 IRWIN: 299–300; © 1992 IRWIN and Eda Čufer: 301; © 1975 Ivan Martin Jirous: 56–65; © 1966 Milan Knížák: 120–21; © 1993 Katarzyna Kozyra: 255; © 1996 Oleg Kulik and *Moscow Art* magazine: 349–51; ©1982 Laibach: 294–97; ©1993 Vladislav Mamyshev-Monroe and *Kabinet* magazine, St. Petersburg: 234–42; © 1989 Wojciech Marchlewski and *Dialog* magazine: 271–77; © 2001 Suzana Milevska: 182–91; © 1996 Viktor Misiano: 347–49; © 1965 Alex Mlynárčik: 86–87; © 1983 Andrei Monastyrski: 175–81; © 1980 Museum of Soviet Unofficial Art, Jersey City: 72; © 1991 New York University and the Massachusetts Institute of Technology: 102–19; © 1996 *NU: SIKSI Index—The Nordic Art Review*, Stockholm: 345–47; © 1995 Anatoly Osmolovsky and *Radek* magazine: 318–25; © 1997 Bojana Pejić: 325–39; © 1998 Piotr Piotrowski: 226–34; © 1966 Marko Pogačnik and Iztok Geister: 92–95; © 1983 Petr Rezek: 220–25; © 1995 Rutgers University Press, New Brunswick: 76–77; © 1984 Scipion Nasice Sisters Theater: 297–99; © 1990 Nedko Solakov: 277–80; © 1997 Soros Center for Contemporary Art, Bucharest: 53–56; © 1974 *Sovetskaia kul'tura*: 72–73; © 1971 Piotr Stanislawski: 199; © 1997 Tallinna Kunstihoone, Tallinn: 15–29; © 1992 Walker Art Center, Minneapolis, Minnesota, USA. Reprinted with the permission of the author: 154–61; © 1993 *Wprost*: 251–53; © 1997 Igor Zabel and *Art Press*: 354–61; © 1993 Slavoj Žižek: 285–88; © 1995 Artur Żmijewski: 242–50; © 1993 *Życie Warszawy*: 250.

Index

Trustees of The Museum of Modern Art

This publication was generously sponsored by
The International Council of The Museum of
Modern Art. Additional support was provided by
The Trust for Mutual Understanding.

Produced by the Department of Publications,
The Museum of Modern Art, New York

Edited by Joanne Greenspun
Designed by Gina Rossi
Production by Christopher Zichello
Printed and bound by Passavia Druckservice GmbH,
Passau

Published by The Museum of Modern Art,
11 West 53 Street, New York, New York 10019
www.moma.org

Library of Congress Control Number: 2002112020
ISBN: 0-87070-361-7 (MoMA)
ISBN: 0-262-08313-2 (MIT Press)

Distributed by The MIT Press,
Massachusetts Institute of Technology,
Cambridge, Massachusetts 02142
http://mitpress.mit.edu

Printed in Germany

Cover: Dimitrije Bašičević Mangelos. *Energija.* 1978.
Acrylic and oil on globe made of wood, metal, and
printed paper, 20¼ × 14 × 13¹⁄₁₆" (51.4 × 35.6 × 33.2 cm).
Courtesy Peter Freeman Inc., New York

Frontispiece: Komar & Melamid. *Don't Babble.* 1974.
Oil on canvas, 35½ × 24" (90.2 × 61 cm). Collection
Richard Karasik. Courtesy Ronald Feldman Fine
Arts, New York

DATE DUE